Fort Union and the
Upper Missouri Fur Trade

Fort Union and the Upper Missouri Fur Trade

BARTON H. BARBOUR

University of Oklahoma Press : Norman

Also by Barton H. Barbour

(ed.) *Tales of the Mountain Men* (Santa Fe, 1984)
(ed.) *Edward Warren* (Missoula, 1986)
Reluctant Frontiersman: James Ross Larkin on the Santa Fe Trail, 1856–1857
  (Albuquerque, 1990)

Published with the assistance of the National Endowment for the Humanities, a federal agency which supports the study of such fields as history, philosophy, literature, and language.

Library of Congress Cataloging-in-Publication Data

Barbour, Barton H., 1951–
    Fort Union and the upper Missouri fur trade / Barton H. Barbour.
        p.   cm.
    Includes bibliographical references and index.
    ISBN 0-8061-3295-7 (cloth)
    ISBN 0-8061-3498-4 (paper)
    1. Fort Union (N.D.)—History—19th century.   2. Fort Union Region (N.D.)—History—19th century.   3. Missouri River Valley—History—19th century.   4. Fur trade—North Dakota—Fort Union Region—History—19th century.   5. Fur trade—Missouri River Valley—History—19th century.
    6. Frontier and pioneer life—North Dakota—Fort Union Region.
    7. Frontier and pioneer life—Missouri River Valley.   I. Title.
    F644.F6 B37 2001
    978.4'73—dc21

                                                    00-056827

The paper in this book meets the guidelines for permanence and durability of the Committee on Production Guidelines for Book Longevity of the Council on Library Resources, Inc. ∞

2 3 4 5 6 7 8 9 10

To Warren, for the past,

and to Jennifer, for the future

Contents

Illustrations

FIGURES

MAP

Preface

I often had the feeling that I was bucking the current of contemporary historical thought as I wrote and revised this manuscript. Fur traders are not quite the celebrities of early western history that they once were. Indeed, if current popular opinion on Kit Carson's career is any indication, their role has been reversed from heroic to villainous. I decided to write about Fort Union and its people not to reestablish a heroic luster for fur traders, but to render their world and its meaning in realistic tones. Using this post—possibly the best documented one in the United States—as a lens for examining several aspects of the western American fur trade seemed like a good idea. The fort's story also became a vehicle for testing the validity of some historical interpretations of the trade in general and of a few especially significant events.

Several themes emerged from my investigation. I discovered that Fort Union's residents constructed not just a habitation, but a community with a distinctive social organization that effectively maintained an informal communitarian legal system. The general contours of Fort Union's society originated in a centuries-old fur trade tradition, but a particular time and place—the Upper Missouri country from 1830 to 1867—gave it a special character. The long thread of continuity in the fur trade was broken when Fort Union ceased to exist, and its demise signaled the termination of a very old process in North American, and United States, history.

I concluded that the relationship between fur traders and the government has sometimes been oversimplified and that closer examination yields a more complex and subtle story. I spilled considerable ink over the question whether Pierre Chouteau, Jr., & Company exercised a monopoly. Not only do I think that they did not, but I have also introduced comparative evidence, based on the experience of the Hudson's Bay Company, suggesting that if they had achieved such a monopoly, both the trade and the development of Indian policy might have been better conducted than they were in the United States.

Another theme I develop is that after 1860 the changing political atmosphere in the United States—the rise of Lincoln's Republican party—spelled the end of the old-time American fur and Indian trades. Ironically, when Chouteau's company was exiled from the Upper Missouri—allegedly for Confederate sympathies—it was replaced by a set of scoundrels whose strategy, tactics, and commitment to the trade make the older company's behavior appear almost sterling by comparison. No other American fur company so stoutly supported the advance of natural sciences, ethnology, or the arts, and none offered more assistance to the government than Chouteau's.

Likewise, I concluded that some recent scholarship overemphasizes the idea that the trade destroyed Indian life and culture. Many factors shaped the train of events by which the United States dispossessed Indians of their lands, and merely blaming fur traders leaves too much out of the explanation. I found that the trade met mutual needs and that Indians and Euro-American traders often meshed their disparate cultures and lives in meaningful ways. I attempted to identify areas in which the trade altered or eroded traditional aspects of Indian life and offered analysis of such changes.

I hope this history of Fort Union will help explain how the traditional fur trade operated, why it was important, and how its collapse coincided with the rise of "modern" America after the Civil War. I also tried to frame the Upper Missouri trade in a big-picture context, since national trends and events very definitely affected the trade and Chouteau's company.

Based largely upon a fresh reading of documents pertaining to the Upper Missouri trade and traders' dealings with the government, this history is bound by no particular theoretical approach. I was more interested in "reconstructing" the story of Fort Union than in "deconstructing" it. I take the view that most of the documents I cited mean pretty much what they say and that too much can be made of ulterior motives, hidden agendas, and other strange extractions visible—and comprehensible—mainly to readers with an avant-garde approach to historical scholarship.

I have been at some labor to offer a lively narrative, leavened with sufficient background material to aid readers who are not deeply immersed in fur trade studies. If this book conveys Fort Union's story in an engaging fashion, and points to some new ways to look at what I think are fascinating aspects of western American history, it will have succeeded.

Acknowledgments

I wish to thank several institutions and individuals for assistance in completing this book. In 1990 I was the recipient of the University of New Mexico Arts and Sciences Dean's Doctoral Year Fellowship, which funded the bulk of my research. The documentary bedrock for this book, and several illustrations, came from collections of the Missouri Historical Society. The society's staff, especially Martha Clevenger, offered friendly guidance during the weeks I spent at Saint Louis and never winced at my requests to photocopy thousands of pages of documents. Likewise, the staff at the Minnesota Historical Society, notably Ruth Bauer, provided congenial assistance while I worked there. Charles Rankin and the staff at the Montana Historical Society invited me to speak at a conference in 1992 and shared with me their knowledge of the Upper Missouri. Joseph C. Porter and David Hunt of the Joslyn Art Museum in Omaha allowed me to examine the Maximilian-Bodmer Collection, and the museum permitted me to use illustrative material. The Midwest Jesuit Archives at Saint Louis, Missouri, provided access to the De Smet papers as well as two illustrations. The Boston Athenaeum allowed me to quote from Isaac Sprague's diary, which is in their collections. I also wish to thank the staff at the National Archives in Washington, D.C.

Professor Paul A. Hutton directed my doctoral dissertation work, encouraged me to refine the piece for publication, and offered sound advice throughout the process. Special thanks go to Alan R. Woolworth, researcher emeritus at the Minnesota Historical Society, and William Lass of Mankato, Minnesota, who headed me in the right direction early in the research process. I am grateful to have profited from their many years of experience. The late John C. Ewers, ethnologist emeritus at the Smithsonian Institution, also offered guidance in the initial stages of my work. William J. Hunt, Jr., of the National Park Service's Mid-West Archeological Center in Lincoln, Nebraska, shared his vast knowledge with me, put me on the trail of useful information, and shared illustrations. My colleagues Cheryl Foote and Hana Samek-Norton offered encouragement as revisions came and went over the years, and I also benefited from numerous conversations with my good friends Mel Yazawa and Dick Etulain, both at the University of New Mexico.

I am deeply grateful to two organizations based in Williston, North Dakota: the Friends of Fort Union and the Fort Union Association. Both provided financial aid and enthusiasm for this project at crucial points. In particular, I would like to thank Marv Kaiser and Bud Hagen for their support and advice. Likewise, I am indebted to the staff at Fort Union Trading Post National Historic Site, especially former park superintendent Paul L. Hedren, for inviting me to undertake this work in the first place and for many wise suggestions and continued support over several years, and to Orville C. Loomer, who treated me to an overflight of the region in 1990. I also wish to thank John N. Drayton, director of the University of Oklahoma Press, for his patience and support. Finally, I offer a word of thanks to my wife, Jennifer, who helped me revise the manuscript. Without her continued support, and that of my son, Vachel, this book might never have appeared. Whatever errors of judgment and interpretation may lie herein are my own.

Fort Union and the
Upper Missouri Fur Trade

Introduction

Fort Union, the Upper Missouri Outfit's flagship post, played a commanding role in Upper Missouri affairs for almost four decades. No other trading post within the contiguous United States existed for so long. In 1966 the U.S. Congress designated the site of the old post near Williston, North Dakota, a unit of the National Park Service to commemorate the importance of the western fur trade. By 1995—after years of archeological excavation and archival research—the fort was almost fully reconstructed.

Pierre Chouteau, Jr., his partners, and his employees made the Upper Missouri Outfit (UMO), a component of John Astor's American Fur Company (AFCo) from 1828 to 1834, the most powerful United States presence in the Northern Plains between 1830 and 1865. Fort Union lay at the western edge of a commercial network extending from the Northern Plains south to Saint Louis, east to New York and Washington, D.C., and even further to London, Paris, Leipzig, and Canton.

Fur traders were the first entrepreneurs in western North America, and their business generated much information that was later used to advance national expansion. The trade's enduring imprint was etched on Americans' self-conscious construction of their "national character," on their folklore, and on their impressions of Indians. It helped promote domestic manufacturing, generated capital to fuel the growth of American

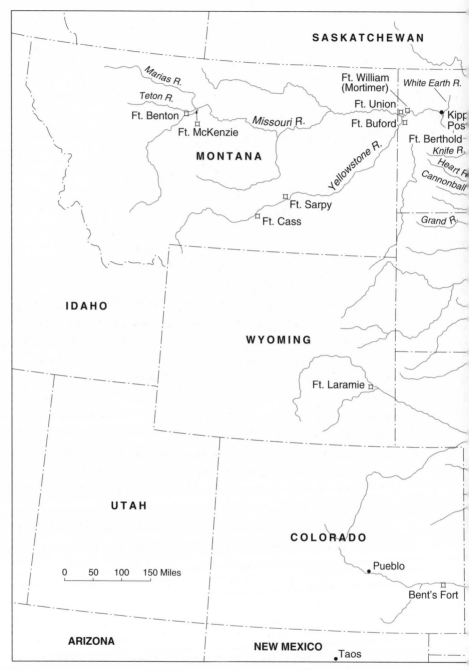

The Upper Missouri River Fur Trade Country, 1830–67

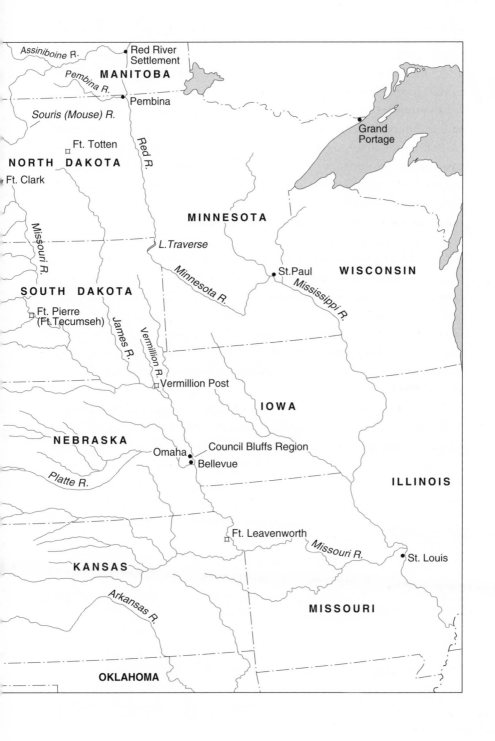

commerce and trade, and helped lay the foundations for modern joint-stock companies. It also provided international connections that affected banking, trade and finance, and diplomacy.

More than a century before the United States purchased Louisiana and began to develop that region's economic potential, events took place far to the north that would influence the destiny of the Upper Missouri and Pacific Northwest regions. The Governor and Company of Adventurers of England Trading into Hudson's Bay, called the Hudson's Bay Company (HBC), had been chartered by King Charles II in 1670. Holding exclusive proprietary trading rights throughout Rupert's Land—the enormous watershed of Hudson's Bay—the "Great Company" did not yield its title until confederation made Rupert's Land part of Canada in 1870. Some unknown wag long ago declared that the company's initials stood for "Here Before Christ," in testimony of its power.[1] Headquartered in London, this joint stock company was the greatest mercantile success in early Canada. After merging with its North West Company rivals in 1821, the HBC began a rough-and-tumble competition with United States outfits for Northern Plains and Rocky Mountain furs that continued until about 1850.[2]

The newly unified HBC threatened to hamstring the United States fur trade and disrupt the government's diplomacy with Indians, partly because it consolidated commerce, sovereignty, law, and Indian affairs under a unitary authority. In the United States, where no analogous entity appeared, Indians, traders, Indian agents, and soldiers often operated at cross-purposes, generating problems for all.

Before the 1860s, fur traders' activities and institutions constituted the primary source for Indians' exposure to American society and culture. Because Fort Union was in business for so long, it offers an opportunity to investigate Indian-white relations in the years preceding the United States' military conquest of the Northern Plains. When federal civilian and military agents appeared in sufficiently large numbers to affect the course of events, the "traditional" fur trade became a casualty to about the same degree as the Indian cultures that supported it. By the late 1860s the old-time fur and Indian trades had vanished, their places taken by a government rationing system for Indians, an emigrant trade for overlanders, and military sutlers' stores for troops in the region.

Fur traders first appeared on the Upper Missouri in the 1730s, but Indians had lived there for at least ten thousand years. Some tribes devoted much time and energy to farming, while others relied mainly on hunting and did no planting. Linguistic, social, and religious differences abounded, and deep antagonisms echoed sharp differences in Upper Missouri tribal life. Beginning about 1700, tribes that had formerly dwelt east of the Mississippi moved westward, at least partially in response to various intratribal and Indian-white conflicts. From east and west, tribes converged on the plains.

The Assiniboines and Crees became the principal native traders at Fort Union. They had been allies for a century before moving from the forests southwest of Hudson's Bay onto the plains. Generations of experience with Hudson's Bay and North West Company men had attuned them to the commercial fur trade long before they resettled near the Missouri River about 1800.[3]

Assiniboine and Cree middlemen had profited by selling used trade goods to the Blackfeet and Gros Ventres de la Prairie, though the lucrative second-hand trade required travel to HBC posts over great distances. Other Upper Missouri tribes also sponsored commercial ventures to Hudson's Bay; for example, the Mandans visited York Factory in the late seventeenth and early eighteenth centuries.[4]

The Crees and Assiniboines moved south partly because of their activity in the pemmican trade. Pemmican, the *voyageurs'* food, was made from crushed dried buffalo meat, dried berries, and grease melted together and packed into rectangular hide sacks. Highly nutritious and easily transported, pemmican remained edible for years. When over-hunted bison herds retreated southward, the Assiniboines and Crees followed. Eventually, instead of trading pemmican with the HBC, the two tribes traded robes with the Americans on the Missouri. The HBC traded few robes because of the high costs of transportation to their bayside York Factory, but even before the steamboat era, Americans at Fort Union moved thousands of robes down the Missouri River.[5]

Trade formed an important theme in Assiniboine and Cree life. Their visits to Fort Union took place within a ritualized context that reached far back in time, reflecting a long continuity in fur trade protocol. It seems fitting to ask here, Did the fur trade benefit Indians, or did it force them into dependence on the whites' goods? One answer is that fur traders and their business "generated a cycle of trade, violence, dependence, and poverty for American Indians."[6]

Advocates of the "dependency theory" argue that white traders gradually attained near-total economic control over Indians, which fostered a decline in the Indians' independence and ensured their loss of sovereignty to the United States. Traders are cast as willing agents in the government's plan to undermine or destroy Indian cultures. This simple assessment is flawed. The historical record does not support the conflation of fur traders with the U.S. Army and government; instead, it shows that they had dissimilar views and divergent interests. It is also important to differentiate the few hundred fur traders on the plains from the many thousands of white men and women who came after they were gone. An emphasis on unidirectional dependency is likewise misleading.

The fur trade demanded mutual reliance among all participants: white men did not tan buffalo robes, and Indians did not make guns, steel knives, and so on. Interdependency percolated through every aspect of life, and it characterized North America's fur trade frontier almost everywhere. In time, that interdependency corroded and vanished, mainly because it did not conform to the United States' cultural and political imperatives. Still, the trade probably had dual effects: it made Indians' lives easier, but it also necessitated a reliance on exotic products from an alien, industrializing world.[7]

Implicit in the dependency argument is the troubling assumption that Indians failed to make wise choices about their use of trade goods or alcohol and realized too late, if ever, that they had been duped and were about to be overwhelmed. Arguing that white traders' greed and moral degeneracy were the principal causes of Indians' impoverishment would seem to suggest that Indians could not control events, make rational decisions, or operate as partners in the trade. To employ a bit of modern jargon, this argument "disempowers" nineteenth-century Indians, yielding little more than a new wrinkle on the old face of "poor Lo," a derogatory nickname for culturally moribund Indians derived from Alexander Pope's poem *An Essay on Man*.

Indians were partners, and they were willing to trade common articles such as bison robes for luxury and utilitarian goods that would otherwise have been impossible to procure. Moreover, by the early eighteenth century Indians had already become keenly discriminating customers who could easily discover defects in trade merchandise. Indian men and women were active participants in the trade who influenced its institutions and economics, and their demand for a broad range of high-quality goods was taken seriously at fur companies' headquarters.[8]

Edwin T. Denig, a UMO trader, believed the Assiniboines had "been greatly changed for the better" as a result of the fur trade, which had "promoted the general cause of civilization." In his judgment, trade introduced them to a different world and "set them to thinking, to show them their uncultivated state, and to implant a desire to improve" their condition. In Denig's view, the "conversation and instructions [that Indians] received from the traders has increased their knowledge, elevated their desires, and stimulated their industry." Still, he found the slow pace of change among Indian societies "vexatious and discouraging." Ideas about Indian culture were freighted with ethnocentric contradictions even for Edwin Denig, who married an Indian woman and helped raise mixed-blood children.[9]

Denig expected trade to be a vehicle for the Indians' cultural transformation. He believed "the change from savage to civilized life and occupations must be gradual, accompanied by instruction, education, and practical experiment." He thought Catholic missionaries could also be effective agents of change if they dedicated themselves to teaching young natives "agricultural and pastoral pursuits" and if they sent a few Indians east to be trained as medical doctors. In the meantime, Indians would continue to hunt game, which was gradually declining, and trade at Fort Union or other posts. If government or philanthropists failed to take action, however, Denig feared that Indians would "by a sudden pressure of emigration, and a consequent annihilation of game, become the drudges of the whites, destroyed and degraded by their great banes, whiskey and smallpox."[10]

Fur traders were an important source of whiskey, but hardly the only one. Any land bordering "Indian Country" could be a distribution point for alcohol. Army sutlers and soldiers likewise contributed to the flow, as did white emigrants moving westward who gave or sold whiskey to Indians. Fur traders and a few missionaries thought that many bad influences stemmed from emigrating whites on the plains, who killed game, spread diseases, and mistreated Indians.[11]

Most tribes attributed magical properties to liquor that made it particularly appealing. It may also have served as a vehicle to achieve a temporary suspension of the rigid social constraints that marked Indian life. Not all Indians used alcohol, but among the Upper Missouri tribes that did, Denig claimed about 1853, "from a long period of actual observation and experience we can safely say that the whole number of deaths arising from the consequences of intoxicating drink does not amount to 100 during the past 20 years, from and including the Sioux to the Blackfeet." Denig's estimate cannot be authoritatively verified or refuted, since no one else in the region kept a count.[12]

Whiskey floods in the Upper Missouri country usually coincided with episodes of intense trade competition and may have been more closely linked to the nature of competitive capitalism than to Indians' unquenchable thirst for the stuff. As fur traders themselves argued, under a more monopolistic system liquor would likely have created fewer problems. Finally, whether the use of liquor was moral or immoral, legal or illegal, Indians wanted it, and few refused when it was offered for consumption. In this they differed not at all from whites, except that white people seem to have been much more prodigious drinkers. An ironic trade-off was also involved, as John C. Ewers suggested many years ago when he wrote: "Perhaps the Indians' contribution of the 'coffin nail' offsets the Europeans' gift of 'fire water.'"[13]

Because of the trade, everyday tasks probably became less burdensome, while burial offerings, costume and makeup techniques, hunting, and warfare were modified to some extent. Indians made rational decisions about adapting new materials and technologies to their uses. Men who hunted bison and women who tanned robes each benefited from the trade. Rudolph Friederich Kurz, while at Fort Union in 1851, mentioned that women robe tanners received "a share in the dressed skins, which they exchange for clothes, ornaments, and dainty tidbits." Edwin Denig stated that sometimes Crow men and women divided their skins before exchanging them for goods so that "either trades for what they like best."[14]

In the end, it was not the fur trade that demolished the old ways of life for Plains Indians. It was the U.S. Army, carrying out orders from the government, which in turn reflected the will of the American people. Commerce did not subjugate and impoverish Plains Indians; military force and the erosion of the native land and resource base did. Fur traders had nothing to gain by the destruction of bison herds, but white soldiers, "settlers," and town builders did. And, as some traders knew but hardly dared say, a government-sanctioned monopoly based on the HBC model might have reduced both use and abuse of alcohol as well as other problems related to unbridled competition beyond the United States' frontier when no coherent Indian policy existed.

When the Hudson's Bay and North West Companies amalgamated, a number of traders, clerks, and other employees from both companies lost their jobs. In 1821 three of them—Kenneth McKenzie, William Laidlaw, and Daniel Lamont—joined with Joseph Renville, James Kipp, and Robert Dickson to launch a new outfit, with the spread-eagle name of Columbia Fur Company, intended to operate chiefly south of the Canadian border.[15]

Columbia Fur offered stiff competition to John Astor's AFCo in the Minnesota Valley, while to the west on the James River (Rivière au Jacques) and the Upper Missouri it battled a well-entrenched Saint Louis firm, Bernard Pratte and Company, in which Pierre Chouteau, Jr., was a partner. To oppose Astor, Columbia Fur built four posts in the Minnesota Valley, several trade houses at Lake Traverse and at Green Bay on the western shore of Lake Michigan, and one at Prairie du Chien on the Mississippi. To compete with the Saint Louis traders, in 1822–23, Columbia Fur placed several posts along the Missouri. The largest, Fort Tecumseh, stood at the mouth of the Teton River (today's Bad River). All could be supplied from the outfit's headquarters at Lake Traverse, the source of the Red River, athwart the divide between the Red River, which flowed northward toward Hudson's Bay, and the Saint Peter's (Minnesota) River, which flowed southeast to the Mississippi.[16]

Inspired by Dickson's pioneering ventures among the Teton Sioux, and strengthened by McKenzie's aggressive leadership after 1823, Columbia Fur traders soon reached the Mandan villages. John Astor planned to extend the AFCo operations westward from Michilimackinac,

Kenneth McKenzie. Self-styled "King of the Upper Missouri," McKenzie played a crucial role in creating Fort Union, inaugurating steamer traffic on the Missouri, making a "gentlemens' peace" with the Blackfeet, and operating an illegal whiskey still at Fort Union. *Courtesy Missouri Historical Society, Saint Louis.*

Pierre Chouteau, Jr. Descended from one of Saint Louis's founding French families, Chouteau became a leader in the fur trade following the War of 1812. He ran and in 1834 purchased the American Fur Company's Western Department. *Courtesy Missouri Historical Society, Saint Louis.*

but that meant he must have access to the Missouri, and to do so he needed a foothold at Saint Louis.[17] Shortly after the War of 1812, Astor had begun courting Saint Louis traders, seeking a deal that would allow him to push up the Missouri. Saint Louis's leading French mercantile families repeatedly rejected his offers, but the federal government's Indian factories also obstructed his path.

Proponents believed that a system of Indian "factories"—government-subsidized trading posts run by factors—would benefit the nation and Indians alike. British traders routinely defied the 1783 Treaty of Paris by trading with Indians in the Old Northwest and sometimes encouraged them to commit depredations against Americans. An orderly Indian trade system, the argument ran, would diminish British traders' illicit profits while bringing Indians more effectively under the influence of the United States and reducing the threat of frontier bloodshed. Factories also offered Indians an alternative to private traders, whose goods might be shoddy, whose prices were widely variable, and who often gave or sold Indians liquor. Initiated in 1796, the factory system was supposed to help the "savages" become "civilized," partly by fostering their dependence upon white mens' goods.[18] Astor's chief objection to Indian factories was that they limited private enterprise at certain points, mainly along the Mississippi, where American entrepreneurs found easiest access to the fur trade frontier.[19]

When Astor contacted General Charles Gratiot (cousin of Pierre Chouteau, Jr.) of Saint Louis early in 1814 to discuss the factories, Gratiot encouragingly responded: "The Indian trade will have in future to be carried on by a Compy to become profitable[.] as it stands now it is too precarious for any body to hazard anything unless the factories were to be abolished." Astor set out to remedy these two nagging problems: the impediment of government trade houses, and an inefficient business organization at Saint Louis.[20]

Astor, a critic of the factory system since at least 1807, intensified his attack after a company reorganization in 1817. By out-trading the factories and enlisting the aid of influential politicians such as Missouri's Senator Thomas Hart Benton and Michigan territorial governor Lewis Cass, Astor prevailed, and the factory system expired in 1822. His deputy and lobbyist Ramsay Crooks applauded Benton for "destroying the pious

monster" and clearing the path for the AFCo to muscle its way into Saint
Louis and the Missouri River trade. By 1823 only one major loose end
remained: American Fur must convince the creoles that cooperation
would pay better than resistance.[21]

During October 1821, Ramsay Crooks informed Astor of his intention
to open a Saint Louis bureau and instructed Samuel Abbott at Prairie du
Chien to "proceed this fall to Saint Louis, there to remain until you obtain
a *complete* list of the goods usually found in the retail establishments at
that place. Ascertain everything that may be of advantage to us, and, as
soon thereafter as may be convenient to yourself, pursue your journey to
New York."[22]

While Crooks gathered intelligence on the fine points of supplying
the Missouri River trade, Astor still lacked firm commitments from the
Saint Louis men. Crooks wrote in November that "preliminary arrangements are made for prosecuting the trade of St. Louis and the Missouri
next season. . . . You now do no business with them worth attending to,
and any scruples we have before entertained in regard to embarking in
their portion of the trade, ought not to be indulged in any longer."[23]

In April 1822 the AFCo opened its Saint Louis branch office. Crooks
assured Astor that he would not attempt too much in the first year, that
he meant only to "tamper with the Missouri traders on a moderate scale,
in order to secure them for the following year." This "tampering" constituted the first stirrings of the AFCo's future Western Department, and
it may have hastened the making of a deal.[24]

In 1822 the firm of Berthold, Chouteau, & Pratte signed a one-year
contract with Crooks to sell furs to and purchase goods from the AFCo.[25]
The next year a new partner, Jean-Pierre Cabanné, joined the firm, and
it was renamed Bernard Pratte & Company. Social and economic relations between Astor's men and the Saint Louisans were further solidified
in 1825 when Ramsay Crooks married Bernard Pratte's youngest daughter,
Emilie.[26] In December 1826, Bernard Pratte & Company became the sole
western agents for Astor's company.

With Joshua Pilcher's Missouri Fur Company bankrupt, William Ashley's
brigades working Rocky Mountain streams far to the west, and the Frenchmen in Saint Louis engaged in preliminary arrangements with the AFCo,
Astor prepared for his debut in the Upper Missouri. The troublesome

Columbia Fur Company, however, would not go away. In just a few years and on a relatively lean budget, Columbia Fur had completed the groundwork upon which the Upper Missouri fur trade rested during the next three decades.[27]

From posts strung along the Missouri between Council Bluffs and the Yellowstone, the Columbia Fur Company traded with several tribes judged to be under British influence. William Tilton and James Kipp built Tilton's Post at the Mandan village of Mih-Tutta-Hang-Kush late in 1823, but the nearby Arikaras, fearing that the newcomers were out to usurp their middleman role on the Missouri, forced its abandonment the following spring. James Kipp established a new post closer to a Mandan village at the Big Knife River and in 1826–27 advanced another 150 miles up the Missouri into Assiniboine country, setting up Kipp's Post at the mouth of the White Earth River.[28]

Crooks estimated in 1826 that competition with McKenzie's outfit did American Fur "an annual injury of ten thousand dollars at least." Verification of this claim is impossible, since no Columbia Fur Company financial records have survived, but it is known that the outfit was backed by Saint Louis merchants who were equally hostile to Astor's company and to the Chouteau-Pratte clan.[29]

Much of the company's income stemmed from the previously under-exploited buffalo robe trade, and Columbia Fur's gross take from 1825 to 1827 ranged between $150,000 and $200,000 annually. Marketed in the west and the east, buffalo robes were made into sleigh and carriage robes, hearth rugs, and men's overcoats. Characteristically, when Astor became interested in robes in April 1827, he wrote: "About Buffalo I think they will do if you can get the whole and not otherwise. . . . I mean . . . at least 5/6 of them so as to have the command of the market."[30]

Recognizing that McKenzie and his partners' robe trade showed promise, Crooks and Astor opened negotiations with the upstarts. In Crooks's view, the choice was either a formal division of territory or incorporation. Crooks and McKenzie sparred over the issue of territorial division between April 1826 and early the following year, with no results. Astor enjoined the frustrated Crooks, who complained that McKenzie's demands were "too great," to keep trying, as "it will be better than to carry on one opposition after another."[31]

Final talks had to wait until McKenzie came downriver with Columbia Fur's harvest of robes and skins. McKenzie insisted that two or three of his partners be included in the deal, and he wanted the AFCo to "employ [Columbia Fur's] people in preference to our own on the Missouri and St. Peters." Crooks hoped that McKenzie might "consent to leave the whole of them to their fate, and come over to us himself." Next, Crooks discussed the potential sale with Columbia Fur's money men, Saint Louisans named Collier and Powell, who demanded that Astor purchase all their remaining goods at cost plus 20 to 25 percent. An outraged Crooks flatly refused their proposal, concluding that further discussion was pointless. In one of many letters he wrote that summer, Crooks informed Astor on June 27, 1827: "All my sincere efforts to arrange with the Columbia Fur Company have proved abortive. We must now fight harder than ever."[32]

Crooks's pessimism proved exaggerated, for the two concerns struck a bargain within a few days. Perhaps because the chief negotiators, Crooks and McKenzie, were fellow Scotsmen, they "were disposed to be as conciliatory towards each other as was consonant with duty." Besides, Columbia Fur was being hounded by its principal creditors, Collier and Powell, who Crooks heard were "sick of the business and somewhat cramped in means." The deal was finally made on July 6, when Crooks penned a letter to Astor describing the settlement. Columbia Fur ceased to exist, and some of its employees might transfer to the AFCo. Collier and Powell gave up the Indian trade for four years, and the AFCo bought their trade goods, absorbed transport costs to the Upper Missouri, and paid them 12.5 percent profit on their imported goods.[33]

With the Columbia Fur Company rechristened the Upper Missouri Outfit of the AFCo's Western Department, Astor and Crooks had cause to celebrate. Astor had united his vast capital and grandiose vision with Chouteau's acute organizational mind and McKenzie's vigorous field tactics. Pierre Chouteau, Jr., became the department's chief executive, while McKenzie assumed management of the UMO. He retained several former associates—James Kipp, William Laidlaw, and Daniel Lamont— as well as a new man, David D. Mitchell, for the UMO.[34] Five years of maneuvering had secured a formidable combination of finance, management, and experience.

The amalgamation assured Astor's AFCo a large profit from the Missouri River trade. Building on Columbia Fur's experiences, McKenzie began to refine his strategy for maintaining dominance in the region. Central to that strategy was the need for a large, impressive, and well-stocked upriver fort that would advertise the UMO's power. Fort Union would become McKenzie's grandest achievement. As the premiere trading post on the Upper Missouri, it symbolized John Astor's reach at its westernmost extreme.[35]

From this point on, many fur traders referred to Astor's outfit simply as "the Company," while the term *opposition* covered any other competitors. Opposition men faced intimidating, often insurmountable odds in marshaling capital, manpower, resources, and political connections. Successful competitors came and went, but the Company remained.[36]

Astor retired as director of the AFCo in 1834, selling the Northern Department to his agent Ramsay Crooks, who legally retained use of the company name. The Western Department went to Bernard Pratte & Company, soon to be renamed Pratte, Chouteau & Company.[37] In 1839, following the death of partner Bernard Pratte in 1836 and subsequent sale of his son's interest, the company became Pierre Chouteau, Jr., & Company. Under this name it remained in business until 1865, when it was sold.

DYNAMICS OF THE UPPER MISSOURI FUR TRADE

Fort Union was a regional collection and distribution center and a terminal point in a global enterprise. It affected, and responded to, business decisions made thousands of miles away at banks and auction houses in New York, Montréal, London, and Leipzig. Occasionally, Fort Union's fur shipments were large enough to influence prices at European auction houses.

Making money in the fur trade was a difficult and expensive proposition. Sometimes competition reached such intensity that profits practically vanished. High costs, high risks, and complex infrastructure are not easily discernible in the prosaic exchange of a handful of beads or a striped blanket for a buffalo robe at some remote trading post in

"Indian country." Some observers view the trade as nothing more than an unsavory backwoods ripoff whereby venal white men conned unsuspecting natives. In reality, success in the chancy economics of fur trading required that interrelationships among Indian, mixed-blood, and white traders be reasonably amicable. No less vital to victory, however, were large amounts of capital, access to worldwide networks for supplies and sales, and dependable connections with allies inside the government.[38]

The simple passage of time could impede success in the fur and Indian trades. Early-nineteenth-century communication and transportation networks dictated the speed at which the business moved. Three or more years might pass before money spent on trade goods found its way back to the credit side of fur companies' ledger books. An elaborate system of credit and interest arrangements fueled the fur and hide business, enabling traders to ship huge amounts of goods from Italy, France, Belgium, England, Germany, and the United States deep into North America's interior.

Transoceanic freight and insurance charges, as well as currency exchange premiums, consumed capital and contributed to high operating costs. So did payments of U.S. customs duties at New York or New Orleans, warehousing fees, and the expense of transporting goods to western cities with wholesale and distribution capabilities, notably Saint Louis. Passing time also threatened bales of furs, which might be severely damaged by insects or rodents while in transit or in storage. Merely sitting in stuffy, humid warehouses awaiting transportation encouraged improperly put up packs of furs to rot.

Labor costs also generated substantial overhead expenses for fur companies. Before steamboats began to ply the Missouri in 1831, boatmen hauled merchandise upriver to trading posts in ungainly keelboats. Sixty feet in length, and weighing several tons, these boats carried twenty to forty tons of freight. French inhabitants of Louisiana or Canada constituted the vast majority of keelboatmen. A single man's annual wages ranged only from $130 to $150, but Pierre Chouteau, Jr., like some other traders, hired roughly one hundred boatmen each year. Keelboats could be purchased for about $135, but with crews of ten or twelve, operational costs amounted to a considerable sum.[39]

The Keel-Boat, from "Remembrances of the Mississippi," *Harper's New Monthly Magazine*. Before as well as after the advent of steamer traffic on the Missouri, these unlovely but effective craft moved goods and men up or down the river. *Courtesy Missouri Historical Society, Saint Louis.*

Fur traders staked their future profits against the probability of losses during transportation. Keelboats and steamers regularly fell prey to the Missouri's myriad snags, typically with losses of fifteen thousand to forty-five thousand dollars.[40] Wrecks were liable to occur at any point in the transport network, whether on the Mississippi or Ohio Rivers, on the Pennsylvania or Erie Canals, or on the high seas. Consequently, fur traders purchased domestic and international shipping insurance, paying premiums of 2 to 3.5 percent of the value of goods shipped. With so many shipments of merchandise moving through Saint Louis, a fledgling insurance industry appeared there as nervous investors purchased insurance for cargoes destined for trade in Indian country."[41]

Traders occasionally passed out substantial amounts of goods to purchase "protection" from Indian nations along the river or those who controlled overland routes to trading posts. Fur traders likewise bowed to the native tradition of giving gifts to signal the beginning and end of trade sessions by proffering a gratuity, sometimes tobacco and liquor, sometimes coffee or tea and biscuits. White and Indian traders created mutually beneficial liaisons that were adjusted according to need. This practice might disrupt or reshape internal tribal politics to some degree, but native traders also exercised some leverage. Indians' reciprocal "gifts" of robes and furs, usually worth 100 to 150 robes, might be withdrawn if traders failed to produce their fair share of presents. Indeed, according to Edwin Denig, Indians expected about double the value of the robes they offered.[42]

Few early-nineteenth-century business organizations in the United States were capable of shouldering such heavy risks and overhead expenses. The AFCo was the first large integrated corporation in the United States, and against its success the strategy, tactics, capital, and effectiveness of its competitors must be measured. The Upper Missouri was just one theater of operations in John Jacob Astor's campaign to capture the entire North American fur trade.[43]

It is a bit misleading to describe Pierre Chouteau, Jr., & Company's business simply as the fur trade of the Upper Missouri. The Upper Missouri trade was actually composed of three distinct but interrelated commercial ventures: fur trapping, the Indian trade, and freighting contracts with the U.S. government. Each component produced income for Pierre Chouteau, Jr., & Company.

Fort Union's bourgeois outfitted trapping expeditions principally between 1830 and 1839. Euro-American, Indian, and mixed-blood beaver hunters were outfitted with traps, provisions, ammunition, horses, and camp equipment at Fort Union or other UMO posts. Changing fur market conditions, and changing fashion, made trapping expeditions less necessary after 1840.

The Indian trade entailed the exchange of Euro-American manufactured goods for buffalo robes and other peltries. There was also a brisk trade in dried or fresh meat and other foods that helped supply Fort Union with provender. Traders sometimes purchased skillfully crafted artifacts such as lances, bows, pipes, and decorated leather clothing and accessories as highly prized "keepers" or for eventual sale to eastern and foreign collectors. Visiting scientists, artists, and naturalists avidly sought Indian manufactures, and so did some employees at Fort Union and elsewhere. In its varied forms, the Indian trade constituted Fort Union's leading money-maker.

Freighting government annuity goods provided a third source of income for Pierre Chouteau, Jr., & Company. The company transported and stored tons of goods destined for Upper Missouri tribes following the conclusion of federal treaties, a process that began in 1825 with the Atkinson-O'Fallon expedition and continued beyond Fort Union's occupation. Because these three undertakings boosted the company's profits, as well as its influence among Indian tribes and with the federal government, they merit a closer look.

TRAPPING EXPEDITIONS AND
FORT UNION

Federal laws prohibited whites from trapping animals in Indian country, which meant land west of the Mississippi, north of the Arkansas, and east of the central Rockies claimed but not yet incorporated by the United States.[44] But whites conducted many trapping expeditions in Indian country, and their activities came under congressional scrutiny more than once. Revisiting that investigation of fur trapping helps explain why practice did not follow policy.[45]

In 1824, Senator Thomas Hart Benton of Missouri, chairing the Senate Committee on Indian Affairs, took testimony regarding white trappers' invasion of Indian lands. Few Euro-Americans set traps in Indian country before 1822–23, when William Ashley and Andrew Henry's brigades inaugurated large-scale, highly profitable trapping. By 1824 their success raised legal questions concerning potential repercussions from this new and expanding activity. Respondents explained that white trappers jeopardized both international and domestic tranquility. Although the "factory system" of government trade houses expired in 1822, British influence among Upper Missouri tribes still threatened to defeat U.S. policy aimed at the Assiniboines, Crees, and Blackfeet, many of whom lived south of the "medicine line" separating the United States and Canada.

When the committee queried Richard Graham, a Delaware and Shawnee agent, about American citizens' "hunting and trapping on Indian lands," he answered that these activities produced "the most unhappy effects upon the minds of the Indians," who viewed game as whites did their domestic animals. Consequently, Graham observed, it would not be "unreasonable to suppose, that they will not only steal from, but murder those who are depriving them of their only means of subsistence." To eliminate this problem, he suggested that the government restrict fur traders to specific locations and "not permit them to attend the Indians on their hunting parties, as they at present do, many of them carrying with them their traps. . . . The Indian would then know that every white man found on his lands, at any other place than the trading establishment, was a trespasser, and might be taken up and brought to the agent."[46]

Joshua Pilcher, vainly struggling to wring success out of his dying Missouri Fur Company, explained that his men trapped on Indian land but claimed that an established norm of Indian hospitality permitted "traders, travellers, or others, killing what was necessary for their subsistence." He admitted that "the trapping done [was] not under any license; the one we receive from the Government is to *trade*," but he added that "Messrs. Berthold, Chouteau, and Pratte, of St. Louis . . . have also been, and are still largely engaged in the trapping business."[47]

Questions about Ashley and Henry's license had already stirred concern among Indian agents, notably Upper Missouri agent Benjamin O'Fallon.

Writing to Secretary of War John C. Calhoun in April 1822, O'Fallon suggested that whites might be permitted to trap on land belonging to Indians with whom the government had no treaty arrangements, but only until "foreign" (that is, British) influence was eliminated. Thereafter, "hunting and trapping should be prohibited and our traders confined alone to a fair and equitable trade with them." O'Fallon envisioned government use of trappers to achieve a national security aim, but once the objective was gained he wished to end trapping and establish trading posts instead. This thorny issue was temporarily laid aside when William Clark, an influential expert and O'Fallon's uncle, offered Calhoun his opinion that "the license granted to Genl Ashley and Majr Henry I am inclined to believe will not produce any disturbance among the Indian tribes with whome we have much intercourse." Clark, and the majority of government men, had agreed to wink at fine legal distinctions between trapping and trading. Put simply, the business of trapping on Indian land was entirely illegal.[48]

Despite Indian resistance and a governmental licensing system initiated partly to rein in traders, the 1830s saw the greatest invasion of trapping outfits ever to appear along the Upper Missouri. More importantly, the government's decision not to enforce its own law exemplifies what can happen when economically and politically powerful men share overlapping interests and close relationships. Parallel interests, along with conflicting ideas about the proper place for Indians in the republic, helped create and perpetuate a dysfunctional ethical flexibility that tainted the Office of Indian Affairs and impeded the flow of justice for the remainder of the century.

Far from the rarified atmosphere of the nation's capital, trappers continued their illicit practices. Kenneth McKenzie tried to secure the "mountain trade" during the 1830s. From 1829 to 1839 he outfitted trapping and trading brigades, usually led by Étienne Provost, Lucien Fontenelle, or Andrew Drips. McKenzie's tactic, intended to trump upstarts such as the Rocky Mountain Fur Company, helped reduce competition, but his expeditions often lost money for the company.[49]

McKenzie scored a prodigious coup in 1830 when he opened trade with the Blackfeet. Thanks to the skillful diplomacy of a veteran trader named Jacob Berger, the Blackfeet permitted the UMO to build a post in 1831 on the Marias River. Some Blackfeet torched Fort Piegan in 1832, and the Company built a new post, Fort McKenzie, a few miles away. It tapped the rich Blackfeet fur resources, reduced the influx of undesirable free trappers, and produced well for a number of years.

In part, McKenzie acted as a spoiler who sought to make trapping less appealing to potential competitors. But he also served a larger cause by denying the formidable HBC an opportunity to cultivate Blackfeet animosity against Americans. This important achievement pleased the national government almost as much as it did the UMO. Ever since Lewis and Clark's expedition the Blackfeet country had been celebrated for its excellent fur resources, but the tribe was notoriously anti-American, and their enmity was unquestionably fueled by British traders.[50]

The UMO's high-intensity trapping campaign resulted in overhunting of beaver and temporary depletion but did not bring higher prices. Haberdashers developed new hat styles using silk instead of fur felt and fur flocking and found cheaper sources of felt-quality fur, such as the ratlike South American nutria. As beaver prices gradually lost value, the trade shifted in response. When beaver harvests declined, the Upper Missouri trade grew more dependent on buffalo robes and on Indians who collected and processed them. A journal entry made at Fort Union on May 5, 1835, highlights the change: "As the beaver trade for the last three years has been regularly declining notwithstanding every facility and encouragement we have given the Piegans, it appears that our sheet anchor will be Robe trade. . . . and by encouraging the Blood Blackfeet and others to make Robes, articles which they now obtain as luxuries will become necessaries and they will be compelled to remain on the Missouri in order to procure them."[51]

By 1840, as participants recognized, the era of the mountain men was over, but trapping for beaver and other mammals never entirely disappeared from the area around Fort Union. Well before 1850 beaver fur prices plunged so low that trapping practically ceased, but by 1851 beaver populations were on the rise, and "a great many" were reputed to be in the vicinity of Fort Union. Beaver skins were traded even in the 1860s, although prices had long since fallen from an all-time high of about six dollars a pound to about fifty cents.[52]

In the competitive atmosphere of the American fur trade little effort was directed toward conservation of fur resources. During the 1820s, however, the HBC attempted to boost beaver populations by limiting or curtailing hunts in certain areas. The program was most effective in areas where competition was least serious. The conservation policy was jettisoned in the HBC's Saskatchewan District because of intense competition with Fort Union.[53]

INDIAN TRADE AT FORT UNION

Fort Union's Indian trade made it the keystone of a regional trade network. Cree, Assiniboine, Crow, and Blackfeet customers, all buffalo hunters and robe makers eager to acquire Euro-American utensils, cloth, and weapons, kept the UMO in business.

In order to maintain the flow of robes to Saint Louis, traders encouraged Indians to produce more than were required to satisfy their immediate desires for trade goods. At Fort Union, accounts with Indian as well as white traders were figured in terms of the standard exchange medium, buffalo robes. One robe's value was calculated at "an imaginary value of $3 each in the country." To illustrate, in 1851 a 3-point blanket (a coarse but durable English woolen measuring roughly four by six feet) cost three robes. Two robes bought a two-gallon iron-bound brass kettle, while three inexpensive butcher knives could be had for one robe. A robe also purchased a yard of red or blue woolen stroud cloth or a hundred loads of powder and ball. Good horses might fetch ten or more robes, and guns were similarly expensive. Other fur values were calculated in proportionate fractions of robes, with so many raccoon, fox, or beaver skins equaling one robe.[54] Robes sold at Saint Louis for about six dollars.

Many trade goods did become more necessities than luxuries, and certain items displaced old-time native tools and equipment. Iron and steel knives and axes have obvious advantages over stone or bone tools. Substitution of brass or iron kettles for pottery of native manufacture may have occurred in as brief a timespan as a single generation in many tribes.[55] Ribbons, scarves, glass necklace and embroidery beads, shell and bone hair tubes, mirrors, paints, brass rings and bracelets, and dozens of other types of goods quickly found acceptance among native customers. Smoothbore flintlock weapons, called North West guns, offered no real advantage over bows and arrows for hunting buffalo and made a difference in warfare when only one side possessed them. Guns became badges of status and evidence of symbolic links between Indians and traders, but bows and arrows remained popular weapons until multiple-shot breechloaders were perfected in the 1860s.[56]

Traders encouraged Indians to collect robes and furs by advancing "credits" to hunters each fall. Traders might provide a gun, ammunition, traps, a kettle, a blanket, or other goods to Indian hunters in the expectation that their catch would be traded at Fort Union. Indians often insisted that purchases in a given year be credited against the next year's fur harvest. Traders could refuse these requests, but only at the risk that the Indians might trade elsewhere. Sometimes the tactic worked, though Denig observed that "our books are full of unpaid debts of 20 years' standing, and would make a handsome fortune if the value could be realized." Native hunters frequently ignored credits, knowing that traders were not likely to press too hard for collection.[57] Credits proved vexatious and difficult to collect and in many cases were simply written off as losses.

The robe trade accelerated culture change. As Indian men and women became enmeshed in an international web of production and consumption, they used hardware such as knives, fleshing tools, awls, and needles to streamline the hide tanning process, thereby promoting production surpluses. Native responses to the fur trade probably included a rise in plural marriages by Indian men as a means of maximizing robe production. (Polygamy was common among Indians; men often married their wives' sisters, and endemic intertribal warfare had created gender imbalances resulting in a "surplus" of women.) Ancient communitarian structures such as traditional community bison hunts may have begun to erode as tribal members developed individual or family-based patterns of production and consumption. Marriage and other social and economic connections between fur traders and Indians likewise altered internal tribal politics. Trade chiefs, wives, kinfolk, and members of "soldier" societies who defended fur traders all had a hand in undermining older native ways.

Traders at Fort Union congratulated themselves and let the government know that they had "weaned" the Assiniboines and Crees from British influence. Like the Blackfeet, the Assiniboines and Crees found economic opportunities at Fort Union, and trading robes there simply represented a rational business decision. Fort Union's traders inserted themselves into a well-established economic system, but they never forgot their obligation to establish and maintain good relationships with tribes whose bales of robes were vital to the fur company's success.

The decline in the population of bison is an important aspect of western North American history and in the Indian trade at Fort Union. The near disappearance of the animals has generated a great deal of finger-pointing, some of it likely misdirected. Fort Union's robe traders operated on different principles, and had different objectives, than did the hide hunters of the late nineteenth century. It is quite possible that Fort Union's robe trade may have had little to do with the herds' destruction, while disease may have been a leading factor. Some contemporary observers believed that bison numbers were visibly declining as early as the 1830s and 1840s, but current estimates suggest that by 1860, close to the end of Fort Union's existence, the northern and southern bison herds' combined population still amounted to near twenty million. Two decades later, they may have numbered about four million, but by 1883 practically all were gone. Anthrax, brucellosis, tuberculosis, and other bovine diseases transmitted by Texas cattle driven to the Northern Plains after the Civil War may have devastated the herds.[58]

In comparison with robe traders, professional hide hunters and the U.S. Army each had a more deleterious impact on the herds. Bison and Indians were so closely entwined in the military and public imaginations that their fates seemed linked. In the late 1860s U.S. Army generals ordered a methodical slaughter of bison in order to cripple Indians' resistance efforts, and American hide hunters began exterminating them about 1870.[59] There is little question that the fur trade—as prosecuted by both whites and Indians—reduced many game animal populations in North America. Perhaps it is more a tribute to the animals' remarkable ability to survive under intense pressure than to any humane considerations that none of the creatures targeted by the fur hunters has become extinct. In the twentieth century these animals' greatest enemies were likely to be farmers and ranchers unwilling to yield a portion of their land to nonprofitable varmints.

ANNUITY CONTRACTS

Pierre Chouteau, Jr., & Company, and its predecessor, Pratte, Chouteau, & Company, received numerous government freight contracts to carry annuities to Upper Missouri tribes, as well as occasional contracts for military supplies. Chouteau & Company gained a major advantage in the scramble for contracts when the steamboat *Yellow Stone* ascended the Missouri to Fort Tecumseh in 1831 and to Fort Union in 1832, effectively opening navigation on the Upper Missouri. Government officials, lacking the means to move tons of promised treaty goods up the river, had no feasible alternative to using the fur traders' transportation network, and they knew that Indians would be displeased if government failed to meet its obligations. The UMO owned several steamers and contracted the services of other vessels over the years.

Chouteau & Company won several contracts during the 1830s, and by 1839 the company saw them as necessary not only as sources of profit but also as a tool for keeping competitors out of the transportation business. If Chouteau could monopolize the contract trade, there would be less incentive for others to enter the costly and risky business of steamboating. Several documents from the year 1839 cast light on these issues.

John F. A. Sanford was the company agent who most often dealt with the government during the 1830s and 1840s. Sanford's name may be familiar to some readers as the defendant in an unsuccessful freedom suit brought to the Supreme Court in 1857 by his former slave, Dred Scott. More to the point here, Sanford worked for the Office of Indian Affairs from 1826 to 1834 and was a dedicated Indian agent who spent much time in the field. Eventually frustrated by governmental ineffectiveness, he transferred to the private sector, joining Chouteau's organization early in 1835. Among the important men with whom Sanford dealt at this time was the "Godlike Daniel" Webster, who received various "loans" from Astor or Chouteau and generally worked sub rosa on behalf of the company. Sanford's extensive acquaintance with the Office of Indian Affairs ideally suited him to lobby for Chouteau's interests. Three years earlier, Sanford had married Chouteau's daughter, Emilie, at Saint Louis. This doubtless enhanced his relationship with Chouteau, but it also fueled some critics' allegations of intrigue with the company. Emilie died in 1836, but Sanford's loyalty to Chouteau continued for the rest of his life.[60]

Early in January 1839, Sanford toured Washington, New York, and Baltimore buying merchandise and pressuring the Office of Indian Affairs to grant Pierre Chouteau, Jr., & Company a contract to carry seventy thousand dollars' worth of Indian goods. Upon arrival at Washington, he noticed an advertisement calling for bids immediately. Caught off guard, Sanford quickly submitted a preliminary proposal to the Indian Office. He then warned Chouteau that T. Hartley Crawford, newly appointed commissioner of Indian affairs, was "determined to do things in his own manner" and explained that "our delegation" might be forced to "take steps to thwart him." As Sanford saw it, Chouteau & Company must bid on the contract to "prevent others from embarking in this kind of business." If the Office of Indian Affairs denied the contract, then the company should "positively decline transporting [the goods] upon any terms." He promised to "do the best I can to have the contract or baulk any other *bidder.*"[61]

Disbursing agent Major Ethan Allen Hitchcock complained to Crawford on February 8 that the "American Fur Company" (Pierre Chouteau, Jr., & Company) "very nearly monopolized" the upriver trade and tried to thwart the emergence of competitors. Nonetheless, Hitchcock admitted that if no other outfit had the wherewithal to deliver goods, the government could only with "manifest absurdity" charter a vessel, and so Chouteau might as well get the contract, since conditions "did not afford to the Govt. any control over the competitors for the trade."[62]

Chouteau & Company avidly sought government contracts for nearly thirty years, sometimes as the only bidder. The company shipped Indian Office goods to the Sioux and Winnebagos on the Upper Mississippi, to the Omahas, Poncas, Otoes, Missouris, and Pawnees on the middle Missouri, and to several Upper Missouri tribes.[63] Freight contracts probably more than offset the costs of steamboat navigation on the Mississippi and Missouri Rivers, especially when lobbyists' efforts went according to plan.[64]

American Fur Company Headquarters, 1835, ink on paper by Clarence Hoblitzelle, 1897. *Courtesy Missouri Historical Society, Saint Louis.*

Pierre Chouteau, Jr., & Company's broad experience and excellent connections with foreign and domestic suppliers enabled them to provide goods of generally unimpeachable quality. The company also purchased goods in such quantities that it often received discounts not available to other merchants.[65] The federal government had no alternative but to deal with Chouteau for annuities and other purchases. Joshua Pilcher, while superintendent of Indian affairs at Saint Louis in 1840, recognized this when he inspected a Chouteau bid proposal featuring a display of goods. Pilcher informed Indian Commissioner Crawford that "all minor articles are Superior to the samples placed in my office to be bid upon; while all the more important articles are fully equal to any in my possession."[66] Another aspect of federal ineptitude appears in one of Ramsay Crooks's letters to Chouteau, his "Cher Cousin." Crooks ridiculed the "snail-like activity that so generally distinguishes the operations of the 'Indian Office,' at Washington" and observed that the Indians on Lake Superior were "not much pleased with the punctuality of their 'Great Father,' who they think treats them more like step-children, than his legitimate offspring."[67]

Some degree of mutual dependence between Chouteau & Company and federal Indian agents and superintendents was inevitable. But this does not convincingly demonstrate that Indian agents and fur men were co-conspirators. "Symbiosis" more appropriately describes the relationship. In this case a monopoly existed by default because only one organization possessed the capacity to meet government obligations in a timely manner.

Even Chouteau's company endured the uncertainties of political upheaval within the Indian Office whenever a political party lost control of the executive department. In the 1840 election the Whig William Henry Harrison defeated Democrat Martin Van Buren, and Chouteau's men failed to have Joshua Pilcher, a former employee and a Democratic "Bentonite" friendly to their interests, retained as superintendent of Indian affairs at Saint Louis.[68]

Chouteau's men scrambled to secure an acceptable alternative. With Saint Louis fur traders divided into Whig and Democrat camps, a bitterly contested campaign ensued, each faction supporting a veteran fur trader. The principal contenders were well acquainted. Charles Keemle, a

Democrat newspaperman, had been a clerk in Pilcher's Missouri Fur Company. Chouteau's outfit hedged its bet by supporting two former employees, the Democrat Pilcher and the Whig David D. Mitchell.[69]

Ultimately, Chouteau & Company were satisfied when Mitchell was appointed superintendent. Mitchell had begun his fur trade career in Astor's Western Department in 1828 and soon joined the UMO. With Chouteau's warm support, David Mitchell had purchased Daniel Lamont's share of the Upper Missouri Outfit in 1835 and served as bourgeois at Fort Union in 1838. Perhaps he still held his share in 1840. As superintendent, Mitchell would preside over a beefed up federal liquor law enforcement effort from 1843 to 1846, while Andrew Drips, another UMO veteran, worked as a federal temperance agent. When the Saint Louis Superintendency was superseded by the Central Superintendency in 1851, Mitchell retained his position and headed the Central Superintendency until Alfred Cumming took over in 1853.[70]

Whether they were in the company's vest pocket (as critics have asserted ever since) or not, a handful of intelligent fur traders helped to orchestrate government Indian policy for over a quarter of a century. The Indian Department benefited from these men's years of practical trade experience and their firsthand knowledge of Indians. Sanford, Pilcher, Mitchell, and Drips had helped make the Upper Missouri trade profitable, and their careers lent them credibility as expert private-sector advisors and federal employees. If they were also men on the make, willing to shift from private to public arenas in their quest for individual gain, they were no different than other "expectant capitalists" in the Age of Jackson. It is worth noting, incidentally, that Chouteau's fur company experienced far less employee turnover than the Indian Office. Lack of continuity in federal service is one reason why Indian policy developed chaotically in the nineteenth century and was often ineffective.[71]

Chouteau's UMO constituted the most authoritative American presence in the Upper Missouri from 1829 until at least 1860. Economic enterprise, not governmental authority and policy, initiated relations between Indians and white Americans in the region. Given the company's clear view of its interests and objectives, large-scale organization, experienced and knowledgeable partners and traders, and strong connections with influential politicians, it is no wonder that Chouteau &

Company took the lead on the Upper Missouri and left the government floundering in its wake. Many years passed before the federal government found it possible, and necessary, to gain the upper hand. In the interim, annuity contracts met the government's immediate needs and buttressed the prestige of Chouteau's company.

TRADE GOODS AND PROFITABILITY AT FORT UNION

Fur traders' diplomacy with Indians, no matter how carefully contrived, would lead nowhere if the right kinds and quantities of goods were not on hand when Indians brought robes or meat to trade. Keeping Fort Union supplied required meticulous inventory taking and the timely submission of detailed requisitions for a new season's goods. No freight moved along the frozen Missouri during the winter, but traders could not afford to wait until the spring thaw to place orders. In order to assure adequate stocks of merchandise for the coming year, it was necessary to dispatch the "winter express" to Saint Louis. Traveling alone under dangerous weather conditions, the express man carried orders to company headquarters.

Distant forts, such as Fort McKenzie or Fort Cass, sent off an expressman in November or December. At each downriver fort he collected orders, and he usually reached Saint Louis in February or March. Clerks forwarded orders to eastern cities as well as to Britain and the continent. Two or three months later European goods arrived at New York, where company agents or commission houses dispatched them to Chouteau's warehouses at Saint Louis, along with domestic orders placed in New York, Philadelphia, and elsewhere. By May or early June the season's goods were ready to be hauled up the Missouri.

Near the beginning of Fort Union's career in 1829, a UMO order for English goods amounted to $35,862.76. Packed in nearly two hundred bales, cases, and casks, the shipment included 164 "pieces" (bolts) of scarlet "saved list" cloth (a narrow, white-edged woolen used for breechcloths and other purposes), 191 pieces of indigo blue saved list cloth, several thousand pairs of English woolen point blankets in mixed colors

Saint Louis, 1832, after L. D. Pomarade, frontispiece in *Pictorial St. Louis*, by Richard N. Compton and Camille N. Dry (Saint Louis: Compton & Company, 1876). This image shows the bustling inland port at about the time Fort Union was built. *Courtesy Missouri Historical Society, Saint Louis.*

and sizes, over eight hundred dozen "warranted" and six hundred dozen "common" scalping knives, and hundreds of dozens of "Wilson's" butcher knives. Also included were thousands of variously sized gun and pistol flints, Indian awls, and fire steels; raw brass and iron; and several cases of English North West guns.[72]

Extant records for the trade of 1830 reveal imported purchases amounting to at least fifty thousand dollars. To this must be added tariff duties, which had been rising for years. The 1816 tariff levied a 25 percent duty on most imported woolen goods and 15 percent for other imports. An 1824 protective tariff, setting a 33⅓ percent rate on imported cotton and woolen goods, was raised still higher when the May 19, 1828, "Tariff of Abominations" set the duty on woolens at 45 percent and placed similarly high duties on other products. The total of duties paid on imported goods by the Western Department of the AFCo is unknown, but an average annual rate of 25–35 percent probably is not out of line.

It is impossible to calculate precisely the costs of building, staffing, and supplying Fort Union for its first year in business. Supposing a work force of about 120 men with overall wages of about $21,500, roughly $16,000 in inventory, and a few thousand dollars spent on tools, hardware, and other materials, one arrives at an estimate of approximately $40,000 in 1830–31.[73]

The payoff quickly justified the investment. Fur sales were strong in 1829, while Fort Union was probably in the planning stages. By December 23, AFCo President William B. Astor wrote to Pierre Chouteau, Jr., that the Western Department's furs received to that date had sold for $136,850.54.[74] In July 1831 the UMO of 1830 was credited with at least 14,584 robes from the Yellowstone, though this figure falls far short of the total UMO harvest of robes, furs, and skins. By June 1832, Fort Union posted sales of at least eight thousand robes and 4,603 pounds of beaver skins, totaling well over $42,000 when other skins, buffalo tongues, and castorum are included. A year later Fort Union's inventory amounted to $23,330.75, far above those of Forts Cass and McKenzie.[75]

In the summer of 1832 the Western Department's inventories showed Fort Union holding roughly three-fifths (about thirty-one thousand dollars) of a total of nearly fifty-three thousand dollars, evidence of its leading role in the trade. Fort Pierre, the next largest post, had an inventory of about twenty thousand dollars.[76] Inventory values were calculated by doubling the purchase prices of goods to account for mark-up.[77]

The UMO's profits amply rewarded its proprietors. Net proceeds in 1834 reached $134,800, an impressive total. Fort Union's inventory for 1834 included roughly $50,000 in trade goods on hand, as did that of 1835.[78] In 1835 the UMO gathered more than twenty-two thousand robes and many other furs and skins. In 1836 over thirty thousand robes were shipped for sale, and in 1837 more than forty-three thousand UMO robes went to market.[79]

To trade for these robes, in 1834 the steamer *Assiniboine* carried about twenty-one thousand dollars' worth of goods to Fort Union. In 1835 the steamer *Diana* hauled around twelve thousand dollars in goods, and in 1836 the same vessel brought about sixteen thousand dollars' worth of merchandize to Fort Union. Similar amounts of goods came each year through the 1840s.[80]

Fur and skin sales from the UMO of 1854 grossed nearly $150,000 in 1855, resulting in profits of about $44,000.[81] In 1856 the UMO for 1855 yielded $147,000, of which Fort Union had contributed about $44,000. Forts Berthold, Clark, and Pierre jointly returned about $43,000.[82] Even in the 1860s the company continued to do well. Net proceeds of robe sales ranged between $90,000 and $200,000 from 1860 to 1864. Obviously, Chouteau & Company did not retire from the Upper Missouri trade in 1865 because profits were down.[83]

CHAPTER ONE

The Construction of Fort Union

Late in the autumn of 1829, crisp days and chill nights shimmering with the aurora borealis portended the onset of another blue-lipped Northern Plains winter. From dawn to dusk gangs of boisterous Upper Missouri Outfit men toiled, digging trenches, cutting and trimming timber, and hauling stone near the confluence of the Missouri and Yellowstone Rivers. In anticipation of the cold season they hurriedly raised the log palisade walls of a fortified trading post. Their bosses had already paced off lines forming a great quadrangle about sixty feet from the water's edge. On the advice of the Assiniboine nation, the white men chose an elevated prairie on the Missouri's north bank six river miles, but only three by land, above the mouth of the Yellowstone. The site was a good one. Coulees east and west of the proposed stockade would carry rainwater to the river when the intense thundershowers typical of the region threatened to flood the place. Safely above the high-water mark of the Missouri's spring rise, the chosen spot was close to a lush bottomland plentifully stocked with cottonwood for palisades, interior buildings, and firewood.

The post would be called Fort Union. Constructed roughly two years after the Columbia Fur Company joined hands with John Jacob Astor's American Fur Company and was renamed the Upper Missouri Outfit, it became the centerpiece of the AFCo's Western Department. Its builders, if they judged rightly, might soon take command of the fur trade from the Upper Missouri clear out to the Rockies. A permanent trading post for the Assiniboines, Crees, and other Missouri River tribes upriver from the Sioux and Mandans could keep potential competitors at bay. Fort Union, its builders undoubtedly hoped, would eliminate the costly and unpleasant necessity of buying out other small opposition outfits. The new post would also make an excellent staging area for launching trapping brigades into the Rocky Mountains. Offering access to an immense region loaded with fur-bearers, the Missouri-Yellowstone system was ideally suited for transporting men, furs, buffalo robes, and supplies up or down the rivers.

Early in 1830 about 120 employees were hired to ascend the Missouri and finish the new post. Because it was built in haste to serve the trade, its structural weaknesses would soon cause problems. Nevertheless, the two key players in its inception, Pierre Chouteau, Jr., and Kenneth McKenzie, had cause to celebrate. In a bold stroke they had placed a post within striking distance of some of North America's richest beaver country. The gamble paid off handsomely. Fort Union produced bountiful profits and played a starring role in Upper Missouri history from 1830 until 1867.

Although Fort Union soon would be reckoned the "vastest of the forts the American Fur Company has on the Missouri," details concerning its first year or two are sketchy. Even its location has been a matter of dispute, because the UMO built more than one post in the vicinity within a short time. In 1833, Prince Maximilian, a German naturalist, was told that "Fort Union was begun in the fall of 1829." Ten years later, when America's greatest bird-watcher, John James Audubon, summered at Fort Union, he heard the same date. But Charles Larpenteur's oft-quoted Upper Missouri narrative gives a date of "about the year 1827." According to Larpenteur, Kenneth McKenzie's party failed to reach the Yellowstone's mouth, so they established a preliminary wintering post "at the mouth of White River . . . 150 miles below the Yellowstone. . . . The following year [McKenzie] went on to the mouth of the Yellowstone, where the chief of the band of the Rocks [Assiniboines] had desired him to build."[1]

The confusion in dates apparently arises from the fact that two posts— Fort Floyd and Fort Union—were established in the same general region between 1827 and 1829. Construction of Fort Union began while Fort Floyd was still being used. Fort Floyd's location and the source of its name are both mysteries, and today its probable site lies submerged somewhere behind North Dakota's Garrison Dam. The name of the post may be traceable to several bills placed before Congress between 1820 and 1829 calling for American occupation of the "Oregon country." Their author was Virginia representative John Floyd, a distant relative of Sgt. Charles Floyd of the Lewis and Clark expedition.

Fortunately, for most of Fort Union's career the documentary record is rich. Thousands of pages of ledgers, inventories, and business correspondence have survived, as have a number of journals written by men who visited or worked there. These documents preserve the information needed to describe construction phases of the fort, re-create its residents' lives, and evaluate its significance. No drawing was made until 1832, but numerous images appeared thereafter, establishing a graphic record of Fort Union's architectural changes over time. More recently, National Park Service archeologists have unearthed a wealth of information concerning construction details. Before examining the post's physical appearance, however, it is necessary to back-track a bit and outline the circumstances that brought it to life.

As soon as he took charge of the UMO in 1827, McKenzie yearned to plunge into the mountain trade, mindful as he was of "General" Ashley's successes a few years earlier. But the Western Department's directors, believing a rush to the mountains was premature, persuaded McKenzie to "first establish a permanent post at the mouth of the Yellowstone, which would afford a safe and convenient base for the operations of the upper country." In mid-September 1828, McKenzie sent the keelboat *Otter* from the Mandan villages upriver to the mouth of the Yellowstone "to establish a post for the Assiniboine trade." Fur trade historian Hiram Martin Chittenden surmised that McKenzie sent James Kipp along to oversee construction of the fort, which began about October 15. Chittenden continued: "This post, the first that the American Fur Company built above the Mandans, was not named Union, as is generally supposed, but Fort Floyd. 'Fort Union' was first applied to a post built in the year 1829, about two hundred miles above the mouth of the Yellowstone. The correspondence of the American Fur Company is clear upon this point. But before the close of 1830 the name 'Floyd' had been abandoned and 'Union' had been permanently settled upon the post at or near the Yellowstone."[2]

In May 1829, McKenzie wrote a letter from Fort Tecumseh to William Laidlaw and Daniel Lamont, likely at Saint Louis, stating that "the people of the Yellowstone arrived on the 11th instant" with some three hundred packs of buffalo robes, muskrat, and beaver. More furs were forthcoming, but the point here is that the fur-laden boat descended from Fort Floyd. No mention was made of a Fort Union in this letter.[3] In 1994 National Park Service archeologist William J. Hunt, Jr., offered a persuasive case for locating Fort Floyd near the mouth of the White Earth River, identifying it as the site usually called "Kipp's Post," which stood about one hundred miles down the Missouri from Fort Union.[4]

McKenzie remained at Fort Tecumseh or had returned by July. In a letter to Pierre Chouteau, Jr., he mentioned William Vanderburgh's arrival on July 4 "with 30 men, whom I intend will leave here about the middle of this month for the upper country although I consider the party very weak to go into that country at this present time." McKenzie apparently hoped to send both river and land parties up the Missouri to the Blackfeet. But neither an anticipated contingent of men from Montréal nor a boat from Saint Louis had yet arrived, and he thought the "risk would be too great" to send a weak party. If McKenzie was considering the Three Forks area, his fears were reasonable. The Blackfeet, suspected by most American fur traders of being under British influence, vigorously opposed the incursions of Americans, and routinely plundered those who entered their country. In 1831, Joshua Pilcher, while employed as a government Indian agent, reported to Congress on the number of casualties in the fur trade and the Santa Fe trade, charging the Blackfeet with the deaths of at least fifty-one Americans between 1822 and 1829 and the theft of thousands of dollars' worth of goods and horses.[5]

Fur trading forts were inventoried each spring to determine what goods and provisions should be ordered for the coming season. Although records of the earliest Fort Union are scarce, a few surviving inventories provide clues to the relative importance of UMO posts. An inventory taken at Fort Floyd on April 29, 1829, listed only $1,496.19 worth of trade goods on hand, and $213.03 worth of "articles in use," such as adzes, planes, draw knives, and other tools, as well as cooking gear, harness, live-stock, and the like. Fort Floyd was a small post, but the inventory indicates that it remained operative that year. By comparison, Fort Tecumseh's inventory in May listed goods and articles in use valued at better than $28,000.00. Even Vermillion Post's $2,262.15 inventory was substantially greater than that of Fort Floyd.[6]

The earliest explicit references to Fort Union appear in a day book kept at Fort Tecumseh and in a letter penned by Kenneth McKenzie. Writing under a dateline of "Fort Union 5th May, 1830," McKenzie noted that an *engagé* named "old Giguerre" had contested a charge on his account for some tobacco received at Fort Tecumseh "last summer," adding that Giguerre "also denies a charge made by Mr. Chardon at Fort Floyd of a Buffalo Robe." This is the only document in which both Fort Union and Fort Floyd both appear. A few days later, on May 19, a clerk at Fort Tecumseh named Jacob Halsey noted that "At 4 P.M. Hugh Glass and Francis Viond with 9 men arrived from Fort Union, they came in a skiff & wooden canoe & were sent in quest of horses &c." The men continued rounding up horses for Fort Union, and on May 23, "in the morning Mssrs. Glass, Viond, Minton, Holliday, Degray & Lachapelle left here with 12 men and 58 Horses and Mules for Fort Union, Yellow stone river." The men did not get very far on their way before they uncorked a keg of alcohol. On the next day, Halsey wrote, "Last evening Joseph Villandre one of the Yellow stone party returned to exchange a Kettle which had been fired through by Lamont Lamotte [*sic*]—It appears from Villandre's statement that the party encamped early and were all taking a frolick when the Kettle was broke."[7]

By May 1830, and possibly for some time earlier, McKenzie resided at Fort Union. Construction at that time must have been well enough along to provide structures adequate to house men, supplies, and trade goods. About 120 men, nearly one-half of that year's 258 engagés, were posted at Fort Union, making it by far the most heavily staffed AFCo post. McKenzie arrived at Fort Tecumseh on July 15 "with a Keel boat laden with furs & peltries." The next day Halsey left the fort with McKenzie's Saint Louis–bound party. On July 22 they passed the keelboat *Twin Males* heading upriver to Fort Union with merchandise, and on July 25 they resumed their journey down the Missouri on the keelboat *Otter*.[8]

Returning from Saint Louis to Fort Union later that autumn, McKenzie and about ten other men reached Fort Tecumseh on October 9. Along the way they had somehow lost track of a number of horses destined for service at Fort Union or in the mountains. The party remained at Fort Tecumseh for over a month before McKenzie and Thomas Dickson left for Fort Union.[9]

The "King of the Upper Missouri" had not yet attained regal stature in 1830.[10] McKenzie's lack of influence was demonstrated when he blundered into an unpleasant confrontation with the Arikaras. Most fur traders considered the Arikaras to be dangerously unpredictable, but the tribe's hostility reflected a calculated response to the growing number of traders whose presence imperiled their traditional position as river trade middle-men. After departing from Fort Tecumseh on November 14, McKenzie and his men stopped at the Arikara villages where the AFCo maintained a post run by Richard F. Holliday. Two days after McKenzie's party left the village, some Arikara warriors halted them "in open day and their Saddles, Blkts. [blankets] Tomahawks &c were forcibly taken." Holliday became aware of the mishap when "one of the partys Mules returned to the Ree village with an arrow sticking in his head." It was later reported that the "Rees" had taken "every thing they had except their horses—and they took one of them."[11] Despite such difficulties, McKenzie and his UMO men were determined to persevere. Within a few years they did exactly what the Arikaras feared, supplanting that tribe's economic power with their own. Still, the transition was relatively peaceable; warfare between Arikaras and traders ceased after 1830.

Fort Union's initial construction was only one phase of a continuing process that never entirely ceased as long as it was occupied. The post was subject to many repairs and modifications, but by far the most extensive alterations occurred about two years after it was first built. Beginning in 1832 the UMO men entirely rebuilt the fort on a grander scale, completing the work in 1835. National Park Service archeologists designate the two posts Fort Union I and Fort Union II, and modern-day visitors can tour a reconstructed Fort Union II.[12]

In 1832, George Catlin wrote a description of Fort Union I and painted the first of only two known pictures of the original post. Catlin had arrived at Saint Louis in 1830, seeking to paint Indians whom he believed would soon pass into oblivion. Two years later he secured a berth on the AFCo's *Yellow Stone,* the first steamer to challenge the turbulent Upper Missouri. Upon reaching Fort Union in mid-summer, Catlin exaggerated its dimensions, writing, "The American Fur Company have erected here, for their protection against the savages, a very substantial Fort, 300 feet square, with bastions armed with ordnance." He judged it "the largest and best built establishment of the kind on the river, being the great or principal head-quarters and depot of the Fur Company's business in this region."[13]

The next year, Prince Maximilian of Wied-Neuwied and his companion, a skillful Swiss artist named Karl Bodmer, came to Fort Union. Among Bodmer's many splendid Upper Missouri images, one depicts the fort as viewed from the heights overlooking it to the north. His penciled field sketch, which was the basis for an aquatint engraving included in Maximilian's *Atlas,* is the best available illustration of Fort Union I.[14]

Kenneth McKenzie, William Laidlaw, and Daniel Lamont dominated the UMO hierarchy, but they were not truly the builders of Fort Union. French-speaking creoles of Missouri (formerly Upper Louisiana) and French Canadians provided the necessary know-how and labor. As a result, Fort Union's buildings echoed the French Colonial vernacular architectural traditions with which the workmen were familiar. James Kipp's previous fort building experience makes him a likely choice as the author of the ground plan. The quadrangular perimeter formed a parallelogram to make the best use of level ground at the site and avoid slopes that would cause drainage problems. Oriented more or less toward the compass points, the fort measured approximately 178 feet on the north and south walls, and 198 feet on the east and west walls, rather less than Catlin's estimation.[15]

Palisades at Fort Union I offered protection from attackers and unwelcome guests as well as from the high winds typical of the region. Pickets were hewn from the trunks of broad-leaved cottonwoods that constituted the principal timber in an area otherwise dominated by prairie grasses and shrubs. The construction technique was what Frenchmen called *poteaux-en-terre,* or "post-in-ground." Workmen dug long trenches a few feet deep into which they set vertical timbers, usually left round at the

Fort Union at the Mouth of the Yellowstone River, by Karl Bodmer, 1833. Bodmer's original penciled field sketch shows a stack of lumber outside the post to be used in the expansion that soon followed. *Courtesy Joslyn Art Museum, Omaha, Nebraska. Gift of the Enron Art Foundation.*

bottom and hewn flat on their exterior faces. Then they jammed heavy stones around the posts and filled the trenches with hard-packed earth to secure the palisade. In French settlements of Missouri such walls were often strengthened by a wooden plate, or stringer, nailed or pegged along the top. Saint Louis creoles were expert at this style of construction, and they had long used cottonwood as a building material.[16]

Archeological work at Fort Union indicates that this technique was used at the site, though some conclusions about construction at Fort Union I remain speculative. Almost certainly the tall cottonwood palisades were the first elements to be completed. Because of strong prevailing northwesterly winds, builders installed two massive timbers to anchor the fort's north wall. Even so, Fort Union I was rather flimsily put together. Practically all of the pickets lining the north wall were made of narrow sawn planks measuring only about nine by three inches. Additional posts helped to prevent the wall from being blown over, but the structure remained weak.[17]

Fort Union I featured bastions or blockhouses located at opposing corners of the palisaded enclosure. Bastions appeared in many western fur trading posts and served a variety of purposes. In military terms, bastions provided projecting structures from which raking gun-fire would thwart attackers' attempts to approach or scale the walls. Bastions certainly lent traders' forts a martial appearance, but they were intended more to awe Indians than to function defensively, and no genuine "siege" ever took place at Fort Union. Charles Larpenteur remarked that the bastions at nearby Fort William, erected in 1833 by an "opposition" company, "were built more for amusement than for protection against hostile Indians."[18]

Fort Union's bastions served as watchtowers, storage rooms for armaments and ordnance, and occasionally as an artist's studio, and they also offered pleasant vantage points from which to enjoy the sweeping panoramic view or a cool evening breeze. No evidence has been found to indicate that bastions at Fort Union I were made of stone; probably they were built of cottonwood in a "log cabin" style. Archeologists discovered that the palisades for the later Fort Union II were completed before bastions were added at the northeast and southwest corners, but ground disturbance related to the second post's construction made it impossible to tell much about what had happened earlier.[19]

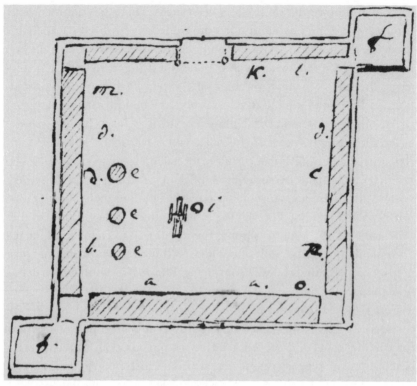

Prince Maximilian's sketch of Fort Union's layout, 1833. *Courtesy Joslyn Art Museum, Omaha, Nebraska. Gift of the Enron Art Foundation.*

Karl Bodmer made his pencil drawing of Fort Union I on July 2, 1833, as preparations were afoot for a major expansion of the post. Bastions (Prince Maximilian called them "blockhouses") appear at the northeast and southwest corners. The image shows rooftops of the bourgeois's, or chief factor's, house close to the north wall and a storehouse at the west wall, as well as a gate in the north palisade wall, a tall flagpole at the center of the plaza, and a true blockhouse over the main gate facing the Missouri.

Prince Maximilian's journal further illuminates the scene. He drew a crude plan of the fort that identifies various structures. Noting that the new fort was nearly finished, he continued: "The fort itself is a quadrangle, the outer sides of which are eighty-four of my paces in length. On the southwestern and northeastern corners there are small blockhouses with a pointed roof on top, and all the fencing consists of sturdy poles, placed close together, fifteen to sixteen feet high, over which small chevaux-de-frise have also been constructed to prevent climbing over."[20] He remarked that the original bourgeois house was of "one story with four glass windows on each side beside the door. There are also more apartments in the attic. This house is quite nicely built, like all the other houses of cottonwood lumber, for no other building wood is available here." No complete images of the first bourgeois house are extant, but the roof line visible in Bodmer's sketch and Maximilian's description each lend support for the supposition that it resembled early Saint Louis houses in its poteaux-en-terre or *poteaux-en-sole* ("post-on-sill") construction. Characteristic of such dwellings was a steeply pitched hip roof, known as a *pavillon* roof to French Canadians as well as to Mississippi Valley creoles.[21]

Along with the structures already noted, Maximilian observed stores for both whites and Indians, carpenters' and tailors' apartments, a forge, rooms for employees, a warehouse for furs, and a stable. He also saw, at the center of the open space within the fort, three Assiniboine buffalo hide lodges "inhabited by several whites and their families." The prince complained that the interior of the fort was filthy because fifty or sixty horses were picketed inside the compound each night to prevent their theft, and he noted that Kenneth McKenzie planned to erect a corral "so that the courtyard will always remain dry and firm."[22] In fact, poor drainage in the plaza would continue to create a mucky problem for a number of years, as various means were initiated in an attempt to prevent the area from becoming a foul quagmire during wet weather. The simple boardwalk visible in an 1866 photograph of the bourgeois house suggests that no permanent solution was ever discovered.

A twenty-four- by twenty-one-foot ice house immediately to the west of the bourgeois house was "well filled with ice during the winter, which supply generally last[ed] till fall." Containing a good ten days' supply of fresh meat, the ice house was especially useful during the sweltering summer months. In 1833 opposition trader Robert Campbell recorded that the ice house had a plank floor upon which was stored lumber (perhaps for the current rebuilding project) and a rope ladder leading through a trap door to the cellar, where ice was kept.[23]

"Interior Fort Union, Montana," Carbutt, Chicago, Illinois, Publisher; Illingworth and Bill, Photographers, "with Capt. Fisk's Expeditions, 1866." One of only four known stereographic photos taken at Fort Union, this one shows the bourgeois house in its final year. Sagging roof beam, deteriorating chimneys, missing window glass—all suggest that the old house has seen better days. *Courtesy Montana Historical Society, Helena.*

Probably some of the hastily built structures that Maximilian saw were replacements for several along the western palisade that went up in smoke when a fire threatened to destroy the entire fort on the night of February 3, 1832. Writing to David D. Mitchell at Fort Clark a week and a half after the fire, Kenneth McKenzie described the damage. Awakened by shouting around midnight, McKenzie rushed from his room to find flames attacking "the range of buildings forming the West quadrangle of the fort (120 ft. by 24 ft.) and occupied by the clerks, interpreters, mechanics, & engages, with their families of squalling children not a few." Caused by hearth embers that fell between rough floorboards, the fire first appeared in "Mr. Chardon's room, originating beneath the floor," but, "there being unfortunately a free communication under the whole range, and much rubbish accumulated there, it was almost simultaneous in every apartment. . . . The inmates were awakened by a suffocating smoke and the opening of the doors for escape, caused a rush of air which fanned it to an almost immediate & unconquerable flame." Lost in the inferno were "trunks of wearing apparel, all the buffalo tongues of the year, near a thousand of sawn plank, the labour of two men for six months, stored to season in the lofts, rifles, pistols, white [that is, albino] beaver skins," personal belongings and "a cellar full of small [whiskey?] kegs." Had it not been for a favorable east wind, "the whole fort must have gone." The gunpowder stock was safe, no one had died, and within four hours the blaze was under control. When day broke, McKenzie sent men out into sub-zero weather to cut new pickets and build "shelter for the houseless." Pickets were soon installed, but it took months to rebuild quarters and storage rooms. "In our wooden houses," McKenzie concluded, "I fear we are all too little cautious of this good servant but terrible master & enemy *Fire*. I hope my loss will be a lesson to every post on the river."[24]

Since McKenzie remarked that the pickets were replaced within five days, one can assume that his workmen probably used the same relatively shaky poteaux-en-terre technique described above. Digging a trench and setting heavy pickets during mid-winter on the Northern Plains was no easy task, and the thermometer had plunged to forty degrees below zero on the night McKenzie wrote to Mitchell.

At any rate, the end of the original fort was already near, and the enlarged complex would be far more striking. Karl Bodmer's sketch of the post in the summer of 1833 shows stacks of timber lying along the northern palisade of the fort that can only be waiting for use in the expansion soon to get underway.

Fort Union II, which can be viewed as a reconstruction by present-day visitors, is much better documented in both the historical and the

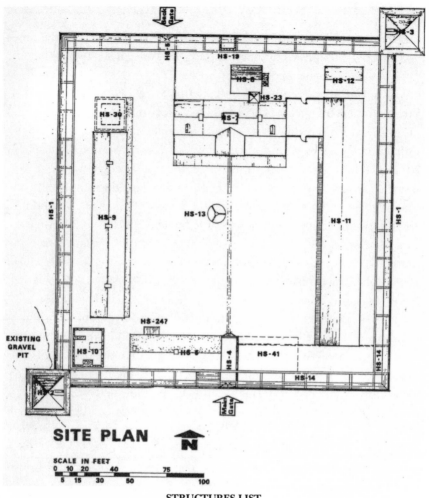

SITE PLAN

N

SCALE IN FEET
```
0  10  20      40      75
   5   15   30    50           100
```

STRUCTURES LIST

HS-1   Palisade
HS-2   Southwest Bastion
HS-3   Northeast Bastion
HS-4   Front Gate
HS-5   Back Gate
HS-6   Indian-Artisan House
HS-7   Bourgeois House
HS-8   Kitchen
HS-9   Dwelling Range
HS-10 Blacksmith Shop
HS-11 Store Range
HS-12 Powder Magazine
HS-13 Flagstaff
HS-14 Stables (adjacent to South Palisade)
HS-15 Stable, Buffalo Calves (adjacent to North Palisade)

HS-16 Hen House (North Palisade)
HS-17 Artist's Studio (North Palisade)
HS-18 Cooper's Shop (North Palisade)
HS-19 Milk House, Dairy
HS-20 Charcoal House (South Palisade)
HS-21 Building and Pens, Outside
HS-22 Building East of Ravine
HS-23 Bell Tower
HS-24 New Tower (1853)
HS-25 Cemetery, Outside
HS-26 Distilling Building, Outside

HS-27 Kilns, Outside
HS-28 Fence, Structures, Outside
HS-29 Carpenter Shop
HS-30 Ice House
HS-31 Army Storerooms
HS-32 Army Sawmill
HS-33 Army Root House
HS-34 Second Army Root House
HS-35 Army Winter Quarters
HS-36 Army Officer's Quarters
HS-37 Army Blacksmith Shop
HS-38 Army Ice House
HS-39 Army Corral
HS-40 Adobe Store
HS-41 Warehouse

Site Plan of Fort Union, indicating all of the major structures within the post's walls. *Courtesy National Park Service, Midwest Archeological Center, Lincoln, Nebraska.*

archeological records than its short-lived predecessor. Numerous illustrations, a few lengthy verbal descriptions, and a wealth of archeological data allow a detailed re-creation of the fort's construction history. One of the best accounts is a report prepared for John James Audubon by Edwin Thompson Denig, a UMO employee and an exceptionally astute chronicler of the Missouri River fur trade. Another one was written by Audubon's traveling companion, Isaac Sprague. Rudolph Friederich Kurz, a UMO employee during 1850–51, created a gem of information: a detailed journal accompanied by many excellent line drawings. There is no paucity of sources on structural details of the second Fort Union.

The enlarged fort, including bastion walls, would measure about 237 feet from east to west and about 245 feet from north to south. For security's sake, the new palisades for the larger enclosure were probably built while the former walls still stood. The redesigned structure exhibited a few innovations, based upon experience and intended to ensure greater longevity for the palisades. The new palisades were made of large, square-hewn cottonwood pickets that rested upon a sandstone and mortar foundation. A second improvement, which came a bit later on, was an interior framework of stout beams to lend additional support for the heavy palisades.

Denig called Fort Union "the "principal and handsomest trading-post on the Missouri River" in a meticulous description he presented Audubon on July 30, 1843.[25] He remarked that the twenty-foot-high pickets were "founded upon stone" and that the fort measured 220 by 240 feet. Rudolph Kurz, writing in 1851, observed that "the palisades of this fort are not driven into the ground, as in Fort Berthold, but are fitted into heavy beams that rest upon a foundation of limestone."[26]

The newly built palisades of 1833 looked sturdier than they really were. During the night of December 15, just one month after completion, a fierce wind flattened substantial portions of the north and west palisades. Kenneth McKenzie immediately called for modifications. Subsequently, according to Denig, the palisades were buttressed by "an open framework in the inside, of sufficient strength to counterbalance their weight, and sustained by braces in the form of an X, which reaches in the inside from the pickets to the frame, so as to make the whole completely solid and secure, from either storm or attack."[27]

The efficacy of the bracing system under battle conditions remained untested, but it did defend the palisades from further assault by the Upper Missouri's frequent heavy winds. Still, soft wooden construction materials failed in the punishing climate, and the problem recurred in later years. Rudolph Kurz noted in 1851 that "at this place palisades are further secured by supports of crossed beams on the inside, so that they cannot be blown down by the wind. Nevertheless, it happened once during my stay that on the western side, where the supports were badly decayed, a violent wind did force them down before the new beams were ready."[28]

Safety dictated that the large quantities of gunpowder necessary for the fort's trading and hunting be stored in a powder magazine whose substantial construction required the skills of a journeyman mason. A Saint Louis stonemason named Peter Miller was engaged for the Upper Missouri on April 15, 1831, as a "boatman" to be transported aboard the steamer *Yellow Stone*. In all likelihood, this was the man, identified only as "Miller," who erected the magazine in 1833 and who McKenzie explicitly mentioned in connection with other masonry work at Fort Union.[29]

Denig called the twenty-five- by eighteen-foot magazine "perhaps the best piece of work, as regards strength and security" in the entire fort. Its vaulted limestone walls, four feet thick at the base, grew to nearly six feet in depth at the top, above the curve of the arch. "The inside," Denig wrote, "presents a complete semi-circular arch, which is covered on the top with stones and gravel to the depth of 18 inches. The whole is covered with a shingle roof through which fire may burn yet with no danger to the powder within." Double doors, the exterior ones tin-lined, protected the magazine's valuable but deadly contents.[30]

The massive stone bastions, the most imposing architectural elements of Fort Union II, were not completed until early October 1834. The same mason who built the powder magazine, Peter Miller, was contracted to build the bastions. Although not entirely satisfied with Miller's work on the bastions, Kenneth McKenzie tried to keep the mason on hand. In this effort he failed. Miller left Fort Union on October 9, having by then apparently seen enough of life on the Upper Missouri. At that time McKenzie wrote that "Miller has finished the bastions & starts today for St. Louis. I offered him $300 he asked $450 for a year. His work is inferior in finish to Pow[der] Mag[azine] but in other respects I think it is according to contract."[31]

The two-story whitewashed stone bastions would have been visible for miles. With three-foot-thick walls nearly thirty feet in height, railed balconies that "served for observatories," and shingled roofs painted Turkey red and surmounted by "weathercocks, one a Buffalo bull, the other an Eagle," these must have been a wondrous sight. In the northeast bastion were "placed opposite their portholes one three-pounder iron cannon and one brass swivel, both mounted, and usually kept loaded, together with a dozen muskets in case of a sudden attack from the Indians." Plenty of ammunition was stored in each bastion, though the southeast one mounted "but one small swivel." Large American flags snapped and swirled in the prairie breeze from poles atop the bastions' elegant roofs. By 1860 a crude third-story room had been added to the southwest bastion, and it remained until at least 1866.[32]

Of equal splendor, and only slightly less conspicuously visible, was the elaborate new bourgeois house. This served as the residence for the superintendent, his clerks, a few craftsmen or "mechanics," and any distinguished visitors who happened to be on hand. In 1986, National Park Service archeologist William J. Hunt, Jr., and his crew uncovered evidence that an entirely new bourgeois house had replaced an earlier one. Some foundation stones showed marks of a mason's hammer, which would date its construction to "sometime between 1831 and October of 1834," when the mason left. Mortar used in the foundation contained bits of yellow-painted plaster and other tiny artifacts indicating that its construction probably occurred sometime after the original fort was built. As well, trenches and post ends unearthed just outside the new foundation are thought to represent the first bourgeois house's foundation.[33]

The house stood near the center of the fort's north wall. Its rear wall lay about a dozen feet from the palisade, and its front door faced the river gate. The building looked as though it might have been plucked out of Saint Louis and dropped nearly two thousand miles away. Denig stated that it measured "78 feet front by 24 feet depth," and presented a

very imposing appearance, being neatly weather-boarded, and painted white, and with green window-shutters; it is roofed with

Bourgeois House, Fort Union, by Rudolph F. Kurz, September 1851. This wonderfully detailed image includes the notations "P. J. De Smet's Room" and "Authors Room." *Courtesy Midwest Jesuit Archives, Saint Louis, Missouri.*

shingle, painted red to preserve the wood. In the roof in front are four dormer windows, which serve to give light to the attic. The piazza in front adds much to the comfort and appearance, the posts are all turned, and painted white. It serves as a pleasant retreat from the heat of the day, and is a refreshing place to sleep at night when mosquitos are plenty. . . . The interior of the building is handsomely papered and ornamented with portraits and pictures.[34]

The lower story of the bourgeois house comprised four large rooms divided by a central hallway. The largest room on the eastern side sheltered the superintendent, and a smaller adjoining room served as the business office. The western side contained a roomy mess hall and clerk's quarters. Upstairs, a large attic provided guest rooms, a tailor shop, and a saddle and tack room.

Workers remodeled the bourgeois house in the years following its construction. From 1843 until at least 1847 it had four gable windows on the second story roofline, but no front porch. Sometime between 1847 and 1850 a spacious two-story porch was built, and part of the second story's roof was raised, providing more commodious upstairs rooms. An observation platform was also added at the center of the roof. Rudolph Kurz's drawings of the house made in 1850–51 illustrate its appearance when completed. By the middle 1860s the roof sagged badly, window panes were missing, and the place must generally have been in an advanced state of disrepair.

In front of the bourgeois house, at the center of the parade ground, or plaza, stood a sixty-three-foot flagstaff, presenting a distinctly nautical appearance complete with a crow's nest platform and rope trusses. Denig thought the flagstaff "the glory of the fort" and noted that it sported "an immense flag which once belonged to the United States Navy." Perhaps this was the same sixteen- by twenty-foot "American Ensign" the UMO purchased in 1833 or 1834 for twenty-seven dollars. Surrounding the flagstaff was an octagonal fence enclosing a small garden, twelve feet in diameter, containing lettuce, radishes, and cress. Beside the garden squatted a small iron four-pounder cannon that bellowed on special occasions. As Denig wrote, "it is customary on the arrivals and departures of the Bourgeois, or of the boats of gentlemen of note, to raise the flag, and by the firing of the cannon show them a welcome, or wish them a safe arrival at their point of destination."[35]

Kenneth McKenzie's construction crew, or later workmen at the fort, erected, a few paces north of the bourgeois house, a kitchen where meals were prepared for elites such as the bourgeois, clerks, and visitors. At some point a belltower was added to the kitchen structure. Years after McKenzie left, sometime between 1851 and 1858, workers built adjacent to the southwest bastion a timber-framed tower sheathed with planks that was used for a flagpole and an observation deck.[36]

A variety of small rooms were built beneath the overhanging braced framework, which supported a promenade or gallery running along the palisades. Five structures that Denig identified inside the north wall in

1843 included a stable for buffalo calves "which are annually raised here," a hen house, a "very pleasant room intended as an artist's work-room," a cooper's shop, and a milk house and dairy that boasted a few milch cows. Beneath the west and south walls, respectively, were a storage area for the blacksmith's coal and ten stables, "in all 117 ft. long and 10 ft. wide," capable of holding fifty horses. Also under the palisade walkway were storage sheds for harness equipment, tools, and fresh or dried meat. These sheds, shops, and livestock pens were probably made simply by nailing boards to the bracing beams and were thus easily modified according to changing needs.[37]

Just west of the main gate on the south, or river, side of the fort was a house measuring fifty by twenty-one feet and divided in two sections. At the west end was a "blacksmith's, gunsmith's, and tinner's shop," and to the east was a "reception room" for visiting Indians. Reflecting the traders' security concerns, this arrangement made trading sessions or diplomatic meetings possible when "the Indians were troublesome, or too numerous" to be allowed inside the fort. Indians entered the reception room after passing through the first of two sets of heavy double gates, twelve feet wide and fourteen high, that controlled access to the enclosure.[38]

Within the first set of gates a picket-lined open space, measuring about twelve by thirty-two feet, provided admittance to the reception room but not to the fort's parade ground. Often the outer gates would simply be left open during business hours. The actual exchange of goods for furs and other products was customarily done through a small window in the Indian trade room, located adjacent to the reception room, which opened onto the reception room's entry passage. A second window, on the fort's exterior wall, could be opened for trade if additional security was required. Atop the outer gates, during the 1840s, was a large and colorful oil painting, executed by an engagé named Jean-Baptiste Moncravie, depicting "a treaty of peace between the Indians and whites."[39]

Modifications of Fort Union's accommodations for visiting Indians were slated for 1851. Rudolph Kurz wrote on December 1 that he and Denig planned to construct an "Indian lodge" in the fort. "When the Indians are at the fort in such numbers an especial need is felt for a room of good size with a large fireplace, where the redskins can be quartered en masse. As things are now, they have to be crowded into at least five rooms already occupied."[40]

Ranged along the east and west palisades were two large buildings that met a variety of needs. On the east side was a "perfectly waterproof" warehouse measuring about 127 by 25 feet, "very strongly put together, weather-boarded outside, and lined with plank within. It has also cellar and garret." At the north end was a small storage and luggage room. Next was a retail store to sell goods to employees and other white men. The prices of the goods were "fixed by a tariff or stationary value, so that no bargaining or cheating is allowed." Beside this was the main wholesale warehouse room, some 57 feet in length. Then came a storeroom for meat and supplies, and at the southern end was a room in which buffalo robes and other furs were pressed into compact bales and then stored. This room, Denig remarked, could hold between twenty-eight hundred and three thousand packs of buffalo robes, or practically thirty thousand robes.[41]

In the shadow of the west palisade stood a barracks for employees measuring 119 by 21 feet and containing six apartments "of nearly equal size." This building, a single-story, shingle-roofed affair about 15 or 20 feet in height (rebuilt after the 1832 fire), was "perhaps not quite so strongly built" as the warehouse, but "sufficiently so as to suit all purposes." Two rooms, likely at the north end nearest the bourgeois house, were clerks' quarters. The next room housed the fort's hunters, and into the southerly three rooms crowded several common hands and their families. Each of the long buildings at Fort Union was probably constructed in the poteaux-en-terre style.[42]

With so many employees and visitors on hand, the people at Fort Union produced substantial amounts of refuse as well as human waste. No unambiguous documentary reference to latrines or outhouses survives, and the tentative conclusion is that people simply went outside the fort to relieve themselves, used chamber pots, or possibly used some form of a privy within the fort. Only one archeological feature has been identified as a "latrine," but evidence dates it to 1860 or later. Employees threw trash in several dumps located outside the north wall of the fort and one inside the southeast corner of the fort. These dumps, to the delight of archeologists, produced bottles, bones and food scraps, glass beads, and other artifacts from the fort's occupation. It is known that the bosses periodically called upon employees to straighten up the fort inside and out. Still, what with thousands of hides and robes in storehouses, heaps of kitchen and butchering scraps lying around, and employees' careless personal sanitation practices, Fort Union probably exuded quite a nasty stench at times, especially during the hot summer months.[43]

Charles Larpenteur, a longtime UMO employee and later a trader on his own hook, took the credit for initiating a garden at Fort Union sometime about 1835. By 1843, when Denig described the flagstaff garden mentioned above, there were two others as well. Closest was a small garden adjacent to "old Fort William," a post originally built three miles downriver in 1833 by Robert Campbell and William Sublette's opposition outfit. After Campbell and Sublette sold out to the UMO in 1834, it was dismantled and reconstructed about two hundred yards east of Fort Union to become quarters and a corral. The small garden plot furnished peas, turnips, radishes, lettuce, beets, onions, and other vegetables. "The large garden," Denig continued, "half a mile off, and below the fort, contains one and a half acres, and produces most plentiful and excellent crops of potatoes, corn, and every kind of vegetable, but has not been worked this year [1843]."[44]

The Upper Missouri's rigorous climate resulted in fairly rapid deterioration of soft structural wood throughout Fort Union. Cottonwood has a twisted grain, and it fared poorly under alternating periods of extreme dryness followed by rain, snow, and sub-zero weather conditions. Routine replacement of warped and crumbling structural elements was unavoidable, and the fort's appearance was altered over time in major and minor ways as necessity or whim dictated. Nevertheless, by 1835 the post had pretty much assumed the form it retained until its demolition in 1867.

Fort Union was much more than a squalid and ephemeral place where shoddy goods were traded for furs over a few years, only to be carelessly abandoned. Instead, it was calculated to convey the impression of power, solidity, and permanence. Its owners meant it to be a magnet for customers and a grand stage on which to perform the trade ritual, even under conditions that demanded high security. The post provided housing and workplaces for a diverse community, isolated and exposed, in the Upper Missouri "wilderness." Though in certain basic respects—

Fort Union, by Rudolph F. Kurz, 1852. This splendid view of the interior of the post conveys a sense of the kinds of activities that might be seen every day within the bustling post and shows many architectural details. Courtesy the Thomas Gilcrease Institute of American History and Art, Tulsa, Oklahoma (Reg. No. 1326.1093).

Architectural rendering of Fort Union at the time it was occupied by soldiers in 1864. *Courtesy National Park Service, Fort Union Trading Post National Historic Site.*

Old Fort Union, about 1864. This crude, cartoonlike image, although grossly distorted, gives an idea of how the riverside landing might have looked when soldiers briefly occupied Fort Union. *Courtesy Montana Historical Society, Helena.*

maintaining quarters, procuring food, and the like—its populace could be defined as self-sustaining, it would not have existed had there been no fur trade. The trade required a wide variety of goods, but since few articles sold at Fort Union were manufactured locally, the Missouri River became Fort Union's lifeline to the metropolis of Saint Louis and points east. From distant marketplaces in the United States and far-off Europe and China came demands that translated into a steady flow of goods and furs up and down the river.

Communication with Saint Louis was sporadic. The Upper Missouri's climate forced a seasonal rhythm on the trade that no one at the post could alter. With river navigation closed from November to March, only the hardiest travelers would risk a winter journey afoot or by dog train,

Fort Union, as painted upon bed ticking by an employee of the American Fur Company, about 1864. Unreliable in much of its detail, this image nevertheless shows an attached stock pen on the north side of the fort and several keelboats on the Missouri. *Courtesy Montana Historical Society, Helena.*

and then only when crucial letters concerning goods or supplies needed for the next year's trade had to move down the ice-choked river. Until well after 1832 the appearance of steamboats remained a rarity. Even during the warm months isolation and insularity were central themes of life at Fort Union.

Economic success, according to the views of the men who ran the post, necessitated a strictly hierarchical social structure. Mid-nineteenth-century fur men's lives shared many similarities with those of French, English, and Dutch fur traders 150 or 200 years earlier. Based as it was on hoary tradition and long experience, social organization at the post was far from casual. Two generations among some Upper Missouri frontier families called Fort Union home before it decayed to a desolate hulk when Indian-white wars erupted in the 1860s. Most of the folk who lived

there recognized that isolation estranged them from "civilized" areas elsewhere, yet they retained, or created, a sense of community that was insep-
arably woven into the architectural fabric of the fort. Because of its
lengthy occupation, and because its inhabitants constituted a unique
mixed community in "Indian Country," Fort Union offers opportunities
to examine some of our notions about frontier life and its effects on
people and institutions.

CHAPTER TWO

Artists, Scientists, Explorers, and Missionaries at Fort Union

As outposts of white "civilization" on the Upper Missouri, Fort Union and other trading posts occasionally sheltered visitors who had little or nothing to do with the trade. By design, Pierre Chouteau, Jr., subsidized and supported the investigation of American natural history, geology, and ethnology during the first half of the nineteenth century, coincident with the rise of American scientific institutions. For more than thirty years Chouteau offered Fort Union's rustic hospitality to scientists, artists, journalists, missionaries, and government explorers traveling on the Missouri.

Among its distinguished visitors were Duke Paul Wilhelm of Württemberg, George Catlin, Prince Maximilian of Wied-Neuwied, Pierre Jean De Smet, John James Audubon and his companions, Governor I. I. Stevens of the Pacific railroad surveys, Captain William F. Raynolds of the army's Topographical Engineers, and the ethnologist Lewis Henry Morgan. They came for various reasons: to catalog "unknown" flora and fauna, to ponder the Indians' origin and paint their portraits before their anticipated disappearance, to spread the saving grace of the Christian God among the heathen, and to survey and map the West. These visitors' experiences tell us much about Euro-American conceptions of, and interests in, the early West.

Without the patronage of Chouteau, his partners, and a few other traders, men such as Catlin, Prince Maximilian, and Audubon would have found it difficult indeed to pursue their studies. The Chouteaus' sponsorship for governmental exploration dated from the senior Pierre's advice and aid to Lewis and Clark. Years later, Pratte, Chouteau, & Company and Pierre Chouteau, Jr., & Company extended credit to John Charles Frémont's expeditions of 1839 to 1844 that resulted in the West's first reliable emigrant "road maps." Likewise, in 1861, Captain Raynolds found food, lodging, and helpful information at Fort Union.[1]

The support of Pierre Chouteau, Jr., emanated from practical as well as altruistic sources. In part it served self-interest, for the favorable publicity accompanying his generosity to artists, scientists, and explorers blunted some of the criticism directed at less high-minded behavior among his UMO functionaries. Chouteau's liberality toward the "Pathfinder," Frémont, endeared him to the West's most powerful politician, Missouri Senator Thomas Hart Benton, whose daughter Jessie was Mrs. Frémont. But Chouteau's interest in intellectual matters was genuine, and his commitment to advance knowledge about the West produced solid results.

Possessing one of the finest libraries in Missouri, Chouteau must have seen books as repositories of knowledge, not mere emblems of affluence.[2] He and his eldest son, Charles, were proud founding members of the first scientific academies at Saint Louis. In numerous cases Pierre, Jr., arranged for Indian artifacts, animals, and geological specimens to be shipped down the Missouri. These materials went principally to the Saint Louis Academy of Science or, after 1849, to the newly endowed Smithsonian Institution.[3]

UMO men Edwin Denig, Alexander Culbertson, James Kipp, and Francis Chardon offered their learned guests expert advice and aid in collecting natural history specimens and Indian artifacts, and a few became corresponding members of the Saint Louis Academy.[4] Denig stands out as the leading scholar among Fort Union's traders. He penned a description of Fort Union for Audubon in 1843, prepared several mammal specimens for Culbertson to "put into any museum you think propper" in 1849, and authored several ethnological papers. In 1853,

Denig wrote a comprehensive report on the Assiniboines for Henry R. Schoolcraft of the Office of Indian Affairs, and he also wrote on the Sioux, Arikaras, Crows, and Crees. A good deal of Denig's work was later plagiarized by Ferdinand V. Hayden, a paleontologist who examined the Upper Missouri between 1853 and 1857.[5]

Alexander Culbertson, a UMO veteran with twenty years of intimate acquaintance with the Blackfeet, promoted science when he persuaded his younger brother, Thaddeus, to travel up the Missouri in 1850. Young Culbertson conducted the first geological survey of the Mauvaise Terres, South Dakota's spectacular badlands. Ironically, Thaddeus, a tubercular whose trip up the Missouri had temporarily restored his health, perished from dysentery just a few weeks after returning home to Chambersburg, Pennsylvania. The Smithsonian Institution published portions of his journal in 1851 and the entire piece a century later.[6]

No white men knew more about the Upper Missouri's land and people than did the fur traders. A few perceptive traders recorded information about the changes taking place among the Indians, a transformation for which they were partially responsible. Thanks to their native wives and their exposure to Indian societies, fur traders were better prepared than their bookish visitors to recognize significant data about Indians and about a world that they knew could not continue indefinitely. Denig and his associates were capable proto-ethnologists who undertook the first reliable field work in the Upper Missouri. Their reports, intended to help the government shape an enlightened Indian policy, gathered more dust than critical acclaim because government officials generally ignored their advice. Nevertheless, their reports combined informants' data with personal observations, thus establishing stylistic and methodological foundations for future students of American Indian life.[7]

The first scientist to visit Fort Union was Duke Friedrich Paul Wilhelm of Württemberg, Germany. A nephew of King Friedrich and a student of natural science in the Humboldtean tradition, he was more interested in painting animals and birds than Indians. Duke Paul traveled to the upriver region in 1823 and again in 1829–30. On his second trip, the duke stayed at Fort Union and other UMO posts. Unfortunately, next to nothing is known of his activities while at Fort Union in 1830.[8]

Far more familiar is George Catlin, a visionary entrepreneur who achieved fame as the first artist to visit the Upper Missouri country specifically to paint Indians. Born in Wilkes-Barre, Pennsylvania, in 1796, Catlin moved to Philadelphia in 1820. Abandoning an unsatisfactory legal career, he sold his law library, declared himself a painter, and soon became a successful miniature portraitist. By 1822, Catlin had fallen under the spell of Indian portraits in Charles Willson Peale's museum, and his life changed. The enterprising artist decided to create an "Indian Gallery and Museum" of his own to preserve the splendor of the "vanishing Americans" and in the process generate an income. In 1828, Catlin married Clara Gregory of Albany, New York, where the couple lived briefly, but his crusading zeal proved stronger than the attractions of domestic life. In 1830, cognizant that the government's new Indian policy called for all Indians to be removed beyond the Mississippi, George Catlin determined to go to Saint Louis and begin making pictures of "wild" Indians who were untainted by the vices and abuses of whites.[9]

Upon arrival at Saint Louis, Catlin presented himself to Superintendent of Indian Affairs William Clark, whose connections with fur traders would prove useful. Clark approved of the young artist's plans and liked his paintings. Clark's nephew, Benjamin O'Fallon, and Indian Agent John Dougherty invited Catlin to accompany them on brief trips to the upper Mississippi and the Kansas country to paint Indians. Meanwhile, Catlin made portraits for fashionable Saint Louis elites, and it became only a matter of time before he encountered Pierre Chouteau, Jr. John Sanford, then courting Chouteau's daughter Emilie, met the artist and introduced him to the fur magnate. To Catlin's delight, Chouteau invited him to be his guest on the second voyage of the steamer *Yellow Stone* in 1832. With the permission of the secretary of war to visit agencies along the Upper Missouri, and with Chouteau's assurance of support, Catlin prepared to embark on the *Yellow Stone* early in March. As Catlin envisioned it, his life would be "devoted to the production of a literal and graphic delineation of the living manners, customs, and character of an interesting race of people, who are rapidly passing away from the face of the earth—lending a hand to a dying nation, who have no historians or biographers of their own."[10]

It would prove difficult for the artist to square his romantic and humanitarian instincts with the realities of life among fur traders and Indians at Fort Union. Catlin departed Saint Louis on March 26 and arrived at the Yellowstone around June 17, where he saw a "very substantial Fort" whose "bastions armed with ordnance" belched a welcoming salute when the *Yellow Stone* arrived at the landing.[11] Kenneth McKenzie offered Catlin the second story of one of the bastions for a studio. The artist later claimed that "the cool breech of a brass twelve-pounder" made a "comfortable seat" while he worked in the heat of June and July. Artillery pieces were certainly present at Fort Union, but they were considerably smaller than twelve-pounders.[12]

Fascinated with Kenneth McKenzie, Catlin characterized him as a "kind hearted and high minded Scotchman" who seemed to live the life of a medieval baron. As a privileged guest, Catlin took his meals at the "first table" with McKenzie and the clerks. The table, he exclaimed, "groans under the luxuries of the country" and included plenty of buffalo tongues, beaver tails, and other meat. Coffee, bread, and butter were absent, but the iced madeira and port wines accompanying supper offset those deficiencies.[13]

When he was not painting, Catlin occasionally tasted the excitement of frontier life. He tried "running" buffalo with Francis Chardon and drew a picture showing Chardon flying over his stiff-legged horse's head as a wounded bull angrily faced him. Catlin's painterly skills earned him a magician's reputation among the Indians. "My painting room," he wrote, "has become so great a lounge, and I so great a 'medicine man,' that all other amusements are left off, and all other topics of conversation and gossip are postponed for future consideration. The chiefs have had to place 'soldiers' (as they are called) at my door, with spears in hand to protect me from the throng, who otherwise would press upon me; and none but the worthies are allowed to come into my medicine apartments, and none to be painted, except such as are decided by the chiefs to be worthy of so high an honor."[14]

Catlin took up the traders' offer for a free berth on the *Yellow Stone* and quarters at Fort Union, but he made a point of paying for his purchases there and elsewhere. By limiting his indebtedness to the fur traders, he retained some independence in expressing his opinions. Eventually his admiration and concern for Indians led him to condemn the fur traders for their irresponsible sale of liquor. He also grew sharply critical of government policies. Catlin reveled in the long upriver journey that he imagined took him backward in time, but he was horrified to find Indians living in "the most pitiable misery and wretchedness," caused, he believed, by the "contaminating vices and dissipations introduced by the immoral part of *civilized* society." In his view, the Indians' deteriorating conditions were consequences of the fur trade.[15]

According to Catlin, the traders on this "blasting frontier" destroyed the fundamental fabric of life for the "sons of Nature" whose culture he so extolled. To prove his point he marshaled an impressive case study for the devastating results of an Indian's exposure to "civilization." The parable was that of Wi-jun-jon, a distinguished Assiniboine whose name meant "In the Light," though Catlin incorrectly recorded it as "The Pigeon's Egg Head." In 1831, Wi-jun-jon traveled with a few companions to see the "Great Father" at Washington, D.C. Wi-jun-jon and his fellows passed through several large cities, spent time in the nation's capitol, and at length returned home in 1832 on the *Yellow Stone*, profoundly impressed with the whites' numbers and accomplishments. Catlin recorded Wi-jun-jon's transformation in a remarkable "before and after" painting. One side shows Wi-jun-jon as a well-dressed Assiniboine in his own village, and the other depicts him upon his return. Puffing a cigar, resplendent in a military costume supposedly given him by President Andrew Jackson, he sports a top hat and parasol, while whiskey flasks peep out of both trouser pockets. Thereafter, traders customarily referred to Wi-jun-jon as "General Jackson." The Assiniboines initially found his stories about the whites amusing, but in time his people came to regard him as a nuisance and ultimately deemed him an evil magician and outrageous liar. Three years after his marvelous trip, one of his tribesmen "loaded a musket with the straightened handle of an iron pot," murdered him, and then scalped him. Ever the showman, Catlin purchased Wi-jun-jon's scalp from a trader and later regularly exhibited it to gaping audiences while denouncing the pernicious effects of "civilization" upon Upper Missouri natives.[16]

When eastern newspapers printed some of his letters (which in 1844 came out in a two-volume memoir of his western travels), Catlin found himself at odds with the company upon whose largess he had depended. He had indicted the traders as irresponsible monopolists and implied that they deliberately spread disease among the Indians. "These traders," he wrote, "in addition to the terror, and sometimes death, that they carry into these remote realms, at the muzzles of their guns, as well as by whiskey and the small pox, are continually arming tribe after tribe with firearms." In January 1833 he wrote to his former benefactor, Pierre Chouteau, Jr., to defend his statements. Catlin had recently spoken at Cincinnati with Bernard Pratte, who told him his letters had irritated the fur traders. Pratte apparently complained that Catlin's remarks were liable to "excite the public attention to something like competition in the Fur Trade, by inducing them to undertake an opposition to the Am. Fur Company." The artist apologetically observed that he meant no harm and that he was aware of his obligation to Chouteau. Then, in a bizarre about-face, he heaped praise on the traders. Referring to an as yet unpublished letter concerning "the policy of the Government in protecting and encouraging that Institution," he recalled,

> I spoke of the vast importance of the efforts of that Company in meeting and opposing British influence which is already advancing to an alarming degree amongst the numerous and powerful tribes of Indians on our Frontier, and of securing to the U.S. a share of the Fur Trade of our own Country. I spoke also of the enormous expenditures and immense liability to heavy losses and also of the prohibition of Spiritous liquors in that Country which must inevitably result in a complete annihilation of the Company's business & even greatly jeopardize the lives of persons employed in it, if that prohibition should still be continued in force.

Catlin's advocacy for Indians had unfortunately crashed on the shoals of his own entrepreneurial plans.[17]

In June 1833, Catlin published a letter defending and applauding the AFCo's presence in the Upper Missouri that (in Brian W. Dippie's phrase) "tortured logic" to make its points and displayed the jangling crosscurrents of his mercurial mind. Somewhat mollified, Pierre Chouteau, Jr., permitted the artist to warehouse his collection at the Company's building in Saint Louis, but Catlin's relationship with the Company was souring rapidly. The end came in 1835 when Catlin criticized the Northern Department's operations under Henry H. Sibley, who later became a territorial delegate and the first governor of Minnesota. Sibley despised Catlin and applied the full weight of his influence to ensure congressional refusal to purchase Catlin's Indian gallery when it came up for sale in the late 1840s and early 1850s.[18]

Catlin was the first artist to work in the Upper Missouri, the first to depict Fort Union, and the first to attempt to create a thorough visual record of Plains Indians. During his five-month voyage in 1832 he produced nearly 170 paintings, including landscapes, portraits, and village scenes. Though he worked so rapidly that he often ignored details, his paintings and letters constitute a valuable resource for historians and ethnologists. Catlin's prose, highly colored by romanticism, advocacy for the Indians' cause, and self-aggrandizement, must be read with caution. He exaggerated the amount of time he spent in "Indian Country," but his description of Fort Union and anecdotes about life there offer a lively account of its early years. His western travels began in 1832 and ended in 1837, the year a horrifying smallpox epidemic almost destroyed several Upper Missouri tribes.

Little wonder that Catlin's sensitive mind turned to contemplate the darker side of Americans' obsession with "progress" and "improvement." His speculations on the meaning of the "West" and the deep resonance of the frontier in American consciousness preceded the appearance of Frederick Jackson Turner's frontier thesis by half a century. "Few people," wrote Catlin, "even know the true definition of the term 'West'; and where is its location?—phantom-like it flies before us as we travel, and on our way is continually gilded, before us, as we approach the setting sun." Even more striking is his Turnerian observation that "the Frontier may properly be denominated the fleeting and unsettled line extending from the Gulf of Mexico to the Lake of the Woods . . . which indefinitely separates civilized from Indian population."[19] In his varied roles as self-promoting entrepreneur, Indian advocate, wilderness preservationist, and critic of government policy, as well as in his ambiguous

relationship with the fur traders, Catlin reflects the contradictory ideology of Young America that fostered simultaneous admiration and
loathing for Indians.

In the spring of 1833 another prince and another painter came to Fort
Union. Over the next year the German Maximilian of Wied-Neuwied and
Karl Bodmer, a Swiss artist, assembled a spectacular collection of
materials related to Upper Missouri Indians and the fur trade. Maximilian
prepared a meticulous travel narrative, and no artist ever duplicated the
ethnographic detail captured in Bodmer's Indian portraiture, the magical
clarity of his landscapes, or the precision of his natural history illustrations. Only Audubon's 1843 animal and bird paintings compare favorably
with Bodmer's natural history studies. The Maximilian-Bodmer collection excites admiration and wonder simply because of its robust splendor,
but even more important is the fact that, like Catlin, they visited Fort
Union before the smallpox ravages of 1837.

Prince Alexander Philip Maximilian of Wied-Neuwied studied natural
science under Johann Friedrich Blumenbach of Göttingen, whose most
famous student was Alexander von Humboldt, the first truly modern
earth scientist. By 1832, when Prince Maximilian decided to travel to the
United States, he had served in the Napoleonic Wars and in 1815–17 had
roamed Brazilian jungles collecting natural history specimens and
studying native cultures. The Brazilian foray was a dress rehearsal for a
more ambitious project. Maximilian wanted to study the "wild" Indians
of North America to determine whether they represented an initial or a
terminal phase in the human evolutionary process.[20]

When the prince published his book on Brazil, he prepared his own
illustrations, but friendly critics advised him to find a more capable artist
for the proposed American adventure. By the happiest of coincidences,
Maximilian met twenty-three-year-old artist Karl Bodmer in January 1832.
Quickly perceiving that Bodmer was "very skilled in landscape drawings,"
Maximilian persuaded him to take the job, with the understanding that
all of Bodmer's work would become the prince's property.[21]

On May 18, Maximilian, his servant David Dreidoppel (a veteran of
the Brazilian voyage), and Bodmer set sail for America. After they landed
at Boston, a leisurely trek across the eastern United States brought them

at length to Saint Louis on March 24, 1833. During the intervening months Maximilian visited New Harmony, Indiana, where fellow scientists Thomas Say and Charles-Alexandre Lesueur provided a practical introduction to frontier America and its people. Meanwhile, Bodmer traveled to New Orleans, where he made his first paintings of Indians.[22]

In Saint Louis, the prince and Bodmer sought out the men who would be able to facilitate their trip beyond the frontier. Maximilian carried letters of introduction to William Clark and retired fur trader Jean Pierre Chouteau, the father of Pierre Chouteau, Jr. On March 25, Maximilian and Bodmer examined Clark's "Indian Museum" and stood by as Clark entertained Sauk, Fox, and Winnebago dignitaries. Later that day Maximilian decided to do his field work in the Upper Missouri, but when he broached the idea to Kenneth McKenzie, the bourgeois was noncommittal. The following day, Superintendent Clark invited the Europeans to meet the famous captive Sauk chief Black Hawk at Jefferson Barracks. On March 27, Maximilian again probed McKenzie, with some anxiety, for the Scotsman still vacillated, and Maximilian had heard that the *Yellow Stone* "never takes passengers, and therefore it is still uncertain whether we will travel on it."[23]

The next day, the prince met Captain William Drummond Stewart of Grandtully, Scotland, another veteran of the Napoleonic wars who made several excursions to the American West. Stewart urged him to head for the Rockies, but Maximilian preferred the less strenuous river highway. McKenzie used his friend Stewart as an intermediary to inform the prince that "the principal reason for hesitation about our traveling on his ship was that we would perhaps not always abide by company prices" for goods purchased in the Upper Missouri. Maximilian assured Stewart of his good faith and waited for a response. To pass the time, he and Bodmer visited the studio of Peter Rindisbacher, another Swiss artist who painted Indian subjects, from whom the prince purchased three watercolors and a colored lithograph.[24]

Finally, on March 30, Stewart informed the prince that McKenzie was ready to talk. At the Company's offices Maximilian and Bodmer met with McKenzie and Pierre Chouteau, Jr. The fur men agreed to let Maximilian and his associates travel under McKenzie's care "to their fort on the Yellowstone River and winter there at the foot of the Rocky Mountains." With the deal concluded, Prince Maximilian and Bodmer hastily prepared for their trip.[25]

During the next frenzied days, the Europeans purchased equipment and a small stock of Indian trade goods and requested that William Clark issue a passport allowing them to stop at military posts and Indian agencies along their route. Benjamin O'Fallon procured copies of Clark's maps of the West for Maximilian and showed some of Catlin's work to the prince and Bodmer at his home. On April 3, Maximilian arranged with McKenzie to purchase additional Indian goods "at the fort, where I could have them at a better price than elsewhere." McKenzie and Chouteau also agreed to deposit twenty-five hundred dollars on account for the prince, cash being useless in the upriver country. Two days later Maximilian inspected the *Yellow Stone* and dispatched three crates of artifacts and specimens bound for Europe. By April 9, with their gear safely stowed, the prince and his assistants were ready to go up the Missouri.[26]

When the steamer pulled away from Saint Louis the next day, its passengers included Pierre Chouteau, Jr., his wife and daughters, Kenneth McKenzie, and a newcomer, Alexander Culbertson, beginning his fur trade career. Also aboard were about one hundred UMO engagés headed for various trading posts and a few Indians returning from Saint Louis or points east where they had gone to conduct business with the federal government.[27]

A voyage up the Missouri in steamboating's early years taxed the skills of the most capable pilots. The rapid current, swollen by spring floodwaters and thick with snags, sawyers, and logjams, demanded unremitting vigilance to avert disaster. In some of Bodmer's images, the muddy river's channel is so densely packed with snags that it appears impassable. But the vessel survived the ordeal and, after a run-in at Belle Vue with government officers over some whiskey on board, the *Yellow Stone* steamed on to Fort Pierre, arriving on May 30. A week later, Maximilian, Bodmer, and Dreidoppel transferred their gear to the more agile *Assiniboine*, which carried them past Fort Clark to dock at Fort Union on June 24.[28]

"At 6:30," wrote Maximilian in his diary, "we reach the mouth of the Yellowstone River, which is in no way inferior to the Missouri in width." Gazing at the hills covered in fresh prairie grass and the river bottom

The Steamer Yellow Stone on the 19th April 1833, after Karl Bodmer. This image, reproduced from Maximilian's Atlas, shows the Yellow Stone stranded on a sandbar while a small boat removes some of its cargo in order to allow the vessel to float free. Courtesy Joslyn Art Museum, Omaha, Nebraska. Gift of the Enron Art Foundation.

cloaked with willows and cottonwoods as twilight approached, the prince penned his first impressions of Fort Union: "The American flag waves brightly in the last rays of the sun. Bunches of horses graze everywhere. . . . We come closer. Cannons thunder at Fort Union; ours respond. On shore we are received by Mr. Hamilton, an Englishman who has lived here several years, several clerks of the company, and a large number of *engagés*. . . . On the seventy-fifth day after our departure from St. Louis we cast anchor before Fort Union."[29]

After disembarking, wrote Maximilian, "we called on Mr. [James Archdale] Hamilton, who has been living here, and we inspected Fort Union rather thoroughly. We were given quarters in the Superintendent's house, and our baggage was brought there. Today we still slept on the *Assiniboine*." Catlin, too, had enjoyed chatting with Hamilton, a sophisticated expatriate Englishman who he thought "a complete storehouse of ancient and modern literature and art." (Hamilton was a strange bird. Once, in a fury, he threw a brand new silk neckerchief into a fireplace because an admiring Indian had touched it. Always dapperly attired, he stood out from the fort's populace because he bathed and changed his shirt every day. Stories circulated that he was of noble lineage but had gotten mixed up in some scandal that forced him to leave home.) The next day, engagés off-loaded trade goods and stowed eight thousand buffalo robes and roughly sixty-two hundred wolf and fox hides bound for Saint Louis. Maximilian was told that Fort Union traded nearly forty-two thousand buffalo cow robes a year, while Indian consumption and trade at British posts to the north accounted for many more. He also heard that Fort Union's residents consumed between six hundred and eight hundred head a year for food. Natural losses from predators or during floods, when hundreds of bison might drown while trying to cross a river, added to the rate of buffalo reduction. Selective hunting, as he noted, endangered the herds, because it "can certainly diminish the species significantly, especially since only cows are shot. The Indians for the most part say the whites are responsible for the decrease."[30]

The prince soon discovered that meals at Fort Union were "very plain" in comparison to those served on the steamer, which had included "good white bread, crackers, various kinds of always fresh meat, various vegetables, beans, potatoes, fruit, preserved fruit, buffalo tongues, venison of elk, deer, antelope, always fresh." At the time, Fort Union had no garden, and Maximilian concluded that "vegetables do not thrive here, neither potatoes nor corn, for the region is too dry." Nevertheless, local pears and cherries were available, and McKenzie kept a bull and five milch cows at the fort. There were also swine, chickens, a male goat, and plenty of catfish in the Missouri. Two days after landing at Fort Union, the *Assiniboine* set off for Saint Louis, laden with the past year's fur harvest. The entire community turned out for the boat's departure, and some engagés rolled a couple of small cannons outside the fort to blast a farewell salute.[31]

While Bodmer painted and Dreidoppel collected plants and animals to send back to Germany, the prince busied himself purchasing Indian artifacts. For this purpose he supplemented his Saint Louis Indian goods with fifteen pounds of tobacco and six gallons of whiskey from Fort Union's store. The tobacco cost seventy-five cents a pound, while for the liquor he paid McKenzie's "bargain" price of forty-eight dollars rather than the standard ninety-six dollars. "Up here," he wrote, "they sell their wares to their own people at enormously increased prices. The Indians are said to obtain whiskey at 3000 per cent." He purchased a Crow warrior's outfit from McKenzie, and from Francis Chardon he bought a scalp, allegedly that of the Arikara who had murdered the mountain man Hugh Glass. Soon Glass's scalp itself passed through Chardon's hands and into Maximilian's collection. The Europeans were not above grave-robbing in order to satisfy their acquisitiveness. Dreidoppel and Bodmer, on July 4, inspected the forest a few hundred yards upstream from Fort Union where the Assiniboines placed their dead in trees. Though he was "gripped by revulsion," Dreidoppel managed to get away with a recently deposited Assiniboine skull, while Bodmer painted a watercolor of the desecrated burial scene.[32]

Maximilian and his associates observed with "indescribable interest" the comings and goings of Indians who traded at Fort Union. Some Assiniboines arrived on June 27 in grand martial array, hundreds of warriors leading the way, drumming, singing, and firing flintlock guns into the sky. Refulgent in war paint, badges of honor, and costumes trimmed in colorful porcupine quill embroidery, some of the men impressed and frightened Maximilian; others seemed "rather wretched and dirty," which he heard was "the general reputation of the Assiniboine." In their wake

An Assiniboine woman works in front of the skin lodge of a chief. From Maximilian's *Atlas*. *Courtesy Missouri Historical Society, Saint Louis.*

followed a multitude of snarling canines dragging loaded travois, superintended by scores of women and children. Just outside the walls, the
band halted while a few trade chiefs entered the fort to receive a customary treat of watered-down whiskey and tobacco. Prince Maximilian
noticed that despite intense July heat, many Indians wore buffalo robes
or "long overcoats made of thick white woolen blankets, mostly with a
blue border." As the principal men and traders smoked pipes of friendship, Assiniboine women laid out the camp and erected lodges. During
the two-day liquor spree that followed, Maximilian traded alcohol for
many artifacts.[33]

On the evening of July 5, Fort Union hosted a rare and spectacular
event that probably typifies "King" McKenzie's sense of humor. "When it
was dark," wrote the prince, "Mr. McKenzie prepared an entertainment
with a few firecrackers and rockets for the entire crew assembled in front
of the fort. The former were aimed into the most closely packed crowds
of *engagés* and other people, who were completely unfamiliar with these
things; and one can readily imagine the panicky fear and laughter that
resulted from this."[34]

On July 6, the Europeans moved on to Fort McKenzie, some five
hundred miles up the Missouri, to investigate the Blackfeet. With them
went Alexander Culbertson to replace David D. Mitchell as bourgeois at
the post. Remaining briefly at Fort McKenzie, the travelers wintered downriver at Fort Clark, where Maximilian nearly died from scurvy as he and
Bodmer froze while they studied the Mandans and their neighbors. When
spring came they returned to Saint Louis, then went on to New York to
embark for Europe in July 1834. The venture had been fabulously successful.
Bodmer had produced nearly 250 images, the prince had filled several
notebooks, and they had sent many crates to Europe packed with botanical,
ethnological, and zoological specimens. Maximilian's ghoulish method of
acquiring skeletons notwithstanding, no other nineteenth-century traveler
amassed as extensive and important a collection of Upper Missouri Indian
materials. Maximilian published his *Travels in the Interior of North America*
between 1839 and 1843 in German, French, and English editions, each
with an atlas of stunning aquatint illustrations prepared under Bodmer's
supervision. This work memorializes the energy and diligence of its cre-
ators and the vanished people from that time whose images it preserves.

Only when the photographic camera made its debut in the West would such precise details in portraiture, costume, and material culture again be recorded.

John James Audubon (1785–1851) was already reputed to be America's most distinguished naturalist when he decided to travel up the Missouri. His path-breaking study, *The Birds of America*, appeared in 1838; in 1841 the final volume of his *American Ornithological Biography* was published at Edinburgh. By 1842 a prosperous Audubon acquired a handsome estate on the Hudson River, to which he might easily have retired. But the fifty-eight-year-old bird-watcher yearned to see the Upper Missouri, so in 1843 he persuaded several young men to accompany him as assistant naturalists on his final adventure. Audubon's companions included Isaac Sprague as artist, Edward Harris as ornithologist, John G. Bell as taxidermist, and Lewis M. Squires, "no naturalist, though a tough, active, and very willing person." Sprague, Harris, and Audubon recorded their experiences during the trip.[35]

Six years earlier, smallpox had wasted the Mandans, Blackfeet, and many other tribes, permanently altering tribal balances of power. Gathered into a single village, remnants of the Mandans, Arikaras, and Hidatsas cowered before their Lakota enemies. Military and diplomatic power had slipped away from the Blackfeet, and they no longer threatened fur traders. Coincidentally, intensified competition for fewer robes destabilized the trade, and whiskey—the leading trade article among myopic new-comers in for the short run—flowed in greater quantities than ever. Desirous of regaining control over an ineffective western Indian policy that had been drifting for years, the federal government dispatched more agents and soldiers to keep tabs on Indians and fur traders alike. Into these surroundings came Audubon, Sprague, Harris, Bell, and Squires to collect mammal specimens for Audubon's last great work, *The Viviparous Quadrupeds of North America*, which would be published between 1845 and 1848.

Leaving Philadelphia on March 12, the five men traveled by rail, coach, and steamer, arriving at Saint Louis two weeks later. Armed with letters of introduction, Audubon called upon Pierre Chouteau, Jr., and his partners, who treated him "extremely kindly." "The Chouteaux," he wrote, "supplied us with most things, and, let it be said to their honor, at little or no profit." Like Maximilian a decade earlier, Audubon encountered William Drummond Stewart, now Sir William, who was making lavish preparations for his own final excursion to the Rockies. Stewart, fixated as always on the mountain men, tried to talk Audubon into going along, but the aging naturalist declined.[36] Instead, Audubon arranged with the "American Fur Company" for a berth on its steamboat. Unusually severe weather created a lengthy delay, but on April 25, Audubon's party boarded the *Omega*, captained by Joseph Sire and piloted by Joseph LaBarge. Audubon watched as J. B. Sarpy, "book in hand," ticked off the names of one hundred engagés hired for upriver service, while a clerk handed each man the standard equipment, a "blanket containing the apparel for the trip."[37]

High water, high wind, and sandbars impeded progress during the first weeks of travel. The *Omega* passed Fort Leavenworth on May 3, and six days later it stopped at the Indian agency at Belle Vue, where the agent searched the vessel for liquor. Joseph LaBarge's memoir included an unlikely account of the inspection, wherein Audubon provided the inspectors with free drinks while Captain Sire's men used a small trolley to roll the liquor kegs from one side of the hold to the other. Isaac Sprague and Audubon each recorded a more believable version. Sprague stated simply that a detachment of dragoons inspected the vessel while the naturalists were out shooting birds. Audubon wrote that he spent two hours chatting with Captain Burgwin, the officer in charge. If the steamer's crew hoodwinked soldiers, the naturalist was probably not involved in the fraud.[38]

A more serious incident occurred on May 22, when a number of Indians identified as Santee Sioux hailed the *Omega* near Handy's Point. Indians customarily solicited gifts from passing steamers and usually got them, but this time the traders were nervous and the Sioux warriors belligerent. When the steamer kept going, the Indians opened fire, several balls piercing walls and doors on the vessel. No one was injured, though a sleeping engagé snapped to wakefulness when a musket ball tore through his trousers and smashed into a nearby trunk. Audubon kept two spent musket balls as souvenirs.[39]

According to Joseph LaBarge, Audubon "was not a popular traveler," and the naturalists' haughty demeanor did not endear them to the steamer's crew or engagés. Apparently, when Audubon's "botanist" (Labarge rendered his name as "Mr. Prou," though no such person can be identified) bragged he could identify any plant, Étienne Provost decided to play a practical joke and put him to the test. Concealing a sprouted kernel of Indian corn in his hand, Provost displayed a few leaves and challenged the easterner to identify it. The scientist thumbed through his books in a vain effort to name the plant. Confounded, he opined that it was likely a new species, at which point Provost triumphantly shook the dirt from the roots and the botanist admitted defeat.[40]

Forty-eight days of river travel brought the *Omega* to Fort Union on June 12. As cannon boomed the usual greeting, Audubon met superintendent Alexander Culbertson and the "gentlemen of the fort," who treated him to "some first-rate port wine." The next day their gear was transferred to the same quarters that Maximilian and Bodmer occupied a decade earlier, a room Audubon described as "small, dark, and dirty . . . with only one window, on the west side." Dissatisfied with their room, two days later the scientists moved to a "larger, quieter, and better one," possibly on the second floor of the bourgeois house. Soon after their arrival, Edward Harris, who had some medical training, made himself useful by prescribing treatments for some of the fort's residents "consumed with defects too bad" for Audubon to name, presumably gonorrhea.[41]

Culbertson went out of his way to assist and entertain the visitors. He and his wife—a Blackfeet named Natawista Iksina (Medicine Snake Woman)—and several other men and women from the fort staged mock buffalo hunts and feats of shooting and horsemanship that astounded Audubon. Culbertson killed a large wolf and then, swinging low over his saddle, snatched it up at a gallop. Again at full speed on a Blackfeet mare, Culbertson loaded and fired his flintlock fusil eleven times within less than a mile. Later, he offered the naturalist several more wolves that he killed while they scrounged at night among trash heaps outside the fort. When Audubon attended a fandango that went on until one o'clock in the morning, Culbertson played the fiddle "very fairly," one "Guepe" played the "clarionette," and "Mr. Chouteau" played a drum "as if brought up in the army of the great Napoleon."[42]

Culbertson offered the naturalists more than displays of gunning, riding, and musical entertainment. He gave Audubon some decorated

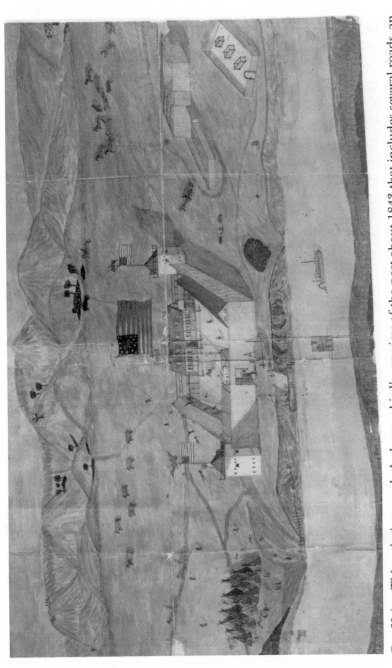

Fort Union. This painting on cloth shows a bird's-eye view of the post about 1843 that includes several roads, an Indian camp, the river landing, and what is probably "Old Fort William" to the east of the fort. *Courtesy Midwest Jesuit Archives, Saint Louis, Missouri. De Smetiana Collection.*

Blackfeet stirrups, a knife sheath, a pair of leather breeches, and a crupper and presented "splendid" examples of native clothing to Audubon's assistants. He also assigned several clerks and hunters to chaperon the scientists, show them the country, and protect them from danger. One was the famous mountain man Moses "Black" Harris, who shot specimens for Audubon.[43] James Kipp gave Audubon an elk horn bow, "a complete dress of a Blackfoot warrior," and an Indian saddle. Edwin Denig—whose wife, Deer Little Woman, was an Assiniboine—helped Audubon plunder an Indian grave to secure an Assiniboine skull, just as Bodmer and Dreidoppel had done ten years earlier. Denig and Audubon dropped the coffin from its perch, twisted the head from the body, and then left the remains scattered about on the ground. Possibly remorseful, Audubon noted that his assistants tried and failed to replace the coffin in its tree. He planned to rebury it the following day, but his journal is silent on the outcome.[44]

Audubon's party seems to have been busy day and night killing every animal that came under their gun sights. The naturalists collected hundreds of specimens and made many drawings using a camera lucida. This boxlike device employed a lens and mirror to project a sharp image of an object onto paper crisscrossed by grid lines. Once the image was carefully traced, it could easily be reproduced on a larger grid pattern. Sprague used the camera lucida to prepare sketches that Audubon later enlarged and colored for his book. In gratitude for the bourgeois's generosity, Sprague painted portraits of Culbertson and his wife, with some assistance from Audubon, and presented them to the Culbertsons along with a painting of Fort Union. Sprague kept another painting of the fort that was eventually published with Audubon's journals.[45]

Audubon, who generally expressed contempt for Indians, was favorably impressed with Culbertson's wife. He described her as a "princess" of the Blackfeet nation, a stunning horsewoman and a gracious host. But when Natawista Iksina painted Squires's face one day for fun, Audubon thought he resembled "a being from the infernal regions." Audubon recorded a characteristically negative evaluation when some Assiniboines came to Fort Union in early July. To Audubon the Indians seemed "miserably poor, filthy beyond description, and their black faces and foully smelling Buffalo robes made them appear to me like so many devils." Mrs. Culbertson likewise indulged in negative cultural stereotyping. Evidently proud of her own pure tribal blood, she regarded the mixed-blood hunters from the nearby opposition post of Fort Mortimer as innately inferior, remarking that "all such no-color fellows are lazy."[46]

Audubon's distaste for Indians harmonized with his enmity for his predecessor, George Catlin, whom he lambasted as a charlatan. Catlin had made a point of paying his own way and eventually grew critical of the Company. Surviving expense records of Audubon's venture up the Missouri, while scanty, suggest that he, too, repaid his hosts. But the trip may have helped persuade the aging naturalist that Chouteau's company knew best and that liquor laws should be adjusted to meet their wishes, for so he wrote in his journal.[47]

By early August the scientists had completed their work, and a new keelboat, the *Union*, was loaded with specimens. On August 15 Audubon's party left Fort Union, along with Alexander and Natawista Iksina Culbertson with their infant daughter, Étienne Provost, J. B. Moncrevier, and four engagés going downriver to be mustered out. The keelboat, beset by wind and rain, arrived at Saint Louis in mid-October, and Fort Union's bird and animal life had a chance to recover.

Rudolph Friederich Kurz, the only trained artist ever to work for the UMO, left a wonderful visual and journalistic record of his time at Fort Union. An introspective and sensitive intellectual, Kurz emerges as one of the most engaging characters in the post's story. He had met Karl Bodmer in their native Switzerland and was inspired to follow in Bodmer's footsteps. In 1846 Kurz came to America intending to "give from [his] own observation a sincere portrayal of the American Indian in his romantic mode of life." Though his mission sounds remarkably Catlinesque, Kurz wrestled with conflicting impressions of the myths and realities concerning Indians once he signed on with the fur company. Perhaps swayed by the opinion of Fort Union's traders, Kurz dismissed George Catlin as a "Yankee humbug" who painted "silly make-believe" scenes. Nevertheless, Kurz remained a staunch defender of Indians' rights to life, land, and humane treatment, and he was sharply critical of Christian missionaries and the American government.[48]

Lacking the wherewithal to finance his ambitious undertaking, Kurz had knocked about Missouri for more than four years, producing relatively little. By the spring of 1851, abandoning prospective plans to travel to Fort Laramie and the Great Salt Lake, Kurz determined to go up the Missouri essentially on his own. In June 1851, while resting at Belle Vue, Kurz met "W. Picotte and A. Culbertson," whose permission he asked to board a steamer bound for the Upper Missouri. During their conversation, Picotte and Culbertson convinced Kurz that only a stay of "two or three years at a fort" would yield the experience he desired. Persuaded, Kurz boarded the *St. Ange* and signed on as a clerk destined for service at Forts Pierre and Union. For seven months during 1851–52 he kept a journal that describes his experiences in captivating detail. His drawings offer an impressive graphic record of the fort's architecture, inhabitants, and customers. Kurz's journal and illustrations offer readers a unique first-hand glimpse of everyday life in the fur trade and constitute the best source material for Fort Union in 1851 and 1852.[49]

During the 1850s other artists and explorers came to the Upper Missouri, but their arrival coincided with major changes coming from the East that would rearrange the fur traders' world. On March 2, 1853, after pondering the question of a transcontinental railroad for years, Congress passed a bill calling for the army to survey several prospective routes. Sectional competition as well as geography necessitated multiple surveys, but many Americans, including Secretary of War Jefferson Davis, hoped that one route would emerge as clearly superior. Leading the northernmost survey between the forty-seventh and forty-ninth parallels was Isaac Ingalls Stevens, who served concurrently as governor and Indian agent for Washington Territory and chief of the survey. Cloaked with the authority of an Indian agent, he planned to make treaties with Indian tribes along the route whereby they would assent to the road. Among Stevens's soldiers and scientists was John Mix Stanley, a civilian artist who produced most of the illustrations that accompanied Stevens's report.

Stevens's expedition departed Saint Paul on June 6, 1853; crossed Minnesota's prairies to the range dividing the Mississippi and Red Rivers; and continued on to the Missouri. Stanley accompanied the main party, but a second detachment headed up the Missouri from Saint Louis aboard the steamer *Robert Campbell,* landing at Fort Union after a forty-two day trip.[50]

The main party arrived at Fort Union on August 1, where they remained for ten days. When Stevens saw Fort Union, its bourgeois house and "store" were each two stories high. Some interior structures were made of adobe bricks and others of wood. Ranged along the interior walls were "shops and dwellings of the blacksmith, the gunsmith, the carpenter, the shoemaker, the tailor, and others." Stevens wrote: "These mechanics are mostly French half-breeds, and have half-breed or Indian wives, and many children."[51]

Like Audubon a decade earlier, Stevens considered Alexander and Natawista Iksina Culbertson gracious and engaging hosts. "Mr. Culbertson," wrote Stevens,

> has occupied the position of chief agent of the company during the past twenty years, [and] has under his supervision not only Fort Union, but Forts Pierre and Benton also. He is a man of great energy, intelligence, and fidelity, and possesses the entire confidence of the Indians. His wife, a full-blood Indian of the Blood band of the Blackfoot tribe, is also deservedly held in high estimation. Though she appears to have made little or no progress in our language, she has acquired the manners and adapted herself to the usages of the white race with singular facility. Their children have been sent to the States to be educated in our best schools.[52]

Edwin Denig and Alexander Culbertson, whom Stevens had met at Saint Louis, assisted the survey by providing food, wagons, and equipment and by persuading Indians not to molest the explorers. Nevertheless, Assiniboine skeptics were not assuaged by Stevens's glib assurances that their "Great Father" would see that his "red children" did not suffer when the railroad traversed their lands. "We hear," one old man spoke, "that a great road is to be made through our country. We do not know what this is for . . . but I think it will drive away the buffalo." Time would verify the old man's suspicions.[53]

During their stay, Stanley painted a view of Fort Union and exposed several daguerreotype images of Assiniboines that "greatly pleased" the natives. These daguerreotypes—the very first photographs made in the region—vanished, possibly when a fire at the Smithsonian Institution early in 1865 destroyed many of Stanley's paintings and sketches.

Between August 2 and August 9, while small parties surveyed the immediate region, some engagés helped Stevens's men build several "Pembina" or "Red River" carts. Built entirely of wood, these screeching two-wheeled open wagons were pulled by a pair of horses or oxen and could carry five or six hundred pounds of freight. The traders sold oxen to the expedition, offered information and advice, and loaned the surveyors a few hunters and guides. Stevens was grateful for the "good offices of the Indian women at the two posts, the wives of the factors and officers of the companies, who fitted us out with a good assortment of moccasins, gloves, and other guards against the severity of the weather in the fall and winter." Bound for the Three Forks of the Missouri, and on to the Snake and Columbia Rivers, Stevens and his men would need plenty of warm clothing.

On August 9 two advance parties left Fort Union for Fort Benton; Stevens's main party left the next day. An eastward-bound contingent under Lieutenant Rufus Saxton, the last of the railroad surveyors, passed by the fort early in October. Saxton had crossed the Isthmus of Panama and proceeded north to San Francisco and then to the Columbia River before turning east to establish a supply camp west of the Rocky Mountains at Father De Smet's Saint Mary's Flathead mission. On September 22, having bought an eighty-foot keelboat named the *Blackfoot* at Fort Benton, Stevens and twenty-odd men floated down to Fort Leavenworth, arriving on November 9. Not surprisingly, Stevens thought his route offered the best possibilities; he and his officers also emphasized the ease of Missouri River navigation and advised that a military post be built at the Yellowstone.[54]

The railroad survey marked a major turning point in western American history. Hard-headed pragmatists, a new generation of Topographical Engineers and government-sponsored scientists conducted a "great reconnaissance" to advertise the possibilities for resource exploitation on a scale that would dwarf that of the fur trade. When the Civil War erupted in 1861, plans to construct a transcontinental railroad were temporarily shelved, and the old-time Upper Missouri trade gained a few more years of life. But at war's end the railroads surged west. With them came industrial technologies, a stronger military presence, and increased Anglo-American settlement, all of which signaled the end of a florescent era in Plains Indian culture and of trading posts like Fort Union.[55]

During the later 1850s and 1860s Fort Union sheltered military explorers, artists, missionaries, sportsmen, and one more notable scientist. The War Department was eager to find out more about the upper Yellowstone River in order to develop a military strategy regarding the region's Indians and their dealings with railroad builders and emigrants. In 1859 Congress appropriated sixty thousand dollars for an initial survey to be carried out by Topographical Engineers Captain William F. Raynolds. Among the few white men who knew anything about the upper Yellowstone were the old mountain man Jim Bridger and Robert Meldrum, a Chouteau trader with the Crow nation. Both offered to help Raynolds.[56]

Raynolds's *Report on the Exploration of the Yellowstone River* details his expedition's progress and describes conditions in the Upper Missouri. Booking passage on two Western Department steamers, the *Spread Eagle* and the *Chippewa*, his party departed Saint Louis on May 28, 1859. The steamers carried Chouteau & Company's goods as well as tons of annuities for the Sioux, Blackfeet, and other Upper Missouri tribes. Raynolds was authorized to distribute goods promised to the Sioux under the provisions of General William Harney's 1857 treaty. Most Sioux bands, however, rejected the treaty signed by their Yankton kin and let Raynolds know that they opposed his expedition. Bear Rib, a Hunkpapa Sioux, warned Raynolds that all whites had better steer clear of Sioux country, and he repeatedly expressed unwillingness to allow the expedition to pass through his land. Raynolds threatened that Sioux resistance would cause the President to "send soldiers and wipe the entire nation from existence." The Sioux grudgingly acquiesced in order to receive the goods promised two years before by Harney.[57]

Raynolds's party circled the northern Rockies, the two-year tour taking them through the Bighorns, South Pass, Pierre's Hole, and the Three

Forks; on to Fort Benton; and down the Missouri past Fort Union in August 1860. While the expedition wintered in 1859–60 on the Upper Platte, Bridger entertained Raynolds with tall tales in the mountain style, replete with petrified trees and animals and gigantic diamonds that shone like the sun. Because of a late departure and the onset of winter, Raynolds himself never saw the upper Yellowstone. The geysers and other natural wonders that Bridger and Meldrum told about remained in the realm of fable for another dozen years.[58]

On his return trip, floating from Fort Benton down to Fort Union in a fifty-foot mackinaw boat, Raynolds observed several small parties of wolf hunters who appeared oblivious to the potential for conflict with Indians. Curiously, Raynolds was troubled about the apparent decline in bison and expressed fear that "this noble animal" would be extinct within a generation. He believed that overkilling of cows for robes was the principal cause, but he also thought that "the immense number of wolves in the country, which destroy the young" was a serious problem. As a remedy, he suggested a "prohibition of the trade of buffalo robes and a premium upon wolf skins." The explorers rested at Fort Union for one week, acquiring another mackinaw boat to carry their now enlarged party. The newcomers were Lieutenant John Mullins's contingent, which had traveled overland through Crow country from Fort Benton to Fort Union, where they sold forty worn-out horses to Robert Meldrum.[59]

At Fort Union a row occurred between Captain Raynolds and Indian Agent Bernard Schoonover that exemplifies the antagonism and cross-purposes under which soldiers and Indian agents often labored. Schoonover, it seems, told some Sioux, already in an ugly mood, that if they were dissatisfied with the quality or quantity of their annuity goods, it was Captain Raynolds's fault.[60]

Raynolds's subordinate, Lieutenant Henry E. Maynardier, had arrived at Fort Union on August 1. Robert Meldrum welcomed the party and gave the lieutenant some provisions while his men set up camp near the mouth of the Yellowstone. The amiable Maynardier and his men exchanged pleasantries with the residents of Fort Union while he awaited Raynolds's arrival. On August 4, he wrote,

Major Schoonover, Indian Agent, and Mr. Wray, Clerk of Fort Union, paid us a visit, accompanied by the ladies of the fort. We prepared a dinner of the scanty materials in our possession, and made some trifling presents to our Indian friends, after which we went to the fort and enjoyed a ball given in our honor.

Although the ladies were the daughters of the forest, they were attired in the fashionable style of the States, with hoops and crinoline, and exhibited as much grace and amiability toward us, their guests, as could be found in the saloons [salons] of any city in the land.

I was as much pleased as surprised to find in what good order and geniality the people of the fort lived, and I must specially record my grateful sense of the uniform kindness and hospitality received both here and at the other posts of the company. Mr. Meldrum, who was in charge of the post, was unremitting in his attention to our wants, and was well assisted by his clerk, Mr. Wray. Both these gentlemen proved that, however rude may be the surroundings and associations of daily life, true warm-heartedness and civility can be found under the roughest exterior.[61]

The explorers departed Fort Union, amid the customary cacophony of blazing guns, on August 15. Maynardier bid adieu to his "kind friends at Fort Union, with many regrets," while Raynolds was probably only too glad to escape the mean-spirited Agent Schoonover.[62] Not all of Maynardier's memories were quite so pleasant. On the way downriver a haughty Blackfeet Lakota warrior, The Little Elk, unaware of the actual numbers of the whites, taunted Maynardier at Fort Berthold: "We don't want to see any white people or any steamboats, because the goods the steamboats bring up make us sick. . . . The Blackfeet [Sioux] and Oncpapas can whip the whites; you have not many soldiers, and we have enough to kill any party you can send against us." White soldiers, no less arrogant, also contributed to the tense and ominous mood then prevailing in the Upper Missouri.[63]

Three more artists came up the Missouri to Fort Union between 1858 and 1861, a voyage that by then had become almost routine for young

Fort Union, ca. 1860, showing the third-story addition on the southwest bastion and an odd gazebolike structure outside the north wall. *Courtesy University of Wyoming, American Heritage Center.*

men desirous of painting the West. Carl Wimar, William Jacob Hays, and William de la Montagne Cary traveled in the footsteps of George Catlin and Karl Bodmer, becoming the last painters to visit Fort Union. Both Company and opposition men assisted or tolerated the artists, who must have provided a bit of diversion in the traders' often monotonous lives. These artists and their companions left written and pictorial accounts of the trip that offer glimpses of events at Fort Union during the closing years of its life.

Carl Wimar, a German immigrant to Saint Louis, decided to travel upriver in May 1858 on the steamer *Twilight.* Also aboard were Henry Boller, clerk for the opposition firm of Frost, Todd, & Company; two German Lutheran missionaries, Jakob Schmidt and Moritz Braeuninger; and two Indian agents, Alfred J. Vaughn and Alexander Redfield. Wimar's journal, later published in German at Saint Louis, offers nothing about Fort Union. He did note, however, that he and his fellow traveler, Constantin Blandowski, had unsuccessfully tried to associate themselves with the "American Fur Company" men rather than the Indian agents, whom the Indians ridiculed and despised. Wimar arrived at Fort Union on June 23, remaining until July 6, when he went up the Yellowstone with Blandowski, Agent Redfield, Alexander Culbertson, the Lutheran missionaries, and a few others to visit the Crow nation. Wimar returned to Fort Union by the end of July, spent three more weeks there, and left for Saint Louis and a successful career painting western scenes.[64]

Many of Wimar's Indian portraits and landscapes have survived in private and museum collections. One dramatic canvas, *Indians Approaching Fort Union*, depicts the fort with its former opposition post, Fort William, in the distance. Of far greater potential value was the fact that Wimar carried a camera with him. Regrettably, not one of his nearly one hundred ambrotype images is extant today. It is tantalizing indeed to speculate on the content of those vanished blinks of the camera's eye.[65]

A New Yorker, William Jacob Hays, went west to paint Indians in 1860. Leaving Saint Louis on May 3 aboard the steamer *Spread Eagle*, he arrived at Fort Union on June 15. Hays spent just a few days at Fort Union, but two sketches of the post, dated June 16 and July 11, have survived. One shows the southwest bastion with a wooden third-story addition atop the original stone structure and a large fur press outside the south wall on the

Carl Wimar, photograph by A. J. Fox, 1857. Wimar was one of the last artists to visit Fort Union. *Courtesy Missouri Historical Society, Saint Louis.*

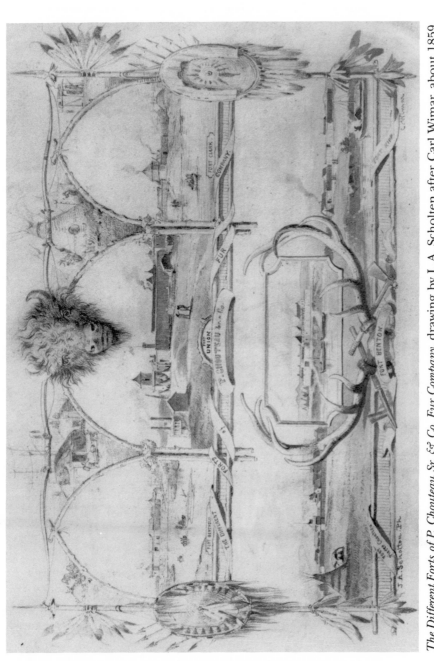

The Different Forts of P. Chouteau Sr. & Co. Fur Company, drawing by J. A. Scholten after Carl Wimar, about 1859. Fort Union is at the top center. *Courtesy Missouri Historical Society, Saint Louis.*

riverbank. Because of fears of a Sioux assault while Hays traveled down-river on the *Key West*, "three cannons were kept loaded with grape for more than a week, while every man on board kept his fire-arms loaded and ready for use at a moment's notice." The vessel was not attacked, and the worried artist reached Saint Louis by early August.[66]

The next year another New Yorker, William de la Montagne Cary, made a trip to the west. In April 1861, as Confederate guns blazed away at Fort Sumter, Cary and two companions, W. H. Schieffelin and Emlen Lawrence, headed for Saint Louis. They carried plenty of camping gear and a letter of introduction to the leading patron of Upper Missouri artists, Pierre Chouteau, Jr., who put them on a company steamer.[67]

The three young men survived an unnerving experience some miles above Fort Union on May 19, when a crewman's lust for liquor proved fatal not only to himself, but to the steamer *Chippewa* as well. Foolishly lighting his way with a candle, the man broached a keg of alcohol in the dark hold of the vessel that evening. Volatile whiskey fumes ignited, burning the man so badly that he soon died. Worse still, the blaze quickly spread forward to threaten three hundred kegs of DuPont's gunpowder. A few minutes later, luckily after the captain grounded the steamer and the terrified passengers stampeded off the stricken boat, the *Chippewa* was no more. With a stupendous blast audible for miles, she deposited tons of scorched goods in treetops along the Missouri. Cary escaped with his life, but the inferno consumed about eighty of his sketches.[68]

With his shaken companions, Cary rafted back down to Fort Union. There they remained for "six long weary weeks" before making their departure upriver to Fort Benton. They eventually journeyed west to the HBC post Fort Walla Walla and on to San Francisco, where they booked passage on a vessel back to New York. Cary's only known illustration of Fort Union freezes a tense moment from 1861 when some Sioux raiders made a dash on the fort's horse herd, escaping with several head. Cary claimed that he participated in repelling the attack. This was not the first time that Indians, presumably Sioux, raided Fort Union. In February of that year Pierre Chouteau, Jr., wrote: "Try and find out which of the Bands made the attack on Fort Union. We must try and obtain redress in some way or other. Major Schoonover who was in the midst of the fray has fully reported the whole matter to the Superintendent of Indian Affairs."[69]

William de la Montagne Cary's six months of field work, pleasant or otherwise, yielded source materials for a long career as an illustrator and gallery artist in New York. He died in 1922, the last surviving painter who saw the Upper Missouri before the reservation era. Cary's work is largely imaginative and lacks the wonderful detail of Bodmer, or the exuberant freshness of Catlin. Still, Cary and his friends' "boyhood idyll," as one authority described it, contributed to the documentary record of Fort Union.[70]

Two noteworthy sportsmen also found an outlet for their craft at Fort Union. John Palliser, an Irishman who later became famous for his work with the British North American Exploring Expedition of 1857–60, came to Fort Union in October of 1847 and stayed the winter. He published in 1853 a reminiscence of the sojourn that provides the only glimpses by an outsider of life at the post during the cold season. *Solitary Rambles and Adventures of a Hunter in the Prairies* chronicles his horseback trip up the Missouri in the company of the "hardy old veteran" James Kipp, who despite his sixty-odd years still made annual trips up the river to Fort Union from his farm at Independence, Missouri.[71]

Far less savory a character was Lord George Gore, another British adventurer who from 1854 to 1856 financed a lavish hunting expedition and carried on an illegal trade with the Crows on the Yellowstone. This latter activity embroiled him with the Indian Department, and he was ordered out of the country. Before he left, however, he managed to alienate the men at Fort Union when they offered to sell him two flatboats to go back down the Missouri. Thinking the traders' price exorbitant, the enraged sportsman piled most of his goods and equipment outside the front gates and set them aflame in a gesture of contempt.[72]

Upper Missouri Indian agent Alfred Vaughn, writing from Fort Pierre on November 9, 1856, complained to Superintendent Alfred Cumming at Saint Louis that Lord Gore had angered the Hunkpapa and Blackfeet Sioux by "passing through the heart of their country [with a large party of men, horses, and oxen] killing and scattering the small quantity of game which is their only means of subsistence." Vaughn's letter was transmitted to the commissioner of Indian affairs at Washington, George H. Manypenny.[73] Eventually there was talk of initiating legal proceedings to seize Gore's booty—robes, furs, hides, and elk horns—illegally removed from the Indian country, sell it, and reimburse the Indians for their losses. Existing records are silent about whether this occurred.[74] Lord Gore epitomizes the worst kind of Upper Missouri traveler—crass, arrogant, and insensitive—but he was a fairly representative precursor to later western "dudes" such as the Grand Duke Alexis and Theodore Roosevelt, who recklessly overhunted in their zeal to have a jolly time, thereby hastening the end of freedom for Plains Indians.[75]

The last scientist to visit Fort Union was Lewis Henry Morgan. Morgan earned fame as the "father of modern ethnology" in 1851 when he published *The League of the Ho-de-no-sau-nee, or Iroquois*, but he was eager to learn about western Indians' social structures. Consequently, he journeyed through Kansas and Nebraska in 1859 and 1860. The following year, he traveled from Saint Paul across the prairie to Fort Abercrombie and then took a small steamer, the *Pioneer*, down the Red River to the HBC's Fort Garry. In order to round out his experience, Morgan wanted to see the Upper Missouri and the Yellowstone. His opportunity came in May 1862, when he left Omaha aboard the steamer *West Wind* and transferred to the *Spread Eagle*, bound for Fort Benton.

Morgan disembarked at Fort Union on June 9, describing it as "an old-fashioned Fort" rude in appearance but "roomy and quite respectable" within the palisades. While gathering data from natives and fur traders, Morgan heard about an unusual pet at the post. Robert Meldrum kept an immature beaver at Fort Union, where several native women "took turns in nursing it at their breast until it began to bite occasionally when they gave it up." The creature survived, and Meldrum presented it to Alexander Culbertson's daughter, Fanny. Morgan, evidently impressed, wrote: "They are fine pets, cleanly and harmless, and become very tame and affectionate. I must get one." By late June, Morgan reached Fort Benton, where "about 70 men, women, and children" lived. During a remarkably swift 750-mile downriver journey from Benton to Union, Morgan claimed that the steamer reached a speed of almost twenty-five miles an hour, the trip requiring only sixty-eight hours. When Morgan arrived at Sioux City on July 3, he learned that sickness had carried off two of his three small daughters. "Our family is destroyed," he lamented.

"Thus ends my last expedition. I go home to my stricken and mourning wife, a miserable and destroyed man."[76]

Weathering this personal tragedy, Morgan continued his distinguished scientific career, writing numerous books and articles on Indian life. His discussions with natives, mixed-bloods, and white fur traders in the Upper Missouri yielded reliable information that he incorporated in his path-breaking comparative studies of American Indian society. He also published *The American Beaver and His Works* in 1868, the first book entirely devoted to that animal; it was based largely on information he had acquired along the Missouri River.[77]

Men of the cloth likewise found shelter and assistance at Fort Union over the years. Carrying on a centuries-old North American frontier tradition, various Christian sects attempted to missionize the western Indians. Among the last areas within the continental United States to undergo this process were the Upper Missouri and northern Rocky Mountain regions. The ecclesiastical invasion began in October 1831 when three Nez Percés and a Flathead accompanied a Chouteau company brigade led by Lucien Fontenelle and Andrew Drips to Saint Louis. These Indians, the story goes, were the first from the mountain tribes to set out to gain information about the white men's God. Though all four died before returning home with the whites' promises of timely attention, other deputations went east to contact willing missionaries. With the appearance of Marcus and Narcissa Whitman, Samuel Parker, Henry and Eliza Spalding, Jason Lee, and other Protestant missionaries in Oregon by the middle 1830s, the missionary frontier reached the Upper Missouri and the Rockies. Most American missionaries ignored the intervening Plains Indians and moved clear out to Oregon, where other white Americans lived and the earth yielded splendid farm crops. The Flatheads and other would-be Christian tribes in the meantime remained unchurched, but eventually their calls were heeded.

By the end of the 1830s Catholic churchmen amplified their far western missionary program. Catholics had an advantage in that virtually all the French-speaking fur company employees nominally shared their faith and welcomed missionaries. The best known Catholic missionaries were two Jesuits, Pierre Jean De Smet and Nicolas Point. Among all

Pierre Jean De Smet, S.J. A diligent missionary, De Smet got along well with the fur traders and visited Fort Union several times between 1840 and 1864. *Courtesy Missouri Historical Society, Saint Louis.*

Upper Missouri proselytizers, the Jesuits maintained the best relationships with the fur company and with the region's inhabitants. Father De Smet envisioned a great mission system for the Plains Indians based on earlier Jesuit experience in seventeenth-century Paraguay. When his mission among the Potawatomis at Council Bluffs failed, De Smet concluded that better prospects lay to the west. Proximity to the whites and to their horrid whiskey, he believed, had irrevocably polluted the Potawatomis. If he could just persuade one untainted tribe to adopt his mission scheme, De Smet hoped, others would gradually follow and his holy endeavor would succeed.[78]

De Smet, like other missionaries on the western frontier, relied on the good will of Saint Louis fur traders for transportation and other assistance in Indian Country. Indian agents supplied another, considerably less potent, source of protection and aid. In April 1840, De Smet accompanied a fur brigade under Andrew Drips to the final Green River trade rendezvous. Marching on to Pierre's Hole, he triumphantly preached to the Flathead nation and in his enthusiasm baptized several hundred Indians, who surely had little idea that this act implied they must bury their old gods. Many Indians, assuming that the whites' powerful technology reflected analogous potency in the spirit world, adopted the new religion not to supplant but to augment their own. Besides, they hoped the "Black Robes" would protect them from enemies and share with them the defensive or curative magic of religious medallions, rosaries, and crucifixes.[79]

Several months after his sojourn with the Flatheads, De Smet appeared in the Upper Missouri, stopping briefly at Fort Union in late September. The missionary described it as "the vastest and finest" of the Company's Missouri River posts, noting that "the gentlemen residing there overwhelmed us with civilities." Each time he visited Fort Union over the years, De Smet baptized all the mixed-blood children he could find.[80]

De Smet got on well with the traders and apparently believed they were in the main decent and responsible men. In April 1841, Pierre Chouteau, Jr., & Company extended him unlimited credit, "with a view to aid in your laudable undertaking," and wished the missionary program "entire success." De Smet developed warm associations with Edwin Denig and Alexander Culbertson, with whom he corresponded for several years. He sent them books and religious instructional materials; they helped him by sharing information about the native tribes and occasionally forwarding Indian artifacts.[81]

Sectarian rivalry for souls was by no means absent in the Upper Missouri. Interdenominational hostility among Christians was an important, and corrosive, aspect of the western missionary frontier, and Indians soon realized that this new religion was neither uniformly accepted nor free from vicious competition. In 1852, Father De Smet voiced his fear that Jim Bridger's two mixed-blood children might fall into the hands of Protestants if they were not speedily sent to good Catholic boarding schools. Henry Spalding a few years earlier had complained that Jesuits deliberately conspired to undermine the Protestants' crusade in the Oregon country, and he even intimated that Catholics had instigated the Cayuse destruction of Marcus Whitman's mission community at Waiilatpu in 1847.[82]

Despite intermittent visits to Fort Union or elsewhere in the West, much of De Smet's work consisted of fund-raising for missions in Missouri, a task at which he proved singularly adept. As the years fled, De Smet's idea for a mission system gradually evaporated, the victim of underfunding, lack of administrative support, stiff competition from other sects, and growing tensions between the government and Indians. This left the Catholics solidly established in Missouri but did little for western Indians, except perhaps to begin driving a wedge that divided many tribes into what would soon be denominated "friendlies" and "hostiles," or "progressives" and "traditionals." By the time of De Smet's final visit to Fort Union aboard the *Nellie Rogers* in 1863, unrest among the Sioux had reached a dangerous pitch, and he realized that his longtime desire to establish a Sioux mission would never become a reality. The rush of miners into Montana's gold fields brought "all the vices and excesses of our modern civilization; especially as understood and practiced by our American pioneers." These "pioneers," in De Smet's judgment, were more of a threat to the Indians than the traders had ever been.[83]

Nicholas Point, another Jesuit, spent seven years in the West. Point left his native France for Kentucky in 1835 and subsequently moved to Louisiana in 1837 to found Saint Charles College. In 1840 he was ordered to Saint Louis, where he arrived just in time to take a hand in De Smet's establishment of missions for the western Indians.[84]

Point, De Smet, and four other Jesuits left Westport in a large wagon train, bound for the Oregon country, captained by John Bidwell and guided by Tom Fitzpatrick. For the next six years Point served in the Coeur d'Alene and Flathead missions, but declining health led him to petition for removal to the East. He and De Smet, seeing in Blackfeet enmity an obstruction to the success of their Flathead mission, opened negotiations with the Blackfeet in 1846, hoping to forge a peace between the nations. In August of that year Father Point arrived at Fort Lewis, Chouteau & Company's Blackfeet post. In the next few months he baptized some six hundred persons and helped cool Blackfeet hostility toward Americans, who moved across the plains in ever increasing numbers. When spring arrived, Father Point received permission to return East, and he headed down the Missouri on a barge for Fort Union. There he boarded the steamer *Martha*, reaching Saint Louis in early August.

As both journalist and artist, Point documented his voyage down the Missouri to Fort Union. When he left Fort Lewis on March 18, 1847, that post was in the process of being dismantled and relocated a few miles downstream, to be renamed Fort Benton.[85] Father Point arrived at Fort Union on the first of April, his barge receiving the usual cannon salute and mass greeting. He made numerous sketches along the way, including one of the *Martha*, one of Fort Union from the south, and one of the interior, showing the bourgeois house before it was remodeled for the last time. He also made portraits of the Culbertsons, Malcolm Clark, and old Jacques Berger, who had been instrumental in opening the Blackfeet trade in 1830. Point was a self-trained artist whose naïve style exudes the mysticism of his faith. His charming paintings provide a valuable addition to the pictorial record of Fort Union and constitute an interesting collection of ethnographic illustrations.[86]

Not all missionaries fared as well as De Smet and Point. Two German Lutherans, Johann Jakob Schmidt and Moritz Braeuninger, failed miserably, but their experience is illuminating and instructive. These two were jointly sponsored by synods at Saint Sebal, Iowa, and Neuendettelsau, Bavaria. Both had been in North America for several years, seeking a suitable field for their endeavors. When an 1857 mission effort in Canada fizzled, the disappointed priests moved to Detroit. There they encountered an Indian agent named Alexander Redfield, who invited the Lutherans to accompany him to Fort Sarpy in the Crow country, three hundred miles above Fort Union.[87]

The steamer *Twilight*, chartered for Frost, Todd, & Company (an opposition outfit), left Saint Louis for the Upper Missouri on May 23, 1858. On board were the two missionaries, the artist Carl Wimar, Indian agents Redfield and Vaughn, numerous voyageurs and mechanics, and a few women and children. The *Twilight* boasted an impressive steam calliope that blared music at each landing and usually sent Indians fleeing for cover from the outlandish sound. In just one month the *Twilight* docked at Fort Union, which Schmidt described as "beautiful . . . the best looking on the Missouri we have seen so far."[88]

Their admiration soon turned to disgust, for the steamer had dropped off a goodly supply of liquor along with the expectant missionaries. By the next morning the Assiniboines were too drunk to receive their annuities, a situation that caused the missionaries "unspeakable pain" and depression. The alcoholic frolic continued for two more days, prompting Schmidt to observe, "The white workers are so drunk they cannot work." Even the veteran factor at the Crow post, Robert Meldrum, couldn't get results, for his engagés were "drunk and full of foolishness." Just a few days before the keg was broached, the Germans pridefully (and inaccurately) thought it was "great that we are the first missionaries among these wild western Indians" and were zealous to prevent them from falling into "the hands of the Romans." Their tune quickly changed. The Indians now seemed "dirty and depraved in body and soul," and the fur traders were nothing but a "godless rabble."[89]

The priests experienced the utmost difficulty in adjusting to social conditions on the river and relating to the people working at Fort Union and living elsewhere in the Indian country. The gritty reality of life on the Upper Missouri stood glaringly in defiance of the missionaries' cherished, if unsubstantiated, hopes. Especially after James Kipp warned them that the Crows were the "wildest of all Indians," and Agent Redfield obligingly told them that the Crows were "morally perverted" prostitutes and fornicators, who committed "shameful acts man with man," the Germans became "surprised and scared."[90]

In the end, misguided faith got the better of common sense, and the missionaries bound themselves to fulfil their destiny. That destiny led first to Fort Sarpy and subsequently, late in 1859, to an unavailing mission among the Crows at Deer Creek Station about sixty miles up the North Platte from Fort Laramie. Captain William F. Raynolds, wintering near Deer Creek before he continued west, pitied the destitute missionaries and their companions, whom he described as "God-fearing and devoted men, but ignorant of the world as well as of our language, and in consequence poorly fitted for the labors they had undertaken." Raynolds played the good samaritan to the Lutherans, loaning them money and giving them some work repairing barracks for his men. Finally, in the spring, Schmidt and Braeuninger moved on to Powder River. There, amid internal discord, frustration, and gloom, Braeuninger met a lonely death at the hands of some Hunkpapa Sioux in July 1860. After a feeble effort to maintain the isolated and ineffective mission, by 1867 the Iowa synod admitted defeat and recalled the survivors. The German Lutherans' inexperience, coupled with their persistent inability to adapt to conditions during a time of aggravated tensions between whites and Indians, as well as among Indians, had doomed the mission.[91]

While it may be argued that Schmidt and Braeuninger simply made a poor show of it, it should be borne in mind that even the most widely admired churchman, De Smet, utterly failed to establish an effective western missionary system. No matter how high-flying the rhetoric of proselytizers, of whatever stripe, the outcome in practically every case remained the same: the missionaries departed, abandoning their missions as though they were hopeless candles burning in a hostile night. In some instances missionaries blamed the fur traders for their own failures. And yet, ironically, even moderate success in the mission effort must in part be chalked up to encouragement from the very traders who later seemed lukewarm, or worse. When at last the priests and ministers moved on to hawk their goods elsewhere, they left the Indians to work out their own destinies. In their wake, the departed missionaries also left a dangerous threat to native tribal cohesion, for Christian ideology was not without its charms. Whether Christianity made more or less difficult the Indians' transition from "free" sovereigns of the soil to "unfree" inmates on wretched prisons of reservations cannot be precisely quantified, but it seems fair to assert that wherever the new religion took root, it divided and enfeebled native nations by disrupting their social and cosmological worlds.

Few years went by at Fort Union without the appearance of some artist, scientist, explorer, missionary, tourist, or sportsman. Some made outstanding contributions to science, art, or ethnology, while others left tragic or reprehensible legacies. Certainly, the number of verbal descriptions and illustrations they produced has helped preserve a lively interest in Fort Union and the people whose lives it influenced. When George Catlin arrived in 1832, the Upper Missouri was nearly pristine. The land bore few scars after several millennia of human occupation. The Crees, Assiniboines, Blackfeet, and Sioux had no reason to suspect that the cosmos as they knew it was soon to be vaporized. Despite the traders' merchandise and the periodic visitation of epidemic disease, native cultures remained viable, and the tribes retained confidence in their ability to defend themselves against white intruders, should it come to that.

Catlin and those who followed him left a composite record of life at Fort Union between 1830 and 1865. In part, the record is a tragic chronicle of the effects of liquor and disease, the gradual reduction of the buffalo, and the first stirrings of an eventual American military conquest. But the same accounts also richly document the beauty, the freedom, and the grandeur of American Indian life on the Northern Plains before the reservation era. Moreover, these accounts and images, along with a wealth of surviving business records related to Fort Union, make it possible to reconstruct, to some degree, the vanished society of fur traders, Indians, and mixed-bloods on the Northern Plains.

CHAPTER THREE

Fort Union's Society

Western North American trading posts served strictly economic objectives and generally had nothing to do with military affairs. Business was the dominant theme, and fur trade history is essentially one of profit and loss. But the trade could not function unless a certain number of people lived at or near the trading posts. A few large, semipermanent posts housed civilian communities whose members constituted a society peculiar to the fur trade frontier. Fort Union, a designedly grand installation set in a stark physical environment, deeply influenced political, economic, and cultural affairs for two generations of Upper Missouri country residents. Only two other nineteenth-century posts within the United States were of comparable significance: Bent's Old Fort on the Arkansas (1834–49) and the HBC's Fort Vancouver on the Columbia (1825–49). Fort Union outlived both.

Fur traders' society was conjured out of economic decisions made by men whose frame of reference was built on ledger books, shipping lists, and global market conditions. Yet for people who worked at Fort Union, the fur trade was more than a business, and the post was their home. Their community differed markedly from either of the "parent" cultures upon whose margins it existed. Euro-Americans and Native Americans alike had reoriented themselves in response to the trade. Mixed-race marriages had always been permitted, even encouraged, in the fur trade country but were almost universally deemed repugnant wherever Euro-American culture was dominant. Nineteenth-century fur traders were among the most racially tolerant Americans of their time. Perhaps this was partly because their business necessitated multiple levels of coopera-tive interaction among people who did not fully comprehend each other's culture. Perhaps also the behavior and temperament of certain white men fitted them equally for the trade and for life with native people and may furnish connections that run unbroken through centuries of the fur trade.

Popular-culture versions of the fur trade often feature mountain men as the key players. A reconstruction of community life at Fort Union tells a different story, one that more accurately reflects the notion that the fur trade created a society with special characteristics. Fort Union was no ephemeral hovel, quickly erected and as quickly abandoned, intended to shelter a gang of hard-bitten mountain men between one Homeric adventure and another. Instead, its population was ethnically diverse and sexually balanced to a considerable degree. Families were integral to its social structure. Women and children were always part of everyday life at Fort Union, and native wives played an important role in shaping rela-tionships between the traders and their customers.

Within Fort Union's walls dwelled people bound together by shared experiences: life's pleasures and privations, birth, disease and death, and the daily demands of the fur business. Residents defined and gave shape to their isolated community deep within Indian country, but the post's social order likewise reflected its proprietors' requirements. Apart from infrequent scientific or artistic visitors, no one lived there who was not bound by an engagement of one form or another.[1]

As an economic colony of its Saint Louis owners, Fort Union dimly prefigured what future Americans would call a "company town." Debt peonage was not the Chouteau company's objective, but mobility and other options of most employees were to some degree dictated by their employers and by their reliance on Company transportation. Hunting and gardening produced food for basic survival needs, and the post's community was in this sense self-sufficient. Were it not for the trade, however, there would be no Fort Union; the community's economic health depended on its Missouri River lifeline to metropolitan fur markets and supply centers at Saint Louis, in the eastern United States, and in Europe.

Fort Union never experienced growing pains. Traders showed no interest in acquiring land to expand settlement, and so dodged one of the conflicts that poisoned relations between Indians and whites. Likewise, Fort Union's limited farming operations were restricted to only a few small garden plots over the years. Labor requirements determined the post's population, which fluctuated seasonally but must seldom have exceeded one hundred souls. Including residents at various satellite posts such as Forts McKenzie and Benton, and a handful of temporary winter posts, Fort Union's regional "community" probably amounted to fewer than three hundred persons.

Four decades of occupation wrought change to the landscape surrounding Fort Union, though less than might be imagined. The most visible change would likely have been a reduction of bottomland forest adjacent to the post. Construction and repairs consumed cottonwood and other timber, as did the shipyards (*chantiers*) that annually turned out keelboats, flatboats, pirogues, and rafts. Vast amounts of wood went into fireplaces for heating and cooking, but much of that might be collected during the Missouri's spring flood, when tons of dead wood and snags floated downstream. If firewood failed, buffalo chips supplied a ready alternative fuel source. When Fort Union was torn down in 1867, the surrounding landscape probably appeared much as it ever had. No fur traders' comments on this topic have survived, but it is fair to assume that big trees were scarce along the river bottom. Contemporary photographs depict a wide variety of shrubs and grasses in the immediate vicinity. Local environmental changes related to Fort Union's lifetime bear little comparison to those that came later, when farmers' plows, ranchers' cattle, engineers' dams, and oil drillers' rigs redefined the Missouri River and the Northern Plains.

Fort Union housed a remarkably cosmopolitan society, one that included sundry European ethnic groups and members of half a dozen Indian tribes. Upon arriving at Fort Union in June 1833, Prince Maximilian observed "people of all nations gathered here, Americans, Englishmen, Frenchmen, Germans, Russians, Spaniards, Italians, about a hundred in number, with their mostly Indian or half-breed wives and children."

"Trading Post, Fort Union," Carbutt, Chicago, Illinois, Publisher; Illingworth and Bill, Photographers, "with Capt. Fisk's Expeditions, 1866." The two rude buildings seen here may be the ones for which the Northwestern Fur Company claimed they had paid one thousand dollars in 1867. Several lodges of unidentified Indians are visible in the background. *Courtesy Montana Historical Society, Helena.*

Almost two decades later, in 1851, Rudolph Friederich Kurz echoed the prince's assessment, hearing "English, French, Spanish, and German" spoken, as well as "Assiniboin, Crow, Herantsa, Cree, Mandan, and even Blackfoot." Kurz's list of nationalities comprised "Canadians, Americans, Scotchmen, Germans, Swiss, Frenchman, Italians, Creoles, Spaniards, Mulattoes, Negroes, and half-Indians."[2]

Most of Fort Union's populace were engagés, an all-male contract labor force, mainly Canadians of French extraction, hired for one- or two-year stretches. Engagés represent a traditional fur trade subculture whose roots reach back to the seventeenth century. Canadians enshrined the voyageur and the *coureur de bois* ("woods runner") as pillars of their folk culture, but Americans are less aware of the voyageurs' significance in early-nineteenth-century U.S. history.

"Creoles" (French who remained in North America after the fall of New France), *métis* (mixed-bloods of European–Native American descent) and "French Canadians" built forts, maintained and stocked them, and helped keep them supplied with provender. According to fur traders, French Canadians' strength, endurance, and tractability made them the finest boatmen. When an 1816 law banned Canadian traders from U.S. soil, John Astor explained to Secretary of State James Monroe that he still required "the use of Canadian Boatmen, as Our Citizens will not submit to the hardships and habits of living which they have to endure." Ramsay Crooks added that they were "indispensable to the successful prosecution of the trade. . . . Tis only in the Canadian we find that temper of mind to render him patient docile and persevering in short they are a people harmless in themselves whose habits of submission fit them peculiarly for our business."[3]

Fur company agents actively recruited francophone *habitants* each year from Canadian parishes along the Saint Lawrence, especially around Lachine and Montréal, for service in the western trade. Gabriel Franchere, born in Montréal and one of the "Astorians" of 1810–13, regularly furnished Canadian laborers for John Astor as well as Pierre Chouteau, Jr. After 1842, when Ramsay Crooks's "American Fur Company" (the former Northern Department) went bankrupt, Franchere shared Chouteau's office space in New York City and served as the Western Department's principal Montréal labor contractor until his death in 1863.[4]

In Rudolph Kurz's view, inherited from Fort Union's elites, the genuine HBC-style coureurs de bois outshone the *mangeurs de lard* ("pork eaters") who made up the bulk of engaged labor at Fort Union. "Pork eaters" were common hands hired at Saint Louis to move goods up or down the Missouri, while coureurs de bois—more experienced backwoodsmen—generally remained in the fur country for years at a time. Competitive labor market conditions sometimes induced fur companies to boost salaries to acquire highly skilled Canadian boatmen. In March 1832, Ramsay Crooks wrote Chouteau that "Mr Franchere at Montreal . . . in

"Trading Post, N.W. Fur Co., Fort Union, Montana," Carbutt, Chicago, Illinois, Publisher; Illingworth and Bill, Photographers, "with Capt. Fisk's Expeditions, 1866." This exterior view of the post shows a badly damaged northeast bastion and the recently added third story on the southwest bastion. Note also that the foreground is covered with a variety of shrubs and grasses, even after thirty-six years of occupation. *Courtesy Montana Historical Society, Helena.*

consequence of the increase in wages which we authorized him to give [has] but little doubt of his procuring at least 50 Boatmen for your Department."[5] In the same year William Clark approved a request from Pierre Chouteau, Jr., to allow ninety-three men already at various posts in the Upper Missouri to remain for an additional eighteen months. All but eleven bore French surnames.[6]

Hispanic engagés, most likely from New Mexico, also found employment at Fort Union and other UMO posts. Kenneth McKenzie in 1829 complained about the Company's hiring of, as he spelled it, "Spanairds." After railing about two Hispanic deserters, he fumed: "I hope they will be taken up and punished as they merit, I hope you will not engage any more Spanairds [*sic*] for this outfit. they are worthless rascals." Two Hispanos, Antonio Sisnairo (Cisneros) and Joseph Maria (José Maria), accompanied Fontenelle and Drips's mountain expedition of 1831–32. Isidor Sandoval was hired as a voyageur and posted to Fort Union in 1830. Evidently the same man was at the fort in 1841, when Charles Larpenteur mentioned a "Spaniard" named Isidro Sandoval. The next year Isidor the Spaniard was killed during a fight with a notorious bully, Alexander Harvey.[7]

Both Larpenteur and John Audubon alluded to an unidentified "Mexican" who turned up at Fort Union in 1843 with "His India," or Indian wife, about to give birth. The man had recently deserted from Fort Van Buren, the UMO Crow post on the Yellowstone at Rosebud Creek. Larpenteur, pitying the pregnant wife, gave the man work, though he described him as "only fit to herd horses." The unlucky man deserted again with his wife and child, only to be badly mauled by a juvenile grizzly bear. Subsequently returned to Fort Union, the injured escapee was sentenced to a flogging at the flagpole, but Larpenteur says the punishment was waived.[8]

Larpenteur, like McKenzie, at times denigrated Hispanos, but he also admitted that "Spaniards" were "remarkable for their activity and skill amongst horses." Ethnic bias aside, Hispanos were respected as superior horsemen and wranglers. At least three Hispanic wranglers worked at Fort Union in 1851–52. One anonymous old man tended cattle, and despite his seventy-odd years, he still possessed the "keenest, quickest eyesight" in the fort. Somewhat better known are José Ramusio, whose name was anglicized to "Joe Ramsay," and "Joe" Dolores. Dolores, nicknamed "Spagnole," was a horse guard and part-time trapper who lived at Fort Union with his Mandan wife and may be the unidentified "Mexican" who stumbled into the grizzly bear. Ramsay was a hunter at Fort Union for about twenty years and stayed on after Chouteau sold the fort in 1866. About that time, during a hunting excursion Ramsay's gun barrel burst, severely injuring one of his arms. Of no use to Chouteau's successors, he was turned out to fend for himself. Some Assiniboines took him in, and he spent his last years under their care. Another Hispano, "Philip" Alvarez, did tailoring and other jobs at Fort Union during its final years.[9]

Hispanos also brought adobe construction techniques to the Upper Missouri. Fort Benton was built almost entirely of adobes, as were some outbuildings at Fort Union. In 1867, Charles Larpenteur employed two Hispanos, "Phil Lovatto" and "Raphael," to mold several thousand adobes for a new store outside Fort Union and for another at Fort Buford. Though well beyond the optimal climatic range for adobe construction, mud bricks apparently lasted long enough in the Upper Missouri to make their use feasible.[10]

Several African-American engagés lived and labored at Fort Union. Best known is James P. Beckwourth, a mulatto from Virginia who first came west with William Ashley's 1824 brigade and signed on with the UMO in 1833. His several years in the mountains had resulted in close ties with the Crow nation, and he even claimed they named him a chief. Kenneth McKenzie attempted to capitalize on Beckwourth's influence by hiring him to make certain the Crows traded with the UMO. Eventually McKenzie found another Crow expert, Robert Meldrum, who was perhaps easier to deal with, and Beckwourth retired from the Upper Missouri in 1836.[11]

Charles Larpenteur, working at Fort Union in 1834, encountered "two waiters, one a negro," serving dinner in the bourgeois house. One of these men may have been "Alfred," a "Negro" who was associated with, or belonged to, John F. A. Sanford. There was also a John Brazo, whom Larpenteur described as "a mulatto . . . a man of strong nerves and a brave fellow, who had on several occasions been employed to flog men at the flagstaff."[12]

Kurz identified two black men at Fort Union in 1851–52. One was "Auguste," about whom nothing is known. The other was "Jim Hawkins, a negro from Fort Union," who in 1851 ran off to Fort Pierre, where he found work as a cook. Alexander Culbertson apparently brought Hawkins up the Missouri, though the man had at one time been employed at Belle Vue post under Peter A. Sarpy. Hawkins worked out an uncommon labor arrangement. "He is really the slave," wrote Kurz, "of someone in St. Louis and is required to pay a certain sum to his master every year; the balance of his wages he may spend as he likes. Here he is free, it is true, but the company must be responsible, more or less, for his life."[13]

Engagés included good men and bad, but little more than their names survives in Company records. In the 1830s common engagés received from $200 to $260 for an eighteen-month stint in the Upper Missouri. The standard tour of duty included three to five months of upriver travel, winter and spring spent in the *pays d'en haut*, and a shorter return journey to Saint Louis the next summer. Before departing from Saint Louis, each engagé received a small advance called an "equipment," the cost of which was deducted from his annual wages. A typical equipment included a three-point blanket, one and one-half yards of stout blue woolen stroud cloth, a butcher knife, a silk handkerchief, a rough checked shirt, and a few pounds of tobacco. Billed at inflated Upper Missouri prices, these supplies cost about seven dollars. In 1829 an average engagé's annual wage was roughly $140. A keelboat pilot of proven skill might earn $700 for the year and a double equipment. Traders and interpreters received from $350 to $600 annually and a new suit of clothes. By 1831 most contracts were written for eighteen-month terms, but annual wages amounted to about the same. Wages increased slightly over the next several years; by the late 1830s an engagé could expect perhaps $160 a year.[14]

The bourgeois and clerks encouraged hard workers to reengage when their contracts ran out, and some contracts extended for up to five years at a stretch. On the other hand, malingerers might find themselves on the next available keelboat or steamer headed down the Missouri, forfeiting whatever wages stood unpaid in the ledgers. Post managers kept lists of men whose engagements had expired, sometimes as a means of warning Company agents at Saint Louis against rehiring certain individuals. The rosters include notations such as, "A great villain," "lazy, not worth half wages," "a Great Skulker," "very so so," "of no use for this post," and "a Damn'd rascal." Poorly rated men would likely be passed over in favor of those who received compliments such as "good man," "very good man," or, rarely, "excellent."[15]

Sometimes the Company retained energetic and able engagés by offering increased wages and benefits such as better board and lodging. Engagés who were "qualified in the mercantile line or in languages and prove to be honest and shrewd" might in time be promoted to clerks, bourgeois, or agents as they worked their way up the corporate ladder. Many engagés, however, were liable to run off at a moment's notice, and the bourgeois kept a close rein on his laborers. To maintain control over his rough and rowdy engagés, every one of whom was "armed and, though not courageous in general, was nevertheless, touchy and revengeful," a bourgeois had to be tough and cool-headed. His authority also depended upon loyal clerks for moral and, if it came to it, physical support.[16]

Not all engagés were interchangeable drudges. Some were artisans whose skills commanded premiums at Fort Union. Carpenters, blacksmiths, tinsmiths, gunsmiths, boat-builders, and tailors found work year in and year out. In 1832 or 1833, during Fort Union's initial construction, Peter Miller, a stonemason, and Antoine Luteman, a carpenter and part-time mason, directed construction of the bastions and the powder magazine. Two engagés, Samuel Holmes and "Saucier," worked as laborers for the mason. Although Miller's wages were relatively high, when he completed his work in October 1834 he returned to Saint Louis, declining McKenzie's offer for another year's service. Indeed, Peter Miller disliked being at the fort enough to desert temporarily in 1833 after trying to persuade two other men to go along.[17]

Antoine Luteman, a Saint Louis carpenter who helped finish the bastions, arrived at Fort Union in the spring of 1832, apparently remaining until 1835. Kenneth McKenzie described "Old Luteman" as a good worker, "slow but sure." Rock work, framing, flooring and shingling new buildings, and setting paving stones in the dairy kept Luteman and his helpers busy. Other engagés carted stones or chopped and hauled timber that sawyers cut into planks in saw pits outside the fort.[18]

Coopers, tinsmiths, and blacksmiths were highly skilled journeymen engagés. In a shop near the bourgeois house, coopers fashioned barrels and crates to store or transport trade goods, food, and other materials. Fort Union's first tinsmith arrived in December 1833. With soldering irons, sheet iron and tin, and various tinner's tools he fabricated kettles and other tinwork and made repairs as well. Tinware sold at Fort Union included coffee boilers, basins, cups, funnels, candle molds, plates, lanterns, and nutmeg grinders. With a resident tinsmith on hand, these trade items would be more regularly available, presumably at lower costs than those ordered from the East or from England. James Archdale Hamilton, standing in for Kenneth McKenzie during an absence, wrote in December 1834 that "our tinsmith will now be able to furnish the river with tin kettles. Please inform us the quantity of each size required for Fort Pierre and its dependencies." Only a few months earlier, Hamilton had complained "there is not half enough tin in [the] St. Louis order, and there is not enough here for more than a months work."[19]

Good blacksmiths were indispensable at Fort Union. Blacksmiths forged functional and decorative hardware, repaired traps, made tools and equipment, and undoubtedly did gunsmithing as well. At some point before 1843, a blacksmith and a tinsmith probably worked in tandem designing and fabricating two large decorative weather vanes to adorn Fort Union's bastions. Constructed with iron bases surmounted by three-dimensional embossed tin figures, one depicted a galloping buffalo and the other an eagle with outspread wings.[20]

Tailoring was another skill in constant demand. Fort Union annually stocked assorted textiles and finished clothing for sale to employees and Indians. Engagés received a few yards of woolen cloth as part of their equipment, and many took further advances on their wages in cloth. The combined demands of Indians, elites, and engagés created a need for common as well as fancy tailoring. In 1835, James Archdale Hamilton complained to Pierre Chouteau, Jr., & Company that "Chiefs Coats could easily have been made here had Mr. McKenzie sent the lace promised."[21] Indian and mixed-blood women made and sold moccasins and other leather items such as shirts, trousers, and coats. "Country-made" clothing, a product of bicultural interaction, blended Euro-American tailoring and textiles with Indian construction and decorative techniques to create beautiful garments adapted to Upper Missouri life. In 1836, Charles Larpenteur recorded payments of a few dollars "for tailoring" and for "making pantaloons." In 1843, John Audubon's quarters were next door to the fort's hired tailor on the second floor of the bourgeois house. The tailor's shop was located there mainly to ensure that tools and materials were not pilfered by "Indian visitors." Rudolph Kurz in November 1851 bought a winter suit of buckskin trousers and a coat made "with hood, 'metis fashion,' and sewed throughout with sinew" from "Madam Bombarde," an engagé's wife.[22]

Some garments and other articles were made by Indians for sale to the traders and engagés. While Rudolph Kurz worked at Fort Clark, he traded Pierre Garreau, a mixed-blood interpreter, "a bolt of calico for a man's buckskin shirt, elaborately ornamented, and a woman's shirt-dress made of two whole bighorn pelts; each of these, at the current price, was valued at $12." Kurz, a diligent collector, bought bridles, knives and scabbards, tomahawks, moccasins, gauntlets, sashes, necklaces, and saddles. In one case he traded James Kipp "a flask of cherry brandy and two pounds of candy 'kisses' for his Mandan woman" in exchange for "six beautiful arrows for my elk-horn bow."[23]

By the 1850s men at Fort Union apparently poked fun at the practically extinct class of "mountaineers" by burlesquing their attire and behavior. This provided an opportunity for native tailors to sew outfits for sale to employees who went down the Missouri to visit the "States." Many engagés arrived at the settlements sporting expensive and highly decorated buckskin suits made at a trading post and parodying Indian yells and dances in order to impress gullible town-dwellers.[24]

Craftsmen and hunters, valuable to the fort and difficult to replace, held intermediate positions between engagés and elites. Like artisans, good hunters occasionally bargained for better wages, since their specialized skills were necessary for the fort's survival. Hunting and meat processing were year-round, labor-intensive activities that kept individuals and some families continually employed.[25]

Post superintendents, partners in the Company, traders, and clerks constituted a self-conscious "upper class" of educated and literate residents. Their work involved personnel and operational management, record-keeping, day-to-day store-keeping functions, and diplomacy with Indian tribal leaders. A surprising number of these men left journals, memoirs, or extensive correspondence. No written account by a member of the post's lower social echelon (if ever one existed) has survived.

During the years that Pierre Chouteau, Jr., & Company operated Fort Union, the bourgeois were generally men of Anglo-Scottish descent, though there were exceptions. Charles Larpenteur, born at Fontainebleau, France, occasionally superintended the fort but never gained a partnership. Edwin Denig, a Pennsylvanian of Danish extraction, and Alexander Culbertson both entered the Company's service in 1833. Engaged for three years for two thousand dollars as clerk and trader, Culbertson later became chief agent. Denig ran Fort Union intermittently from 1843 until the early 1850s. Practically all of the resident managers married Indian women and had families, a topic addressed later in this chapter.[26]

When the Columbia Fur Company and Chouteau's organization merged in 1827, several bourgeois or agents—Kenneth McKenzie, William Laidlaw, Daniel Lamont, and James Kipp—became profit-sharing UMO partners. All but Kipp were Scotsmen, and all spent time at Fort Union, though McKenzie achieved the greatest notoriety. Energetic and ambitious men, their residence in the upriver country helped ensure smooth business operations and steady profits for the Company and for themselves. As Rudolph Kurz observed, "Agents and bourgeois form, so to speak, a company of their own in so far as they all agree to buy goods from the stockholders at a stipulated price in which is included interest and transportation charges."[27]

Kenneth McKenzie, the arrogant "King of the Upper Missouri," emerges as the standout among Fort Union's bourgeois. It was he who kept Columbia Fur strong enough to force Pierre Chouteau, Jr., to the bargaining table. McKenzie was not the first man to visualize the potential of a fort at the Yellowstone, but he gets the credit for turning vision into reality. Like Chouteau, he quickly grasped the relationship of steamboating to profit and power in the Upper Missouri and made the new technology his servant. His business acumen is indisputable, and if his methods were sometimes raw, they were effective.

On the other hand, McKenzie must have been a bit of a megalomaniac. He evidently came to believe that his escapades—and his power—in the upriver country were immune to threats from the nation's petty laws and regulations. So it was that he rationalized his distillery project at Fort Union and reputedly encouraged some Crow warriors to steal furs from the Rocky Mountain Fur Company and then sell them at Fort Union.

There are more amusing aspects of McKenzie's personality and his reign. Here, after all, was the man who first brought fireworks, lots of them, to Fort Union. He also introduced Upper Missouri people to expensive novelties such as a magic lantern and an electrical spark generator. In 1832 or 1833 he ordered from England a "good complete suit of armour (coat of mail, etc)." For this he was willing to pay the considerable sum of fifty or sixty pounds sterling, though there is no evidence he ever wore the getup. In 1833 he ordered fifty bogus "peace medals," of the "size and thickness of Government medals," stamped with the visages of Pierre Chouteau, Jr., and John Astor. These he intended to pass off to Indians as identical to the ones bearing likenesses of presidents of the United States. By 1838 the cat was let out of the bag, and the Indian Department ordered the UMO to quit impersonating the government. This order was ignored. McKenzie obviously delighted in playing the grand host at Fort Union, especially with princes or other dignitaries as his guests. And, while he always served himself well in the trade (he died a rich man in 1861), he remained unshakably loyal to his company until a lawsuit over back pay developed in 1849. For all of these reasons, McKenzie takes the prize as the bourgeois archetype. Blinded by self-delusion, however, the "King" slipped up badly at Fort Union a few times, and his outrageous gaffes became more memorable than his achievements.[28]

Clerks, possibly the busiest workers at Fort Union, were likely candidates for advancement within the organization. Clerks spent several years mastering the skills requisite for their entry-level management positions. They customarily took orders from above, passed them along to lower-echelon workers, and were expected to see that the work was properly performed. Clerks communicated with bourgeois and engagés every day, and at Fort Union their lodgings were next door to the quarters of the rank and file.

A clerk had to be literate and possess some mathematical know-how. He plumbed the mysteries of double-entry bookkeeping and had to keep a close eye on engagés' balances at the retail store, lest a man's bill outrun his wages. When that happened, an engagé would be most liable to desert. Providing backup for the boss when he dealt with drunks or trouble-makers was another aspect of the clerk's apprenticeship. The clerk's life must have seemed an endless round of errand running, inventory taking, requisition writing, and locking and unlocking store-room doors and the fort's gates. When Indian bands came to Fort Union, clerks were especially harried, what with trade, entertainment, squabbles, and crowded conditions inside the post. Overworked young clerks found an incentive for continued service and loyalty in the hope that they might rise in the organization and retire as traders, superintendents, or partners.

Chouteau Fur Trade Medal, 1843. Bogus peace medals such as these enhanced the standing of Chouteau's company with Indians long after the government ordered it to cease using them. *Courtesy Missouri Historical Society, Saint Louis.*

Stocking larders and feeding residents at Fort Union required a substantial expenditure of time and energy, providing work for many people. Buffalo meat was monotonously central to the diet, and residents annually consumed roughly 280,000 pounds of meat. Sometimes, because of migration, bad weather, drought, or prairie fires, buffalo wandered far from Fort Union, rendering casual subsistence hunting impractical. As a hedge against food shortages, traders purchased vast amounts of dried meat along with robes when Indians butchered the animals in fall and spring hunts.[29]

No matter how ingeniously prepared, dried meat had a limited appeal. Professional hunters provided the fort's populace with a reasonably steady supply of more appetizing fresh meat. Some men, such as Joe Ramsay (José Ramusio), worked as hunters for more than twenty years, growing old in the service. Killing buffalo may have been exclusively men's work, but women usually performed the bloody job of skinning and butchering the animals and then cutting the meat into sheets to dry in the sun. This was hard work and could be dangerous if the women happened to get caught on the *large* (the open prairie) by roving enemies out for scalps or captives. Hunting parties, commonly comprised of about twenty persons, transported fresh or dried meat to Fort Union in Red River carts.[30]

Hunting combined work, sport, and amusement. Hunters preferred to kill buffalo by running them. Riders dashed across the prairie at a full gallop on fleet horses and closed in on wild-eyed bison, loading and firing their smooth-bore Northwest guns as rapidly as possible amid choking dust and deafening noise. Good buffalo runners—horses with excellent native characteristics bolstered by specialized training—fetched premium prices and were carefully tended and guarded against theft. Full-time hunters were inordinately fond of this exhilarating routine, but Kenneth McKenzie, Alexander Culbertson, and other elites were equally keen for the chase. This was high excitement, to be sure, replete with danger. Ravines and animal burrows threatened horses and riders. Enraged buffalo occasionally gored a rider or disemboweled his horse. A too hastily loaded fusil could explode, maiming or killing the hunter. But among devotees of "running," the thrill eclipsed all hazards. In a more prosaic tactic, called the "approach," hunters sneaked up on bison and shot them from concealment.[31]

Fishing in the Missouri River also provided entertainment, a useful source of protein, and a respite from buffalo meat. Fish hooks and lines could be bought at the retail store, and a seine (a net that was set in the river for a fish trap) was sometimes used. Anglers caught catfish, suckers, walleyes, and saugers.[32] Other protein sources included domestic cattle, swine, goats, chickens and their eggs, and sometimes dogs. Pigs performed the dual function of supplying food and serving as efficient garbage scroungers. Their slop trough, located just outside the fort walls, attracted numerous wolves that also scavenged the offal. This circumstance offered a source of amusement to men who either shot the wolves or "fished" for them from atop the walls using lines and hooks baited with meat.[33]

The diet at Fort Union included many species of native plants and wild animals aside from buffalo. Buffalo berries, chokecherries, wild plums, serviceberries, wild currants, gooseberries, and grapes made seasonal additions to the larder and prevented scurvy. Somewhat surprisingly, there is no evidence that scurvy ever afflicted fur traders at Fort Union, though it nearly killed Prince Maximilian at Fort Clark in 1834, and several soldiers died from it at Fort Union in the 1860s. Deer, elk, antelopes, bears, rabbits, ducks, geese, pigeons, and prairie chickens provided a welcome variety of meat and helped conserve dried buffalo meat for leaner times.[34]

A vegetable garden first became productive under the watchful care of Charles Larpenteur in 1835. Indeed, the small garden may well represent the first farming ever attempted in the confluence region; no Indians practiced agriculture that far up the Missouri.[35] Garden seeds appear in a number of requisitions for trade goods, and crops such as potatoes, radishes, corn, peas, onions, cucumbers, pole beans, and watermelons added variety and nutrients to the inhabitants' diets. Environmental limitations on the garden's output included a short growing season (about 120 days), aridity, and insect invasions. Raids on the garden by Indians or by opposition men sometimes resulted in premature harvests, or none at all. In August 1835, Larpenteur noted that some Assiniboines would have stolen all of the corn and potatoes had it not been for the timely intervention of some "Indian soldiers." Edwin Denig estimated that relatively abundant harvests occurred only once every three years but reported that in the summer of 1838 the large garden plot half a mile below the fort produced 450 bushels of potatoes and "many other vegetables." Interest in the garden may have waned with the passage of time, but in 1851, Rudolph Kurz noted that potatoes were still cultivated.[36]

In addition to what could be hunted, grown, or gathered around Fort Union, many other foodstuffs came up the Missouri. Flour, crackers, pilot bread, rice, tea, coffee, chocolate, honey, molasses, salt, pepper, raisins, and other comestibles were commonly on hand, as were spices such as cinnamon, nutmeg, mace, and cloves. Some of these foods were used in the trade, but most were likely consumed by residents. Large quantities of alcohol of differing grades and under several names—brandy, whiskey, rum, shrub, wine, high-wine, and straight—appeared almost every year, destined for consumption by the post's residents and Indians alike.[37]

Aside from keeping body and soul together, foodstuffs delineated and reiterated Fort Union's hierarchical social order. Engagés were generally issued only lyed corn, "grease" (lard), and fresh or dried buffalo meat. Such a limited diet may have encouraged desertion. In 1834, Jacob Halsey at Fort Pierre complained to William Laidlaw that thirteen "Porkeaters" had deserted, remarking that "the scoundrels have no good reason for leaving us, they have been well treated in every respect we having always been able to give them plenty of good dry Buffalo Meat and corn." Clerks, traders, and bourgeois, by contrast, enjoyed such delicacies as canned oysters, chocolate, almonds, dried and brandied fruits, catchup, preserved herrings, and capers.[38]

High-status employees were served better food, and they dined at tables in the mess hall set apart from the engagés. Variable quality of food and drink, and physical distance separating elites from the rank and file in the dining room, reminded every resident of his or her respective place. Fort Union's sharply drawn social lines were deemed necessary to maintain order and the chain of command at an isolated post where, in actuality, distinctions among men were relatively small.

Food also played an important role in the Indian trade. Visiting Indians received a preliminary "feast" of coffee and biscuits before serious trading commenced, and sometimes "feasts" marked the conclusion of a trading session. Feasts and gifts, traditional elements in the trade ritual, symbolized hospitality and reaffirmed cordial relationships with Fort Union's native trade partners. Traders periodically groused about Indians' begging for food or presents, but they accepted the practice as necessary for profitable trade and pleasant relations.

Women, children, and family life were prominent elements in the fur traders' society. Women—as laborers, craftswomen, translators, mothers, wives, and sexual partners—helped to create Fort Union's social culture and maintain its profitability. No woman left an account of life at Fort Union, and any evaluation of womens' lives at the post must be divined mostly from evidence in mens' records, whatever lapses and biases they may contain. Indian and métis women, perhaps more than men, established the bicultural common ground that supported the distinctive traders' society.

Children play an inconspicuous role in Fort Union's surviving records, but their continual presence is certain. Father De Smet found many children when he visited Fort Union in 1840, 1846, 1851, and 1866. In a mass baptism on July 20, 1851, De Smet counted twenty-five mixed-blood children at the post. In 1852, three fathers—W. Hodgkiss, "Champagne," and "Paquette"—purchased daguerreotypes of their children (two daughters and two sons) who had been sent to Saint Charles, Missouri, probably to attend school. The children presumably returned to Fort Union, but their photographs have disappeared. Charles Larpenteur made a rudimentary census on June 20, 1864, that enumerated seventeen "half-breed" children at the fort.[39]

Practically all of the superintendents, traders, clerks, and engagés at Fort Union had Indian or mixed-blood wives or companions. Marriage according to "the custom of the country" was recognized as legitimate by Indians and whites. Some fur traders used "country" marriages strictly as a convenient avenue to sexual gratification or to solidify connections with a certain tribe. Indian families frequently offered young women, and some men even "loaned" their wives, to the fur traders for permanent or temporary unions. Sexual intercourse symbolized hospitality and signified bonds of friendship and association between individuals as well as different cultural and ethnic groups.

Indian and mixed-blood women may well have found life with the traders less arduous and risky than it would have been otherwise. Adjusting their native life, and to a degree their traditional roles, to life within the fort usually brought greater security and comfort and easier access to materials such as cloth, tools, and decorative items. In turn, their kinfolk expected open-handed hospitality at the fort, which occasionally over-taxed the food supply or traders' patience and led to complaints about Indian freeloaders' constant demand for gifts.

Many fur-trade marriages were permanent relationships marked by genuine commitments and lifelong bonds of affection. The status of men and women at Fort Union determined the selection of spouses and marriage arrangements, and what constituted acceptable behavior among engagés was not necessarily so for those above them. According to Rudolph Kurz in 1851, "unfaithful women are now become a common-place—nobody thinks much about such occurrences." He further noted, with evident bias, that "much depends on the girl's parents, whether they come of good family and enjoin upon their daughters the duty of being loyal to their husbands. Indian women who marry engagees are not valued at the purchase price of a horse; therefore they do not regard themselves bound in duty to remain. Such Indian women are, as a rule, the riffraff. Children born of such unions inherit, as a matter of course, bad rather than good qualities of their parents; on the other hand, halfbreed children of clerks and traders are a credit to the white race."[40]

Francis A. Chardon, who ran the Mandan post at Fort Clark for many years, was a callous and crude man. His first native wife, a Sioux woman named Tchon-Su-Mons-Ka, died on April 24, 1837. A few months later, during the smallpox epidemic, on September 22, his young son Andrew Jackson Chardon perished. At that point Chardon had an Arikara wife, but in June 1838 he "divorced" her and concluded to "buy myself a Wife, a young Virgin of 15—which cost $150." One of his employees, lecherous eighty-year-old Toussaint Charboneau of Lewis and Clark fame, behaved in as repellant a manner as Chardon. Charboneau inaugurated his final "marriage"—to a fourteen-year-old Assiniboine prisoner purchased from some Arikaras—with what amounted to a gang rape followed by a drunken "charivaree." Whites were not alone in committing such outrages. Kurz (among others) mentions that a number of Indian tribes, such as the

Hidatsas, Assiniboines, Pawnees, and Comanches, customarily gang-raped women captives and licentious or unfaithful wives.[41]

On the other hand, some marriages between traders and Indian women were quite successful. About 1837, Edwin T. Denig, chief clerk and bourgeois at Fort Union, wed an Assiniboine named Deer Little Woman, whose brother, First To Fly, was a noted chief. Denig already had one mixed-blood child from an earlier "country" marriage. His first son, Robert, was born between 1833 and 1837, perhaps to a Sioux woman. Denig noted that the mother lived near Fort Pierre, but Robert stayed with his father at Fort Union.[42]

Rudolph Friederich Kurz worked as a clerk under Denig at Fort Union in 1851–52. At first, Kurz had mixed feelings about the man. He heard at Fort Clark that Denig was "a hard man, liked by nobody, not even here; he keeps two Indian wives . . . squanders all he has on them; begrudges anything paid the employees, is never satisfied, etc." Later, when he was transferred to Fort Union, he first found Denig a "rather prosy fellow" but was soon "pleasantly surprised," possibly because of the lavish dinner that Denig served him. Kurz's views continued to vary, nevertheless, for he was subject to substantial swings of opinion.[43]

Denig and Deer Little Woman had two daughters, Sara (1844) and Ida (1854), and a son, Alexander (1852). Although Denig's kinfolk in Pennsylvania felt disgraced by his marriage to an Indian, he stood by his native wife. He also married his wife's younger sister. This "custom of the country" would have raised no eyebrows, and it may indeed have been necessary, because Deer Little Woman suffered a disabling injury sometime before 1851. Still, Denig's polygamy created some problems. He found it difficult, according to Kurz, to dissuade the younger sister from socializing with less respectable women in the fort. But Denig had too much "kind feeling" toward Deer Little Woman to "cast her off" (along with her sister), which would have accorded with native custom. Eventually, it seems, the younger woman went her own way, and Denig and Deer Little Woman were married under American law at Saint Louis in 1855.[44]

In the early 1850s the Denigs sent their eldest son, Robert, to Chicago for schooling. By 1856, concerned about their other children's need for security and education, the Denigs quit Fort Union for the Red River settlement in Canada, which was something of a retirement community for fur companies' aged employees. Many mixed-blood families did likewise rather than suffer abuse and humiliation in "civilized" locales where white prejudice was far more openly expressed.

Alexander Culbertson first came up the Missouri in 1833. Like his long-time friend Denig, he hailed from Pennsylvania. Culbertson became bourgeois at Fort Union in 1840 and soon married Natawista Iksina, a Blackfeet chief's daughter. Culbertson was about thirty, while Natawista Iksina was about fifteen years of age. The couple had three daughters: Nancy (1848), Francisca (1851), and Julia (birth date unknown). Rudolph Kurz described Mrs. Culbertson as "one of the most beautiful Indian women," having "much presence, grace, and animation."[45]

After becoming chief agent of the UMO posts in 1848, Culbertson accumulated a fortune from the fur trade and other investments, reputedly as much as three hundred thousand dollars. Eventually, in 1857, the family moved into a lavish house in Peoria, Illinois, though they still made annual trips up the Missouri. Their daughters were educated at a convent in Saint Louis and at a Moravian seminary for women at Bethlehem, Pennsylvania. Within a decade Culbertson squandered his wealth in a series of unwise investments, and by 1866, bankrupt and hounded by creditors, husband and wife returned to the Upper Missouri. A few years later the marriage broke up. Natawista Iksina returned to her people in Canada, and Culbertson died in 1879 at his daughter Julia's house in Nebraska. Despite the ups and downs of cultural and economic stresses, this fur-trade family stayed together for more than a quarter century.[46]

A few fur traders had Indian wives in the pays d'en haut and white wives elsewhere, whom they might occasionally visit. James Kipp was married for some years to a Mandan woman, and the couple had several children. Kipp was not only a hopeless alcoholic (Kurz said Kipp's addiction cost him at least two fortunes), but he also was concurrently married to a white woman who lived at Liberty, Missouri, with their children. In 1851, after apparently wrestling with his conscience for some time, he paid a visit to his wife in Missouri, leaving his Mandan wife and their children at her village near Fort Berthold. By that time, thanks to Kipp's age and alcoholism, his former clerk, Denig, had been promoted over him.[47] Kenneth McKenzie lived with several Indian women over time and had at least one mixed-blood son, Owen, who was an adult by the mid-1840s.

McKenzie later at Saint Louis married a white woman with whom he had two daughters and a son.[48]

Many engagés married Indian or mixed-blood women and raised families at Fort Union. One engagé, nicknamed "Jack Ram," and his wife allegedly had twelve children living at Fort Union in 1834. Sometimes the fort's population overtaxed the food supply, and people were sent away temporarily to fend for themselves until supplies were replenished. In January 1852, Edwin Denig, finding the "first and second tables so overcrowded with bourgeois, clerks, interpreters, hunters, workmen, and horse guards," decided to send out a "starvation band." The hunting party went a few miles away to the confluence of the Missouri and Yellowstone Rivers, where deer were plentiful. Away from the watchful eye of the bourgeois, they enjoyed their sojourn, "feeling quite at ease, camping in two tents with their women and eating all the choice portions of the game they kill."[49]

Life at Fort Union revolved around work and trade, but its populace found time to enjoy a variety of entertainments. Native games of chance, card games, betting on horse races, drinking, feasting, and affairs of love offered welcome diversions. The upper echelon of traders hunted for sport or as a display for guests. Indian dances and ceremonial events provided entertainment, but they also bolstered the close ties between traders and natives. In August 1835 the Girl Band (*Gens des Filles*) of the Assiniboines conducted their sacred Medicine Lodge ceremony at Fort Union. Charles Larpenteur and six other men helped the Assiniboines cut lodge poles in the nearby forest and later participated in the ceremony.[50]

Another cause for celebration was the arrival of a steamboat, which almost always meant a few days of heavy drinking and carousal. Steamers also brought up eagerly awaited bundles of newspapers, almanacs, books, and letters from traders' friends and families, all of which helped relieve the boredom and loneliness of frontier life. Feasts and liquor sprees for the fort's employees often accompanied holidays such as Christmas and the Fourth of July as well.

Considerable socializing took place between residents of Fort Union and members of opposition outfits, despite Company policy designed to eliminate competition.[51] Rudolph Kurz described several "balls" that he attended at Fort Union and at the nearby opposition fort during 1851. Balls at Fort Union took place in the "main hall," the mess room on the first floor of the bourgeois house. The spacious room with its whitewashed and wallpapered walls would be cleared of most furniture and "decorated . . . as brilliantly as we could with mirrors, candles, precious fur skins, and Indian ornaments." Edwin Denig provided fiddle music and Kurz beat a drum, while Indian and mixed-blood women, mostly dressed "according to European mode," gracefully danced waltzes and cotillions with their partners. At one soirée Denig's younger wife sported "a rose-colored ball gown in the latest fashion, direct from St. Louis." Occasionally engagés sponsored their own dances, for which they paid the costs.[52]

Men and women found other ways to kill time at Fort Union. Residents and visiting Indians regularly consumed substantial amounts of alcoholic beverages. Boredom, physical and psychological stress, and isolation probably help explain why drinking was popular. Some employees qualified as full-blown alcoholics, but not everyone had ready access to liquor. Engagés generally lacked both the means and opportunity to get drunk very often. Engagés were permitted to charge alcohol purchases against their wages at the retail store, but traders knew that a heavy debt might persuade a man to desert.

The upper echelon had more to spend and paid lower prices for liquor. McKenzie, Denig, Kipp, Culbertson, and their guests habitually imbibed brandy, madeira, gin, or good whiskey. Engagés, their families, and visiting Indians made do with a few drams of watered-down raw alcohol, called "Indian grog," that sold for eight dollars a gallon. Even so, it seems that few people at the post passed up an opportunity to get drunk.

"Drunking Sprees," as Charles Larpenteur called them, could be expected to take place when steamers arrived, when hunters returned, or when trappers sold furs to the Company. "Balls" and holidays likewise offered the hope that the bourgeois might broach a keg. Petty squabbles might turn ugly, and deeper hostilities could erupt into bloody fights when the community engaged in wholesale inebriation. Nonetheless, a drunken crowd at Fort Union probably behaved pretty much like one in the settlements down the Missouri, or anywhere else in the United States. A few residents even considered Fort Union safer than the settlements.

Recalling drunken behavior he had seen in Missouri and Georgia, Kurz concluded: "Though one is beset by perils in the Indians' domain, the dangers here do not compare with those that threaten one's life in the United States."[53]

More innocent pastimes sometimes brightened people's lives at Fort Union. In 1831–32 a gadget known as the "electrifying machine" arrived. This popular contemporary parlor-trick device was in effect a small electrical generator. When an operator turned a crank or pedal, the machine produced a current that made sparks or shocked unsuspecting victims, to the delight of onlookers. In 1844 it was still on hand, for the "electrical machine" appears in that year's inventory. For reasons unknown it was broken by 1846, though clerks dutifully listed it in inventories for several years thereafter.[54]

Another unusual device appeared in 1833. Kenneth McKenzie bought a costly "magic lantern" and set of glass slides at Philadelphia and shipped them up the Missouri. McKenzie paid $50.00 for the magic lantern set, while extra slides cost a hefty $2.50 each. Using a reflective plate behind an oil lamp to project images against a wall, this contraption brought the first "picture-shows" to the Northern Plains and must have fascinated residents and Indians. The magic lantern remained at Fort Union until at least 1851, when it vanished from inventories. Another "first" occurred in 1833, as mentioned earlier, when the UMO purchased three crates of fireworks at New York and sent them to Fort Union. Costing roughly an engagé's annual wages, the assortment included "pound Rockets," "Roman Candles," "Bengola Lights," "Serpents," "Pinwheels," "Jacks in the Box," a "Chinese Fan," and lucifer matches. Years later, in 1843, John Audubon noted another fireworks display on Independence Day.[55]

Card games and other amusements provided after-hours diversion for people at the fort. Playing cards, sold at the trade counter, furnished the materials for many a hand of poker, the "American game." Rudolph Kurz, who disliked poker because betting favored those with more to risk, observed that "as no money is in circulation here the gamesters stake their credit at the store; they gamble their wages. . . . To keep the score they use grains of corn." In 1833 a set of tenpins and three balls was sent to Fort Pierre, and employees at the opposition company's Fort Mortimer played backgammon in 1843. Perhaps these games were played at Fort

Union, too. Native guessing games and games of chance, as well as story-telling, were also popular diversions for men and women.[56]

Residents kept pets for companionship as well as for utilitarian purposes. Many dogs lived and worked at Fort Union. Useful to hunters, they also pulled travois in the warm season and *carrioles* (sleds) in winter. Sometimes they got out of hand, as when Charles Larpenteur "killed seven dogs for having torn the hog to pieces" on June 1, 1835. Edwin Denig kept a large dog named Natoh ("Bear") for years and commissioned Rudolph Kurz to paint its portrait in 1851. A hunter named Morgan used three dogs, two of which were named Bull and Badger. When Natoh died following a vicious fight with Badger, Denig acquired "three splendid wolfhounds" to pull a carriole. House cats, though rarely mentioned, were welcome guests, principally for their ability to reduce the fort's rat population. Edwin Denig owned a trained parrot named Polly, whose vocalizations delighted visiting Indians. A few wild animals temporarily stayed at the fort, either as pets in training or to await shipment downriver to Pierre Chouteau, Jr., or other persons. A juvenile grizzly bear, which once broke its chain and ran amok, was at the fort briefly in 1851, as were an eagle and a semitame wolf. Buffalo calves were occasionally allowed to roam inside the fort as well.[57]

A few men at Fort Union played musical instruments, and music proved useful both as entertainment and as a means to stymie trade competitors. Edwin Denig and Alexander Culbertson each played the violin, and Culbertson also played the clarinet. In 1840 he ordered a "10 key'd B Clarionet" with silver keys, and Denig ordered a bugle. "Jews Harps," a triangle, violin strings, and a tambourine also appear in orders or inventories.[58]

By the mid-1840s, traders sometimes presented musical performances designed to reel in customers. With competition for Upper Missouri robes at its zenith, Indian agents tried to enforce a federal law prohibiting traders from doing business at Indian camps, a practice called "going *en dérouine*." In order to beat the law during the winter of 1844–45, Fort Union traders posted mounted pickets on the heights above the Missouri with instructions to look for incoming customers and signal the direction of their arrival and the number of horses needed to collect robes. Traders and clerks then marched off, armed with musical instruments such as "a clarionette, a drum, a violin, and a triangle, besides the jingling bells on the sled." These flag-waving parades, aided by whiskey, music, and the hard sell, usually persuaded Indians to bring their robes to Fort Union.[59]

Numerous contracts signed with X's attest to the fact that most engagés could not read, but some employees were literate and a few were highly educated. For educational, practical, and recreational purposes, Fort Union housed a small library. Kenneth McKenzie ordered "sundry books" in 1833, listing a medical text as "Thomas' Practice," and others as "Conversations on Chemistry" and "Conversations on Natural Philosophy." During the smallpox epidemic in 1837, Charles Larpenteur resorted to "Doctor Thomas' Medical Book" for information on inoculation. Other volumes known to be present were the "Boy's Everyday Book," a Spanish grammar and dictionary, a copy of *Don Quixote*, and a book on mixing dyes used in tinting porcupine quills.[60] Some of the men passed around literature of a more titillating nature, too. Francis A. Chardon complained to Jacob Halsey in 1836 that he had nothing to read except "Kipps Bible," though he had recently examined a copy of the pornographic classic *Fanny Hill* belonging to Alexander Culbertson.[61]

Later on, in 1851, Rudolph Kurz evidently had a partial set of the *Viviparous Quadrupeds of North America* by Audubon and Bachman. Kurz and his associates read and discussed Harriet Beecher Stowe's *Uncle Tom's Cabin* when it first appeared in serial form in *The National Era*. Books, newspapers, and other reading material kept residents abreast of national and international events and helped pass time during the long plains winters, or when business was slow.[62]

Health conditions at Fort Union were reasonably good, but sickness and injuries were unavoidable. Colds, infections, gunshot and stab wounds, frostbite, and broken bones occurred with some regularity. Gonorrhea, which Larpenteur dubbed the "Blackfoot Sqwaw [*sic*] complaint," was a painful but treatable affliction. Traders stocked medical and surgical instruments, vegetal and chemical remedies, and opiated pain-killers to treat residents and sometimes Indians as well.[63]

Epidemic disease was rare but devastating. Cholera, smallpox, and influenza, the most dangerous ailments, killed Indians, mixed-bloods, and whites. Most deadly by far was smallpox. This plague periodically swept over North America, but when smallpox ravaged the Upper Missouri in 1837, thousands of Indians died, permanently affecting Upper Missouri history.

The disease arrived in June 1837 aboard the Company's steamboat *St. Peters*. Those on board included several Indian women and Jacob Halsey's mixed-blood wife and three-year-old son. By the time the vessel reached Fort Union on June 24, people were already dying. Halsey's wife had recently delivered a daughter and was lying in when the smallpox appeared on her. Writhing in agony, she fell from her bed, ruptured a blood vessel and hemorrhaged. She and her infant soon died. Halsey, less seriously affected, eventually recovered.[64]

But then the pox came to Fort Union with terrifying ferocity. Charles Larpenteur and others grasped at every means available, however limited, to check the spread of the disease and to warn off Indians who came to trade. On the same day that Halsey's son got the smallpox, Edwin Denig was stricken with an unidentified violent fever, probably a mild case of the disease. Denig, however, was the only man on hand possessing any surgical skill. With him incapacitated, it fell to Larpenteur to make a critical decision: whether to attempt a risky vaccination program to mitigate the worst effects of the disease. Larpenteur desperately scanned "Doctor Thomas' medical book" for guidance on vaccination and inoculation as people around him sickened and began to die. He became convinced that lives would be spared if residents were exposed to vaccine matter, which supposedly yielded mild cases with good chances for recovery. Meanwhile, people at the fort fell into utter panic, all fearing for their lives.[65]

In an atmosphere of ignorance, inexperience, horror, and necessity, Larpenteur launched his "inoculation" program. On July 12, seventeen patients, mostly women, received matter from a scab on Halsey's arm. In the end, "about 30 Indian Squaws and a few white men" received the vaccine. "Inoculation," in this instance, simply meant rubbing pus from Halsey's sores into cuts made in other peoples' arms. This amounted merely to a transfer of the disease in its active state. Larpenteur's fatal error grew out of confusion, for proper vaccination required a preparation made from cowpox matter, which was less virulent than smallpox.

Within a week it was dreadfully clear that the attempted cure had backfired. All of those inoculated developed extreme cases and were sequestered within the fort. The stench of disease grew so heavy in the quarantined area that residents stumbled about with vials of camphor pressed to their noses. Some of the afflicted went mad and attempted to escape the fouled precincts of the fort, but the gates were locked so no one could enter or leave. Soon the surrounding prairie was thickly strewn with the stinking corpses of dead Indians, among whom the devastation was far greater. Ramsay Crooks, writing from New York, later informed Pierre Chouteau, Jr., that "at Fort Union all was wretchedness and despair—the Prairies covered with dead bodies, and the whole atmosphere tainted. . . . [The Indians] are very humble and submissive, begging the Whites not to desert them in their misery." Many Indian men, horrified by the disease's effects, killed their families and then themselves as the Upper Missouri endured the most nightmarish episode in its recorded history.[66]

All told, within Fort Union twenty-seven people apparently fell ill. In the end, however, only four people died: the tailor's Indian wife, Baptiste Contois (a Red River métis), another engagé's wife, and Larpenteur's wife, whose pox-ridden body swarmed with maggots for two days before she expired. In the midst of the horror two hundred Assiniboines showed up to trade. It took, Larpenteur wrote, "one of the best interpreters that the whole Missouri can afford" to talk them into staying outside the fort.

Even so, trade continued, and contaminated goods helped distribute smallpox among Indians at Fort Union and elsewhere. One opportunity for the disease to spread came when some Assiniboines stole a few horses from old Fort William. Then the pox broke out on a keelboat in charge of Alexander Harvey en route to Fort McKenzie. He paused at the Judith River and prepared to turn about while awaiting advice from superiors at Fort Union. But with the Blackfeet insistent upon trade, Harvey's boat proceeded on, and the disease spread up the Missouri.

By mid-August 1837 the smallpox had largely run its course. Larpenteur was embittered, for it seemed that his every effort had availed naught. His journal entry on the tragedy concludes with a grimly sarcastic remark: "Theres noculation for you—mildest kind—one case out of six hundred."[67]

Fort Union lost some people, true, but Indian losses ran vastly higher, though details are lacking. Some tribes never recovered from this epidemic. Jacob Halsey estimated that "at least 800" Assiniboines and "at least 700" Blackfeet died. The Crows were more fortunate this time; they heeded the traders' advice and avoided Fort Cass. D. D. Mitchell estimated Blackfeet and Assiniboine mortality to be "at least four-fifths"; others estimated "ten in twelve." Dramatically affected were the Mandans and the Hidatsas, who formerly lorded it over their Arikara neighbors. After the epidemic, the situation was reversed. Chardon estimated that three-quarters of the Hidatsas had died, but the Mandans were "virtually annihilated," having only about thirty survivors. They never again wielded significant power. Even so, when Chardon calculated that more than eight hundred Arikaras (he usually called them "the Horrid Tribe") had died, he rejoiced: "What a bande of RASCALS has been used up."[68]

This was neither the first nor the last invasion of smallpox. The 1837 epidemic has attracted historians' attention because of its thorough and striking documentation by George Catlin, Francis Chardon, and others. Nevertheless, from 1780 (and possibly much earlier) to 1860 smallpox came roughly every twenty or thirty years.[69]

By late 1856 smallpox was again on the Upper Missouri. In December, Alfred Cumming, the superintendent of Indian affairs at Saint Louis, recommended to George H. Manypenny, commissioner of Indian affairs, that Dr. Ferdinand V. Hayden, then at the Smithsonian Institution, should be sent up with the steamer carrying annuity goods in order to vaccinate Indians. A few days later, Upper Missouri agent Alfred J. Vaughn informed Cumming that the danger seemed to be past, but the Arikaras and Mandans once more sustained heavy losses. As often happened, government agents failed to gather full information on events taking place. James Kipp wrote from Fort Union in January 1857 to inform Chouteau & Company that the disease was among the Blackfeet, far up the Yellowstone. Assiniboines, Crees, Crows, Sioux, and the Red River settlement were likewise suffering, and "thousands of Indians have fallen victims to this dreadful scourge." The Sioux near Fort Pierre, in anger and frustration, stepped up their ongoing warfare against the Arikaras and Hidatsas.[70]

Asiatic cholera, another faceless killer, first swept over the nation and the frontier in 1833, claiming over five hundred victims at Saint Louis alone during the summer. In the same year it made its way to the Upper Missouri aboard the *Yellow Stone*. John Dougherty, the Indian agent at Bellevue, nearly died before recovering, but his subagent perished along with two blacksmiths, the interpreter and his wife, and several others. Dougherty's son, John, died "at the Blackfeet"; so did several fur company men and many Indians. Cholera appeared again in 1849–51. Influenza, though seldom fatal to whites, killed many Indians. Edwin Denig, noting that about two hundred Crows died of influenza about 1852, blamed the deaths on their own medical practices, such as the use of shamans and sweat lodges.[71]

Disease played a tragic role in altering conditions in the Upper Missouri. Despite folkloric allegations, however, there is no credible evidence that traders at Fort Union deliberately spread smallpox or other diseases among their customers. Such a course would have been economic madness on the traders' part, and it is worth remembering that diseases also killed traders and their families. Heavy population losses among Indians resulted from biological isolation in North America and immune systems that succumbed to imported diseases. Consequently, epidemics struck with cataclysmic fury. The smallpox epidemic of 1837 was but one of many, and it is likely that far more destructive outbreaks had occurred two centuries earlier. Indeed, early-nineteenth-century Upper Missouri Indian populations may still have been recovering from massive population collapses in the seventeenth century caused by smallpox emanating from the Valley of Mexico.[72]

Did fur traders live under a form of law and order, or were they anarchic reprobates, willing to kill at the drop of a whiskey bottle? Numerous anecdotes convey the impression that fur traders, especially mountain men, knew no law beyond that of the tooth and the claw. They are often reduced to pasteboard figures resembling a nineteenth-century version of Hell's Angels. Arguably true in some cases, as we shall see, these myths obscure some important realities. Distance from courtrooms and lawyers rendered access to the regular legal system impossible, but Fort Union did not tolerate anarchy. Instead, it was governed by a system of informal law common throughout the Upper Missouri. Transgressors who violated certain standards of behavior that were acknowledged as vital to the community's welfare were punished, sometimes severely.

Engagés stood on the lowest rungs of Fort Union's social ladder, but they were not devoid of legal or informal protection of their rights. If an engagé fell ill and could not work, he might still receive the full amount of his wages, provided that the Company found no major faults in his conduct. On the other hand, an ailing engagé paid for his medical expenses, though the Company furnished room and board. If an engagé was caught trading for robes and furs on his own hook, he was liable to be charged for the Company's presumed loss, but his wages were not otherwise affected.[73]

Engagés occasionally did trade among themselves, to make petty profits or to beat the Company's inflated prices. Many an engagé who purchased too freely at Fort Union's retail store found himself with little to show at the end of a year's labor. In 1830, probably a typical year, engagés' indebtedness to the Company ranged from about 10 percent to better than 90 percent of their wages, though few men squandered their money so unwisely as the latter. The average laborer's debt stood at between 20 and 30 percent. Given the high prices charged for goods, it is not surprising that some enterprising engagés brought items to sell to other employees.[74]

Although the Company discouraged the practice, petty trading became enough of a problem in 1850 that William Hodgkiss at Fort Pierre complained about the "quantity of Baggage the men are allowed to bring up in the Steam B[oa]t." When Hodgkiss examined some trunks belonging to men who had died or deserted, he was in for a surprise: "The quantity of Mdze found was really astonishing—in one chest we found 80 lbs. Tobacco & 40 lbs sugar and coffee—in another 120 Yds. Calico all in dress patterns, besides clothing, Knives, Beads, Hdks [handkerchiefs], &c &c of every description, they bring these things here, sell them to the men in such a manner that we cannot detect them in it . . . thereby saving all their wages, and getting . . . every thing they need in this country at St. Louis prices." Hodgkiss believed that if the practice were curtailed, the Company would realize "a difference of $1000 per year in our payments alone at this post."[75]

The chief guardians of law and order were the bourgeois and his clerks. Sometimes, however, the community undertook extraordinary enforcement measures in its own behalf. Such an event occurred at Fort

Union in the summer of 1836, when employees rose up against the Deschamps family. The Deschampses, Canadian mixed-blood hunters and interpreters, had on several occasions raped, robbed, abused, injured, or murdered Indians and whites at the post. Old François Deschamps was the patriarch of this sinister and reputedly incestuous clan. It was widely known that during a bloody territorial skirmish in 1816 between Hudson's Bay and North West Company men, he had killed Governor Robert Semple of Lord Selkirk's Red River colony.[76]

In July 1835, fed up with their manifold offenses in general but aggravated specifically by the Deschampses' treatment of his consort and an attempt on his own life, an engagé named Gardepied angrily confronted the elder Deschamps in Charles Larpenteur's room. Larpenteur, who happened to be out tending the garden that morning, later asserted that four men conspired, "unknown to me, to kill Old Man Deschamps and his eldest son, François." Young François, about thirty years old, worked as an interpreter and "ate at the table with the boss and the clerks." Within just a few seconds, Gardepied smashed old François' skull with a rifle barrel, then dealt the younger François a severe blow. While the bleeding son cowered beneath a bed, Gardepied snatched out a concealed dirk and disemboweled old François. When Larpenteur returned, he and some other employees persuaded Gardepied to spare young François's life, and the affray ended, temporarily. On the surface, a mediated truce was achieved, but beneath there writhed a malevolent spirit.[77]

About a year later, on June 28, 1836, in the midst of a drunken spree attending a steamboat's arrival, "Mother Deschamps" induced her sons to exact vengeance. They murdered one of Gardepied's allies, a man named Jack Kipling, who dwelt at the adjacent old Fort William. Kipling's terrified daughter arrived at Fort Union about midnight "crying bitterly" and pleading for help. When some engagés went to examine Kipling's corpse, the Deschampses opened fire on them.

At that point "eight or ten" employees collectively decided to eradicate the Deschampses, declaring "that not one should excape." The enraged men "applied to Mr. McKenzie for permition [sic] to destroy them all," and when he "made them no reply they all threatened to lieve [sic] the fort." Correctly interpreting McKenzie's lack of opposition as tacit approval, the men armed themselves with muskets and even dragged a small cannon from the fort, determined to rub out the Deschampses. Upon approaching Fort William, the men demanded that the Deschampses release several Assiniboine women, "their squaws . . . whom we did not want to kill for fear of the tribe." This was done, and a few hours later eight Deschamps family members lay dead or were incinerated in a burning room at Fort William.

Among the dead was old "Mother Deschamps," who mistakenly assumed that her daughter's marriage to trader David D. Mitchell would qualify her for some clemency. When she stepped out of the old fort, holding aloft a peace pipe, an engagé named Mayotte shot her through the heart; one of the Deschampses then shot him through the neck. Only two women (Mitchell's wife and her younger sister) and two young boys were spared, and they soon left, lucky to get away with their lives. "Such was the end of this troublesome family," wrote Charles Larpenteur, "after which peace and comfort were enjoyed." The restoration of order had cost Fort Union one man dead and one wounded.[78]

William Fulkerson, the Mandan subagent, evaluated the affair in a letter to Superintendent William Clark at Saint Louis. This "treacherous [and] quarrelsome" family, he wrote, "always acted in concert, and effected their purposes by force." Fulkerson informed Clark that the "whites and the balance of the half-breeds . . . arose in mass against [the Deschampses], with a determination of extinguishing the whole family, and insuring greater safety among themselves for the future." Violent though it was, this event bluntly demonstrated that consensus underlay community law enforcement at Fort Union.[79]

Another incident from the autumn of 1836 illustrates the importance of horses to Fort Union's residents and the role of community law regarding livestock. The post maintained a herd of fifty to one hundred horses, watched over by a few engagés. One day in September, two horse guards, a "Spaniard" and a "Dutchman," decided to desert and made off with the finest horses of the lot, one of which happened to be a buffalo runner belonging to Kenneth McKenzie.

The deserters tried to steal a ferry to cross the Missouri but bungled the attempt. Then the stolen horses ran off and returned to Fort Union. (Charles Larpenteur claimed this was because they had "more sense than their new masters.") The deserters had no choice but to surrender themselves. McKenzie had them clapped in irons for several days, during which they were "tried, convicted, and sentenced." Each man was to receive twenty-four lashes (in his published memoir Larpenteur says it was thirty-nine) and be sent down the river.

Ethnicity seems to have figured in sentencing and punishing these men. The "Spaniard," who Larpenteur characterized as "an old thief" whose "hide was brown and tough," got the full count of stripes. The "Dutchman," who whimpered and whose "fair and tender" skin bled too easily, had his sentence reduced by half. But the floggings reflected more than the boss's irritation over the theft of two superior animals. Charles Larpenteur, despite his bias, described the gravity of the crime in terms the community would have accepted. "Every person about the fort," he wrote, "from the head man down to the cook was much vexed and saw that no [one] but a villanous [sic] Spaniard would expose a Fort like this to starvation for in this country living is depended altogether on Buffalo Meat. None but talk and grumbling and saying of what would be Done with them if they were caught was done the balance of the day."[80]

Larpenteur also tells a tale featuring one Augustin Bourbonnais, a UMO boatman hired in 1832. Bourbonnais completed at least one engagement; four years later, as a "free trapper," he was trading furs at Fort Union. In November 1836, puffed up and drunk after selling five hundred dollars' worth of furs, he tangled with Kenneth McKenzie. Bourbonnais, a "stout and good looking young man" with a "fine head of yellow hair which takes the eye of the squaws," repeatedly tried to seduce the "King's" young Assiniboine wife. When she informed McKenzie of this, he warned Bourbonnais off, but to no effect. McKenzie soon caught the two in flagrante delicto in his own bed and cudgeled Bourbonnais out of the fort. Bourbonnais, boasting that he would kill McKenzie, strutted about for several days, brandishing "his riffle [sic] pistol and a Large Club."[81]

Meanwhile, McKenzie stayed inside, hoping the storm would blow over. But when Bourbonnais threatened to burn down Fort Union, McKenzie was obliged to take action and convened a "court martial." McKenzie, the clerks, and the traders agreed that Bourbonnais endangered everyone at the post and thus merited killing. The engagés, too, were consulted, and they unanimously concurred: Bourbonnais had gone too far. To complete the "legal" process, all the French-speaking men signed a paper "certifying that Mr. McKenzie was Justifiable in taking the mans life anyplace he might meet him." McKenzie requested the engagés to apprise Bourbonnais of the "court's" decision "in order to get him to leave the Country," again without effect. McKenzie then posted guards atop the bastions with orders to neutralize the threat. According to Larpenteur, the "mulatto named John Brazo" shot Bourbonnais through the shoulder one Sunday morning. The disabled man was carried into the fort, where Edwin Denig dressed his wound. By spring's arrival, Bourbonnais was well enough to be sent down the Missouri, away from Fort Union.[82]

As Bourbonnais's case suggests, McKenzie tolerated a degree of challenge to his authority as bourgeois. Whatever may have been McKenzie's affections for his "country wife," it was only when Bourbonnais's threats potentially jeopardized the entire populace that the boss took action. More was at stake than the "King's" love life, or hypersensitivity about his position. Once again, as in the Deschamps killings, community law enforcement required that consensual judgments be made concerning community security. To Rudolph Kurz, the logic of community law at Fort Union was clear: "One can easily understand why people in these wilds rarely resort to process of law. Among the promiscuous white inhabitants of this region there are many rough and vicious characters. . . . Every man is armed; every man protects his own house and property; with knife or shotgun he requites every insult. One who loves his life guards against giving offense. . . . One hears among white people hereabouts, therefore, fewer violent disputes, and witnesses fisticuff fights less frequently than in civilized States, for the reason that, knowing the deadly consequences, people guard against giving cause for strife."[83]

Sometimes fur traders and their families became embroiled in native fights as well. One longtime employee at Fort Union, Zephir Rencontre, married for thirty years to a Yanktonai woman, in 1851 lost both wife and daughter, the victims of two young Mandans on a horse-stealing raid near Fort Lookout. Killings like this resulted from intertribal animosities that perpetuated blood feuds in which any enemy was fair game.[84]

Sometimes Indians assisted fur traders when trouble was afoot. Whenever natives visited fur posts, certain Indians designated as "soldiers" guarded goods and protected traders. This practice minimized the potential for violence and made killings a rarity. Indians who served in this capacity gained status and received rewards to ensure their continued good efforts.

Fur traders in the Upper Missouri depended on alliances with Indians, as the following episode illustrates. In September 1830 an engagé named Pierre Goselin traveled from Saint Louis to Fort Tecumseh with P. N. Leclerc and Baptiste Defond. The small party encountered two Yankton Sioux, who said they, too, were headed for Fort Tecumseh and wished to accompany the white men. In the afternoon of September 25, the Yanktons suddenly set upon the whites, severely wounded Goselin with an arrow, and ran off. Leclerc, seeing no other option, left the steadily worsening Goselin with a few days' rations and hoped for the best. Leclerc and Defond arrived safely at Fort Tecumseh, but Goselin never turned up and was presumed dead.

On October 9 more Company men arrived from Saint Louis, Kenneth McKenzie among them. When he heard about Goselin's murder, McKenzie declined taking direct action, preferring to wait until the federal Indian agent arrived. Here was a delicate and dangerous situation: Yanktons had never killed a trader, but one of the alleged killers soon turned up with a Yankton party at Fort Tecumseh. McKenzie continued to stall. Then, on October 27, a Yankton ally of the traders mortally wounded the Indian believed to have slain Goselin. The other Yanktons grew angry but did nothing and left the following day. In gratitude, McKenzie "dressed the Indian who risked his life so much for us—he was presented with every thing to ornament himself with," including a sword.[85]

The UMO's community, in the broadest sense, included people at several forts and outposts. UMO employees developed marriage ties with women from a variety of tribes, but Indians often viewed their tribal neighbors as enemies to be destroyed. Consequently, the traders faced the challenge of balancing business affairs, diplomatic relations with Indian nations, and the welfare of the men, women, and children who lived at the forts. In spite of the conflicts inherent in merging these disparate interests, traders generally managed to preserve harmony at Fort Union.

Fort Union and the other UMO posts constituted a unique Northern Plains community. Combining elements from several cultures, they produced a distinctive society that was internally coherent and self-sustaining. Multiethnic societies had long been characteristic of fur trading regions, and in many respects the patterns visible at Fort Union illustrate the continuation of a life-way that had emerged in the seventeenth century.

Wherever whites were a minority of "strangers," they made adjustments to function effectively within the framework of native life. This made economic sense, insofar as it helped to formulate a mutually comprehensible structure for commercial interaction. Although the American federal government sought to exercise authority over the trade, it lacked sufficient "imperial" power to gain control. When France and Britain clashed in the Ohio country or along the Great Lakes a century earlier, fur traders and imperial agents often worked in tandem. This was not so in the Upper Missouri. Congress passed laws in abundance, but they were easily ignored or subverted. Indian agents, virtually impotent in a land where personal power was meaningful, were frequently viewed with contempt by traders and Indians alike. American soldiers in the region before the 1860s were too few and too inexperienced to impress either Indians or fur traders. Consequently, residents at Fort Union were left largely to themselves, and they took a strong hand in maintaining their own society.

In the long run, this social system was doomed, for events occurring on the national stage would have made it impossible to sustain indefinitely. Fort Union's community depended on three uncontrollable variables for its continued existence: an abundant supply of bison, Indians whose nomadic hunting patterns were not interrupted, and a feeble national authoritarian presence. All of these things changed in time, but during the years before the federal government possessed the wherewithal to exercise real power in the region, Fort Union's residents achieved the means of living between very different worlds.

CHAPTER FOUR

Fur Traders, Trade and Intercourse Laws, and Indian Policy

The fur trade may well have been the earliest "big business" in the United States to be federally regulated. A small number of men exercised a great deal of influence over the trade, and no early-nineteenth-century enterprise exceeded its continental or global reach. Federal officials who understood that the trade was linked to a number of national policy issues repeatedly tried to supervise its operations. Fifty years before railroads became important, and a century before antitrust laws appeared, the trade was closely scrutinized and, theoretically, regulated according to frequently revised federal laws. Legislation that was designed to serve the public interest by protecting whites and Indians from price gouging and other abuses, reducing the potential for violence, and creating alliances with Indian nations coincidently provided much of the foundation for national Indian policy before the reservation era began.

Regulatory laws established a licensing system, defined crimes in Indian country, and prescribed fines and other punishments for violations. To ensure good behavior and obedience to the law, the government required that traders file bonds worth several thousand dollars before being licensed. Licenses stipulated specific locations for trading posts; traders were forbidden to roam about in search of customers. The Office of Indian Affairs issued permits to enter Indian land and required that all employees taken beyond the frontier must have its prior approval.

Importation of liquor was always strictly regulated and was ultimately outlawed altogether. Persons suspected of violating liquor laws or committing other offenses could be indicted and tried before federal or territorial courts. Guilty offenders might forfeit licenses and bonds, be fined, or be forbidden to return to the Indian country.

On paper, this must have seemed a comprehensive, orderly system of regulation and enforcement. In practice, however, efforts to enforce federal law in the fur trade country seldom were successful. Several factors help explain why there was a chasm between "good" legislation and effective enforcement. Given the difficulties involved in administering law in the Upper Missouri, genuine success may have been unattainable, but regulation did not fail merely because fur traders, Indian agents, or legislators lacked good intentions. Commercial competition, whiskey selling, and violence all remained largely outside government control. Burdened with its inconsistent philosophical underpinnings, early-nineteenth-century Indian policy also hampered the efficacy of fur trade law. In order to understand why federal legislative management of the fur trade was chaotic, and in the end unachievable, one must begin by examining the trade and intercourse laws and how they worked in the Indian country.

In July 1790, Congress passed the first major trade and intercourse law, the principal elements of which are traceable to the Ordinance for the Regulation of Indian Affairs (1786) and the Northwest Ordinance (1787), both made under the Articles of Confederation, and to numerous imperial and provincial laws passed during the colonial era. The 1790 law provided for issuance and revocation of licenses and bonds, oversight by a commissioner or his appointees, and punishment for crimes committed by whites in Indian country. Congress approved similar measures in 1796 and 1799.[1]

At about the same time, the federal government became directly engaged in the Indian trade, operating an experimental government-supported factory system from 1796 until 1822, when it was jettisoned. Factories were trading posts, managed by federal employees called "factors," that stocked standard Indian goods. Conducting trade with Indian tribes residing along the borders of the United States, the system's designers hoped, would bind those tribes to the national government and prevent abuses by unscrupulous whites.[2]

Government trading posts, although intended for other purposes, had the effect of limiting private enterprise along the eastern margin of the fur trade country. Such a system would be beneficial, it was believed, for several reasons. The British, in defiance of the 1783 Treaty of Paris, not only continued to trade with Indians in the Old Northwest, but also exhorted them to commit depredations against Americans. A government-regulated trade with Indians, the argument ran, would diminish illicit profits of British traders that by rights belonged to Americans and bring Indians more effectively under the influence of the United States, thereby reducing threats of frontier warfare. Factories would also offer Indians an alternative to private traders, who sometimes sold shoddy goods at high prices and who were prone to fleece Indians by making them drunk.

By 1803, Thomas Jefferson and others proposed a new and "beneficial" application for the factories. As Indians got better acquainted with white men's goods, proponents said, they would grow dependant upon them. As a result, the "savages" could more readily be "civilized." Better still, they might be extended enough credit to create massive debts. The only means of eliminating these debts would be "to lop them off by a cession of lands."[3]

The factory system, as contemporary critics argued, resembled a monopoly. No privately owned trading posts were permitted to compete with government factories. But the system was never intended to expand much beyond the frontier of white settlement, and most factories were placed along the Mississippi and a few tributary streams. Even within its limited theater of operations, the system encountered problems. Over-priced and sometimes inferior goods, management that was more incompetent than crooked, illicit but persistent competition, and vigorous lobbying by well-organized and influential outfits such as the American Fur Company all contributed to the system's poor record.

With or without a factory system, however, trade and intercourse laws remained absolutely vital to the Indian and fur trades. This was because early-nineteenth-century lawmakers saw Indian trade and fur hunting collectively as the "fur trade," and the two components remained virtually—and legally—indivisible before 1865. Fur trade legislation, therefore, necessarily affected trade with Indians as well as diplomacy, and here was an area in which the federal government had staked out clear constitutional lines. Government's principal challenge was to maintain sufficient power over private fur traders to allow it to shape its own relationships with Indians. Otherwise, it risked losing command over Indian affairs as well as traders.

Trade laws grew more detailed as Congress tried to keep pace with the rapidly expanding western Indian and fur trades. The Trade and Intercourse Act of 1802 set boundaries for Indian country and included an expanded list of prosecutable violations applying to both whites and Indians. United States citizens were forbidden to hunt, and presumably trap, in Indian country. For the first time, the President of the United States was authorized "to take such measures, from time to time, as to him may appear expedient to prevent or restrain the vending or distribution of spirituous liquors" to Indians.[4]

Legislation notwithstanding, the presence of liquor in Indian country became the most vexatious issue in the development of Indian policy, and it left a thorny historical legacy. Among several complicating factors was that the trade and intercourse laws only applied to lands under federal jurisdiction; states adjoining Indian country were not obliged to control or restrict the liquor trade. In 1808, President Jefferson wrote a letter imploring states and territories to cooperate with the liquor ban, but he was powerless to force the issue. Indians and whites routinely bought liquor outside federal jurisdiction and transported it to Indian country to drink or to sell.[5]

By 1822, after twenty years of economic, territorial, and organizational growth in the fur trade, the trade and intercourse laws needed revision. Several significant changes appeared. The Indian Office could issue licenses to trade west of the Mississippi for terms of up to seven years (previously licenses were not to exceed two years). Maximum bond limits rose from one thousand dollars to five thousand dollars. In recognition of Saint Louis's dominant role in the western trade, a special superintendent of Indian affairs would henceforth reside there. Finally, to beef up enforcement of liquor restrictions already on the books, the new code allowed government officers to build cases on informers' testimony. A trader's bales might be searched "upon suspicion or information that ardent spirits are carried into the Indian countries." If liquor was discovered, the informer and the government each received half of the trader's confiscated stock, while the offender faced forfeiture of his license and bond.[6]

In the opinion of Thomas L. McKenney, head of the Indian Office, more was needed. He believed that sharper legal teeth might hamstring the liquor trade. In 1826 he advised Secretary of War James Barbour that "sound policy, no less than justice and humanity, requires that it should be made a capital offense for any person to furnish spirituous liquors to Indians, *under any circumstances.*" McKenney faced numerous vitriolic critics among politicians and fur traders, and his counsel was seldom heeded. No whiskey seller in "Indian Country" ever felt a hangman's noose.[7]

By the 1830s the "Indian problem" had grown larger, and the government needed a better organizational framework. Congress had passed the Indian Removal Act in May 1830, but the tiny Indian Office staff was inadequate to handle such an ambitious program. Meanwhile, as the fur trade expanded, places such as Fort Union threatened to overshadow the government's power. Liquor still seeped across the frontier, and informers were in short supply.

In 1832, Congress legislated an important new position, the commissioner of Indian affairs. In the commissioner was vested "the direction and management of all Indian affairs, and of all matters arising out of Indian relations." The law also aimed at cost cutting; no new clerks would be hired, and personnel were to be cut wherever possible, especially after Indian tribes were forced west. In the same act appeared the blunt declaration that "no ardent spirits shall be hereafter introduced, under any pretence, into the Indian Country."[8]

Two years later, on June 30, 1834, Congress created the Department of Indian Affairs. The new bureau occupied offices at Washington and sent numerous agents and subagents to Indian country. Indian agents were expected to live with, or at least near, the tribes under their jurisdiction. The president would appoint agents to four-year terms, with the "advice and consent of the Senate." The Department of Indian Affairs was placed under the supervision of the Department of War, where it remained until 1849.[9]

On the same day, Congress passed its last important trade and intercourse act. The 1834 trade law capped half a century of legislation aimed at regularizing the growing Indian and fur trades. It listed many criminal offenses and stipulated that cases involving crimes in Indian country must be heard at federal district court in Missouri. A lengthy section addressed the illegal liquor trade, though it exempted "such supplies as shall be necessary for the officers of the United States and troops of the service, under the direction of the War Department." Horse trading and theft, a ban on private citizen land purchases, location of trading posts, and the role of the military in law enforcement all received detailed attention. The act also explicitly prohibited "any person, other than an Indian . . . [to] hunt, or trap, or take and destroy, any peltries or game, except for subsistence." Violators faced a five-hundred-dollar fine and confiscation of their trapping or hunting gear. This tough-sounding clause suffered from a crippling flaw, for it only applied to "any tribe with whom the United States shall have existing treaties." At that time federal treaties with sovereign Indian nations in the Upper Missouri amounted to only feeble preliminaries.[10]

Congress passed three related measures at the same time. One created the Department of Indian Affairs, the second was the Trade and Intercourse Act of 1834, and the third defined and bounded a "Western Territory," essentially "Indian Country," where tribes displaced by the removal program would be relocated. These bills did not pass without objection. Congressional documents that accompanied the debate illuminate legislators' concerns about the fur trade and the "Indian question." Congressmen recognized that these three bills were "intimately connected . . . parts of a system" but declared the system dysfunctional. Major policy revision was required, according to a House report, since the current structure was "so manifestly defective and inadequate."[11]

Some members feared that the legal foundations of the new Indian Department were "of doubtful origin and authority" and that its operations would be "expensive, inefficient, and irresponsible." Legislation had hitherto been based on "mere usage" rather than on a cohesive body of law. Consequently, the report disclosed in a startling pronouncement, "a majority of agents and subagents of Indian affairs [had] been appointed without lawful authority" for the past thirty years. Certain congressmen evidently believed that the entire edifice of U.S. Indian policy rested on quicksand.[12]

The executive branch assumed the constitutionally defensible power to appoint agents but then drifted into stormier waters because of inadequate provisions for congressional oversight with regard to agents' salaries or tenure in office. Only the Senate, as a treaty-making body, had a role in formulating Indian policy. This, it was feared, led to abuses by agents whose actions lay beyond congressional scrutiny. Indian traders as well as agents could be expected to fall into fraudulent practices under such a chaotic system. The report's assertion was correct, but it is also true that members of the House of Representatives had grown resentful over their minuscule role in Indian affairs.

By 1834, Congress had reconfigured its views on the fundamental relationship between whites and Indians. Policy formerly predicated on the "fear of Indian hostility" gave way to an empowered paternalism requiring "a more liberal policy, as well directed to promote their welfare as our political interests." The new calculus implied a relationship of "the strong to the weak," a sense of wardship over Indians that would henceforth inform all federal Indian policy. Such ideas would be used to justify government's future refusal to concede Indians a legitimate title to their land. Ironically, an "enlightened" federal policy allowed government to brush aside inconvenient notions about native sovereignty while its hand grew more repressive.[13]

After briefly reviewing the legal history of Indian policy, the House committee proceeded to examine "the evils attending the present regulation of trade." Years of argument had failed to bring consensus on the question whether monopoly or competition offered the best basis for conducting Indian trade. Americans' traditional distaste for monopolies was exploited by fur traders who cited the Hudson's Bay Company as a pernicious example of monopolists grown arrogant under a government charter. Competition was presumed to be desirable because it would "guard against extortion, while private capital saved a public loss." Yet it appeared that competition only produced price wars, cutthroat trading, negligible profits, and, ultimately, something like a monopoly. Thus, according to the committee, "small adventurers" were driven from the field, and "as soon as the new competition was destroyed, the most extravagant prices were demanded." To prove its point, the committee estimated that profits in the Great Lakes region reached well above 100 percent.

In this calculation, however, no one considered expenses for freight, insurance, damage, or losses. Perhaps blinded by their ignorance, the committee naïvely suggested that the government might offer goods to Indians "at first cost" (wholesale prices). How this was to be done no member said.

The committee may not have realized how destructive competition could be. A year before it met, for example, trapper Thomas Fitzpatrick was robbed of forty-two beaver skins by some Crow warriors. He complained to his friend and political ally, William H. Ashley, blaming the AFCo for inciting the Crows. Fitzpatrick went on: "In short Genl if there is not some alteration made in the system of business in this country verry soon it will become a nuisance and disgrace to the U.S. So many different companies agoing about frome one tribe of Indians to another Each are telling a different tale besides slandering each other to Such a degree as really to disgust the Indians and will evidently all become hostile towards the Americans I now appeal to you for redress." A pious Fitzpatrick then asked Ashley to help him seek "justice from the honorable members" of Congress. Still, just two weeks later, Fitzpatrick instructed his partner, Milton Sublette, to "Studdy well the articles of profit. Liquor will be much wanted" for the coming trade.[14]

Another absurd suggestion, which stood no chance of realization, was that "private associations" would furnish goods "with no other compensation than a bare indemnity . . . dependent for success more on moral influence than physical coercion." Moreover, since the government never undertook to handle the purchase and shipment of annuity goods itself, it necessarily relied on the existing transport structure of established fur traders such as Pierre Chouteau, Jr., & Company.[15]

Fundamental to this discussion of federal authority in the West is the sometimes unnoticed fact that printed laws are inert. Law enforcement is possible only where coercive power is available; otherwise, laws are mere dead letters. In early-nineteenth-century America, before the era of railroads and telegraphs, physical distance and effective law enforcement were more or less inversely proportional. In cities, police and the populace stood in close proximity, force of one kind or another was readily at hand, and laws were cloaked with a fair degree of enforceability.

But how could federal laws be enforced in the Upper Missouri, thousands of miles from the seat of government? Communication was slow, enforcement costly, and results were meager. Federal troops—infantrymen at stationary posts—were too few for the task at hand and lacked the mobility needed to police a vast region teeming with mounted warriors as well as several hundred fractious traders. Indian agents, a secondary federal presence, possessed no power to enforce laws and little influence over fur traders or Indians. Inadequate allocations of federal funds to support distinct agency buildings, staff, and the like forced Indian agents to bargain for quarters at traders' forts. This placed agents in an obviously difficult situation. Despite the symbiosis of traders and government, basic conflicts of interest persisted. And, because traders actually did exercise power and influence, they tended to ignore laws contrary to their own interests.

The government made many laws but failed to develop significant coercive power in the Upper Missouri until after 1865. Much earlier, fur traders had implanted their informal system of law and behavioral standards, applying it to a region they knew well. Rarely appealing for assistance from the federal government, they saw initiative in federal agents as intrusive and inconvenient. Pierre Chouteau, Jr., & Company, with the largest and oldest investment in the Upper Missouri, usually held the winning hand in the region.

Power made some traders imperious, as their critics charged, but power also vested traders with the means to confront problems, make decisions, and take immediate action beyond the legal frontier. The fur traders' communitarian authority simply filled a legal vacuum, and offered reasonable stability under often volatile conditions. Interethnic dealings were generally smooth, thanks to traders' intimate acquaintance and good relationships with Indians. The federal government offered little to offset the traders' advantages.

Fur traders infringed upon governmental prerogative in the Upper Missouri, true, but in the end the government reasserted its power and marginalized the fur men. That said, a question remains: In the interim, did fur traders demonstrate a capacity to preserve law and order in the Upper Missouri? Part of the answer to this question lies in the nature of the relationship of Pierre Chouteau, Jr., & Company with the federal government, and how it affected legal matters.

Fort Union achieved desirable national security objectives that the government was unable or unwilling to gain at its own expense. As early as 1824, the Congress and Secretary of War John C. Calhoun agreed on the need to erect a military fort near the confluence of the Yellowstone and Missouri Rivers. Its threefold purpose would be to exclude foreign traders, protect American traders, and promote good relations with Indians in the region, some of whom were decidedly bellicose.[16]

In 1824, when the Senate Committee on Indian Affairs solicited Agent Richard Graham's views on "the temper of the tribes towards the citizens of the United States, which have an intercourse with the British," he responded: "Generally unfriendly." Graham continued, "I have always found those Indians, within our territories, who visit British posts, more unfriendly to us, and more difficult to control." When asked if the Missouri River fur trade above the Mandan villages could be secured to American citizens if no fort were built, Graham replied simply: "I think it cannot." Joshua Pilcher, an expert with first-hand knowledge, went further. He said that the Blackfeet and Assiniboines received guns and ammunition from HBC posts on the Assiniboine and Saskatchewan Rivers, used them to attack American trappers south of the border along the Missouri, and traded plundered furs at British posts. Pilcher also advised the committee that the Three Forks of the Missouri was littered with rum kegs bearing the HBC brand and that Britishers sometimes traded inside U.S. territory. Pilcher and Graham believed that American military power concentrated at several fixed army posts would scare off the British company and help assure Americans their rightful share of the trade. If no fort was built, they agreed, the British were liable to get the trade by default.[17]

The army's quartermaster general estimated that it would cost $13,100 to send four companies of soldiers, transported in seven boats manned by fifty boatmen, to build a fort at the Yellowstone. This estimate overlooked the costs of soldiers' wages and provisions and fell considerably short of what the actual expenses would have been. Ultimately, cost estimates were immaterial, for the government built no fort. No soldiers camped on the Yellowstone again until 1855, when General Harney sent Lt. Gouverneur K. Warren and a small party to survey the region.[18]

Private capital, not government policy, brought Fort Union to life about six years after the Senate committee queried Graham and Pilcher.

Thanks to Fort Union, and to the trade goods of Pierre Chouteau, Jr., & Company, the Assiniboines were soon very much under American influence, as were the Blackfeet, who traded at Fort Piegan and its successor, Fort McKenzie. By 1838, Joshua Pilcher observed, Fort Union had severed the cords of loyalty that previously bound the Assiniboines to the HBC, as its satellite, Fort McKenzie, had done for the Blackfeet. The principal reason for the shift, Pilcher thought, was that the Americans developed a big trade in buffalo robes, while the British company did not.[19]

No longer did HBC traders flagrantly violate international agreements, and the threat of serious interference with American trappers and traders on the Upper Missouri vanished. After Fort Union's establishment, the HBC concentrated its borderland efforts in the jointly occupied Oregon country, far to the west, where relatively few Americans trapped or traded. Traders at Fort Union and its dependencies, therefore, had a considerable role in advancing certain national interests.

Congress was reminded of this fact in the 1853 annual report of the commissioner of Indian affairs. The report disclosed that neither the "Blackfeet nor the Gros-ventres have [ever] entered, as is well known, into any treaty with the government," but that "some several years ago they made a friendly treaty with Messrs. P. Chouteau, jr., & Co., to carry on trade with them near the falls of the Missouri." In view of the fact that the national government reaped, at almost no expense, quite tangible benefits as a result of traders' activities at Fort Union, it is not surprising that the government sometimes found it easy to gloss over infractions of the law by these same traders.[20]

Liquor played an important and complex role in the Indian trade. Its presence in Indian country drew plenty of attention over the years, and some high-minded reformers saw liquor prohibition as a worthy moral crusade. Critics indicted traders' brazen disregard of federal prohibition laws, or their callous immorality and greed, and argued that liquor destroyed native people.

There have been claims that thousands of years of biological and genetic isolation rendered American Indians especially vulnerable to alcohol's baneful affects and that they are physiologically predisposed to alcohol addiction. Perhaps further investigation of the so-called "thrifty gene" will shed light on this issue, but more evidence is required to prove the case. It is true that only a few precontact native tribes used alcoholic beverages, and alcoholism is more prevalent today among Indians than any other identified U.S. ethnic group. But it is also plain that alcoholism has afflicted many other Americans, whether in the early republic or in the 1990s.[21]

Most Indians and fur traders who interacted at Fort Union regularly drank liquor. British and American traders alike complained that prohibition would ruin their trade because Indians demanded the stuff, and if their rivals managed to get liquor, they would have the natives' trade, too. The whiskey trade had international ramifications and was occasionally the topic of congressional discussion. Congress passed several prohibition laws in order to deal with the problem, and a number of lawsuits grew out of alleged infractions. This is not the place to examine whether any people ought to drink liquor, or whether one group ought to be empowered to prevent another from drinking. But it is useful to inquire, given the attention the U.S. Congress directed toward whiskey in the fur trade, whether prohibition laws of the fur trade era were successful.

Two incidents occurred in the Upper Missouri during the early 1830s that throw light on legal aspects of the liquor trade and on the relationship between Chouteau's company and the government. Most directly, these events illustrate the difficulties of enforcement, but a more subtle analysis reveals the mechanism of fur traders' community law at work. These liquor cases also present the opportunity to reexamine conventional interpretations of such goings-on and to offer explanations that depart from tradition in important ways.

In the autumn of 1832 a confrontation occurred that amply demonstrated the complexities of enforcing liquor laws in the Missouri River fur trade. In July of that year, after three decades of fence-sitting, Congress had prohibited liquor in the Indian country "under any pretence." At first blush this sounds like an absolute proscription, but actually the law contained gaping loopholes and was far less than comprehensive. Exempted from the law was liquor intended for use by military personnel in Indian country, such as soldiers at Cantonment Leavenworth on the Missouri River near Council Bluffs. There is irony here, since soldiers were notoriously susceptible to the ravages of demon rum, and rampant alcoholism was characteristic of the military establishment on the Indian frontier from top to bottom. Sutlers and Indian agents, as servants of the War Department, were likewise immune to the interdiction. But the fur traders were not, and neither were their customers.[22]

Pierre Chouteau, Jr., seemingly heard about the new liquor prohibition by early July 1832 while returning down the Missouri aboard the *Yellow Stone*. The steamer, according to one witness, had already taken about 1,500 gallons of liquor up the river on her first voyage that spring.[23] Apparently Chouteau had the steamer immediately execute an about-face when it arrived at Saint Louis on July 26. Freighted with a fresh liquor cargo, the vessel hurriedly steamed off to get past the inspection point before enforcement began. Arguing that he had yet to receive positive orders concerning the prohibition, William Clark, superintendent of Indian affairs at Saint Louis, on July 24 permitted Chouteau & Co. to take another 1,072 gallons of "whiskey" up the river, an equivalent of about 11 gallons per boatman. With that gesture Clark set the stage for a serious squabble involving both government officials and private traders.[24]

Enter the opposition trader, Narcisse Leclerc, formerly a Chouteau company man but lately operating on his own hook with financial backing at Saint Louis. The firm was called Valois, Leclerc & Company. Narcisse Leclerc was no greenhorn. He had been on the Missouri at least as early as 1823, working for Joshua Pilcher's Missouri Fur Company, and later he clerked under AFCo man John B. Cabanné. In 1832, Leclerc also received Superintendent Clark's permission to take some liquor up the Missouri. This was not his first year in the whiskey trade, for Valois, Leclerc & Company had been allowed to take liquor up the Missouri to the Arikaras in 1831.[25]

When Chouteau's boat, the *Yellow Stone*, docked for inspection at Cantonment Leavenworth on August 2, the Company was in for a nasty surprise. Soldiers read the new law and duly confiscated every barrel of liquor aboard the vessel. John B. Cabanné, soon to become the storm center in the ensuing flap, observed this unhappy development. He later unctuously professed that he "acquiesced cheerfully in a measure so well calculated to secure peace and happiness among the Indians." Having been relieved of its liquor cargo, the steamer proceeded up the Missouri, and Cabanné disembarked at his trading post near Council Bluffs.[26]

Precisely one month later, on September 2, Narcisse Leclerc's keelboat, the *Atlas*, also carrying some whiskey, stopped at Cantonment Leavenworth. This liquor, actually less than the quantity Clark authorized, was not seized. Two barrels of the whiskey on board belonged to Jonathan L. Bean, subagent for the Sioux. A flabbergasted Cabanné witnessed this irregular proceeding, and events thereafter assumed a most unpleasant complexion.

According to evidence that Valois, Leclerc & Company later placed before the federal district court at Saint Louis, the story ran as follows: Cabanné, realizing that Leclerc had got his liquor safely past the inspection, bristled with anger over the competing company's apparent immunity to the law and determined to take matters into his own hands. Leading a crowd of some twenty gun-toting Company engagés, Cabanné halted Leclerc's keelboat near Council Bluffs. Leveling a loaded swivel gun on the opposition's boat, the AFCo men compelled Leclerc to put off four individuals. Cabanné insisted they were deserters from his company, and he wanted them back. Having acceded to these "arbitrary and Unjust" demands, Leclerc proceeded on, expecting that his troubles were over. But twelve days later, on September 17, Leclerc's boat was again "rushed upon by a party of armed men" and forced to surrender boat and cargo. Peter A. Sarpy, Cabanné's trusted minion, was at the head of the "banditti." Sarpy brusquely informed Leclerc that he acted under authority of the government and was there to confiscate illegal liquor. Sarpy's men commenced a search of the boat, breaking open many bales and packages in the process. With his vessel and goods now in the hands of the AFCo men, Leclerc saw no alternative but to retreat down the Missouri, his trade ruined, his profits dashed. The only recourse, it seemed, was to seek redress through legal channels.[27]

Sure enough, within a few months Leclerc initiated a civil suit against the Company and a criminal proceeding against Cabanné. Meanwhile, legal action was also afoot at the federal level, where it appeared that the Company's bond would be placed in suit. This predicament, wrote Hiram Chittenden, "was certainly a grave one for the company and required all its ingenuity and resources to avert disaster." On the surface, the case seems transparent: the ruthless and conniving AFCo, a bloated monopoly, had smashed a feeble and practically defenseless competitor. But there is much more to the story. A fresh examination of this complicated case exposes some important underlying dynamics. It remains a liquor case, true, but it also illuminates the informal, unwritten law operative in the Upper Missouri country.[28]

One of the principal actors in the Leclerc affair was Alexander G. Morgan, the sutler at Fort Leavenworth. Morgan at one point claimed that the keelboat *Atlas*, detained by Sarpy, was his property. If so, the sutler at Fort Leavenworth was also engaged in the Indian trade.[29] A federal Indian agent, Jonathan L. Bean, also a former fur trader, was likewise involved in the affair. Bean offered Leclerc eight hundred dollars to transport some treaty goods up to the tribes in his Sioux subagency. As it happened, Leclerc's own keelboat was not up to the job, so Bean helped negotiate a deal whereby Leclerc obtained the keelboat *Atlas* from a "Mr. Payne" at Fort Leavenworth.[30] Bean's annuity goods, along with two barrels of whiskey for his personal consumption, had been loaded aboard the *Atlas*, bound for his post at the Sioux subagency.[31]

Cabanné's seizure of Leclerc's keelboat gave Bean, who deeply hated the Company anyway, an opportunity to shrill about the greedy monopolists. On October 10, about one month after the second incident took place, Agent Bean wrote to William Clark. Even though Cabanné had by then already assured Bean that the annuity goods were en route to the Yanktons and Santees, Bean whined that "we cannot hope they will reach here this winter, and thus the poor Indian who is starving and shivering with cold is made to suffer even to death, merely that this overgrown monopoly may gratify a little spite." Now, according to Bean, having "by force of arms" become masters of the region, the arrogant company would proceed to gouge Indians, intimidate agents, and thumb its nose at the laws of the United States.[32]

Agent Bean, as it turned out, had too hastily damned the Company, and his lachrymose solicitude for his native charges rings with insincerity. He later testified that the purloined keelboat *Atlas* arrived at his subagency on "the last day of October or the first day of November." When Company man Joseph Picotte delivered the vessel, it contained "all the public stores in good order." Bean even admitted that the boat "arrived at my post at about the same time that Keel boats ordinarily arrive there for the Indian trade." The only conspicuously absent items were the two kegs of whiskey that Bean himself intended to drink or otherwise dispose of. Kenneth McKenzie, in an obliging mood, immediately replaced Agent Bean's seventy-two gallons of missing whiskey with liquor taken from UMO stores. The Company also canceled the freight charges on Bean's annuity goods. Here was a federal Indian agent who not only recanted his hearty condemnation of the Company, but also willingly abetted the unholy trade in alcohol. So much for Agent Bean's high moral ground.[33]

Bean's strident denunciation of the big company and its role in the Leclerc affair was echoed by William Gordon, another veteran fur trader and sometime Indian agent who also had an axe to grind.[34] Gordon, even according to Valois and Leclerc, became a "partner" at some point *after* their trading license was issued.[35] During the court proceeding, both Cabanné and the prestigious William B. Astor claimed, with fair plausibility, that Gordon had belatedly purchased an interest in the enterprise purely on speculation in the hope that the courts would award a hefty compensation to the parties claiming damages.[36]

A. G. Morgan, the sutler mentioned above, wrote two letters to Cabanné in February 1833 that seem oddly discordant with the harsh blasts he had lately directed toward Cabanné and his company. Morgan assured Cabanné that he understood "your *head* and not your *heart* was to blame," and, though Morgan had suffered financial distress, he sought only "an amicable arrangement of this unpleasant business . . . on liberal principles." Morgan further stated that he "cannot conceive why Maj. Bean feels himself aggrieved at the detention of my boat, it was no personal injury to him, as he got his goods as soon or sooner than if they had proceeded." Morgan even sent Cabanné some molasses and medicines and signed the letter "with sentiments of friendly feeling." In a second letter, Morgan repeated his wish to settle the matter and requested that Cabanné ask Chouteau if he might be interested in purchasing "a large lot of shaved Deer Skins, otter, Beaver, Coon & Bearskins." Morgan was also "desirous of purchasing about $2000 worth of Indian goods *for this place*" and promised to sell any furs he acquired to the American Fur Company. All of this suggests that he no longer wished to trade in opposition to the Company.[37]

When the legalistic smoke cleared, the Company agreed to pay Leclerc ninety-two hundred dollars for his lost trade, chargeable to the UMO's account. Cabanné and Sarpy were ordered out of the Indian country for a year. This was a painful loss for the AFCo—two good traders and a substantial amount of cash—but a more menacing threat still loomed. Since Cabanné and Sarpy traded under the license issued to Pratte, Chouteau, & Company, the Company's bond and license stood in jeopardy. Cabanné, faithful if indiscreet, repeatedly asserted that he had acted entirely on his own, undoubtedly in an effort to shield his employers. Ramsay Crooks and Kenneth McKenzie desperately jawboned at Washington during February and March 1833, hoping to head off the impending disaster. In the end, Pratte, Chouteau & Company retained their license, and business continued to flourish.[38]

The Company survived its first serious brush with federal liquor regulation, but this particular case is freighted with more than a little paradox and irony. The Leclerc-Cabanné affair could scarcely have arisen at a more awkward time. Several of the leading men—Chouteau, McKenzie, Crooks, and even William B. Astor—had been trying to persuade the government that some liquor was absolutely required at the posts above the Mandans. Otherwise, they argued, American traders were going to lose out to HBC men, who had unlimited access to alcohol, and American prestige would suffer. In the midst of these discussions the Leclerc-Cabanné scandal broke like a rotten egg, even as Ramsay Crooks and Kenneth McKenzie spent about two weeks at Washington in February 1833 trying to secure some "modification" of the liquor law. It is important to recognize, however, that these were only the most recent of many negotiations, for some years ongoing among British and American businessmen and their governments, to reach an understanding regarding the use of liquor in the trade.[39]

William B. Astor had written in December 1829 to HBC man James Keith at Lachine, near Montréal, that the AFCo wished to end the border liquor trade but would not go it alone. Sir George Simpson, the HBC's cynical chief field executive in North America, suspected that Astor's overture was merely an indication of the AFCo's inability to control its side of the frontier. Consequently, in September 1830, Simpson declined Astor's offer to cooperate in restricting liquor. Simpson's rejection stemmed from his conviction that even if the two great companies agreed to the deal, smaller and less visible traders would infiltrate the region and fill the empty liquor kegs. Astor supposedly quipped, when he met with Simpson later in New York, "I now see it is of no use to attempt it, as if we did the Hudson's Bay Company would hold the head of the Cow, the American Fur Company would hold the tail of the Cow, and the Petty Traders would come in and milk the Cow."[40]

Until 1833, William Astor urged his government to work out an agreement with the British government to "interdict the use of Spiritous Liquors in the territories of the Hudson's Bay Company." Astor's troubleshooter and lobbyist in Washington, Ramsay Crooks, was a member of the Chouteau clan as well, for he had married one of Chouteau's nieces, Emilie Pratte. Though he personally believed that prohibition was a laudable objective, Crooks did the Company's bidding. He accordingly cautioned the UMO men to be "more than usually circumspect" in the hope that within a year the Company would gain "an equal footing" with the HBC. But if the British government failed to help curtail the liquor trade, Crooks wrote:

> it is enough that our laws prohibit the introduction of Ardent Spirits into the Indian Country, and it is [our] bounden duty to conform honestly thereto, taking especial care that none of our citizens enjoy the benefit which a violation of the statute would give them in competition with us. It might be possible to elude the vigilance of all who watch your operations, and carry in a certain quantity of this liquid poison, but rely on it that sooner, or later, detection will overtake you, and you will then deem all you have gained by it, too dearly purchased.[41]

By that time the Leclerc-Cabanné affair had set congressional passions aflame and led to howls from some quarters for immediate revocation of the Company's license. The uproar certainly bred suspicions about Astor and Crooks's altruistic pronouncements, whether they were sincere or not. After mighty labors among the nation's bureaucrats and politicians, the lobbyists defused the immediate threat to their license and bond. In the summer of 1833, a Missouri court heard the civil case, which was probably settled informally. The point here is that the Company apparently tried to support the humane notion of an outright ban on whiskey even as they bowed, in their view, to unalterable realities of the Upper Missouri trade.[42]

What touched off the Leclerc-Cabanné affair in the first place may actually have been a violation of informal but well understood rules of order among fur traders. Daniel Lamont claimed that four deserters left his boat on the way up the Missouri. Soon thereafter, these same men signed on with Leclerc. It was this affront that initially aggravated Cabanné, though he clearly resented Leclerc's evasion of the liquor inspectors at Fort Leavenworth. In his defense, Cabanné invoked the sacred ideals of property and contracts in order to explain his behavior. The "ordinary hands in the Indian trade," he wrote, "are generally persons without property" who received advances in goods, often amounting to a substantial portion of their annual wages. When a man deserted, a contract was violated and the Company lost money. Moreover, he contended, "the success of the Indian trade depends in a great degree on the faithfulness of those who are employed in the capacity of hands as it would be utterly impossible to supply the places of those who might desert their employers in the Indian country." The main principle at issue, he wrote, was that "in that country far removed from civilized society, and where the process of courts cannot reach, it is the perfect understanding of all persons employed in the trade that those who desert from their employers may be compelled to return to their duty and it is a decided evidence of unkind feeling in one trader toward another to employ the person deserting from his service."[43]

When Leclerc ignored this universally recognized standard of community behavior, Cabanné saw fit to move beyond the normal restraints of both custom and law. His arrogation of power backfired, precipitating a crisis for Cabanné and for his employers. Still, reexamination of the Leclerc-Cabanné affair suggests that "transparent" conflicts might offer heartier fare than the simple parable of a powerful monopoly mindlessly attempting to crush a rival organization at whatever cost. In the fiercely competitive fur trade, where even government employees double-dipped or subverted each other, it should surprise no one that liquor law enforcement remained a losing proposition.

In 1833, just on the heels of the Leclerc-Cabanné affair, there occurred another scandal, the result of Kenneth McKenzie's determination to trade liquor in defiance of federal laws. The source of this controversy was a distillery operated at Fort Union, a foolhardy venture that again plunged Chouteau's company into a legal morass. Notorious in its own day, Fort Union's whiskey mill became a perennial yarn of the Upper Missouri trade. Stripped of its anecdotal glamour, this incident reveals the intransigence of the whiskey problem, but a reappraisal also suggests that historians have misinterpreted the big company's role in the set-to that followed.

Irritated by the preceding year's difficulties, and anticipating serious competition this year, McKenzie decided to circumvent federal laws and eliminate supply problems by manufacturing liquor at Fort Union. He purchased distillery equipment and, when spring unlocked the Missouri in 1833, sent it upriver aboard the *Yellow Stone* or the *Assiniboine*. By July his distillery was fully operational, producing a crude whiskey from bushels of Mandan corn. With so many foes in the vicinity, it was inevitable that someone would blow the whistle on McKenzie. The most likely candidates were William Sublette and Robert Campbell's well-capitalized outfit, which was building Fort William three miles down the Missouri from Fort Union, and a Boston man, Nathaniel J. Wyeth, who passed by during the summer.

Wyeth stopped at Forts Union and William on his way down the Missouri to Saint Louis in August. He had spent several years trying to duplicate Astor's scheme of developing a Pacific Coast fur trading post with connections to China, Hawaii, and elsewhere. Ruined by bad luck, HBC opposition, and his own partners' duplicity, Wyeth was not in the best of moods when he arrived at Fort Union on August 24. But he and his men "were met with all possible hospitality and politeness by Mr. McKensie," who proudly showed the visitors around the fort. In his journal Wyeth noted that "they are beginning to distil spirits from corn traded from the Inds. below. This owing to some restrictions on the introduction of the article into the country."[44]

Somehow, Special Indian Commissioner Henry L. Ellsworth heard about the "King's" latest impropriety in November 1833 and forwarded the information to the new commissioner of Indian affairs, Elbert Herring.[45] According to Ellsworth, "A mountain trapper on his way down the Missouri" told him the AFCo's fort at the Yellowstone had "a distillery of whiskey . . . in the most successful operation—Mr. Sublitz [William Sublette] of St. Louis just from there, says, he tasted the whiskey made there, and found it of an excellent quality." As Sublette explained it to Ellsworth, the Company's justification for the still was that "the law does not forbid *making* whiskey—it only precludes its *introduction*."[46]

Wyeth or Sublette probably revealed the story, for William Clark at Saint Louis and other government officials knew about the still by late autumn. On November 14, Clark requested Pierre Chouteau, Jr., to supply fuller details. Chouteau replied that if the charge contained any truth at all, the violation was "unauthorized by and unknown to the Company," adding that it was "probably greatly exaggerated if not wholly unfounded." In the unlikely event that his employees had exceeded their authority and instructions, Chouteau wished to clarify his company's position. It was true, he admitted, that "the Company, believing that a wild Pear and Berries might be converted into wine (which they understood not to be prohibited), did authorize experiments to be made." But if "ardent spirits have been distilled and vended it [was] without the knowledge, authority, or direction of the Company."[47]

Chouteau undoubtedly dissembled. He knew all about the plan by early 1833. In February, nearly two months before the distillery equipment went up the Missouri, Crooks earnestly enjoined his "cher cousin" to exercise caution following the Leclerc episode. "Every eye is upon us," he warned, "and whoever can, will annoy us with all his heart—It will therefore in my opinion be madness to attempt your Cincinnati project of the *Boxes*, or the *alembique*—try to struggle through the disadvantages under which we must labor in the competition with the Hudson's Bay Company."[48]

Months later, on December 16, 1833, McKenzie crowed to his boss Chouteau that "our manufactory flourishes—we only want corn enough to be able to supply all our wants. The quality is fine but the yield from Mandan corn is small." This was obviously not the first time Chouteau heard about the operation.[49] On the same day, McKenzie bragged in a letter to Ramsay Crooks: "For this post I have established a manufactory of strong water, it succeeds admirably. I have a good corn mill, a very respectable distillery & can produce as fine liquor as need be drank. I believe no law of the U.S. is hereby broken though perhaps one may be made to break up my distillery but liquor I must have or quit any pretension to trade at this post, especially while our opponents can get any quantity passed up the Mo or introduce it as they have done by another route."[50]

By March 1834, McKenzie sang a far different tune. Convinced that Wyeth had tipped off federal authorities about the still, the "King" excoriated him as "a man of many schemes and considerable talent" who "in return for my civilities & furnishing him with a boat to go down to St. Louis, on his arrival at Cant. Leavenworth . . . made some tremendous strong affidavits about my new manufactory."[51]

McKenzie, already stung by a recent rebuke from his boss, felt compelled to defend himself in a letter to Chouteau that laid the blame on Wyeth. Because this letter was critical to later historians' interpretation of these events, the full text follows:

Fort Union
March 18, 1834
Pierre Chouteau, Jr., Esq.
Dear Sir:

If I were conscious of having infringed the laws of the U.S. I would at once acknowledge my error & admit the propriety of your censure. You seem to have lent a willing ear to a marvellous tale of discrepancy in my conduct & proceedings, and admitted as facts, statements which had existence only in the narrators imagination. 'Hear both sides' is no less the duty than the practice of all impartial men. The facts are simply as follows:

An old acquaintance of mine in Red River, Mr. J. P. Bourke addressed me last Spring while in St. Louis a letter (of which I annex you an attested copy) in consequence whereof I purchased a still in St. Louis, & brought it hither & last fall he apprized me of his intention to come or send for it in April next (the coming month).[52]

While here it may have been seen by a person styling himself Capt. Wythe, as under that name a stranger introduced himself to me last summer, & received the accustomed hospitalities of this place. L. Cere was here at the same time & may also have seen the Still, though it is exceedingly improbable that it should have been

seen by either of them, nor is it in the nature of things possible for
them to prove a single allegation they have made. They both applied
to me to sell them liquor. I could not do it, but offered them wine
which they declined purchasing & appeared mortified & displeased.
Independent whereof, the character of the former & the wounded
self-love of the latter in being deemed unworthy of an engagement
for the Am. F. C. would in my mind account for their unwarranted
proceeding.

They have lied gratuitously, I content myself with simply denying
the truth of their allegations. I am Dear Sir yours very truly,

Signed K. McKenzie[53]

Two days later McKenzie again wrote to his boss, elaborating on his
defense. He complained that the HBC sold liquor, adding that Indians
routinely expected liquor as well. He said he could extend the trade if
only he had liquor, but none was available. He claimed that the still was
just like "any other article of Mdze. by the sale whereof I expected to
realize a profit." McKenzie asserted that the distiller operated "on his
own account," but "not a single gallon of liquor has been manufactured
since last fall" (a bit of a stretch, for his distiller fell ill sometime in
December 1833). Protesting again that if he had erred it had been in
perfect innocence, McKenzie concluded by declaring that Wyeth was
"beastly drunk" during the downriver trip and that a man of such
"dissipated habits" could not be taken seriously. McKenzie was hurt, he
added, that an ex parte judgment should be made in this case by a "just
& liberal" government.[54] This letter, like the one reproduced above, is so
full of improbabilities that it serves mainly to make McKenzie's self-
defense appear foolish and clumsy.

So once again, not a year after the last scramble to quell an outcry
against monopoly, the Company found itself hard pressed to explain its
conduct to federal agents. By late February, even before Chouteau
received McKenzie's letters, the crisis had passed. Influential friends in
high places, and fast talking, enabled Chouteau and his men to deflect
the federal axe.

Ramsay Crooks congratulated Chouteau for having the "address to
persuade Judge [Elbert] Herring your *Distillery* at the Yellow Stone was

only intended to promote the cause of *Botany*." But, he warned, "Don't presume too much on your recent escape from an accusation, which might have been attended with serious consequences. . . . your business so much resembles a monopoly that there will always exist strong jealousies against you."[55] In fact, Commissioner Herring was not merely persuaded but was recruited: he had given a silent, approving nod to a "hear no evil, speak no evil" arrangement. Crooks observed, however, that Herring's "*qualified* permission is worth nothing, since *secrecy* is the condition; for if you do use [liquor], it will be known generally, much the same as if you published it in the Missouri Republican." Crooks also pointed out that former congressional allies such as Missouri representative William H. Ashley (now closely associated with opposition trader William Sublette) and even William Clark could no longer be counted on for support. Times had changed, and with change had come new political alignments.[56]

Hiram Martin Chittenden, whose *American Fur Trade of the Far West* (1902) influenced generations of readers, saw this case in a very different way. Most fur trade historians have uncritically adopted his analysis of McKenzie's still and its consequences, but Chittenden's biased account warrants correction.[57] Chittenden unquestionably knew the whole story, but he balked at a full disclosure of the relevant facts and rendered an incomplete evaluation of the distillery scandal. He knew that all the principal business managers—Crooks, Chouteau, and Astor—were aware of the plan, but he focused chiefly on McKenzie's part in the affair.

Chittenden charged private businessmen with complicity but left out government officers, perhaps because their reputations might be tarnished if the circumstances of the case were fully aired. Maybe this explains Chittenden's failure to mention William Clark's permission (discussed above) for the AFCo to take a thousand gallons of liquor up the Missouri. More significantly, quoting the same letter from Crooks to Chouteau that is cited above, Chittenden deliberately declined giving Elbert Herring's full last name, which appears in the original text. He well knew that Elbert Herring was the first commissioner of Indian affairs, yet by referring to Herring as "Judge H——," he masked the commissioner's involvement and conveyed a misleading impression that perhaps this referred to someone else.[58]

Since Chittenden cast McKenzie as the villain in this episode, he was obliged to usher the "King" offstage before drawing the curtain on his morality play. The distillery incident became for McKenzie a "*faux pas* which ended his usefulness in the upper country" and "practically closed McKenzie's career in the Indian country."[59] While it is true that McKenzie retired temporarily to Europe to visit his friend Prince Maximilian at Wied-Neuwied, he soon reappeared in the Upper Missouri, and he retained a lively interest in Upper Missouri business affairs for many more years. Back at Fort Union by autumn of 1835, he remained until at least September 1836 and possibly until spring of 1837.[60]

Late in 1844, McKenzie again returned to Fort Union, perhaps for the final time. He and his wife's brother, George, spent the winter and the following spring at Fort Union on a special assignment. Francis Chardon and Alexander Harvey had murdered several Blackfeet at Fort McKenzie in 1843, seriously disrupting the trade, and McKenzie was dispatched on a delicate mission to restore harmony. Presumably, McKenzie returned to Saint Louis the following spring.[61] He held his partnership in Chouteau & Company until at least 1844, but eventually a falling out occurred, and he filed a lawsuit against Chouteau.

In a case heard before the Saint Louis Circuit Court in November 1849, Kenneth McKenzie sued Chouteau and his partners for ten thousand dollars, an amount McKenzie claimed was due for services rendered during "some seven months" in the Upper Missouri in 1843–44. He also claimed he had been denied a fair share of profits since 1841. The case dragged on for four years, but in 1853, McKenzie emerged victorious. After more stalling, in 1859 he was awarded at least twenty thousand dollars.[62] Contrary to Chittenden's assertion, McKenzie's interest in the fur trade continued until he died at the age of sixty-four on April 26, 1861. While it may be that the distillery affair prevented McKenzie from superintending Fort Union again, he did not retire, nor was his usefulness in the Upper Missouri ended.[63]

Fort Union's operators weathered other liquor law violation suits over the years, but none as spectacular as those related to the Leclerc-Cabanné affair or the distillery. Each of these incidents demonstrates that no amount of unenforceable law could prevent the influx of whiskey into Indian country, especially when "persons of little or no capital" were involved. But the record shows that Chouteau's company also shipped liquor to the Upper Missouri country each year. In 1844, Thomas H. Harvey, superintendent of Indian affairs at Saint Louis, wrote to Indian Commissioner T. Hartley Crawford that harsher punishments should be meted out to fly-by-night traders, since "the seizure and destruction of a few kegs of whiskey is not calculated to deter them from a repitition [*sic*] of the offense." He also correctly observed that the laws forbidding the liquor trade were "in practice a nullity."[64]

The worst offenders were opposition traders in for the short term, seeking a fast profit. These men had no serious commitment to the region, and it is not surprising that they saw no reason to exercise moderation. Apparently even the most heavily capitalized opposition firms, such as Sublette and Campbell (1833) and Ebbetts and Cutting (1843), took the same view. There is no evidence that any of these outfits ever wrote letters to a President or anyone else to request that the whiskey trade be slowed or stopped. Yet the AFCo and its Saint Louis associates were roundly criticized for their abuse of the laws in their own time, and by later historians, while scant attention is paid to their efforts, however ineffectual, to limit the whiskey trade. After all, the government passed prohibition laws but was never able to put the bung back in the keg, much less to banish it. The largest, most heavily invested, and most visible concern in the field would have been the greatest loser had it obeyed the law.

Abundant evidence demonstrates that smaller Missouri River outfits regularly managed to get plenty of liquor past federal authorities. Also, the distant southwest region around Taos in the Republic of Mexico, lying entirely outside federal jurisdiction, provided an alternate source of liquor. Other small communities on the periphery of New Mexico, such as Pueblo, Hardscrabble, and Greenhorn, routinely, if illegally, traded whiskey from the Arkansas to the North Platte Rivers by the early 1830s. The famed whiskey man Simeon Turley at Arroyo Hondo, New Mexico, began to manufacture liquor by 1832, and in 1843 he ordered some new distillery equipment. Interestingly, between May 1838 and July 1840 the large Santa Fe Trade firm of Bent, St. Vrain & Company placed orders with Pratte, Chouteau, & Company for six large-capacity copper stills. Where these were forwarded remains unknown, but there is no record of a distillery at Bent's Fort on the Arkansas. One way or another, there was never a sustained shortage of whiskey in Indian country.[65]

Only once did the government try to crack down on whiskey vendors, and the results were trifling. In the early 1840s a special agent (a former AFCo trader named Andrew Drips) was sent on a fool's errand to end the illicit trade in an enormous region reaching from the South Platte to the Upper Missouri. As he had just one assistant, and no military support, his mission was destined to fail. Even so, by 1844 reports circulated among government officials in Washington assuring them that the flow of liquor had finally been turned off.

Despite claims by opposition traders that Drips was nothing more than the AFCo's stooge, it seems he tried to do a job that would have been exceedingly difficult under the best of conditions. In fact, the situation was hopeless, and he stood no chance whatever of singlehandedly ending the whiskey trade. This did not prevent Indian Superintendents Mitchell and Harvey from telling Indian Commissioner T. H. Crawford that there had been "a wonderful decrease in the quantity of spiritous liquors carried into the Indian country" (1843) or that "the use of ardent spirits among the Indians . . . is being much reduced" (1844). This was simply not so.[66]

The Chouteau concern was soon (1848–49) involved in another liquor lawsuit that jeopardized their bonds covering the years from 1841 to 1845. Instigating this case was Alexander Harvey, a disgruntled former AFCo man and anything but a reliable witness. The Company settled the dispute by hiring several witnesses for the prosecution, promptly shipping them off to the Upper Missouri, and paying five thousand dollars to Harvey and his attorney. The Company was beginning to look like an easy mark, but it was probably less costly to pay off challengers, no matter how unsavory, than to go through the whole messy courtroom and legal routine.[67]

By the late 1850s, competition and liquor both troubled the Upper Missouri trade. The usual complaints continued, but an effective solution remained elusive. Agent Alexander H. Redfield, one of the least competent Upper Missouri Indian agents, warned Acting Commissioner Charles E. Mix in 1858 that "*sharp* and *bitter*" competition led to liquor's "being introduced into the country by Half breeds from Red River and secretly

I think by other parties. To detect or arrest these abuses the Agent has but little opportunity or power." Redfield petulantly added, "I wish the *trade was stopped entirely* and *every Half breed and white man expelled* from the country except the Indian Agents."[68]

Conditions in the Upper Missouri—especially relations between Indians and soldiers—steadily deteriorated after Lieutenant John L. Grattan's command perished in a fight with some Brulé Sioux in 1854. At the time, many politicians and reformers argued that it was fur traders who polluted the Indians with whiskey and incited them to violence. A decade or so later, the fur traders were gone, but the liquor remained, and Indian-white wars began in earnest.

What, one might ask, was the force that kept the illegal trade bustling? In the American mind of the 1830s the ideal of entrepreneurial competition had already become a sacred cow. It was immune to challenges, no matter how inefficient or cut-throat its nature. Lawmakers' deep ideological antipathy toward monopolies led them to reject an idea that might have worked much better in the long run. About 1854 the fur trader Edwin Denig, with obvious reluctance, expressed his opinion to Henry R. Schoolcraft at the Office of Indian Affairs that "there is only one way we know of by which the trade could be placed on a better basis, and that being inconsistent with the principles of our Government, is scarcely worth considering. It is that it should be a monopoly. A charter granted to a body of efficient people who could give bond to a large amount for their lawful prosecution of the trade, and their operations subject to the revision and examination of a competent board of directors."[69]

Even a cursory comparison of the HBC and the American systems of operating the fur trade reveals some reasons for the particularly bitter legacy associated with United States–Indian relations. For one thing, the British company enjoyed a certain advantage simply because England, with its priority in the Industrial Revolution, generally produced better trade goods than did the United States. But other factors were involved as well. The HBC's long-term commitment to Rupert's Land, its heavy capitalization and steady returns, its continuity in economic structure and policy, its resource conservation measures, and its legal authority to restrict or prohibit competition all contributed to a less chaotic and more manageable fur trade.

Below the forty-ninth parallel, things were very different. Government subsidies were practically nonexistent, and private capital was frequently squandered in destructive competition. This led to the ruin of traders and investors, while Indians suffered the consequences of an uncontrollable whiskey trade. The government itself became a casualty, losing control of events as it heaped law upon ineffective law that even the best Indian agents were powerless to enforce. Military men were likewise unable to control the trade. Some tribes repeatedly implored the Great Father to fulfill treaty obligations, ban liquor, and protect them from their enemies, but little help was forthcoming. Others, sensing the confusion and ineptitude of U.S. Indian policy as it existed on the Missouri River frontier, developed a fatal arrogance that led them to believe that whites really were as weak and foolish as they appeared to be.

The most powerful company in the field was Chouteau's. Not surprisingly, it was also the most despised. Its high profile made the Company a target, and Chouteau and the UMO came under repeated attack from competitors as well as government. Ironically, its long tenure in the Upper Missouri had demonstrated that a substantial measure of stability was possible under conditions that approached, but never fully achieved, monopoly.[70] And, to repeat a point made earlier, it is beyond question that the self-interests of fur traders and Indians meshed far more rationally and cooperatively than would those of the land-grabbing and bigoted federal government with the same natives.

After 1860, the Sioux wars and the Civil War, as well as the emerging Republican party, would bring new and powerful pressures to bear upon the Upper Missouri. Within a few more years the old company liquidated its interests in the region, ending one era in Fort Union's history and opening the final chapter in the story of the Upper Missouri frontier fur trade. Before recounting Fort Union's decline, it will be instructive to examine what happened when robust competition—usually considered to be a good thing—occurred in the 1840s and after.

CHAPTER FIVE

"Masters of the Country"?

A recurrent theme in Upper Missouri fur trade history is that
Pierre Chouteau, Jr., built a monopoly so powerful that for many years it
resisted all challengers, including the government. It was the UMO's iron
grip on the region and its people, according to this interpretation, that
caused a righteous public outcry against the Company and eventually led
to its dismantling. As we shall see, the UMO men were not exactly the
"masters of the country," but neither was the federal government.

Charges of monopoly would have struck a responsive chord in the
minds of many Americans. The United States of the 1840s was a nation
of would-be entrepreneurs wedded to free-market economic ideas, always
seeking the "main chance." This was also an era of muscle-flexing nation-
alism, and many Americans recalled that the Revolutionary War had
erupted partly over a rhetorical battle concerning the hated British East
India Company's tea monopoly. Chouteau's outfit had numerous foes,
but the HBC—another British monopoly—seemed to pose an even greater
threat to American commerce and sovereignty along the northern
boundary. With the HBC dominating the Canadian trade and the Astor,
Crooks, and Chouteau outfits controlling much trade south of the border,
critics complained, it was well nigh impossible for other entrepreneurs to
gain a significant "market share" of the business.

It seems ironic, in view of the vitriolic animosity leveled at Chouteau's company in the 1860s by government officials and businessmen, that a few genuine monopolies soon came to dominate American industry, politics, and finance. John D. Rockefeller, Jay Gould, J. P. Morgan, and their associates wielded powers that Chouteau could scarcely have imagined. Had the Upper Missouri fur traders remained in operation a decade or two after 1865, they, too, might have been cheered by public-spirited citizens as "captains of industry."

Instead, historians viewed the Company as a gang of "robber barons" and offered a simplistic analysis that, with endless repetition, became conventional: Pierre Chouteau, Jr., & Company were villains whose nasty monopolistic methods defeated all rivals and defrauded the government, stole from Indians whom they first made drunk, and inhibited the settlement of the West by decent citizens. This conception cloaks the Company with more power than it actually wielded and confuses the various roles of fur traders, Indian agents, soldiers, and politicians. It fails to do justice to a complex story and provides an unsatisfactory basis for evaluation.

In a sense, executives such as John Astor and Pierre Chouteau, Jr., did nothing more—or less—than pioneer organizational and tactical innovations that later made American big business a splendid success. Their own excesses were dwarfed by later businessmen's shenanigans, and there never has been a time—certainly not from the 1840s to the 1990s—when American businessmen were conspicuously attentive to ethics, honesty, or adherence to the law. Had a monopoly of some sort directed Indian trade within the United States, it is possible that some nagging problems, particularly those related to the liquor trade and manipulation of tribal interests, might have been materially reduced.

Neither government, the public, nor businessmen would tolerate a monopoly, and historians err if they unblinkingly characterize the UMO as one. The record amply demonstrates that Chouteau's UMO faced frequent and sometimes costly challenges from opposition firms between 1830 and 1865. It was no secret that company policy aimed to achieve as complete a monopoly in the region as possible. But wishing for a monopoly and securing one are very different things. The record also tells us that opposition firms and some federal government employees damned Chouteau and his men as "grasping monopolists." Men tendering such complaints might easily have been motivated by self-interest or the quest for political advantage. Still, it is clear that Chouteau's company created and retained for many years a commanding position in the upriver Indian and fur trades and in the government-contract carrying trade. But the question persists: Did Pierre Chouteau, Jr., & Company really exercise a monopoly?

Available evidence indicates that the Company never attained a functional monopoly for more than a year or two at a time, and then only during brief interludes between periods of stout competition. It took time for opposition firms to amass capital, purchase goods, arrange for transportation, and establish trading posts in the country. Whenever a competitor failed or sold out to the Company, therefore, a temporary condition of monopoly might prevail, but only by default, and only until a new competitor arrived on the scene.

Seldom was there a shortage of men willing to assume the risks involved in doing battle with Chouteau & Company. The western economic frontier offered a narrow range of opportunities for large-scale investment. Land speculation, lead mining, brokering agricultural products, banking and finance: all were important boosters for Saint Louis's urbanization in the years before modern heavy industry emerged with the Civil War. In each of these highly competitive fields, it was possible for innovative or well-funded challengers to succeed.

Small fortunes made in the fur and Indian trades played large roles in shaping mid-nineteenth-century America's preeminent western city. Most Saint Louisans were aware that the Company generated solid profits every year, and potential competitors must have looked on with mingled envy and appreciation. In actuality, the results of intensified competition in the Upper Missouri trade after 1840 were far more disruptive than any problems that can be linked to Chouteau's supposed monopoly. Unregulated competition was not the only unsettling factor in the Indian trade. Increased military activities, Indian removals, Indian-white warfare, and the westward movement all affected the Northern Plains trade.

The government stepped up its western military program after 1830. Soldiers faced a very difficult job as police and protectors for Indians as well as whites. The frontier was crowded with "migrating" Indian nations forced westward under the Indian removal program. Lands abandoned by ousted natives from Iowa to Georgia rapidly filled with white settlers, too many of whom were lawless ruffians. Whiskey traders and land grabbers rushed into vacated areas as advance agents of an American economic culture largely based on speculation and maximized short-term gains.

But the army mustered fewer than ten thousand soldiers before 1846 and was ill-prepared for its greatly enlarged role. Nonetheless, the army became more prominent in Fort Union's story as the years passed, and as American power grew stronger west of the Mississippi. The blue-coated soldiers could not control events, however, and they often served mainly to fan the growing hostilities between whites and Indians in the Upper Missouri region, especially after 1855.

By the late 1840s the "permanent Indian frontier" that had been established in 1817 was collapsing, the result of a number of contributing factors. Boosters such as Hall Jackson Kelly and a handful of missionaries in the 1830s energized the U.S. occupation of Oregon, which began in earnest in 1842. The overlanders' way was made easier by trappers who had explored the Pacific Northwest and developed a nascent Oregon-California Trail a decade earlier.

To the south, the Santa Fe Trail had been booming since 1821, and with the passing years American economic and imperial interests in New Mexico swelled. In 1846 the United States would invade the Republic of Mexico and wrest from its feeble grip all of the northern provinces from Texas to California, practically one-third of that nation's land. Then came gold strikes in California, unleashing an unprecedented torrent of argonauts and hangers-on who swept across the plains in a reenactment of the ancient search for El Dorado. Each of these events sent disruptive shock waves rolling across the plains, throwing the old-time Indian and fur trades into disarray and offering a glimpse of much greater earthquakes to come as the nineteenth century unfolded.

As of 1830, seven military forts lay scattered along a great arc west of the Mississippi River, stretching from Fort Snelling in Minnesota to Fort Jessup, Louisiana. These forts marked the western limits of the United States' active territorial interests early in the nineteenth century. By the late 1830s the government forced several eastern Indian tribes to move west across the Mississippi, safely beyond the "permanent" frontier. During these troubled years of Indian removals, military force in the West necessarily grew, and the government built more forts. Strangely enough, by the time the army completed a strong line of forts to guard the "permanent" frontier in the middle 1840s, they were already obsolete, expensive casualties of Americans' quest for continental nationhood. As U.S. citizens moved west in ever larger numbers, the government found itself negotiating with native tribes more frequently. A period of intensive treaty-making with many Indian nations, east and west, began in 1825 and continued until 1870.

The government signed its first treaty with Upper Missouri Indians in 1825. A product of the Atkinson-O'Fallon expedition, this omnibus treaty with the Arikaras, Crows, Assiniboines, and about a dozen other tribes informed the natives that the Great Father urged them not to molest whites and would now watch out for them. No mention was made of relocation or land trades. The future would become clearer, if more grim, when another multitribal treaty was negotiated in 1851 at Fort Laramie on the North Platte River.

The 1851 treaty assigned native nations to specified reservations, using federally funded annuities ("gifts" and payments for land sold to the United States) as incentives for the Indians' cooperation. The Sioux, Assiniboine, Gros Ventres, Blackfeet, Crow, Cheyenne, and Arapaho nations were accorded specific tribal boundaries, and from then on the government would deal only with "selected" chiefs (usually this meant individuals inclined to support American interests), "through whom all national business will . . . be conducted."[1]

Such a policy would be utterly unenforceable unless many well-trained, case-hardened soldiers and officers made it stick. Before 1850, that level of military power was simply not available in the West, and Indians saw little or no grounds for fear. General William S. Harney's 1855 expedition to the Upper Missouri made a temporary impression, but almost a decade passed before soldiers came again, by which time Indian memories of Harney's warriors had faded to obscurity.

The American frontier military establishment in Indian country between 1820 and 1850 was flimsy and generally impotent. Military weakness flowed from several sources, including popular fear and mistrust of a standing professional army, poor-quality soldiers, and congressional hesitancy in military funding. The Military Academy at West Point trained a reasonably dedicated and competent officer corps, but the rank-and-file soldiers were no advertisement for military excellence.

Alcoholism reached genuinely alarming proportions. At times as many as 15 percent of the soldiers in a garrison might be found in the guardhouse, charged with drunkenness and related crimes. Most courts-martial between 1823 and 1828 stemmed from alcohol abuse, and roughly one-third of all the deaths in the service were related to drinking and its consequences. Just as in the administration of the Indian trade, efforts to control alcohol consumption in the army failed to ameliorate the problem.

Desertion rates, another critical problem, soared because of harsh conditions, poor food, and low pay. In 1825 almost half of the year's enlistees deserted, and in 1831 practically a quarter of the soldiers in the army were expected to desert. During these years the private soldier's pay amounted to six or seven dollars a month, and paymasters' visits were scandalously rare. Civilian working men of the same era, by contrast, might earn a dollar a day. Even common engagés in the fur trade received almost twice as much pay. Neither soldiers nor engagés, however, could avoid paying excessive prices for goods while serving in Indian country, for both were gouged, either at the sutler's counter or fur companies' retail stores.[2]

A major step toward building an effective western army came in June 1832. Near the end of the Black Hawk War, Major Henry Dodge took command of a rudimentary cavalry consisting of six experimental companies, about six hundred U.S. Mounted Rangers. These cavalrymen looked and acted more like militia than regulars, but their ability to move quickly over the plains impressed Congress. During the spring of 1833, President Jackson signed legislation making the rangers a permanent dragoon regiment, mustering some seven hundred cavalrymen in ten companies. In the summer of 1834, Colonel Dodge led about five hundred horse soldiers—whose ranks included numerous future military luminaries, the wandering artist George Catlin, and a few other civilians—out of Fort Gibson on a tour of the Southern Plains in hopes of awing the Comanches and Pawnees. The troopers' unfamiliarity with the plains environment, aggravated by terribly hot weather and heavy losses from a deadly fever, made their trip an unremitting nightmare. Over one hundred enlisted men perished during that summer's peaceful campaign, and so did General Henry Leavenworth, commander of the Western Division, who came out for the ride only to die at the Cross Timbers on the Canadian River. Out of this near disaster grew the U.S. cavalry that would eventually wage war on Upper Missouri Indians.[3]

Still, two more decades passed before soldiers developed the wherewithal to seriously threaten Indians or fur traders. And when they did come in force after the Civil War, it was unclear whether their job was to protect Indians from the rapidly growing number of white emigrants and farmers or the other way round. Not surprisingly, many soldiers were devoted Indian-haters; relatively few were concerned with Indians' rights or their government's guarantees of protection to Indians under federal treaties.

A direct consequence of the enlarged military presence at western forts was the thorough disruption of whatever stability in Indian-white and intertribal relations had existed under the aegis of fur traders. Indians, for their part, grew angry over numerous unfulfilled treaty promises, the steadily increasing number of unfriendly soldiers, and the threat of forced removal. When construction of transcontinental railroads brought more whites into Indian country in the 1860s, many bison were killed to feed workers, and the herds abandoned some regular grazing areas. The U.S. Army explicitly encouraged the destruction of bison and soon developed a policy aimed at total extermination.[4] The Office of Indian Affairs was for once in harmony with the generals. By the mid-1870s Secretary of the Interior Columbus Delano applauded the bison slaughter "as facilitating the policy of the Government," while General Phil Sheridan cheered Texas hide hunters for "destroying the Indian's commissary."[5]

All these factors finally precipitated a series of devastating Indian wars in the Northern Plains that did not cease until 1890. One might fairly argue, as some scholars have, that good intentions and high-minded morality motivated the orchestration of some elements of government and military Indian policy. But the historical record of the nineteenth century, no less than that of the twentieth century, supports the inescapable conclusion that in the end what mattered most were the interests and goals of white people.

In the years from 1830 to 1865 the UMO remained strong, though its ability to influence or control events waned with the passing years. Between 1835 and 1845, profits continued to outdistance losses as Chouteau & Company campaigned vigorously to consolidate its power and stifle intermittent but disruptive and determined competition in the Upper Missouri. The success of Ashley's and Henry's brigades had lured other trappers into the West, and several outfits tried to force their way into what the Company deemed its exclusive domain during the 1830s. Renewed challenges came in the early 1840s as the nation slowly recovered from the shattering effects of the Panic of 1837 and subsequent depression.

The main opposition in the 1830s came from three sources: the Rocky Mountain Fur Company (1830–34), heir to the Ashley-Henry outfit and bankrolled by Robert Campbell; William Sublette and Robert Campbell (1832–34); and P. N. Leclerc (1832–33), whose outfit has been discussed in an earlier chapter.

Robert Campbell, one of Saint Louis's wealthiest merchants and financiers, posed a continuous threat to the Company from 1832 to 1865. Campbell's fur trading career began in 1825, when he hired on as a clerk with Jedediah Smith's Ashley brigade. He soon developed a close association with Ashley and another newcomer, William Sublette.[6] Aided by Ashley's political and business connections, and Campbell's brother Hugh, a successful Philadelphia merchant who marketed furs, Sublette and Campbell were able and willing to challenge the American Fur Company and its successors.

In the autumn of 1833, Sublette and Campbell built Fort William right next to Fort Union as a calculated nuisance. The tactic was effective, and they sold out at a profit to Chouteau the following year. Fort William actually served as a bargaining chip in a larger game: the potential division of a large and profitable territory. In ensuing negotiations the two outfits came to an understanding that approximated a cartel. Campbell and Sublette would restrict their trade to the Platte River and Rocky Mountain regions, while Chouteau, speaking for Bernard Pratte & Company, promised to focus his operations in the Upper Missouri. In 1834, Sublette and Campbell built Fort Laramie (also called Fort William or Fort John) at the junction of the Laramie and North Platte Rivers, where their business flourished. Still, during several months of competition at the Yellowstone, whiskey had flowed freely while the two outfits did each other financial damage by bidding up salaries for hunters and interpreters, including the miscreant Deschamps family.[7]

After amassing a small fortune and deciding to pursue his political career, in 1826 William Ashley sold out to his former employees Jedediah Smith, David Jackson, and William Sublette. Four years later, Smith, Jackson & Sublette sold out to other veteran mountain men who created the Rocky Mountain Fur Company. In 1834 the Rocky Mountain Fur Company was in turn sold to Thomas Fitzpatrick, Lucien Fontenelle, Jean Baptiste Gervais, Jim Bridger, and Milton Sublette. Backed by Campbell's financial power, these men continued to trap and trade in the mountains, and in 1835 they purchased Fort Laramie from Campbell and Sublette. Two years later, in financial distress, the consortium of mountain men was bought out by Pratte, Chouteau, & Company.

Campbell's hand is visible in all of these opposition firms' doings. His active career as a fur trader in the Rocky Mountains ended in 1835, but he retained lifelong economic interests in the Indian and fur trades, and he competed against Chouteau for government annuity contracts as well. Important as it was, Campbell's full story remains to be told.[8]

During the 1840s more opposition firms emerged as various newcomers and veterans tried to upstage Chouteau. Challengers constructed new posts or revived abandoned posts that functioned for a year or two in the heat of competition. Most faded into disrepair and neglect when they fell under the shadow of the well-entrenched "American Fur Company," but it cost the big company plenty to dislodge its rivals.

One of the most serious threats of the 1840s came from a firm called the Union Fur Company, also known as Fox, Livingston, & Company or Ebbetts, Kelsey, & Cutting. In 1842 the newly organized outfit erected a trade house, christened Fort Mortimer, at the site of old Fort William near the mouth of the Yellowstone. The name honored one of the upstart company's principal backers, an Empire State blue blood named Mortimer Livingston, of the New York trans-Atlantic packet outfit, Fox, Livingston, & Company. During its three years in operation, Fort Mortimer remained a thorn in Chouteau's side. It introduced higher than normal degrees of strife and animosity, and both outfits blatantly flouted the law, flooding the Upper Missouri with illegal whiskey.[9]

The story of this opposition post began in 1840, when an adventurer named John A. N. Ebbetts, backed by a few Saint Louisans, came to trade in the Sioux country. His small outfit sparked no preemptive reaction from Chouteau's company. As a consequence of having been ignored, Ebbetts managed a fair trade and returned to Saint Louis with perhaps 350 packs of buffalo robes. Ebbetts's favorable showing prompted him to seek heavier financing to strengthen his hand against Chouteau. In July 1842 a new opposition firm came to the Upper Missouri, styled Ebbetts, Kelsey, & Cutting. Ebbetts had somehow convinced Fox, Livingston, & Company that profits came easily in the fur country. The New Yorkers took the bait and sank more than ten thousand dollars into the venture, perhaps encouraged by a kinsman, Fulton Cutting, who was to serve as a field manager. Charles Kelsey, the third field man, went up the river chiefly to safeguard his investment of close to twenty thousand dollars, most of which he would lose.[10] By the summer of 1842, Fort Mortimer was in operation. Despite name changes by subsequent owners or operators since 1834, local residents habitually referred to the post as "Fort William," or "Old Fort William." Like its predecessor, Fort Mortimer was built of timber and adobes, so Fort Union's employees called their new competitors "'dobies."

Kelsey soon realized that Ebbetts had overstated the ease with which the "American Fur Company" might be outdone. Charles Larpenteur observed that when Kelsey "saw Fort Union in its full splendor, he could not refrain from remarking to Mr. Culbertson, 'Had I known how the American Fur Company were situated, I would have kept clear of investing in this opposition. . . . I hope you will not be too hard on us.'"[11]

Several writers, including Charles Larpenteur, John Audubon, and his associate Edward Harris, described conditions at the post and how it affected Fort Union's trade. Larpenteur reported that in the spring of 1842, Pierre Chouteau, Jr., came to Fort Union with the distressing news that "a strong Opposition had arrived; the firm was Fox, Livingston, and Co. of New York. . . . This news I did not relish; for opposition is necessarily a great nuisance."[12]

On July 1, 1843, Audubon accompanied Fort Union's bourgeois, Alexander Culbertson, armed with a spy-glass, to nearby Pilot Knob to examine from a discrete distance the sorry state of affairs at Fort Mortimer.

Audubon observed "all the people encamped two hundred yards from the river, as they had been obliged to move from the tumbling fort during the rain of last night." Edward Harris got a closer look at the squalid fort on July 2. An amateur physician, Harris treated the ailing post factor, a Kentuckian named John Collins, who had "not a particle of medicine of any kind in the Fort, not even a dose of salts." Harris found Collins lying in the blazing sun under a ragged skin shelter, apparently outside the fort, which "having again been encroached upon by the river they were obliged to abandon it the night before." The young doctor administered calomel, "salts," some quinine, and "an emetic" to Collins, who was apparently suffering more from malnutrition than anything else.[13]

On July 5, when Harris again visited Collins at the "shanty of a fort," he observed that its inhabitants' food stores were depleted and that they depended "entirely on their hunters for their means of supporting life." By July 8, Audubon found Fort Mortimer's crew no better off: "Mr. Collins is yet poorly, their hunters have not yet returned, and they are destitute of everything, not having even a medicine chest. We told him to send a man back with us, which he did, and we sent him some medicine, rice, and two bottles of claret." A few days later, on July 13, John Collins "sent a man over to ask for some flour, which Mr. Culbertson sent him. They are there in the utmost state of destitution, almost of starvation, awaiting the arrival of their hunters like so many famished Wolves."[14]

Edward Harris concluded that "the success of this opposition to the old Fur company appears to be very doubtful."[15] His prediction of the greenhorns' chances for profits was accurate. Fur prices were already low in 1843, and competition would likely drive profits down as well. Pierre Chouteau, Jr., & Company, determined to rid themselves of "nuisance" outfits like Fox, Livingston, & Company, prepared for a clash. Whiskey constituted the leading trade article among the opposition men. The irresponsible newcomers' trade tactics jeopardized the volatile equilibrium that marked the Indian trade in the 1840s. Chouteau's company never shrank from the use of ardent spirits, but in the absence of unbridled competition right at their back door they probably would have dispensed liquor with greater caution.

Hiram Martin Chittenden credited "the firm of Fox, Livingston, and Company, also called the Union Fur Company . . . [as] the most powerful opposition with which the Upper Missouri Outfit ever had to deal excepting only that of Sublette and Campbell ten years before."[16] The Union Fur Company may indeed have enjoyed the financial support of powerful eastern capitalists, but the outfit's field operations were carried out by a band of feckless incompetents. Aimless swings of stinginess and liberality marked their day-to-day business, and their wanton use of alcohol bespoke plain foolhardiness, shortsightedness, or both. Every experienced fur trader knew and feared the effects of a too-liberal dispensation of liquor to Indians, no matter how friendly. Humanitarian motivations aside, simple self-interest dictated that drunken men—Indian or white— were dangerously unpredictable. More importantly, profits might plunge, since little hunting or trapping was done while the liquor flowed.

Some of the firm's difficulties grew out of their recruitment of disreputable employees. In August 1843, making an extremely late departure from Saint Louis, Fulton Cutting boarded the Union Fur Company's steamer *New Haven*, freighted with sixty tons of goods and provisions to supply forts Mortimer and George. When he finally reached the pays d'en haut, Cutting was dismayed to find that his employees had subsisted during the spring and summer mainly by filching vegetables from Fort Union's garden. John Audubon noted in June that the fields at Garden Coulee, about two miles downriver from Fort Union, had been abandoned as a result of incessant pilfering by hungry and shiftless Union Fur Company engagés from Fort Mortimer.[17]

Larpenteur smugly referred to the newcomers as "green cotton." Not a man to overlook an opportunity to make a bad pun, Larpenteur used the name "Cotton" to poke fun at Fulton Cutting while he was at Fort Mortimer. Eventually, as Larpenteur notes in an oft-repeated tale, "the green cotton commenced to dry." Cutting offered L'Ours Fou (the Crazy Bear), a noted Assiniboine leader, lavish gifts of whiskey and a chief's military outfit. This largesse was intended to erode L'Ours Fou's wonted allegiance to the traders at Fort Union. After accepting Cutting's valuable presents, L'Ours Fou visited Fort Union. There, in a dramatic public display of scorn, he heaved the regalia into the dust and pledged his continued good will to Alexander Culbertson and the UMO.[18]

Nevertheless, Chouteau's company responded to the presence of competitors in the area by stepping up its trade activities and selling more whiskey during the bitterly cold winter of 1843–44. Federal law prohibited traders from entering Indian villages to do business, but the UMO discovered ways around this problem. Late in January, in order to head off the competition's trade, Larpenteur traveled northeast to Woody Mountain with a cargo consisting mostly of five gallons of alcohol. During a several-day spree, Larpenteur happily traded 220 robes for whiskey and just 30 robes for other goods. This provides a stark commentary on the unsavory but expedient, and very profitable, role of liquor in the fur trade.[19]

Even when it came to using raucous entertainment to boost trade, the unimaginative (or untalented) opposition could not match the big company's efforts. During the winter of 1844–45, Fort Union posted scouts to watch for the approach of potential customers, who were free to set up their camps and trade wherever they pleased. When Indians were spotted, Fort Union's traders hastily dispatched a welcoming committee equipped with flags, whiskey, and music. As Larpenteur wrote, "It was almost impossible for Indians to refuse such an invitation. . . . Mr. Cotton found himself about as badly used up this winter as he had been last; he learned that he stood a poor show in opposing the American Fur Company, and that it would take Mr. Ebbitt, or any other man, a long time to get a footing in the country."[20] Despite Larpenteur's dour pronouncement, it seems that the Union Fur Company shipped about 1,150 packs of robes and furs to Saint Louis, a respectable showing in view of the UMO's harvest of 1,270 packs.[21]

By June 1844 the beleaguered opposition men pulled out all the stops they could. One tactic, apparently, was to offer constant encouragement to Chouteau company engagés to desert. Indeed, it seems that at least twenty-two Chouteau men did desert that spring, and more were prepared to follow. "Desertions continued," Larpenteur wrote, "until I was left with but four men all told. . . . Having so few men with me, the Opposition men became very troublesome; so much so that I had to lock the door on them." There was also grumbling about opposition men's having stolen a scow belonging to Fort Union, stealing wood cached previously by UMO steamer crews, and committing other deliberate insults.[22]

Their last-ditch efforts were unavailing, and the roguish traders at Fort Mortimer finally threw in the towel. In May 1845 the Union Fur Company sold all its goods and materials to the UMO.[23] But when Ebbetts and

Cutting retired from their rude hovel at the confluence of the Yellowstone and the Missouri, they left behind over fifty unemployed frontier vagabonds who doubtless continued to irritate people at Fort Union. In short order the wooden wreckage of Fort Mortimer fired the boilers of a Chouteau company chartered steamer, the *General Brooke*, and soon the post had all but disappeared. By 1863, little remained of Fort Mortimer except a chimney or two and a few crumbling adobe walls.

Larpenteur's post-mortem appraisal of the fledgling opposition reveals the arrogance of the upriver region's dominant outfit: "This [1845–46] winter's trade convinced the New York firm of Fox, Livingston and Co. that it was a losing game to oppose the American Fur Company; they came to the conclusion to sell out, and we were again left masters of the country."[24]

What was the significance of Fort Mortimer, and opposition outfits in general, in the story of the western fur trade? Posts like Fort Mortimer represented the extension of venture capital channeled to the developing West during an era of generally vibrant economic growth for the United States. Under the aegis of experienced traders such as Pierre Chouteau, Jr., and his associates, trade houses might flourish for years, earning their backers a fair margin of profit. But when investors such as Livingston and Cutting placed their money at risk in the fur trade, they were likely to lose it. In part, they were crippled by their own inadequate knowledge of the western frontier business climate. Having themselves no practical experience with—and no real interest in—Indians, they unwisely placed their money at the disposal of poorly organized and inept field men. In addition, Fort Mortimer and other opposition posts illustrate some of the liabilities inherent in the United States' poorly defined, constructed, and executed policies dealing with Indians and the western fur trade. Despite federal efforts to control the train of events that would necessarily accompany a westward business expansion, the entrepreneurial activities of American citizens remained largely ungovernable, which created disturbances in the Upper Missouri country. Finally, it should be evident by this point that Chouteau failed to secure an actual monopoly in the Upper Missouri.

In 1846 the Company brought better than four thousand packs of robes and furs, nearly half of which came from Fort Union, down the

Missouri in mackinaw boats and on steamers. The new President, James K. Polk, was a Democrat, and generally Democrats were kind to the Company. But Chouteau expected things in Washington would "go about right whichever side" claimed victory. Nevertheless, 1845 had been a difficult year for Chouteau's Missouri River outfits. An extremely cold winter had driven bison far to the east, and beaver fur prices had declined at London. More trouble came when a fire in New York left Chouteau's office at No. 40 Broadway in ashes, destroying many important records and temporarily bringing his business there to a standstill. Nevertheless, the Company stood in a position of considerable strength, having eliminated a serious competitor. In a final slap at Chouteau, Fulton Cutting charged that Andrew Drips (the special agent commissioned to end the whiskey trade) was merely a stooge who allowed the "American Fur Company" to use liquor, but no one paid attention.[25] The demise of Fort Mortimer, however, did not bring an end to opposition. Another outfit whose financiers (Robert Campbell among them) and field operatives were all fur trade veterans mounted a new assault in 1846.

The new competition, Harvey, Primeau & Company, was formed in July 1846 with capital initially amounting to less than sixteen thousand dollars. One of its principal men, Alexander Harvey, had been on the Missouri since about 1831 and knew the business well. But Harvey's explosive personality made him something of a pariah, even among the rough Upper Missouri crowd. He had murdered a "Spaniard" named Isador Sandoval at Fort Union in 1841, probably for revenge. Sandoval was one of several engagés whose complaints about Harvey's belligerent behavior brought about his temporary dismissal in 1839.[26]

Harvey also had been a principal actor in one of the ugliest incidents ever to occur at the Blackfeet post, Fort McKenzie. During the winter of 1843–44, according to the British-Canadian artist Paul Kane, a Blackfeet warrior of the Blood band named Big Snake sought a "free admission to one of the American forts near the Rocky Mountains." Upon his arrival, anticipating a congenial welcome, Big Snake found the gate "shut rudely in his face by the orders of the commander." Deeply insulted, as Big Snake rode off he vented his anger by killing thirteen of the fort's cattle. This brought the fur traders rushing out of the fort to retaliate. In the ensuing scuffle, Big Snake killed a black slave named Reese, tore off his scalp, and "waved it in derision toward the Americans." The dead slave belonged to Francis Chardon, a veteran trader but a notorious alcoholic. In a vengeful mood, Chardon persuaded Harvey to help him even the score the next time any Blackfeet showed up at the fort. Chardon got his opportunity when some Piegans arrived to trade on February 19, 1844. Following their plan, Harvey touched off a small cannon loaded with musket balls, killing perhaps a dozen and disabling several others, mostly women and children. (On Harvey's first attempt, the cannon had misfired, allowing most of the male warriors to leap out of harm's way.) Chardon shot at least one Piegan with a rifle. Then, according to legend, he and Harvey finished off the wounded and later danced over the scalps of the slain inside their fort.[27]

The Blackfeet thereafter shunned Fort McKenzie, and its profitability vanished. Chardon soon abandoned and burned down the tainted fort. When spring came, he built a new post, named Fort F. A. Chardon after himself, at the mouth of the Judith River. Still angry and aggrieved, the Blackfeet refused to trade. Chardon's career in the Upper Missouri was essentially finished, and he was banished from Blackfeet land. Pierre Chouteau, Jr., dispatched Alexander Culbertson and Kenneth McKenzie up the Missouri to straighten out the mess and restore the Blackfeet trade. This was why Fort Lewis, later moved downstream and rechristened Fort Benton, was established in 1847 as the main Blackfeet post. McKenzie helped to set things right, but four years later he sued Chouteau and his partners for failing to compensate him for his "great inconvenience, & loss to his private affairs, & sacrifice of personal ease."[28]

Harvey left the upriver country for a spell, but not before three of the many enemies he had made during his years as an Upper Missouri bully attempted to settle their grudge against him. James Lee, Jacob Berger, and Malcolm Clark severely beat Harvey near Fort Chardon, where he subsequently sought shelter. Culbertson, hoping to be rid of a troublemaker, paid him off, and Harvey went down the Missouri nursing his bruises and swearing revenge. At Saint Louis, Alexander Harvey told his tale to U.S. District Attorney Thomas Gantt. In April 1846, Gantt delivered indictments against Lee, Berger, and Clark, who were ordered out of the Indian country. Francis Chardon, too, was to be permanently exiled when his embittered former partner in crime, Harvey, accused him of selling liquor to Indians. In the end, no witnesses came down the Missouri to testify on Harvey's behalf, and the assault case against his three enemies was abandoned in April 1847.[29]

Harvey's charges of liquor selling proved more aggravating to the Company. In 1848, District Attorney Gantt placed in suit several bonds covering the years 1842 to 1845 and indicted the Company's partners (Chouteau, McKenzie, Benjamin Clapp, Sylvestre Labadie, John B. Sarpy, and Joshua Brant) for violating the trade and intercourse acts. In addition, he sued the upriver agents (Chardon, Culbertson, Kipp, and Honoré Picotte) and steamer captain Joseph Sire for eight hundred dollars apiece. Altogether, Gantt called for punitive damages amounting to nearly thirty thousand dollars.

By December 1848, Chouteau had hired most of the material witnesses and sent them to the Upper Missouri, safely distant from the courtroom. Moreover, old Francis Chardon had conveniently died at Fort Berthold during the spring of 1848. This happy coincidence enabled Pierre Chouteau, Jr., to inform Commissioner of Indian Affairs William Medill in December 1848 that "One of the persons most obnoxious [that is, Chardon] has within the last year died. . . . The other persons, who were also obnoxious, have been dismissed from our employ, and now are we believe out of the Indian country." Chouteau then went on to assure Medill that "the liquor trade has now no existence in the Indian country."[30]

A month later, Chouteau turned the full power of his persuasive charm toward Indian superintendent T. H. Harvey (no relation to Alexander) and attorney Gantt. Restating his confident opinion that the liquor trade had been stifled, Chouteau wrote that the Indian trade would be "more pleasantly carried on, and more profitable," without liquor. He also intoned, in a pointed reminder, "We have now under various names been engaged in this trade for upwards of forty years . . . we have at all times afforded to the Government all the aid and assistance in our power. . . . We can say without arrogance, that we have been for many years the right arm of the government in the Upper Missouri."[31]

He was right; the government did depend on the Company to transport and warehouse Indian annuity goods as well as to transport, house, and support Indian agents. The liquor case dragged on for several months, but as usual the federal government found it hard to beat Chouteau. In the end, perhaps in a tacit admission of government reliance on the big company, Gantt agreed to a compromise. Chouteau & Company paid five thousand dollars in fines and about two thousand dollars in court costs to get out of the legal scrape, but the Office of Indian Affairs approved its trade licenses for the coming year.[32]

Alexander Harvey had done his best to cripple the Company with lawsuits. At the same time, he competed for its trade. Harvey, Primeau & Company included experienced traders and had the financial backing of Chouteau's leading adversary, Robert Campbell. This was a powerful combination, and the new company was a success. In 1848, Harvey, Primeau & Company shipped over eight thousand buffalo robes to Saint Louis. During 1849 and 1850, Campbell provided them a steamboat, the *Tamerlane*, and brokered roughly seven thousand buffalo robes worth better than twenty thousand dollars. Campbell's arrangements with Harvey, Primeau & Company continued until at least 1855, with Campbell taking a 2 ½ percent commission on sales and with additional capital coming from several leading Saint Louis merchants, such as Thomas H. Larkin, and members of the Barada and Chambers families.[33] This opposition company was tenacious and challenged Chouteau for seven years. But when Harvey died in July 1854, the concern lost its driving force. One of the partners, Joseph Picotte (nephew of Chouteau company man Honoré Picotte) continued the opposition for two years in a desultory fashion, backed as usual by Campbell.[34]

In 1857, Picotte gave up the fight, but Campbell persuaded him to advise yet another opposition, styled Frost, Todd & Company, which continued to compete with Chouteau's outfits. Within two years, Frost, Todd & Company turned their attention toward land speculation and politics in what would soon become Dakota Territory. So by 1859, after decades of fending off one opposition after another, the Company was again left in temporary control of the upper river trade.[35] Chouteau's company, its extensive organization aided by pliant governmental tools, continued for the moment to play the leading role in Upper Missouri affairs.

Successful steamboat captains such as Joseph and John B. La Barge sometimes worked for Pierre Chouteau, Jr., & Company, and sometimes competed for the carrying trade. In 1856, after years of association with

Chouteau, Joseph La Barge left the outfit under a cloud of controversy. La Barge had apparently intervened to prevent a company man from raping or otherwise insulting the wife of a "clerk," who seems to have been Charles Chouteau. La Barge said the assault was made by the bourgeois at Fort Clark, but he refused to discuss the matter with Chouteau and terminated his association with the Company. In 1861, La Barge and his two steamboats (the *Shreveport* and the *Emilie*) became the foundation for an opposition firm called La Barge, Harkness & Company. The next year the *Emilie* found itself in a race to Fort Benton with the Company vessel *Spread Eagle*. Rivalry was so fierce that the captain of the *Spread Eagle* rammed the *Emilie* and almost started a shooting war. When La Barge returned to Saint Louis, he preferred charges against Captain Bailey of the *Spread Eagle*. In the end, Bailey lost his license, but, strangely enough, La Barge helped him get it reinstated just one month later.[36]

In the meantime, developments were afoot in the Upper Mississippi region that would profoundly affect the UMO and Chouteau's future. Beginning with Zebulon M. Pike's expedition of 1804–1806, Americans began to assert their presumed sovereignty in the region, hitherto clearly under the thumb of the Montréal-based North West Company. Pike's men shot a British flag from atop its pole at the Nor'Westers' Leech Lake trading post on February 10, 1806, serving symbolic notice that the tilt of imperialism would ultimately shift toward the United States.[37] National muscle flexed slowly, but within two decades American power was firmly established in what became the state of Minnesota.

John C. Calhoun, while secretary of war in James Madison's administration, had envisioned a great chain of forts extending across the northern frontier and along the Mississippi and Missouri Rivers to offset British influence, protect American citizens, and awe the Indians into peaceful submission. Following the War of 1812, military forts were established at Mackinac, Detroit, Green Bay, Rock Island, Chicago, and Prairie du Chien. The first forts on the new western "permanent Indian frontier" included Fort Smith (1817–33) at the confluence of the Poteau and Arkansas Rivers, Fort Atkinson (1819–27) on the Missouri near Council Bluffs (Bellevue), and Fort Snelling (1820–57) at the confluence of the Mississippi and Minnesota Rivers where Saint Paul, Minnesota, now stands.

Fort Snelling, located within lands claimed by eastern Sioux and Chippewas, played an important role in the administration of treaties and in protecting and extending the fur trade. Of still greater significance, the establishment of Fort Snelling inaugurated the development of a new axis of military, economic, and political power along east-west lines, one that would ultimately eclipse the older north-south axis emanating from Saint Louis. This new orientation would affect the fur trade as well as military affairs. But Calhoun's proposed military fort at the Yellowstone did not materialize until 1866 (Fort Buford); consequently, Fort Snelling's sphere of influence extended all the way to the Upper Missouri and Fort Union.[38]

Fort Snelling's construction was but one of several factors that made the Minnesota territory the eastern terminal of the new east-west axis that reached far into the Northern Plains. There was also the large settlement of buffalo hunters on the Red River of the North at Pembina. Families within that population included French-speaking mixed-bloods, retired veterans of the North West Company, and Orkney Islanders who were former employees of the Hudson's Bay Company. The métis settlement, as surveyed by army engineer Major Stephen H. Long in 1823, lay within U.S. territory just south of the forty-ninth parallel of latitude, but Pembina retained close connections with the HBC.[39]

Hunters and traders at Pembina annually collected hundreds of packs of furs and robes, and they provided immense quantities of an essential food—pemmican—to the HBC, which distributed the meat to its posts throughout Rupert's Land. Beginning in the 1830s, however, relations between the Company and the community began to break down, as the Red River people clamored for free trade. This was a serious blow to the HBC's Canadian hegemony, but the Company suffered even more when Red River men, who formerly comprised the labor force necessary to move goods and furs between York Factory and Red River, initiated cart roads to Minnesota and started marketing their own furs and robes.

The Red River colonists' trade helped nurture an American settlement in the vicinity of Fort Snelling, where half a dozen "Red River trails" terminated. This settlement eventually became known as Saint Paul. A few miles to the southeast, Ramsay Crooks' AFCo had in 1834 set up its first post at New Hope (later renamed Mendota), where trader Henry

H. Sibley prospered and in time built a grand stone house. No lands in the territory were legally open to white men until 1837, but soon thereafter settlement began in good earnest. In 1840 perhaps 700 whites lived in the region, including the garrison of Fort Snelling. By 1849 there were about 4,000, of whom more than 900 lived at Saint Paul. When Minnesota achieved statehood a decade later, it boasted better than 150,000 residents.[40]

Between 1855 and 1863, trade with Red River métis brought almost $1,500,000 into Saint Paul (about 80 percent of its total fur trade), placing it just behind Saint Louis as the leading western fur trade collection point. As many as fifteen hundred Red River carts camped outside the town each summer for weeks at a time, selling their peltry before they headed back north to Pembina or other settlements. In later years, after the robe trade had been exhausted, Red River wheat and other grains continued to flow to the booming twin cities of Minneapolis and Saint Paul.[41]

The old river route from Fort Garry to York Factory had two major flaws, low carrying capacity and high costs, that drove it into extinction. Shipping robes hundreds of miles from Pembina to York Factory had always been expensive, and when the alternative market at Saint Paul appeared, the Red River traders chose to deal with American firms. Despite the French-speaking métis' occasional complaints that American traders charged high prices for inferior goods and that residents of Saint Paul were less civilized than themselves, the Red River traders developed powerful economic attachments to the American side of the border.[42] With nearly six thousand Pembina residents by 1849, that community's trade helped solidify connections from the Minnesota country eastward to the Great Lakes and to New York.

Meanwhile, steamboat traffic on the Upper Mississippi increased dramatically, with hundreds of vessels plying the Mississippi and Minnesota Rivers by the mid-1850s. In addition, the national railroad frenzy of the 1850s and 1860s pushed tracks into Minnesota, further strengthening economic ties with the East and providing new routes for soldiers to go west as well. Railroad tracks first reached the Mississippi River in 1854 at Rock Island, Illinois; two years later a huge wooden bridge spanned the great river, linking the Chicago, Rock Island, and Pacific Railroad to Davenport, Iowa. By 1856 goods could be moved by rail to the Mississippi, loaded onto steamers bound for Saint Paul, and carried to the Red River district in carts. Two years later, the HBC itself imported goods by way of Saint Paul, and by the late 1860s the York Factory route was virtually abandoned.[43]

Competition with Pierre Chouteau, Jr., did not arise solely from other traders. In a very real sense, Chouteau and the UMO found themselves competing more and more with politicians, the army, and the federal government in general. Tradition holds that in the 1860s Chouteau's company was in league with the Democrats, which is to say, Confederates, and this explains why he was denied a license in 1865. Democrats were not the only politicians who catered to fur traders, but it is worth recalling that between 1800 and 1860 the nation elected only two presidents (Harrison and Taylor, both one-term Whigs) who did not profess membership in a "Democratic" party.

True, Senator Thomas Hart Benton, the Gibraltar of Jacksonian Democrats, was generally friendly to the fur men, since they advanced his plans for the conquest of the West and access to the China Trade. It is also true that in 1842, Pierre Chouteau, Jr., had advanced Benton at least a thousand dollars that enabled the senator to purchase a house at Washington, D.C. Several years passed before Benton was able to repay the loan, and Chouteau obligingly carried three long-term notes, so the senator had good reason to grease governmental wheels on behalf of certain Missouri fur traders. By 1846, Benton saw to it that Chouteau would be a beneficiary when the government assumed liability for outstanding claims against Spain and Mexico that predated the war then in progress with the latter nation. Among the largest was that of the ill-fated Auguste P. Chouteau–Jules DeMun trading party, arrested by Spanish soldiers in 1817, which claimed to have lost about thirty thousand dollars on a premature venture to Santa Fe.[44]

One of Benton's political rivals in Saint Louis was "General" William H. Ashley, U.S. congressman and one-term lieutenant governor of Missouri. After his own fur trade successes during the 1820s, some of his protégés tried their luck in the Upper Missouri business. Ashley maintained especially close commercial connections for many years with two former employees, Robert Campbell and William Sublette. Ashley was clearly serving his own business arrangements with Sublette and Campbell when, in a surprise move, he refused to help Astor, Chouteau, and others defeat the 1832 bill that would ban the importation of whiskey into Indian country. Couching his support of the measure in terms that decried monopolies, and dodging the argument that Hudson's Bay men would have liquor whether or not the Americans were allowed any, Ashley masked his real intention. His hope and expectation was that, after the bill became law, his friends would readily defeat federal authority by simply hauling their kegs overland past the riverside inspection points, while the large company's steamboats would undergo regular, rigorous searches. Ashley used his political influence and his reputation as an "expert" on the trade to raise official as well as popular opprobrium against the "American Fur Company" in 1832.[45] As a political defense, Ashley cast himself as an independent Jacksonian. He had often voted contrary to orthodox Democratic doctrine. The National Bank, currency and banking in general, the tariff, land sales—all were issues on which the administration held positions, but at the local level orthodoxy sometimes fractured.

In Saint Louis, factional divisions among competing fur traders shaped local politics as well as Missouri's relationship with the national government. Congressman Ashley's support of the 1832 bill to create the Department of Indian Affairs and to ban alcohol happened to square with the Jackson administration's view, but it more clearly reflected his focus on local economic interests. Thenceforth, Pierre Chouteau and his associates, including John Sanford, John and William Astor, Ramsay Crooks, and Joshua Pilcher, all considered Ashley "a bold adversary" whose guiding stars were his own and Sublette's bank accounts. By 1837, shortly before he died, Ashley was finally forced out of the closet as a Whig, but his political enemies had so labeled him for years.[46] If Ashley used politics to make money, so did many others, including some of the most highly ranked officers within the Indian Department that he helped to create.

Several commissioners of Indian affairs are known to have been crooked or, at the very least, ardently self-serving. Federal appointees, most of whom worked within the executive branch, were tacitly expected to pad their nests while they did the nation's business. The executive department, from the days of Andrew Jackson to those of Benjamin Harrison, tended to view management of the Indian Department as little more than a sinecure for staunch supporters, a choice plum for patronage seekers. Consequently, several commissioners served brief terms in office while waiting for sweeter fruits. Few indeed actually accomplished much in the way of reformulating a badly managed system, and it seems there was a dearth of interest in sincere reform. If the top men in the Indian office behaved in such a manner, it should be no surprise that their underlings often strayed far from the path of strict propriety. It was these men, commissioners of Indian affairs, agents, and subagents—almost all with potent connections to land speculators, sutlers, and government contractors—who constituted a little recognized but genuine challenge to Chouteau's profits and influence in the Upper Missouri country.

Contemporaries of Elbert Herring, the commissioner of Indian affairs from 1831 to 1837, considered him incompetent, though not necessarily dishonest. In actuality, his dedication to President Jackson's Indian removal program persuaded him to employ bribery in land deals, meddle in tribal affairs by refusing to pay annuities, and create fraudulent individual "chiefs" whose "signatures" on treaties bound entire nations to move west.[47] And it was Herring who stood at the helm of the Office of Indian Affairs when McKenzie's distillery at Fort Union caused such an uproar and Herring who consented to the back-room deal that closed the case.

Herring's successor was a Tennessean named Carey Allen Harris, who served from 1836 to 1838. Another Jackson appointee, Harris was a shameless scoundrel bereft of ethical anxieties. Commissioner Harris took a bribe in the form of a "partnership" with other Southerners who speculated in Creek Indian lands that were to be vacated by removals, and he was also implicated in sleazy dealings with contractors who provided annuity goods to Indians in the Old Northwest. All in all, Harris's tenure is memorable for blatant graft and corruption and gross insensitivity to the people whose welfare he was bound by oath to oversee. President Martin Van Buren fired Harris in 1838, replacing him with a Pennsylvanian, Thomas Hartley Crawford, who served until 1845, but charges of corruption in the Indian Department clung to the Democrats for years to come.[48]

William Medill, another Democratic appointee with no experience in Indian affairs, served from 1845 to 1849. His "reform" program—

predicated on the notion that Indians possessed no worthwhile characteristics in their aboriginal state—was highly ethnocentric, but to his
credit he took his job seriously and looked into ways to decrease the
whiskey trade. Medill encountered stiff opposition from traders when he
tried to alter the intercourse laws to prevent cash from being channeled
directly from government annuity funds to traders who claimed that
Indian tribes owed them debts. This was, on the one hand, a direct attack
on a traditional aspect of the Indian trade; many of these debts grew out
of Indian hunters' requests that fur companies advance them credit to
acquire equipment and ammunition for the coming winter hunt. On the
other hand, it was a system open to fraud and abuse, especially evident
in the careers of G. W. and W. G. Ewing. These traders operated in the
Old Northwest and in the Kansas-Nebraska area, and were well known
for their eagerness to swindle the government and Indians alike. The
Ewing brothers argued that Medill's reform efforts were purely politically
motivated and that he was out to ruin Whiggish traders.[49]

James W. Denver, who served intermittently from 1857 to 1859, was
another commissioner who speculated in Indian lands, who was not
above falsifying documents pertaining to land sales, and who considered
fostering intertribal warfare as a method of reducing Mormon influence
over Indians in Utah Territory. His successor, Alfred B. Greenwood,
worked in the Buchanan administration. Greenwood's overt Southern
sympathies helped amplify the popular impression that the Indian Department was firmly in the hands of anti-Union "dough-faces."[50]

Not only were some commissioners eager to get rich while they directed
Indian affairs, but they also sought to undermine the influence that fur
traders developed through years of close association with Indians. In this
respect, "competition" within the fur and Indian trades also involved
power struggles between the government and traders at a time of rapid
national expansion toward the Pacific Ocean. Politics and economics
make natural bedfellows, but it seems clear that most fur traders, and
certainly Pierre Chouteau, Jr., understood that a too-close alignment with
one or another political party could easily become a liability rather than
an advantage.

Political lines drawn in Minnesota Territory also had much to do
with subsequent changes in the Northern Plains fur trade and would

greatly influence affairs at Fort Union. One of the early Minnesota political kingpins was Henry H. Sibley. Sibley's longtime association with Astor and Crooks's AFCo made him wealthy, but also tied him closely to the Democratic party and its customary association with the fur interests in territorial affairs. In Minnesota's elections of 1850, Sibley won the delegate's seat in Congress and Democrats filled most other territorial positions.

In 1856, however, an ideological earthquake dramatically altered the political climate within territorial Minnesota and throughout the nation. Fault lines emerged in the wake of congressional approval of the Kansas-Nebraska Act on May 22, 1854, and a few months later Minnesota almost became the birthplace of the Republican party. As July opened, anti-slavery politicians convened at Saint Anthony with the aim of launching a new party, but its members stopped short, appointing a committee to reconsider the issue. Days later, on July 6, a convention at Jackson, Michigan, officially brought the Republican party into existence.

Several thousand Free Soilers soon gathered in Minnesota Territory, and the balance of power rapidly shifted in favor of the new abolitionist party. By 1857 the Whig party had vanished, leaving the old-time fur interests standing squarely behind the Democrats and Stephen A. Douglas. After achieving statehood in 1858, Minnesota remained strongly Republican and waited with the rest of the nation to see if the union would hold. During the 1860 presidential campaign, Carl Shurz and New York's governor William Seward, both heavyweight Republican fire-brands, stumped in the new state; Lincoln outpolled Douglas by a margin of two to one. Such staunch support for Lincoln meant that Minnesota could look forward to certain rewards, despite the onset of civil war. Sure enough, Minnesota became a fertile field for Republican patronage, and the old Democratic fur men were left in permanently bad odor. It was this new political alignment in Minnesota that ultimately proved fatal to Pierre Chouteau's fur business. Many Republicans viewed Chouteau and his Saint Louis kin with deep suspicion as potential, or actual, Confederate sympathizers. It mattered not that some outfits, even one operating out of Minnesota, were proven to be far less scrupulous than Chouteau & Company. In the final outcome, the truth or falsity of these allegations and rumors was immaterial.[51]

But in the interim, Fort Union and the UMO maintained considerable control over Upper Missouri affairs. During the 1850s Chouteau & Company continued to win government contracts for freighting tribal annuities to the Upper Missouri and elsewhere, though some competitors began to make inroads on this privilege. Upper Missouri agency Indian goods were regularly stored at Fort Union until distribution, and most Indian agents stayed at Fort Union when visiting their charges.

Opposition was just one element among several that complicated affairs on the Missouri River between 1850 and 1860. Steamer traffic mushroomed in that decade. In 1858 more than three hundred steamboats arrived at Leavenworth, Kansas. Many steamers also docked at Sioux City, Iowa, a rapidly emerging commercial center in the late 1850s. In 1860 two Chouteau Company steamers, the *Chippewa* and the *Key West*, breasted the muddy current all the way to Fort Benton, an adobe post some three hundred miles above Fort Union.[52] Western emigration was still in full swing, particularly after passage of the Kansas-Nebraska Act, and Indians were losing patience with the Great Father and his empty promises as throngs of overlanders crept along the congested trails.

Exacerbating matters further, highly publicized gold discoveries in Idaho (1862) and Montana (1863) ignited a frenzied rush that compounded steamer traffic, brought in thousands of new men, and hastened the end of the old fur trading posts and their way of life. Only six steamboats had arrived at Fort Benton before 1864, but between 1866 and 1867 the number reached seventy. For a spell a traveler might count thirty or more on the river between Benton and the mouth of the Yellowstone. In 1865 "1000 passengers, 6000 tons of merchandise, and 20 quartz mills went to Fort Benton." The following year a single vessel among many, the *Luella*, steamed downriver carrying Montana gold dust valued at $1,250,000.[53]

Among other things, these gold discoveries led directly to the opening of the Bozeman Trail, Red Cloud's War, and the end of native sovereignty in the West. The Fort Laramie Treaty of 1868 constituted the federal government's final effort to head off a major war by placing the tribes on reservations, and within a few more years the Northern Plains would become the scene for many bloody confrontations between soldiers and Indians. Impressive success at the gold diggings also meant that Fort

Benton eventually usurped Fort Union's role as the Upper Missouri's leading post. Benton became the main outfitting place for prospectors and emigrants, while the economic importance of the Indian trade declined. Of significance also is that the Missouri no longer was the only way to get to Montana. Many gold seekers arrived at Fort Benton from alternate routes originating at Saint Paul, Minnesota, which by 1860 had become "the logical gateway to the northern plains." Even the HBC in 1859 began to import goods for central Canadian posts by way of Chicago and Saint Paul rather than by the old route through Hudson's Bay itself.[54] The Upper Missouri region was no longer safe from the pressures of an expansive and rapidly modernizing American Republic. The UMO, it should be clear, never achieved a genuine monopoly in the Upper Missouri region. As times changed, however, the fur traders lost ground economically, politically, and institutionally, not only to entrepreneurial competitors, but to the national government as well. Fort Union's days were now numbered.

CHAPTER SIX

The Decline of Fort Union

In the early 1860s momentous disruptions began to shatter the old world of fur traders and the much older world of Indians on the Upper Missouri. After the Civil War the apocalyptic transformation rapidly accelerated. Advancing frontiers and the rise of new states, the growth of western mining and emigration, white encroachment on Indian lands, and increased military presence all created stresses in the trade. The most prominent factor in the Upper Missouri by 1866, however, was the U.S. Army, and it had grown stronger since the 1851 Fort Laramie Treaty.

Indian-white relations in the Upper Missouri began to disintegrate several years before August 1854, when an unlikely event precipitated the first bloody clash in a thirty-year-long war for the Northern Plains. The Sioux Wars began at a Brulé Sioux camp near Fort Laramie. A hungry Indian killed a stray cow while waiting for the late arrival of annuity goods promised after the Fort Laramie Treaty negotiations. The cow killer was High Forehead, a Miniconjou visiting Brulé relatives. The cow's owner, a passing Mormon emigrant, complained to the soldiers. Then a hot-headed twenty-four-year-old West Pointer, Brevet Second Lieutenant John L. Grattan, with twenty-nine volunteers, two field pieces, and a drunken interpreter named Lucien Auguste, blustered into the Brulé camp demanding immediate delivery of the offender. When no one stepped forward, Grattan decided he could lick the Sioux nation with a handful of infantry troops.

The Brulé leader, Conquering Bear, offered horses in compensation for the cow, but the soldiers ignored him while their interpreter insulted the Sioux. As other Indians arrived from the many lodges nearby, tense Brulés squared off with belligerent soldiers. The troopers fired a volley, and a few minutes later Grattan's command lay dead on the banks of the Platte River. Angry Sioux plundered a government annuity storehouse at Fort Laramie and then departed, leaving the fort with its forty-two defenders.

Following the Grattan disaster, Alfred J. Cumming, who had recently replaced David D. Mitchell as head of the Central Superintendency at Saint Louis, warned Indian Commissioner George Manypenny of the "undisguised hostility and contemptuous conduct" of the Sioux within the Upper Missouri Agency. Many Sioux went to Fort Pierre, where they exhorted others to take up arms against the United States, "stating . . . the ease with which they killed the unfortunate party at the Platte." Sioux warriors also pillaged several traders, including one working for Pierre Chouteau, Jr., & Company, to the tune of roughly thirty thousand dollars.[1]

The Grattan debacle only raised the stakes in a contest already in progress. Earlier in 1854 the Hunkpapa and Blackfeet Sioux had refused to accept annuity goods; their agent claimed they preferred "war and stealing horses to receiving presents." About sixty warriors hovered near Fort Union in February, killing a mixed-blood employee of Harvey, Primeau & Company and stealing twenty-six horses from the fort. "Nothing," wrote Agent Alfred J. Vaughn, "short of troops will be of any avail."[2]

Because of unusually mild winter weather, bison were scattered over the plains far from their usual shelter in protective river-bottom forests. With meat scarce, Indians requested the government to send proportionately more foodstuffs than other annuity goods. The Sioux explained that trading robes at Fort Union and elsewhere supplied them with cloth, tools, and the like, and they had no alternative outlet for surplus robes and furs.[3]

Pierre Chouteau, Jr., aware that military policy was taking a new direction, had perhaps guessed that the government was growing tired of playing second fiddle to fur traders. In May, apparently trying to fend off criticism by creating sharper distinctions between traders and Indian agents, he proposed to construct (upon Agent Vaughn's request) separate agency buildings at Forts Pierre and Union. At a cost of $1,250 per agency, each would feature residential quarters and warehouses with shingled pitched roofs, weatherboarded exteriors, and plastered interiors. The Office of Indian Affairs made no response to Chouteau's proposal.[4]

On July 3, Agent Vaughn distributed annuity goods at Fort Union to nine of the thirteen tribes under his jurisdiction, a task made difficult by the fact that Hunkpapa and Blackfeet Sioux intimidated neighboring tribes who stood by the Fort Laramie Treaty, which was intended to make the western emigrant road safe by setting tribal boundaries and allowing the army to build military posts and highways in Indian country. Charles Larpenteur, sensing the futility of the agreement, ridiculed the treaty as "the most absurd I ever heard of—though gotten up by men who should have known better."[5]

Lakota warriors, in the midst of their own expansion into the western plains, often disregarded treaty stipulations. They continued to attack their numerous enemies, and usually they came out ahead. Lakota Sioux warriors were a potent military force and considered themselves naturally superior to their neighbors. From the government's viewpoint, they were intransigent thugs who threatened American citizens as well as other Indians. "It really caused me to weep," wrote Vaughn a month before Grattan died, "at the strong appeals the Mandans Arickaras and Groventres made to me for their Great Father to come to their aid. . . . They hope he will send some 150 well armed and well uniformed men to give those Black Feet and Uncpapas a good whipping." Vaughn agreed with the river tribes that the Sioux deserved a thrashing, but in this case old animosities coincided with the Mandans' and their neighbors' wishes to please the "Great Father."[6]

Vaughn, fearing for his life, dutifully attempted to distribute annuities to the Crows and some Sioux tribes. At Fort Pierre in November 1854 he met with Hunkpapa and Blackfeet Sioux leaders. After hours of talk he handed out some groceries and ammunition. At that moment, Vaughn wrote, "to my utter astonishment a noted scoundrel called and known as Red Leaf drew from his scabbard a huge knife and cut each one of the sacks and scattered the contents in every direction he then threw the Tobacco Powder and Balls in the River and in quick succession forty or fifty guns was fired off all around and about me." Vaughn informed his superiors, calling for immediate action. A few months later, about February 1855, three hundred Hunkpapa and Blackfeet Sioux raided an Assiniboine camp at Fort Union, killing two but losing three of their own men.[7] In May, Agent Vaughn and Alexander Culbertson (who had been appointed special agent to treat with the Blackfeet nation at Fort Benton) both advised that troops should be sent to chastise the Sioux and protect tribes who honored the treaty.[8]

September saw no softening in the attitude of the Hunkpapa and Blackfeet Sioux. At Fort Clark they again humiliated Agent Vaughn and destroyed more presents. Vaughn, in growing frustration, called for a thousand troops, arguing they would do more good than "100 steamboats loaded with presents."[9]

Vaughn remained at Fort Clark until January 1856, then fled to Fort Pierre, badly shaken by another confrontation with the Sioux, this time Yanktonais. Eighty warriors had accompanied Big Head to Fort Clark to claim their annuities. Vaughn obligingly prepared a feast, promising to meet with them the next morning. When day broke, the situation turned ugly.

Upon meeting Vaughn, Big Head grabbed the agent's spectacles and demanded to "see" what presents were left to take. Vaughn led Big Head and five armed men to the storeroom, where the Indians heaped abuse on the agent and ridiculed the government. Meanwhile, Sioux outside the building repeatedly shot their flintlock fusils into the air while the fort's employees cowered in their quarters. For three hours the Indians kept up a continuous fire, killing several unlucky chickens in the fort and discharging a volley at a cat, which managed to dodge the balls. Writing shortly after the Sioux departed, Vaughn blamed the trouble on some nameless "renegade white men and half-breeds" who sold liquor, though he praised the "American Fur Company" for its cooperation and hoped that General Harney's campaign had succeeded in ending the crisis. But Vaughn was losing patience, and moderation, with the Upper Missouri

Agency; it was "only necessary now to exterminate Big Head's Party and one-third of the Blackfeet Sioux and Uncpapa bands to put a quietus upon the Sioux War."[10]

Possibly in an effort to put the best face on things, Vaughn mentioned none of this when he wrote his official annual report in September.[11] No military action was taken against Big Head's band, and they continued to generate anxiety for traders. In March 1857, Charles Galpin wrote from new Fort Pierre that some Yanktonais camped above Heart River were "disposed to be mischievious [sic]" and that "the Oncpapas or some other Indians" had stolen eight horses from the fort. Galpin believed the robbers to be "some of the Big Heads band or perhaps some of the cut hands," who were "much afflicted with the smallpox, which may be the cause of their continually going to War against the Rees and Gros Ventres which renders travelling up and down this river exceedingly dangerous."[12]

Two years earlier, on March 22, 1855, Brevet Brigadier General William S. Harney had received orders to launch a punitive foray against the Sioux to avenge Grattan's defeat. Harney's expedition, mustering about seven hundred dragoons and infantrymen and a few pieces of artillery, departed Fort Leavenworth in August for three months of chasing and fighting the Sioux. A "battle"—more an indiscriminate slaughter of men, women, and children—at Ash Hollow near the North Platte in September broke the spirit of Little Thunder's Brulés, and eventually they came to talk peace with Harney.

About the same time Harney got his marching orders, the quartermaster at Saint Louis was directed to "obtain the most reliable information possible as to the suitableness of Fort Pierre Chouteau, at the mouth of the Bad River on the upper Missouri, for a depot of supplies." Military success would be impossible without a forward base of operations, and building a fort entailed enormous expenses, but perhaps the fur post would serve. One Chouteau employee, John B. Sarpy, thought Fort Pierre unsuited for a military depot, but another, Honoré Picotte, took the opposite view.

The quandary was resolved in April 1855, when General Charles Gratiot, Chouteau's trusted kinsman and ally, persuaded Quartermaster General Thomas S. Jessup to pay Chouteau & Company forty-five thousand dollars for their dilapidated fort in Nebraska Territory. It is difficult to say whether the responsibility for Fort Pierre's inflated price lies mainly with Chouteau or with his cousin Gratiot. Gratiot's long and distinguished military career had been abruptly terminated in 1838 when President Van Buren dismissed him after a clash with auditors over record keeping. For the next eighteen years he held a humble clerkship in the General Land Office, and he may have craved a little revenge. His signature on the sale agreement for Fort Pierre in April 1855 was one of the last he ever wrote; within a month he was dead. On the other hand, Chouteau may have suspected that government activity in the Upper Missouri would ruin his business and seized this opportunity to offset future losses.

Four months after taking possession in June 1855, army surveyors calculated that the post needed $22,022 worth of repairs. Charles Galpin, speaking for the Company, offered to knock three thousand dollars off the purchase price, but no more.[13]

By September it was too late to find a better site, so Harney's men wintered at Fort Pierre. Besides, as Joseph LaBarge pointed out to Pierre Chouteau, Jr., "Had it not been for Fort Pierre and those old buildings as they were called when [Harney] landed there with troops and Government Stores . . . the loss to Gov. would have been two or three times the amount it paid for it [and] . . . it gave them power at once and ample shelter for all stores."[14] After some months of bickering with the army, in February 1856, Chouteau—through his agent John F. A. Sanford—agreed to settle for $36,500, a substantial reduction. The sale price of Fort Pierre, which has rarely been published, appears only once in the vast documentary record, embedded in an otherwise dull letter written in French. Chouteau still profited by the sale, but he appears more cooperative and less unscrupulous than some historians have made him out to be.[15]

In June 1856 the soldiers abandoned decrepit Fort Pierre and moved about 150 miles downriver to build Fort Randall above the mouth of the Niobrara. (Within ten years Fort Randall, itself rotting and overrun with vermin, was abandoned.) In March, Harney made a treaty with the Sioux at Fort Pierre, but the Senate never ratified it, balking at the one hundred thousand dollars required to redeem the government's promises. Treaty or no, the growing number of soldiers at new Fort Pierre meant profits for traders. Charles Galpin observed, "There certainly will always be

Soldiers and other white men passing through this country . . . and their wants are innumerable. their sutlers are never more than Half Supplied and never can be unless he brings about four Steam Boat Loads and large ones at that."[16]

Agent Vaughn's unnerving parleys with the Sioux coincided with another destabilizing sequence of events, some of which related to the impending Civil War. Vaughn, like most agents, wished to reside at some distance from fur traders' forts, the better to serve the government's interest. Agents were in a bind: they depended more on fur companies' hospitality than on inadequate federal appropriations, but performance of their duties often entailed criticism of their hosts. Making a second and final plea for new agency buildings to be erected seven miles below the mouth of the Yellowstone, Vaughn submitted detailed architectural drawings to the Office of Indian Affairs in March 1857.[17]

"Major" Vaughn served in the Upper Missouri agency for five years before becoming the Blackfeet agent in 1857, and he seems to have been one of the region's more conscientious federal agents. At one point he suggested discontinuing the robe trade in order to preserve bison as well as the Indians' way of life. Apparently no one took his idea seriously. Charles Larpenteur, bilious as always, described Vaughn as a drunk, firmly in the pocket of the "American Fur Company," who kept "a pretty young squaw for a wife." Nevertheless, Alfred Vaughn ably served the Blackfeet people for three years, encouraging farming and missionary efforts with some success. But by 1860 politics and place of origin mattered more than ability and efficiency. Vaughn, a Virginian, was suspected of secessionist leanings. In 1861 he lost his position, a victim of political circumstances. By comparison with some of his fellow agents, Vaughn's eight years in the Upper Missouri look productive. Larpenteur described Vaughn's predecessor at the Blackfeet agency, Edwin A. C. Hatch (1855–56), as "a drunkard and a gambler, almost used up by the bad disorder" (that is, syphilis or another sexually transmitted disease). Vaughn's successors at the agency, Henry Reed (1861–62) and Gad E. Upson (1863–65), were incompetent and hostile toward Indians and did little or nothing of note.[18]

In April 1857, Alexander H. Redfield replaced Vaughn as Upper Missouri agent, though he spent much of his time in Saint Louis with his family. When he did visit Fort Clark in June 1858, a young Arikara fired a gun between Redfield's legs. The terrorized agent denounced all the Arikaras as "mad and crazy" and peevishly suggested that soldiers should "teach all these foolish savages to respect the power and dignity of the government." Complaining of liquor law violations by Red River "Half breeds" and others, he called for the discontinuation of the Indian trade and removal of "every Half breed and white man . . . except the Indian Agents." Redfield, like other agents, pointed out that most Indians did not feel bound by the Fort Laramie Treaty because so few had signed it, and he suggested that it be renegotiated. Again like others, he requested the separation of agencies from trading posts, emphatically noting that agents were "entirely dependent on [the traders] for Shelter, food, transportation, protection, labourers, Interpreters, & in fact every thing." After one difficult year Redfield resigned his post to take over the Yankton Agency, but he found his task no easier there. Many whites trespassed on Yankton lands, the military was uncooperative, and removing the intruders proved impossible.[19]

Bernard S. Schoonover, the new Upper Missouri agent, officially assumed his duties in March 1859. Almost immediately he took a two-month leave of absence, but when he arrived at his post in the autumn, he found serious problems. Intertribal relations had moved from bad to worse, with the Sioux becoming increasingly aggressive and "friendly" Indians increasingly fearful. The Sioux rightfully complained that heavy emigrant traffic on the Oregon Trail spoiled hunting, and they feared the consequences of "the different exploring parties penetrating their old haunts." Moreover, influenza and pneumonia were taking heavy tolls among the tribes. Schoonover spent so much time trying to allay their fears that he neglected to submit his yearly account to the Office of Indian Affairs. But he did find time to note, rather pathetically, that "the agent in this agency has no home nor resting place even to lay his head in inclement weather so far as the government is concerned unless he depends upon the charity of the traders."[20]

Depredations by Miniconjou, Hunkpapa, and Blackfeet Sioux continued. The Sioux had long considered the government and the army to be weaklings, and little had been done since 1825 to cause them to alter their views. Consequently, the Sioux routinely harassed traders and travelers by the late 1850s. The only response of the government, which was unable to grapple with the larger issues involved, was to consider the idea of deducting money from annuity payments to reimburse those with claims against the Sioux.[21]

Fort Union itself was no longer immune from outright attack. Occasional horse thefts had occurred in the past, but in 1860 Sioux belligerence took an ominous turn. At dawn on August 22, as the watchman unlocked the gates, some 250 mounted Sioux rushed Fort Union. During the next four hours Schoonover and the fifteen men within the fort stood by helplessly, panic-stricken observers of events beyond their control. The raiders killed twenty-five head of cattle outside the walls and burned tons of stored lumber and hay along with several outbuildings. After setting two large mackinaw boats afire, they cut them loose to drift down the river. The Sioux then attempted to torch the fort, but retreated when Robert Meldrum and Malcolm Clark killed one and wounded several others from atop the wall. Schoonover noted that Meldrum had never taken such action before, but in this case he felt compelled to defend his men and his fort.[22]

Schoonover, the last appointee of the Democrats, soon resigned his position. The new agent, Samuel N. Latta, was commissioned in August 1861 but did not go up the Missouri until the next spring. When the steamer *Spread Eagle* docked at Fort Pierre on May 27, 1862, Latta heard that some Miniconjous and Sans Arcs had stolen stock from emigrants on the Platte and had killed a few Chouteau Company men at Forts Berthold and Union. Latta also received information that seemed to implicate Agent Schoonover in an illegal transfer of annuity goods to Charles P. Chouteau. Latta claimed that Schoonover had permitted Chouteau to substitute government annuity goods for company goods lost when the steamer *Chippewa* burned and exploded in June 1861. (This claim was probably true, although Chouteau eventually replaced the borrowed goods. In 1863, Latta complained again, but apparently no lawsuit developed.) The *Chippewa* also carried a quantity of liquor. In a letter to William P. Dole, Latta mentioned the presence of liquor barrels on the steamer, several of which were rescued following the vessel's destruction. Illegal whiskey aside, Latta expressed his undisguised dislike for Chouteau as "a man who takes every opportunity to denounce the administration."[23]

The biggest news, however, was that despite all efforts, competent or otherwise, by Indian agents to head off disaster, intransigent Sioux had declared war not only on the whites, but also on any of their own people who declined to join them. Bear's Rib, a Hunkpapa friendly to the United States, was such a man, and he trod a narrow and dangerous path. Named a chief at General Harney's Fort Pierre council in March 1856, Bear's Rib was faithful to the spirit of the unratified treaty. But by May 1862 his patience was wearing thin, for all Harney's promises had come to naught. Still, in council with Latta and representatives of the Sioux tribes, Bear's Rib reaffirmed his allegiance to the "Great Father," though he feared for his life and the lives of his followers. A few days later, two Sans Arcs, said to have been Ousta ("One-That-Limps") and Tonkalla ("Mouse"), killed him and a few other Hunkpapas inside new Fort Pierre. Bear's Rib, whom Latta called "the best friend the white man had in the Sioux nation," was dead. Likewise, Little Thunder, the Brulé whose camp General Harney had attacked in 1855, eventually became friendly with the government, and in 1865 he suffered the same fate as Bear's Rib.[24]

Samuel Latta was the first of two Republican appointees to the Upper Missouri during Lincoln's administration. Strangely, the high moral principles that informed Republican abolitionism seemed inapplicable to western Indians and their lands; within a few years the Indian Department earned one of the worst reputations for fraud and chicanery anywhere in government. Driven by his party's ideology, his own crooked dealings, or perhaps out of plain contrariness, Agent Latta aimed to tar Chouteau and his company with the brush of secessionism. In his annual report for 1862, Latta stridently condemned the "old American Fur Company" as "the most corrupt institution ever tolerated in our country." The monopolistic company, he shrilled, cheated the government, enslaved the Indians, and destroyed all competition in their country. Then, apparently unconscious of any irony, Latta added that the company "discouraged them in agriculture by telling them that should the white man find that their country would produce they would come in and take their lands from them." Whether anyone in Chouteau's company actually told any Indian these things, Latta's prediction of what whites would do was accurate.[25]

But there was more. "At Fort Union on the 4th of July," Latta reported,

> a flag with eight stars was run up, and remained up until night. Mr.
> Hodgkiss, who had just come in charge of this post, a Pennsylvanian
> by birth, assured me that on the next 4th he should have every State
> in the Union represented. A discharged Union soldier assured me
> that they were all secessionists at this post, and had threatened his
> life for the part he had taken in the Springfield battle. . . . I do not
> wish to be understood as charging every member or employee of
> this company with disloyalty or dishonesty; a few only can I except,
> however. . . . Secessionists of every grade, height, and color should
> be forced to quit this country. They will, as a matter of course, use
> their influence to the prejudice of the government, and, with those
> Sioux at best ill-disposed towards the white man and his govern-
> ment, are capable of doing much harm.[26]

The ill disposition of the Sioux had much more to do with soldiers,
encroaching white "civilization," and the rise of new political and business
centers in Iowa, Minnesota, and Dakota Territory than with commercial
activities of Pierre Chouteau, Jr., & Company. An Indian war would do
nothing to improve business, and there is no evidence that Pierre or
Charles Chouteau had any dealings with the Confederacy. It would have
been sheer madness for Chouteau actively to align his company with the
Confederacy. He had been too long in the business to make such a foolish
decision, and the likelihood that he did so is remote. Nevertheless, Latta's
charges represented a changed attitude that would accomplish within
two years what twenty-five years of commercial opposition had failed to
do: dislodge Pierre Chouteau, Jr., & Company from the Upper Missouri
permanently.[27]

The government did not immediately take steps against Chouteau.
Other, more pressing problems clamored for attention. Soon after killing
Bear's Rib, hostile Sioux made war on most of their neighbors. Num-
bering about thirteen thousand, the Sioux nation constituted a genuine
threat to the people around them. In 1861–62 they pushed the Crows into
the Rockies, away from their traditional homeland near the headwaters
of the Yellowstone. They attacked the Gros Ventres and Mandans near

Fort Berthold, killing a Gros Ventre leader named Four Bears and several others; they also made off with 175 horses. In August 1861 some Sioux raided the Arikara village near Fort Clark, killing several tribesmen and a white trader. So hard pressed were the Arikaras that in 1862 they moved upriver to Fort Berthold, gradually amalgamating with the Mandans and Hidatsas. The Assiniboines, living "in constant dread of the Sioux," abandoned their lands south of the Missouri and began to spend more time in Canada. The Mandans, Arikaras, Gros Ventres, Crows, and Assiniboines all requested military protection and offered to help destroy the Sioux. Meanwhile, a few thousand contentious Yankton Sioux, still nominally under treaty stipulations, were slated to receive about $70,000 from the government, while "friendly" tribes would get roughly $1.50 for each member.[28]

As conditions in the Upper Missouri and other frontier locales grew more chaotic and dangerous, the federal government's attention remained fixed on the East, where the Union army suffered defeat and humiliation during the initial campaigns of the Civil War. Consequently, Washington failed to notice when Indian-white discord in Minnesota passed the boiling point. Unresolved tensions dating from the 1851 Traverse des Sioux Treaty, by which instrument the eastern Sioux people unwittingly gave away most of their land, burst into violence during the summer of 1862.

Little Crow and hundreds of warriors, mostly Santee Sioux, made bloody raids in August at Acton, New Ulm, and elsewhere in Minnesota, killing many settlers. Citizens of Minnesota and of Dakota Territory were horror-struck at the prospect of an all-out Indian war. Traumatized survivors in Minnesota saw thirty-eight captured Santees executed in a mass hanging at Mankato on the day after Christmas, and Little Crow was murdered in a farmer's field the following summer. But the war fever grew, threatening to set the entire Indian country aflame. Whites clamored for blood, but so did the Plains Sioux, who presumably began to foresee the end to their own bid for power. Perhaps they suspected they would end up like the Minnesota Sioux, imprisoned on "reserves" in Iowa and Dakota Territory.[29]

Anger and resentment soon spread along the Missouri as far as Fort Union, whose residents were no longer able to cultivate crops or keep dairy cattle safe. Indeed, the post was under an intermittent state of siege during its last few years. As Sioux attacks on steamers became more frequent during 1862–63, the government at last admitted there was a problem in Dakota Territory, and in late summer of 1863 it ordered General Alfred Sully to take the field against the Sioux.

For three summers (1863–65) Sully carried out indecisive campaigns intended to punish the Sioux and convince them that the government possessed an army capable of forcing its will upon Indians. In 1863, Sully's infantrymen advanced up the Missouri while General H. H. Sibley moved westward from Minnesota to entrap the Sioux between the jaws of a great vise. Plagued by equipment delays, ill-trained soldiers, and an unusually dry summer that parched the plains and almost drained the Missouri, the pincers movement failed. Sully's campaigns solved nothing; in fact, they exacerbated the situation.[30]

Some of Sully's troops arrived at Fort Union in June 1864 to guard supplies for a post to be built near the Yellowstone. Members of Company I, 30th Wisconsin Infantry, printed at Fort Union a few issues of a newspaper, the *Frontier Scout*, which dutifully covered Sully's 1864 expedition. Before departing Fort Union, Sully decided the decaying fur fort was inadequate for troops and marked out a four-miles-square area close to the confluence of the Yellowstone and the Missouri that would be named Fort Buford.[31]

After Samuel Latta took a position as special agent for the "hostile" Sioux in 1864, the Upper Missouri Agency remained vacant until 1866. Mahlon Wilkinson, another Republican appointee, received the Fort Berthold Agency in early 1864. Little seems to be known about Wilkinson, but it may be that he was related to Minnesota's U.S. senator, Morton S. Wilkinson, a member of the Committee on Indian Affairs in 1865. Given Minnesota's patronage situation and its links to Dakota Territory, it is possible that the senator found employment for a kinsman. What is certain, however, is that Agent Wilkinson's enmity for Charles Chouteau equaled that of his predecessor, Latta.[32]

On July 14, 1864, Wilkinson penned a letter from Crow Creek Agency to Senator James Harlan of Iowa (soon to be named secretary of the interior), who forwarded a copy to William P. Dole, commissioner of Indian affairs. Wilkinson voiced his fears about taking the job, arguing that the "fate of all recent agents" proved the difficulty of his position. Wilkinson's discomfort grew when Charles Chouteau discovered that he had issued a trade license to "Mr. Puett and Mr. Pease." Chouteau objected because the agent lacked authority to issue licenses, and he accused the two traders of peddling government annuity goods to Indians. Father Pierre Jean De Smet apparently agreed, but Wilkinson argued that De Smet, like the fur traders and "all their employees," was "opposed to our Government." Wilkinson also claimed that the company was selling whiskey to "Indians French & half Breeds," but alleged that his witness got cold feet because he was "sure he would not live two weeks after it was known he testified against them." It was one thing to impugn Chouteau's honesty and patriotism, but quite another to question the loyalty of a priest who worked tirelessly to achieve peace between Indians and the U.S. government. Wilkinson, like some other agents, had an ulterior motive for slandering De Smet and Chouteau. It emerges with crystal clarity in Wilkinson's postscript to the letter: "I speak of Albert Puett in my letter as having the License to trade, he is my Bro-in-Law & is as Loyal as I am."[33]

A year later, more soldiers came to Fort Union: Confederate prisoners of war paroled in exchange for service with Abe Lincoln's western army. Several hundred "Galvanized Yankees" of the 1st Regiment, United States Volunteers, arrived at Fort Rice in October 1864 to replace the 30th Wisconsin Infantry and other units ordered to go East. In command was Colonel Charles Dimon, a twenty-three-year-old Radical Republican friend of General Benjamin F. Butler. After a miserable, scurvy-ridden winter, the former prisoners were distributed along the Missouri River, with about fifty men of Company B billeted at Fort Union.

Dimon, an ambitious and fanatical martinet, saw treachery everywhere. He fantasized that not only some of his own troops, but Chouteau's men, too, were prepared to foment insurrection. On the way up the Missouri, vastly exceeding his legal authority, he had a "Whitewashed Reb" shot for muttering an "insubordinate" remark. In December 1864 he placed the Upper Missouri under martial law, imposed loyalty oaths, and placed cronies in command at Forts Union and Berthold, again overstepping his authority. Then, in February 1865, Dimon suspended the regularly licensed Indian trade, placing it in the hands of post sutlers.

Intended to intimidate the fur traders, Dimon's act also symbolized the growing enmity between the War and Interior Departments over Indian policy and its implementation.[34]

Since 1849, Indian policy administration had been lodged in the Interior Department. But the War Department relinquished its control grudgingly, and by 1865 the two bureaus were at loggerheads over several issues. The Indian Office's removal and concentration policies heightened tensions on the plains and elsewhere, creating problems for military men, who faced the difficulties of policing Indians and whites. After 1863, when several thousand miners rushed into Montana's gold fields, clashes between soldiers and Indians grew more frequent. Having military and civil Indian policies in conflict did nothing to ameliorate matters.[35]

Fur traders attempted to preserve their relatively static world as rapid and destructive changes affected Indians' lives around them. Chouteau and his partners most likely would have preferred things to remain just as they had been for decades. There is very little evidence that fur traders strongly supported "civilizing" the Indians, and a shift to farming would undoubtedly have caused some decline in the robe trade. The traders' fortunes, and the future of their unique society, were joined to the future of the Indians. The world they created at Fort Union would fall to pieces if Indians lost their freedom and mobility. Invited or not, governmental power grew heavier. The fur traders' hegemony, which depended on federal neglect, was soon to become a thing of the past. Colonel Dimon set in motion the machinery that wrought this change.

When the Company steamer *Yellow Stone* docked at Fort Rice in May 1865, it brought word of Lincoln's murder. It also carried Charles P. Chouteau, Jr., head of company operations, on a final voyage up the river to oversee the transfer of posts to a new concern called Hubbell & Hawley, or the North Western Fur Company. Dimon became convinced that Chouteau was a rebel sympathizer and treated him accordingly, reportedly threatening to take Chouteau, one of the wealthiest and most distinguished residents of Saint Louis, onto the bank and "shoot him like a dog." The main evidence for Chouteau's supposed Confederate association was the nativist assumption that, as Lewis Henry Morgan wrote in 1862, "the French traders . . . are all secessionists, which shows in a general way that the entire French Catholic element of our population is unfriendly to our government." Even Hubbell and Hawley, staunch if insincere Republicans, were much affronted by Dimon's tactics and reported the matter to General Sully.[36]

In one outburst of sectionalist passion the *Frontier Scout*, Dimon's tool, branded the Indian Bureau "the Slave Power of the Territories." Instead of cooperating to attain national objectives, soldiers and Indian agents went for each others' throats. Colonel Dimon's high-handedness galled even the Republican Indian agent, Mahlon Wilkinson, who complained to his superiors that Dimon's appointees forbade his participation in talks with Indians. Dimon's behavior alienated his most useful allies, Generals Sully and Pope. Reprimanded for his rash conduct and interference with the traders and agents, Dimon lost his command in August 1865 and was replaced by the less abrasive Colonel John Pattee. Nonetheless, by the spring of 1865, Charles P. Chouteau had seen the light; after nearly a half-century in the Upper Missouri, the Company was prepared to call it quits. Old connections were no longer dependable, powerful new Republican men were in office, and they had established new political and economic alignments.[37]

In the political chaos created by partisan bickering in the midst of the Civil War, the Minnesota-Dakota axis of power gained ground, while the older Saint Louis–Missouri River axis declined. Two Mankato entrepreneurs, James Boyd Hubbell and Alpheus F. Hawley, found themselves in a strong position to challenge Chouteau. Late in 1863, Hubbell and Hawley, in collusion with Minnesota Republican politicians and Indian Office men such as Northern Superintendent Clark W. Thompson, won a contract to haul supplies to Santee Sioux and Winnebagos who had been forced west to Dakota Territory after the 1862 Indian-White war in Minnesota.

By autumn the sequestered Indians were starving, and a decision was taken to ship foodstuffs to the Fort Thompson reservation on the Missouri River, some 225 miles west of Mankato. Critics of the operation's timing dubbed the enterprise the "Moscow Expedition," since it took place during brutal winter conditions that inspired jokes about Napoleon's failed 1812 occupation of Moscow. Arriving at Fort Thompson on December 2, Hubbell and Hawley's teamsters off-loaded several tons of rotten food and frozen cattle carcasses for the Indians to eat, then returned to

Mankato. Food shortages continued, and by mid-January 1864, a great soup trough was built to "remedy" distribution problems. Every few days, men tossed cows' heads, lungs, and guts, along with a barrel of condemned flour into the trough, and the whole smelly mess was heated by running a steam pipe to it from a nearby sawmill.

The contractors demonstrated a wholesale contempt for law, humanity, and the welfare of famished Indians, but the "Moscow Expedition" paid off handsomely. Another government contract in 1864 to provide food and goods to the Winnebagos brought the Mankato men more financial success, and encouraged them to solicit a trading license for the Upper Missouri in 1865. Hubbell and Hawley's legacy would include gross overcharges to the government, chicanery, influence peddling in the halls of Congress, and flagrant abuse of their trade privileges.[38]

Hubbell and Hawley, Yankees from Connecticut and New York, respectively, each had solid ties to former Know-Nothings and, more recently, Radical Republicans.[39] Hubbell, perhaps more than Hawley, was a political chameleon whose party allegiance and ideology were flexible at best and deeply cynical at worst. For instance, Hubbell described himself as "inclined to be a democrat," but after his arrival at Mankato he found no opportunity in that party, so he switched to the Republican standard. Hubbell had lived in Georgia for a few years in the 1850s and once wrote, "Had I remained South, doubtless I would have been in the Confederate army." At about the same time, he wrote, "When the Civil War broke out there was great excitement in Mankato. I was one of those that 'came near going.'" But the quest for profits was more important to James Hubbell than patriotism or disunion. Anyhow, he scarcely qualified as a genuine Radical Republican, since he believed that slaves in Georgia were attached to their masters and were "well treated as a rule."[40]

At Washington on February 25, with the blessing of Governor Newton Edmunds of Dakota Territory, Hubbell acquired a license to trade with the Sioux at Fort Sully, with the Arikaras and Mandans at military forts Rice and Berthold, with the Assiniboines at Fort Union, and with the Crows wherever they might be found. This placed Hubbell in direct competition with Chouteau's company. By that time, Charles P. Chouteau faced a hopeless political climate in Washington, D.C., where anyone with real or imagined Democratic ties was viewed with suspicion. Though

Chouteau managed to retain some government freight contracts (doubt-less because the company, as usual, was the sole outfit able to handle that business at the time), the Republican administration denied him a trade license.[41]

While both men were in Washington, D.C., Hubbell heard of the Saint Louisan's distress and found an opportunity to speak with Chouteau. Admitting the futility of pressing his case before a hostile administration, Chouteau proposed to sell out to Hubbell. The two struck a bargain on March 2, enabling Hubbell to purchase the old company's holdings on May 19, 1865. In the March agreement—witnessed by his allies Commissioner of Indian Affairs William P. Dole and Northern Superintendent Clark W. Thompson—Hubbell promised to buy all the UMO's Indian goods at Saint Louis and at "Several Trading Establishments" on the Upper Missouri, excepting Fort Benton, which Chouteau would operate for one more year. The selling price remains obscure, but it was surely a bargain. Chouteau was politically crippled, and wartime disruptions had made it impossible to order many items of standard Indian goods. Hubbell consented to pay a 10 percent advance on the cost of all goods, as well as shipping costs and other charges. In addition, the value of "all articles in use at the several posts" would be determined and included in the price. Trading posts, including Fort Union, were to be transferred "free of Charge." Chouteau agreed to "give up all Indian Trade" but would continue selling goods to Montana miners and fulfilling government contracts for another year. Hubbell agreed to a down payment of twenty thousand dollars in cash and up to an additional twenty thousand dollars, depending upon the final evaluation, with the balance due on January 1, 1866. Available records seem to indicate that Chouteau's Indian stock and three forts, including Union, went for about thirty-three thousand dollars.[42]

Word of the sell-out spread quickly to New York City, where fur trade capitalists were eager to invest now that Chouteau was out of the picture. A few weeks later, Hubbell arrived in New York armed with his trade license, his sutlership for Fort Sully, and his agreement to purchase Chouteau's holdings. The only element missing was money, and lots of it would be needed. Hubbell soon negotiated a partnership with Caleb Francis Bates, a New Yorker, and James A. Smith, a Chicagoan, both of whom were merchants of furs and Indian goods. Bates and Smith were well acquainted, having engaged in joint ventures for several years. Hubbell and Hawley, with considerable field experience, would run the posts, while Bates and Smith would finance the operation, make purchases, and sell furs and robes. The new company, styled the North Western Fur Company (NWFCo), was intended to exist only from June 1865 until "the Spring of 1869, unless sooner dissolved by mutual consent." Initially, Hubbell and Hawley were to receive half the profits and Smith and Bates the other half, despite the fact that Hubbell and Hawley threw in only $10,000, while Bates anted up about $50,000. One year later, Bates had already plunged over $70,000 in the venture and was prepared to commit at least another $80,000. A renegotiation of profit division gave Hubbell and Hawley two-fifths, Bates two-fifths, and Smith one-fifth. As Bates pointed out in a letter to Smith, "Mr. Hawley [and Hubbell] I cannot doubt would if he were within reach accept a proposition which gives him 1/5 Int[erest] in a business of $200,000 Capital in place of 1/4 Int[erest] in a business of $60,000."[43]

One reason why Bates was obliged to sink so much money into the enterprise is that Pierre Chouteau, Jr., about six weeks before he died, disposed of his last Missouri River steamer, the second *Yellow Stone*. The vessel sold in mid-July 1865 for forty thousand dollars, and perhaps old Pierre, Jr., had a laugh at the expense of the fledgling company, which seemingly had counted on using the vessel. "We have sold the Yellow Stone," Chouteau informed Smith on July 26, "therefore can furnish no means of transportation. You will have to Charter or make arrangements with other parties."[44]

The NWFCo, meaning C. F. Bates, then shelled out about $50,000 (Hubbell later said it cost $64,000) for a new steamer named in his honor: the *Frank Bates*. Bates soon advanced $28,000 (Hubbell said $30,000) to buy a second boat, the *Miner*. As luck would have it, the following spring, on April 7, 1866, the *Frank Bates* burned, destroying many NWFCo goods as well as over $38,000 in government Indian goods destined for Blackfeet annuities and for treaty negotiations underway at Fort Laramie. The loss also jeopardized the work of the North Western Treaty commissioners, who concluded negotiations in July with the Crows and Assiniboines at Fort Union and with the Mandans, Arikaras, and Gros Ventres at Fort Berthold. "A failure to comply with existing treaties," wrote Commissioner D. N. Cooley, with unconscious irony, to the new secretary of the interior, Orville H. Browning, "would no doubt lead the Indians to distrust the good faith of the compacts about being entered into."[45]

While the NWFCo attempted to organize its operations, Pierre Chouteau, Jr., & Company wrapped up the bulk of its Upper Missouri business affairs. By the 1860s Fort Benton was the best location to trade for robes, since the bison seemed to be gradually retreating northwestward under a variety of pressures. The Fort Benton outfit of 1862 netted $44,078.14 from sales of robes, skins, and furs. Forts Pierre, Berthold, and Union collectively netted $30,708.24, indicating declining profits at posts where trade was formerly heavy.[46]

Chouteau & Company had long recognized that contracts to transport annuity goods, while they might delay delivery of their own goods, had the virtue of offsetting operating costs of steamboats. In 1854, Pierre Chouteau, Jr., calculated that it had cost about $13,000 to use the steamer *Robert Campbell* in 1853. If the government shipped sixty or more tons of annuity goods, at between five and eight cents per pound (the costs would rise over time), freight charges would about equal the steamboat's operating costs. This system worked especially well when, as was often the case, the Company required two vessels to freight its own goods. Contracts with Chouteau's company stipulated that delays occasioned by delivery of annuity goods at distribution points would cost the government $150 per day for as many as fifteen days. In short, any amount over thirty or forty tons would come close to canceling steamboating's overhead costs. Chouteau emphasized safety, reliability, and experience when placing bids before the government. These advantages, Chouteau believed, along with his company's willingness to store undistributed goods free of charge, "ought to give us some preference over ordinary bidders."[47]

In March 1859, Chouteau & Company received a two-year freight contract for annuities to service the Harney treaty, giving bond for $30,000. That summer the company moved about sixty-two tons of government freight up to Fort Pierre for further distribution to Upper Missouri Indians from Forts Union and Sarpy. The company charged the government $2.50 for each hundred pounds shipped from Saint Louis to Fort Union, $7.25 per hundred pounds sent on from Union to Fort

Sarpy, and $7.50 per hundred pounds of goods sent to Fort Benton. Chouteau's net gain must have amounted to near $13,000, roughly equal to the cost of operating the steamer. Even during the final two years of Chouteau's life, with the curtain about to fall on his UMO, Pierre Chouteau, Jr., & Company appear to have gained better than $44,000 through contracts to transport Indian annuities and government provisions. The company also made at least $2,000 in 1864 transporting soldiers to Upper Missouri posts.[48]

By the time he died, Pierre Chouteau, Jr., was worth approximately one-half million dollars. His diverse investments included land in Illinois, Missouri, Minnesota, and elsewhere; city and state bonds; railroads; mines; and urban real estate in Saint Louis and New York City. Though he never spent much time in the pays d'en haut, Pierre Chouteau, Jr., provided the motive force that kept his company powerful and profitable for more than a quarter-century. Oddly, Chouteau himself died at the time Fort Union was slipping into both physical decay and an economic decline from which it would not recover. Even if he foresaw that the old system of the robe trade was about to end, there is no evidence that either Pierre or Charles Chouteau planned to sell out until their petition for a license renewal was denied. But retire they did, and it fell to the new firm, Hubbell and Hawley's NWFCo, to run Fort Union into the ground.

Hubbell and Hawley, as indicated above, had an unpleasant encounter with Colonel Dimon in May 1865 while en route with Charles P. Chouteau to inventory and take possession of their new forts. Dimon halted the *Yellow Stone* at Fort Rice; arrested Hubbell, Hawley, and Chouteau; and informed Hubbell that he was confiscating all the new company's goods at Fort Berthold for violating the intercourse laws. Hubbell managed to get down the Missouri to Sioux City, where he complained to General Sully, who lent him a sympathetic ear and replaced Dimon with Pattee. Hubbell then went to Fort Union, where the *Yellow Stone* had been sent under guard, to reclaim his goods and proceed with the inventory before taking formal possession.[49]

By July 1866 the NWFCo claimed over $200,000 in merchandise in stock, capitalization exceeding $270,000, and a total operating budget, on paper, of greater than $358,000.[50] Furs and robes accounted for part of the NWFCo's trade, but few records survived, and those indicate meager returns. Between August and October 1865, for example, the company sold only about 1,365 robes (roughly 125 packs), forty-one beaver skins, and a handful of fox, wolf, antelope, rabbit, and mink. From July to December, 1866, a total of 609 beaver skins weighing about one thousand pounds and some wolf, deer, rabbit, mink, and house cat skins netted $4,815.80 at Chicago. In May 1868, eighty-nine bales of skins, including 750 robes, 787 fox, 201 wolf, 257 muskrat, and a few badger, rabbit, skunk, mink, and lynx skins were delivered to Durfee and Peck, traders at Fort Stevenson.[51] Some sources, perhaps from data supplied by Hubbell, reported that the company shipped as many as 20,000–25,000 robes annually, but there is no support for this in surviving records.[52] There is, however, evidence that the company made money in other ways. One source of profit came with the signing of the second Fort Laramie Treaty.

As of 1868 the army's war against Plains Indians had not achieved military success. Eastern reformers' moral outrage increased after 1864, when Colonel John Chivington slaughtered many of Black Kettle's peaceful Cheyennes at Sand Creek, Colorado, and the army forced several thousand Navajos onto a concentration camp at New Mexico's Bosque Redondo. Under pressure, the government shifted the course of Indian policy toward a more "humanitarian" tack, creating an Indian Peace Commission in 1867 that resulted in the negotiation of several new treaties. Of particular importance was one made by Generals William T. Sherman and William S. Harney with the Sioux at Fort Laramie in April 1868.

This treaty grew out of Red Cloud's War, a fight between the Sioux and Montana miners who had illegally opened the Bozeman Trail. Red Cloud won his war, and the government found itself bargaining with the Lakota people at Fort Laramie. The treaty established a Sioux reservation west of the Missouri in today's South Dakota. By the treaty's terms the Sioux gave up much of their land and allowed railroad construction to proceed, and in exchange the government closed the offending Bozeman Trail and a few forts. The government also promised to provide the Sioux and other tribes resident farmers and mechanics, schools, agricultural implements, food, and clothing for thirty years. The Fort Laramie Treaty of 1868 created a government-sponsored contract system designed to supersede the old style of trade carried on at Fort Union.

In September, General Harney, aboard the NWFCo's steamer *Miner*, notified James A. Smith that he had been authorized to purchase and ship an enormous amount of Indian goods and supplies guaranteed under the new treaty: more than 610,000 pounds of coffee, sugar, and bacon; 17,820 sacks of flour; 16,200 sacks of corn; 8,000 pounds of tobacco; and various other items. Altogether this meant that well over 1,000,000 pounds of freight had to be shipped from Saint Louis, Sioux City, and Omaha to the new reservation. Records detailing the outcome of Harney's proposal are scanty, but the *Miner* showed a profit of at least $14,500 for the fall of 1868.[53]

The NWFCo also ran a few sutler stores at military posts. At Fort Totten a trader named Fellowes D. Pease commenced a brewery operation that allegedly netted between twelve thousand and fifteen thousand dollars a year. It was supposed to have been "broke up" by General Whistler early in 1868, but a year later the brewery remained "the best paying institution in the country." The company's resident agent during 1868 at Fort Totten was Captain A. Bassett. This was most likely Adams Bassett, commander of the 4th U.S. Volunteer Infantry, a unit of Galvanized Yankees who had arrived at Fort Berthold in 1865. If so, he was either a double-dipper or had retired from military service to work for Hubbell and Hawley. Bassett observed that "trade is very dull—Provisions are the only articles that are in demand," and the nearby Red River "Half-Breeds" would only take hard money for robes. The old-time method of trading goods for furs was almost done for; if traders denied the Red River men cash, they simply hauled their robes to Saint Cloud, Minnesota, each spring. By March 1868, Bassett traded only 514 robes, 151 wolves, 689 fox, and 250 muskrats.[54]

Bassett complained that "Indian trade here *alone* will not pay," but he thought the mixed-blood trade would if properly supplied and managed. Though his bosses judged him to be a competent trader, Bassett's repeated entreaties for more and better supplies fell on deaf ears. His ill humor could hardly have been alleviated by Fort Totten's officers, who seemed to feel that paying bills was an unnecessary inconvenience. Then, General Terry ordered all sutlers to stop doing business at Fort Totten after July 1, 1868, except for the firm of Brenner & Terry, which happened to include his brother. Bassett thought the sutler trade would pay if it could be monopolized, but he had in mind one of his own, not one for the general's brother. Another headache was the problem of the "Northern Pony Express" mail outfit of C. A. Rufee & Co., which ran up a bill of nearly nine thousand dollars for room and board at Totten and other NWFCo posts. The mail company soon failed, and the NWFCo never collected their due.[55]

Making an honest dollar on the Upper Missouri was not easy after the Civil War. This was an era noteworthy for egregious corruption within the War Department and government generally. Perhaps Hubbell and Hawley were frustrated by competition from nepotistic soldiers and dismal trade prospects because of the impending Sioux wars; perhaps they were just plain crooked. In any event, the NWFCo employed flagrant deception and extortion of the government in its effort to turn a profit. The Chouteau company's excesses pale in comparison to frauds attempted or perpetrated by the NWFCo. The two outfits operated on different principles and with different styles. The new company, unlike Chouteau's, had no long-term stake in the country; it was intended strictly for a short and profitable run. It developed no significant ties with Indians and showed little interest in the Indian trade. Its ethical standards were abysmal (consider the 1863 "Moscow Expedition"), and it offered nothing of value to the government or science in exchange for its privileges in the Upper Missouri, something no one could say about Chouteau & Company. Hubbell & Hawley's sleazy take-the-money-and-run mentality betokened a new style of business conduct characteristic of the Gilded Age.[56]

Typical of Hubbell & Hawley's tactics was a claim emanating from their dealings with Indians at Fort Union. In March 1866, P. L. Gaban and H. S. Archdale witnessed a peculiar document asserting that the NWFCo provided forty-two barrels of beef, sixteen barrels of pork, 100 pounds of coffee, 130 pounds of sugar, and 3,600 pounds of flour to starving Gros Ventres, Arikaras, and Mandans. The paper, signed by Poor Wolf (Gros Ventre), Crow Chief (Arikara) and Long Mandan (Mandan), came into agent Mahlon Wilkinson's hands soon thereafter. On September 26, Wilkinson procured the signatures of other "witnesses," including White Shield and Bear That Ain't Afraid (Arikara); Crows Breast (Gros Ventre); and Red White Cow, Bear on the Water, and Crow Chief (Mandan). Crow Chief had formerly been identified as an Arikara. According to the document, when the Indians were starving, the NWFCo ("Mr. Pease") generously provided them with food, and now the Indians wanted their "Great Father to pay for it." Furthermore, the signers wanted the Great Father to "pay Mr. Pease & not send us so many goods next year," presumably so "Mr. Pease" could sell them more of his own goods. Wilkinson endorsed the bill for $4,014 and sent it to Indian Commissioner D. N. Cooley.[57]

The matter did not rest there. In council at Fort Berthold on July 27, Governor Newton Edmunds presented the Mandans, Arikaras, and Gros Ventres with Wilkinson's bill, now unaccountably swollen to $5,712, "for provisions furnished said Indians, at Fort Union, in the winter of 1865–66." When he solicited testimony from the Indians, Whistling Bear (an Arikara chief) and Poor Wolf spoke up.[58]

Whistling Bear admitted that most of the three tribes' people had been at Union "for one moon." Poor Wolf and Whistling Bear declared that the traders had invited the Indians to the fort and "gave us these provisions to encourage us, and without pay, except our trade." Whistling Bear added, "We gave them Deer skins, Elk Skins and Buffalo robes, which we thought would pay for our rations." Both Indians agreed that the pork they received "smelled bad" and the beef "was stinking so that it could not be used in the Fort." Charles Larpenteur, present as interpreter, was asked what he knew about the meat. He replied that he had bid eleven dollars for eighty barrels of meat at Fort Union the preceding August, before the soldiers left. The NWFCo bid twelve dollars and got the entire lot, though "the meat was spoiled." With language remarkably similar to that applied a few years earlier to Chouteau's company, A. B. Smith (a former NWFCo associate) testified that the NWFCo was "one of the most corrupt and damnable institutions ever tolerated in any age or country" and hoped that the government would "look this matter square in the face and correct the evil." Given the damaging testimony of the Indians, Larpenteur, and Smith, the government refused to pay the NWFCo's claim.[59]

When Fort Buford was built in early 1866 it became a target for harassment by the Sioux, who resented this intrusion into land they had recently appropriated from the Assiniboines. At a time when any soldier who strayed too far from the sentries' guns was liable to be picked off, Fort Union was again in the hands of traders, namely the NWFCo and an obscure little outfit known as Gregory, Bruguier, and Geowey.[60] By September 1866 these three men made an agreement with the NWFCo to share the fort's operating expenses, with Gregory, Bruguier, and Geowey paying one-third of the costs. Including wages, mess, Indian feasts, and defense needs, the average monthly operating expense at Fort Union from October 1866 to April 1867 came to just over eight hundred dollars. Trade continued at a low level, with a few thousand robes and varied furs leaving Fort Union in 1866 and 1867.[61]

Despite the agreement between the NWFCo and Gregory, Bruguier, and Geowey, friction developed at Fort Union. In January 1867, John Kerler, Gregory & Company's resident trader, informed John Geowey that the arrival of Fellowes D. Pease had brought trouble. "As I expected," wrote Kerler, "when Pease came up I cannot get along in regard to business. He won't recognize the agreement Mr. Smith wrote to me. . . . Pease is acting like a crazy man and already scattered most of his goods in camps and runs this fort now at the rate of $1,200 Expenses per month." Kerler may have been angered because Pease had traded nine hundred robes to his sixty, ignoring the agreement to avoid just such problems. Kerler hoped that if he traded carefully, he would have more goods on hand than Pease when trade picked up later in the spring. By that time, "wolfers" were poisoning their prey with strychnine, a commodity in short supply and much desired at Union. Kerler told Geowey he could purchase "about 2,000 large Wolves of trappers at $2—if you bring the cash along." Many, if not most, fur hunters now operated on a cash-only basis.[62]

By April the situation was worse. Agent Wilkinson permitted Pease to tear down two log houses outside the fort, for which Gregory, Bruguier, and Geowey had paid $110, to use for firewood. Wilkinson had also pressured the small company to feast Indians whom Kerler believed were working for Pease. The greatest outrage was that Wilkinson had "shamefully" canceled Geowey & Company's license "just at the time when big trade comes in and Pease is out of goods." Kerler thought (with some justification) that Pease and Wilkinson were in cahoots and that his company's trade consequently suffered a loss of three thousand to four thousand dollars. If only his store were open, Kerler could "trade a big lot and beat Pease all to pieces." But Wilkinson, fearful that Gregory was scheming to take over his duties, would not cooperate.[63]

Clearly, increasing the number of trading outfits at Fort Union brought no improvement in the conduct of the trade. Wilkinson and Pease's behavior merely legitimated anxieties that troubled top-level officers within the Indian Department. "There are evils incident to the trade," wrote Commissioner D. N. Cooley to Secretary of the Interior James Harlan in March 1866, "and temptations to fraud and wrong, in any event, and there is too often reason to suspect collusion with Officers of this Bureau, but such evils, temptations and possible collusions must only increase with the number of traders." With military men, Indian agents, and traders alike scrambling for advantage, there remained no untainted guardian of the law, or of the Indians' best interests. By the time the battle-scarred old "Company" retired, there was little left to feed on but the carcass of the fur trade, and unpleasant indeed were those buzzards who picked its bones at the end.[64]

Trade tensions were not the only problems at Fort Union after Chouteau & Company sold it. For the past two years, Sioux aggression against Fort Buford had kept traders' fears at a high pitch. Twice during July 1864, Sioux raided Fort Union for horses. On July 19 a party stole every horse belonging to Captain Greer's Wisconsin Volunteers, "not more than 40 steps from one of the bastions." None were recovered. Ten days later, seventeen Sioux made off with two horses belonging to some visiting Assiniboines. The Assiniboines, some Gros Ventres, and a few soldiers gave chase, recovered the stock, and killed and scalped one Sioux raider. In April 1865, Sioux raiders killed one soldier and wounded another who were hunting a grizzly bear less than a mile from Fort Union. In August of that year, Fellowes D. Pease purchased the remaining army stores and then departed with the troops, but not before he invited the Crows to come and trade. Charles Larpenteur thought that a bad idea, and events proved him correct. In September, while some two hundred Crows were at Fort Union, their enemies the Assiniboines ran off forty-five horses; during the attack four Assiniboines died and two Crows were wounded. So much for Pease's skill as a tribal diplomat.[65]

On July 18, 1866, a Sioux war party shot two traders from Fort Union on their way to Fort Buford, then attempted to burn down the military post. A few days later, downriver at Fort Berthold, federal peace commissioners (including Charles Larpenteur) were interrupted in the midst of discussions with the Gros Ventres when some Sioux approached. The Gros Ventres dashed off in pursuit, returning shortly with scalps, hands, and feet of their foes. The Gros Ventres, having earlier told the commissioners that they were fools for believing the Sioux would abide by treaties, then said, "Here are your Sioux. . . . They are the very same Sioux with whom you have just been making peace. We finished them with the fine new guns you gave them, and scalped them with your own knives."[66]

Sioux animosity was aimed toward soldiers more than traders. Traders had dealt with them for many years and, even with their faults, had served a more useful purpose than the bluecoats, who seemed to have come with evil intentions. In late November 1866, Crows Breast, the Gros Ventre who had helped derail the NWFCo fraud noted earlier, warned Colonel William G. Rankin at Fort Buford that eleven camps of Hunkpapa, Sans Arcs, Two Kettles, and Blackfeet Sioux, with some Cheyennes, were gathered near the Little Missouri preparing to strike the whites. From December 20 until after New Year's Day the Indians sporadically attacked soldiers at the fort and anyone caught outside, but this time they also harassed Fort Union.[67]

Charles W. Hoffman, a Fort Buford sutler (and perhaps an NWFCo employee), recalled that on December 20 the Sioux attacked Able Farwell, a trader going from Fort Union to Buford, who held them off until soldiers from Buford rescued him. On January 1, 1867, two other "citizens" were attacked; one was killed after emptying his guns at the Sioux. From December until mid-March "there was scarcely a day the Indians did not show themselves," and at one point three thousand Sioux were observed near Fort Buford. Among them was Sitting Bull, who swore he would kill every soldier at the fort. Hoffman wintered at Fort Union, along with about thirty white men and some Assiniboines, who "were kept constantly on regular guard duty day and night" to prevent surprise attacks. Two large candle lanterns with "glazed window sash" were placed outside the walls near each bastion on dark nights to provide better security.[68]

In early spring the traders "had a very narrow escape at Fort Union from all being massacred." A large party of Santee and Cut Head Sioux, led by Thundering Bull, came to Fort Union to discuss trade. This was the first time some of them had been to a post since the uprising in Minnesota four years earlier. The Sioux feasted and danced with some

Assiniboines in the fort's "Indian House," a large room with an open roof to accommodate cooking fires. The next morning, Fellowes D. Pease, whom the Sioux called Omaneche, or "Beans," sent most of his men across the river for firewood and invited the Sioux to a council. When they showed up armed with bows and guns, it became clear that the situation might turn nasty. Sensing danger, Pease bluffed the Sioux by telling them that he would blow up the fort and everyone in it unless they put away their weapons. Meanwhile, Hoffman went to the palisades and gestured wildly for the wood gatherers to return, which they soon did. Facing the traders' guns, Thundering Bear and his warriors gave up the idea of overcoming the white men and left. Later that day, Thundering Bear allegedly told Colonel Rankin at Fort Buford, "Today at the trading post above here [Fort Union] we thought we could kill the few men left in the fort and take what we wanted and go, but Omaneche was too smart for us."[69]

Hoffman later made a statement to the effect that "the hostile attitude of Sitting Bull's Sioux that season not only occasioned great expense in hiring and feeding whites and Indians to guard Fort Union but it virtually ruined our trade with other Indians who were afraid to come into Fort Union on account of the hostiles." With this sort of "evidence" in hand, James Hubbell placed a claim before the government for the defense of Fort Union and for other alleged Indian depredations, including an attack on a wagon train at Knife River in 1864 and the destruction of a trading post on the Niobrara River in 1865. The total for all this came to a whopping $56,470.42. Hubbell maintained that his men had defended "Government property at Fort Union by order of Mahlon Wilkinson, U.S. Indian Agent who was there with his family and a quantity of annuity goods during the winter of 1866–7." Speaking of Fort Union, Hubbell asserted that "our trading post was endangered by the presence of the Indian Agt. and his annuity supplies," and the price for defending these goods was $45,454.70.[70]

Hubbell's claim was initially reviewed by the Senate in 1871. After deliberation, the Committee on Indian Affairs dismissed the outrageous claim. For one thing, examination of Hubbell's claims for provisions disclosed that each "defender" consumed nineteen and one-half pounds of food each day. In addition, the value of Gregory, Bruguier, and Geowey's buildings (worth $110 when they were dismantled for firewood) had been inflated to $2,000. The committeemen decided that the claim had been made by a company "which, by making only feeble efforts to protect their own property, may hope to find a purchaser in the Government." Even at the high tide of Ulysses Grant's corruption-riddled administration, this was simply too much to swallow.[71]

Yet another instance of NWFCo chicanery occurred after the army briefly used Fort Berthold during the Indian scare of 1864–66. True to form, Hubbell billed the army $14,020 for its occupancy of Fort Berthold for twenty-four months. Documents appear to indicate that as late as 1868 the army refused to pay the bill, although the NWFCo continued to pressure the Quartermaster Department. Hubbell also noted that from May 19 until August 22, 1865, Fort Union was occupied by soldiers under Captain Greer. On the latter date, Hubbell's agent Pease bought all remaining military stores and took formal possession of the post. At about the same time, the NWFCo contracted one Amroy B. Smith to manufacture Catlinite pipes for the Indian trade, slated specifically for an anticipated treaty between General Sully and the Sioux. Sully, according to Hubbell, had engaged him to make "5,000 pipes at $5 apiece." The company advanced Smith $2,500 to begin production; profits were to be equally divided. But the treaty never came off, and the company took a "book" loss of better than $3,000 on the project. Much later, in 1902, Hubbell declared that he had traded the pipes to Upper Missouri Indians for one robe each, valued at about ten dollars.[72] Sometime after July 27, 1866, Amroy B. Smith complained to the Office of Indian Affairs about his former colleagues, signing a document in which he excoriated "that priestly and sanctimonious public robber—J. A. Smith, No. 118 Lake Street, Chicago," and the NWFCo generally.[73]

Alpheus F. Hawley, James B. Hubbell, and their NWFCo cohorts made money, but they lacked something that Pierre Chouteau, Jr., possessed. Chouteau had winked, then dissembled, while his men broke several laws, true, and he and his fellow managers were not above using influence peddling or pressure tactics with politicians. But Chouteau traded no shoddy goods or rotten food to Indians, nor did he exhibit contempt for them. To the contrary, his company established high standards for goods that prevailed for decades, and competitors were obliged to follow suit or risk the consequences. Chouteau indirectly aided the government in advancing the western frontier, but he took no hand in driving Indians from their lands as a solution for the "Indian Problem." Moreover, Chouteau's support of artists and scientists over the years suggests that he believed his senior position in the trade and in Saint Louis's community entailed a responsibility akin to republican civic-mindedness. Hubbell, Hawley, and their associates believed nothing of the sort. Ideologically, intellectually, and in the literal context of time, Chouteau was a Jeffersonian; Hubbell and Hawley were "moderns" closer in spirit and substance to men like Jay Gould or Jim Fisk. There were real differences between the old and new styles of doing business in the United States.

The NWFCo employed relatively few men, and little is known about them. Pease, Hubbell, Hawley, Bassett, and Galpin have already been mentioned. Gregory, Bruguier, & Geowey employed perhaps a dozen men at Fort Union in 1866–67. Neither company left detailed records, but it is possible to offer a brief sketch of conditions at the post in its final year or two. Traders such as Fellowes D. Pease, John Kerler, and one "Ingram" received seventy-five dollars a month, while the working hands made between forty-five and fifty dollars per month. A Hispano named Philip Alvarez appears frequently in company records and presents a good example of the diverse jobs a man might do for the firm.

Alvarez made seventy-five dollars a month, better than the average hand. He had built one of the houses outside the fort in May 1866, but he also was a tailor. He made moccasins, leggings, blanket coats, jackets, shirts, and other items. Indeed, so valuable were his skills that the company bought a fifty-dollar sewing machine for Alvarez in December 1866. As a sideline, he purchased strychnine, used to poison wolves, and sold the skins for two dollars apiece to the company. Still, despite his several occupations, wealth eluded Alvarez, and he often wound up in the red at month's end.[74]

There were other Hispanic employees. One, named Phil Lavatta (Lovato), worked for Gregory, Bruguier, & Geowey, as did a man named Rafael Durant (Durán), who made adobes for the company in July 1867. Another employee's name is recorded only as "Miguel," and one, called "Joe Ramsay," was probably the José Ramusio mentioned earlier. French surnames also appear, such as "Pet Shuquette" (Pierre Chouquette or Duchuquette, an interpreter), Louis Bompart, and "Frank Pierre." Several

Anglo-American men, such as George Grinnell (a carpenter) and men named Archdale, Owen, and Graves, also worked at Fort Union in its last year. A man named Pierre Hawk (also known as Black Hawk) engaged as "interpreter and Trader at Fort Union" on May 27, 1866, for seventy-five dollars a month "and ration," to include provisions for his family at cost plus 10 percent. As in earlier years, interpreters commanded a better wage than common hands. Some of these men and their families were at Fort Union when Chouteau owned it and stayed on after it was sold. Joe Ramsay, Henry Archdale, Philip Alvarez, and Tom Campbell all were at Union in 1863, while Louis Bompart, George Kiplin, and Gustave Cagnat appear in Chouteau records for Forts Benton or Berthold that year.[75]

Charles Larpenteur, closely associated with Fort Union over much of its history, was a Chouteau veteran among the NWFCo newcomers. In the spring of 1864, Charles Chouteau had placed Larpenteur in charge of Fort Union. On March 26, Larpenteur left Saint Louis aboard the steamer *Benton*, which he said carried fifty tons of commissary stores and seventeen barrels of company liquor, and he arrived at Fort Union on the last day of May. He served as a trader and as an interpreter for the North Western Treaty Commission. When the *Benton* landed at Fort Union, "the doors were all closed, and not a living object was stirring except some buffalo, pasturing about 300 yards from the fort." Sioux harassment kept the traders more or less penned up in the fort, but the white mens' fears abated somewhat on June 13 when the *Yellow Stone* arrived. Charles Chouteau was aboard, and so was Captain William Greer with a company of Wisconsin Volunteers. On June 20, Larpenteur recorded a "Census of half Breeds families" who worked for Chouteau. His census, the only one known to have been made at Fort Union, included fourteen men, sixteen women (two men each had two wives), and nineteen children ranging from four months to fifteen years of age. Larpenteur "took charge of Fort Union for the last year of the American Fur Company" on July 2, when the *Yellow Stone* passed down from Fort Benton en route to Saint Louis.[76]

When the NWFCo bought Fort Union, Larpenteur was there to take an inventory. Upon the arrival of the Galvanized Yankees, Larpenteur was obliged to turn out his men while the soldiers occupied the fort for two months. In late August, Fellowes D. Pease and the soldiers departed, leaving Larpenteur in charge of only six men "in a place where a company of soldiers had once been thought required for safety." On September 17, 1865, "A. B. Smith" (whom Larpenteur referred to as "the Chicago hypocrite"), Hawley, and Pease arrived aboard the *Hattie May*, ready to take over. Larpenteur, "not liking the proceedings of this new firm," requested a discharge and soon departed, bidding farewell to "many of my old friends among the Assiniboines, who shook hands with me, saying they were sorry to see me go."[77]

Larpenteur returned again to Fort Union in June 1866 as an Assiniboine interpreter for the North Western Treaty Commission and again in June 1867 on the steamer *Jennie* as a trader for Durfee & Peck, in opposition to the NWFCo. His men built an adobe house outside the fort, and during the summer trade they acquired two thousand buffalo robes, nine hundred elk hides, eighteen hundred deer skins, and one thousand wolves. That October, in New York City, Durfee & Peck made a deal with C. Francis Bates of the NWFCo "to prevent Competition and for mutual advantages." The agreement aimed to reduce operational costs through price fixing and to provide "Mutual aid & assistance or protection . . . in case of hostile attack" on either company.[78]

Larpenteur's star, like Fort Union's, was now in sharp decline. According to Larpenteur, Durfee & Peck's agents fired him because of some "jealousies" and "malicious reports" when they arrived on May 18, 1868. By then, Fort Union had been demolished. The story of its final days in the summer of 1867 is best told by Larpenteur, the only eyewitness who kept a running record.[79]

Business was slow in June and July, with occasional visits from Crows, Assiniboines, Yanktonais, and Red River métis to trade a few robes and fresh or dried meat. The Missouri was crowded with steamers and mackinaw boats packed with miners passing up and down between Fort Benton and the States; hardly a day passed without the appearance of at least one vessel. On July 11 two soldiers from Buford murdered one of their fellows, dumping his body into the Missouri after stealing several hundred dollars in cash from the dead man. On July 12 there was a "Great drunken frolic" at Fort Union—no doubt one of the last in a long line—when some liquor was offloaded from the steamer *Agnes*.[80]

On August 2, thirty Sioux appeared, and cannons from both Fort Buford and Fort Union blasted away at them, but there was "No boddy

killed that we Can learn of except two Cows killed and two wounded."
Two days later, "the *Miner* arrived at Union, and left at about one oclock
after having demolished the old Fort Union Kitchen for Steamboat wood.
Fort Union is Sold to the government to build up Fort Buford. . . .
Indians and old Squaws about the establishment all drunk."[81]

Larpenteur hurried his crew to finish the interior plastering (with
white clay and buffalo-hide glue) and exterior mud surface of his new
adobe trade house, complete with a small bastion. Meanwhile, on August
7 "the Soldiers Commenced tairing down the Fort Union," and on
Saturday the 10th, Larpenteur moved out of Fort Union for the last time.
While Phil Lovata and Rafael Duran continued making adobes "to build
themselves a house," Larpenteur had the stock of goods removed from
Union and placed into the new store. A few days later, the old blacksmith
shop was dismantled and taken up to Fort Buford.[82]

In late September trade picked up a bit, and Larpenteur acquired two
hundred buffalo robes, fifty dressed domestic cow skins (an indication
of changing times for the Indians, who sometimes ran cattle on horseback as they had bison), and some three thousand pounds of dried meat
from Indians coming to the fort for their annuities. By then some of the
goods from Fort Union had been taken to the NWFCo's sutler store at
Fort Totten near Devil's Lake. On September 26 all the laborers and the
cook moved down to Fort Buford, leaving only the trading clerks at
Union. The next day ten Sioux raiders surprised some NWFCo men at
work in the hay field, but the only casualty occurred when the white men
killed one of the attackers' horses. Soon, however, the Sioux kidnapped,
and later killed, an Assiniboine woman from a party out to butcher some
buffalo. The Sioux leader Sitting Bull was again in the vicinity, and he
stopped at Fort Union on October 15.[83]

From late October until late November, Larpenteur and his men were
busy hauling logs, sawn lumber, goods, and peltries from Fort Union to
the Indian store at Fort Buford, which was completed on November 25.
On the closing day of the month, Larpenteur wrote that he "hauled two
loads from Union. Nothing left at Union but adobes."[84] This laconic
statement was the final sentence written by a resident at Fort Union.
Charles Larpenteur's departure that day marked the end of almost forty
years of life at the post. He alone, among all of those who had lived there,

knew it in its infancy and in its old age. Larpenteur himself, grieving for his dead children, embittered and impoverished after his life as a trader, died in November 1872 and was buried near his house on the Little Sioux River, about thirty miles north of Council Bluffs, Iowa.

By the time the chill winter winds of 1867 blew across Dakota Territory, Fort Union, the once mighty bastion of enterprise, lay in ruins. Its stone was carted off to build a powder magazine at Fort Buford, its timbers hauled away or consumed in steamers' bellies, its former residents scattered to the four winds.

Old memories died hard for some people. In 1869 a Hidatsa chief named Crow-Flies-High led a dissident band of his people from Fort Berthold to Fort Union's ruins and built a small village nearby. Until the fall of 1884 these Hidatsas lived at the Garden Coulee, once the site of the fort's vegetable garden.[85] When Crow-Flies-High departed, some of the last surviving men and women who retained a living link to the old fur post went with them.

Fort Union had vanished, but no amount of change on the Upper Missouri River could eradicate memories of the post. By the early twentieth century, reminiscences and historical pieces began to appear that documented and commemorated the fort. In 1925 the Great Northern Railroad, along with historical societies in North and South Dakota, Minnesota, and Montana, sponsored a flashy "Upper Missouri Historical Expedition" intended to increase public interest (and tourism) along the Great Northern's route to the Pacific Northwest, which in places paralleled the routes of early French and British explorers, Lewis and Clark, fur traders, and the Stevens railroad survey of 1854. Historians, artists, Indians, railroad magnates, and enthusiastic supporters detrained at various sites to deliver accolades to the past, enjoy demonstrations of native ceremonialism and crafts, and dedicate statues and historic shrines. People began to discuss the idea of rebuilding the old fort, but nobody knew where to find funds for what would obviously be an expensive undertaking. Eventually, the National Park Service acquired the site. In the late 1980s, after historians plowed through piles of documents and archeologists coaxed artifacts and data from the soil, politicians, local boosters, and Park Service administrators launched a program resulting in a near-complete reconstruction of the fort. Thanks to the National

Park Service and to many dedicated citizens around Williston, North Dakota, Fort Union stands again, exhibiting vestiges of its former glory as a historic site and museum.

Why was there such interest in Fort Union? In the early twentieth century, the post symbolized the United States' dramatic "great westward movement," and fur traders were cast as advance agents of a Manifest Destiny that was ultimately fulfilled by the army, farmers, and town builders. This interpretation reflects an outdated "consensus" view of American history that promoted Euro-American cultural imperialism. If this book has succeeded at all, it should be plain that such a simplistic appraisal leaves out many aspects of the post's historical importance. As a staging platform for the scientific and aesthetic "discovery" of the West, Fort Union played a unique role: no other trading post sheltered as many naturalists and artists, and no other fur company equaled the yeoman service of Chouteau's company in this regard.

Something else, however, seems even more significant, because it resonates at a deep and fundamental level in American society. The Euro-Americans, Indians, and mixed-bloods who lived and traded at Fort Union were participants in a social experiment that expressed what we today would call multiculturalism. What they demonstrated was the possibility that people with radically different ethnic, linguistic, and cultural backgrounds could live and work together and merge their cultures in meaningful ways. By 1870 the experiment had unraveled, but it did not do so because of internal or inherent failures. Instead, it went to pieces because the citizens of the United States and their government were devoted to a unitary culture that refused to accommodate the range of differences visible every day at Fort Union.

Fort Union's history reveals considerable irony, and one of the greatest ironies arises from the fact that its social organization required an acceptance of cultural pluralism. Not only did this predate John Collier's application of similar ideas to the "Indian New Deal," but the ethnic diversity that helped the trading post become a success has yet to be broadly accepted in the United States. Modern sociologists tell us that the once popular conception of America as an ethnic "melting pot" has been supplanted by that of the "salad bowl," wherein each component is integrated while retaining distinctive characteristics. If a useful civics lesson can be drawn from the post's history, it may be that people need not necessarily embrace, or fully understand, someone else's culture in order to construct common ground, or admit to a common humanity with their neighbors. A culture—or a nation—that denounces such differences risks fragmentation, and may find itself sacrificing worthy ideals to a wrong-headed urge to impose uniformity on its members.

Notes

INTRODUCTION

1. Peter C. Newman, *Company of Adventurers*, vol. 2, *Caesars of the Wilderness*, 366–72.

2. Marjorie Wilkins Campbell, *The North West Company*, 1, 18–19, and passim. See also Heather Devine, "Roots in the Mohawk Valley: Sir William Johnson's Legacy in the North West Company," in *The Fur Trade Revisited: Selected Papers of the Sixth North American Fur Trade Conference, Mackinac Island, Michigan, 1991*, 217–42, ed. Jennifer S. H. Brown, W. J. Eccles, and Donald P. Heldman.

3. Edwin Thompson Denig, *Five Indian Tribes of the Upper Missouri*, ed. John C. Ewers, 100–101, n. 5.

4. For early Assiniboine trade, see Elliott Coues, ed., *New Light on the Early History of the Greater Northwest: The Manuscript Journals of Alexander Henry and David Thompson, 1799–1814*. (New York: Francis P. Harper, 1897; reprint, Minneapolis: Ross and Haines, 1965). John R. Swanton observed that "the utility of the Cree in the promotion and preservation of the fur trade [in Canada] has prevented that displacement and depletion so common among the tribes of the United States" (Swanton, *The Indian Tribes of North America*, 556). On the Mandans, see Arthur J. Ray, *Indians in the Fur Trade: Their Role as Trappers, Hunters, and Middlemen in the Lands Southwest of the Hudson Bay* (Toronto and Buffalo: University of Toronto Press, 1974), 53–57, 89–90.

5. Interior posts of the HBC sent almost no robes between 1800 and 1815, while the Americans evidently gathered from twenty thousand to two hundred thousand robes annually between 1815 and 1830. Ray, *Indians in the Fur Trade*,

210. See also Elliott Coues, ed., *Forty Years a Fur Trader on the Upper Missouri: The Personal Narrative of Charles Larpenteur, 1833–1872*, 108.

6. Albert L. Hurtado and Peter Iverson, eds., *Major Problems in American Indian History* (Lexington, Mass.: D.C. Heath and Company, 1994), 138. Practically the same words could be found in a dozen or more sources, including writings of George Catlin in the 1830s.

7. See Richard White, *The Middle Ground: Indians, Empires, and Republics in the Great Lakes Region, 1650–1815* (New York: Cambridge University Press, 1991). Earlier writers recognized the same theme: "An outgrowth of these contacts [between Europeans and Indians] was the adoption by each of items from the material culture of the other, and, as a result, each became dependent on the other" (S. Lyman Tyler, *A History of Indian Policy*, 13).

8. See Arthur J. Ray, "The Fur Trade as an Aspect of Native History," in Ian A. L. Getty and Donald B. Smith, eds., *One Century Later: Western Canadian Reserve Indians Since Treaty 7* (Vancouver: University of British Columbia Press, 1978), 7–19; and Toby Morantz, "Old Texts, New Questions: Another Look at the Issue of Continuity in the Early Fur Trade Period," *Canadian Historical Review* 73 (1992): 2.

9. Edwin Thompson Denig, "Indian Tribes of the Upper Missouri," ed. by J. N. B. Hewitt, in *Forty-Sixth Annual Report of the Bureau of American Ethnology, 1928–29*, 457, 465; Denig, *Five Indian Tribes of the Upper Missouri*, ed. by John C. Ewers, 89.

10. Denig, "Indian Tribes of the Upper Missouri," 464, 467, 469.

11. Denig, *Five Indian Tribes of the Upper Missouri*, 21–22, 36.

12. Denig, "Indian Tribes of the Upper Missouri," 465; see also Bruce M. White, "Give Us a Little Milk: The Social and Cultural Meanings of Gift Giving in the Lake Superior Fur Trade," *Minnesota History* 48, no. 2 (Summer 1982): 13. See John C. Ewers, "When Red and White Men Met," *Western Historical Quarterly* 2, no. 2 (April 1971): 135.

14. J. N. B. Hewitt, ed., *Journal of Rudolph Friederich Kurz*, 176; Denig, *Five Indian Tribes of the Upper Missouri*, 157.

15. Rhoda R. Gilman, Carolyn Gilman, and Deborah M. Stultz, *The Red River Trails: Oxcart Routes between St. Paul and the Selkirk Settlement, 1820–1870*, 4, 5; Ray H. Mattison, "James Kipp," in *The Mountain Men and the Fur Trade of the Far West*, ed. LeRoy R. Hafen, 2:201–205; Annie Heloise Abel, ed., *Chardon's Journal at Fort Clark, 1834–1839*, 216–20.

16. Hiram Martin Chittenden, *The American Fur Trade of the Far West*, 1:325; Donald Dean Parker, ed., *The Recollections of Philander Prescott, Frontiersman of the Old Northwest, 1819–1862*, 54–57; Alan R. Woolworth and W. Raymond Wood, "The Archeology of a Small Trading Post (Kipp's Post, 32MN1) in the Garrison Reservoir, North Dakota," in *River Basin Surveys Papers*, numbers 15–20, 247–93, ed. Frank H. H. Roberts.

17. Kenneth Wiggans Porter, *John Jacob Astor: Business Man*, 2:686.

18. Francis Paul Prucha, *American Indian Policy in the Formative Years: The Indian Trade and Intercourse Acts, 1790–1834*, 88; Francis Paul Prucha, ed., *Documents of United States Indian Policy*, 22.

19. The factory system operated from 1796 until 1822. Prucha, *American Indian Policy*, 86; for a general survey see Ora Brooks Peake, *A History of the United States Indian Factory System, 1795–1822.*

20. Porter, *John Jacob Astor*, 2:688.

21. Ibid., 713. Soon thereafter, Astor hired Benton as a "Company" lawyer. William Nisbet Chambers, *Old Bullion Benton* (Boston: Little, Brown and Company, 1956), 110–11.

22. Chittenden, *American Fur Trade*, 1:318.

23. Ibid., 318–19.

24. Ibid., 319.

25. See Janet LeCompte, "Pierre Chouteau, Junior," in *Mountain Men and the Fur Trade*, ed. Hafen, 9:99.

26. Harvey L. Carter, "Ramsay Crooks," in *Mountain Men and the Fur Trade*, ed. Hafen, 9:130.

27. Paul Chrisler Phillips, *The Fur Trade*, 2:409–10.

28. David Lavender, *The Fist in the Wilderness*, 348.

29. Chittenden, *American Fur Trade*, 1:325; Porter, *John Jacob Astor*, 2:746; Phillips, *Fur Trade*, 2:408–409, 413.

30. Phillips, *Fur Trade*, 2:415–17.

31. Ibid., 418.

32. Ibid., 418–19.

33. Abel, *Chardon's Journal*, 199 n. 3; Ramsay Crooks, Saint Louis, July 6, 1828, to J. J. Astor, New York, Astor Papers, New York Public Library; Phillips, *Fur Trade*, 2:419.

34. Parker, *Recollections of Philander Prescott*, 92–94.

35. Abel, *Chardon's Journal*, 199 n. 3.

36. See Richard M. Clokey, *William H. Ashley: Enterprise and Politics in the Trans-Mississippi West*; Dale L. Morgan, ed., *The West of William H. Ashley, 1822–1838*, passim; and Don Berry, *A Majority of Scoundrels: An Informal History of the Rocky Mountain Fur Company.*

37. LeCompte, "Pierre Chouteau, Junior," 9:109; Ramsay Crooks, New York, to Pierre Chouteau, Jr., Saint Louis, January 27, 1841, in Chouteau Collection, Missouri Historical Society (hereafter cited as Chouteau Collection, MoHS).

38. See Patricia Nelson Limerick, *Legacy of Conquest: The Unbroken Past of the American West*, 181–83: "Did [George] Catlin denounce [Kenneth McKenzie] for his avarice and for his cruel role in the decline of the Indians?"; Peter Nabokov, ed., *Indian Testimony: A Chronicle of Indian-White Relations from Prophecy to the Present* (New York: Viking, 1991), 35, where he states that the fur trade "was

followed for many by dependency on white goods. . . . Meanwhile many white traders had proved themselves unscrupulous, manipulating their Native American customers with watered-down liquor . . . and dealing in shoddy, mass-produced goods"; and Calvin Martin, *Keepers of the Game: Indian-Animal Relationships and the Fur Trade* (Berkeley: University of California Press, 1978), who mistakenly supposes that "fur trade scholars are in uniform agreement that over the long run, the trade was a disaster for the Indian tribes involved; severe cultural disruption and often physical dislocation were commonplace." Bruce G. Trigger observes that Martin's "data are totally insufficient to confirm the theory that has been built on them" (Trigger, *Natives and Newcomers: Canada's "Heroic Age" Reconsidered*, 243).

39. Michael Allen, *Western Rivermen, 1763–1861: Ohio and Mississippi Boatmen and the Myth of the Alligator Horse* (Baton Rouge: Louisiana State University Press, 1990), 66–69.

40. When the steamboat *Assiniboine* burned below the Mandan villages in July 1835, Bernard Pratte & Company lost both vessel and cargo, valued at about fifty thousand dollars, because the vessel was uninsured. Larpenteur Manuscript Journals, vol. 2, date of August 3, 1835, in Larpenteur Family Papers, Minnesota Historical Society, Saint Paul (hereafter cited as Larpenteur MS Journals, MnHS).

41. Pierre Chouteau, Jr., Saint Louis, to Ramsay Crooks, New York, May 20, 1840, cited in Grace Lee Nute, ed., *Calendar of the American Fur Company's Papers*, 1:851.

42. Denig, "Indian Tribes of the Upper Missouri," 597, 600.

43. For Astor's schemes, consult Porter, *John Jacob Astor*, 2:771. Annie Heloise Abel saw Astor and his men as "unscrupulous, notoriously selfish, . . . brazen in their defiance of the law, [and] remorseless in their exploitation of the Indians." She also noted that the American Fur Company was "almost the only one that, in any way, compares with the gigantic commercial organizations of today" (Abel, *Chardon's Journal*, xvi, 200 n. 5).

44. This definition differs only slightly from that given in "Regulating the Indian Department," May 20, 1834. See U.S. Congress, House, 23rd Cong., 1st sess., H. Exec. Rep. 474.

45. According to Edwin Denig, only Cree and Crow hunters used steel traps with any regularity in the vicinity of Fort Union. Denig, "Indian Tribes of the Upper Missouri," 538.

46. 18th Congress: 1st Session, Senate Executive Document No. 56, March 18, 1824.

47. U.S. Congress, House, 18th Cong., 1st sess., S. Exec. Doc. 56, March 18, 1824, 18–19.

48. See Clokey, *William H. Ashley*, 80–81; and Morgan, *West of William H. Ashley*, 1–6.

49. LeCompte, "Pierre Chouteau, Junior," 9:110.

50. Gary E. Moulton, ed., *The Journals of the Lewis and Clark Expedition* (Lincoln: University of Nebraska Press, 1993) 8:277. Regarding Fort Piegan or McKenzie, in 1833 Indian agent John F. A. Sanford observed: "Since 18 months a trading post has been established (the first that ever was) in their country where they come and trade amicable. It is the first attempt ever made by American Citizens to trade with them, and has so far succeeded very well" (J. F. A. Sanford, Saint Louis, to William Clark, July 26, 1833, Office of Indian Affairs, Letters Received, 1824–1881 [M234, Roll 750], RG 75, NA [hereafter cited as OIA, LR, with microfilm and roll numbers]). Arthur J. Ray points out that the HBC's Sir George Simpson encouraged Piegan traders and raiders to acquire beaver skins south of the border (Ray, *Indians in the Fur Trade*, 201 n. 23).

51. [James A. Hamilton or Daniel Lamont?], Fort Union, May 5, 1835, to Alexander Culbertson, Fort Union Letterbook, Chouteau Collection, MoHS.

52. See Hewitt, *Kurz Journal*, 81.

53. Ibid., 81, 125; Ray, *Indians in the Fur Trade*, 198–201.

54. Denig, "Indian Tribes of the Upper Missouri," 421.

55. See John A. Walthall, "Aboriginal Pottery and the Eighteenth-Century Illini," 168–69; and Thomas E. Emerson and James A. Brown, "The Late Prehistory and Protohistory of Illinois," 107, both in *Calumet and Fleur-de-lys: Archeology of Indian and French Contact in the Midcontinent*, ed. Walthall and Emerson.

56. Denig, "Indian Tribes of the Upper Missouri," 555. See also Fowler, *Shared Symbols, Contested Meanings: Gros Ventre Culture and History, 1778–1984*, 38–43.

57. Denig, "Indian Tribes of the Upper Missouri," 459.

58. See Kenneth N. Owens and Sally L. Owens, "Buffalo and Bacteria," *Montana: The Magazine of Western History* 37, no. 2 (Spring 1987): 65–67; Rudolph W. Koucky, M.D., "The Buffalo Disaster of 1882," *North Dakota History* 50, no. 1 (Winter 1983): 23–30; and Dan Flores, "Bison Ecology and Bison Diplomacy: The Southern Plains from 1800 to 1850," *Journal of American History* 78, no. 2 (September 1991). One Assiniboine, Dan Kennedy (Ochankugahe), recalled reading an article quoting a 1938 letter printed in the *Regina Daily Star* from a person who saw "masses of dead buffalo, apparently killed by disease, covering several acres" at Cypress Hills, Saskatchewan, in 1883. Kennedy himself saw an identical scene in 1879 but concluded that the killers were agents "sent out by the U.S. Government in order to starve the Indians into submission" (Kennedy, *Recollections of an Assiniboine Chief*, 49–50).

59. See Eugene D. Fleharty, *Wild Animals and Settlers on the Great Plains* (Norman: University of Oklahoma Press, 1995), 46–54; and David D. Smits, "The Frontier Army and the Destruction of the Buffalo: 1865–1883," *Western Historical Quarterly* 25, no. 3 (Autumn 1994).

60. See Janet Lecompte, "John F. A. Sanford," in *Mountain Men and the Fur Trade*, ed. Hafen, 9:351–59. Annie H. Abel displayed a remarkable animosity

toward Sanford in her annotations to *Chardon's Journal,* an assessment not supported by available documentation. See Sanford to Clark, June 20, 1830, and Sanford to Commissioner of Indian Affairs, December 31, 1834 (Roll 884); and Sanford to Clark, September 3, 1833, OIA, LR (M234, Roll 750). An Astor account book in the Chouteau Collection, MoHS, records several sums of money given or loaned to Webster. By 1846, Webster had repaid Chouteau $12,373.80. See "Webster, Daniel," index entry in Nute, *Calendar of the American Fur Company's Papers.* Unfortunately, the microfilm edition does not to contain the letters therein cited.

61. Sanford, New York, to Chouteau, Saint Louis, January 3, 1839, in Chouteau Collection, MoHS. Also included is a copy of the draft proposal for transport of the goods.

62. E. A. Hitchcock, Washington, to G. [*sic*] Hartley Crawford, February 8, 1839, OIA, LR (M234, Roll 752).

63. See Pierre Chouteau, Jr., & Co., Saint Louis, to T. Hartley Crawford, August 5, 1841, OIA, LR (M234, Roll 752).

64. Benjamin Clapp, a Company agent, informed Pierre Chouteau, Jr., that a Winnebago and Sioux contract would mean "some money will be made by this operation, probably a pretty little sum of $3000 to $4000—this matter has been managed rightly this time" (B. Clapp, Saint Louis, to Pierre Chouteau, Jr., March 4, 1843, Chouteau Collection, MoHS; see also T. H. Harvey, Saint Louis, to T. Hartley Crawford, June 26, 1844, OIA, LR [M234, Roll 753].

65. See Henry Chouteau, New York, January 9, 1847, to Chouteau & Valle, Chouteau Collection, MoHS.

66. Joshua Pilcher, Saint Louis, to T. Hartley Crawford, Washington, December 30, 1840, OIA, LR (M234, Roll 752).

67. Ramsay Crooks, Lapointe, Lake Superior, to Pierre Chouteau, Jr., Saint Louis, September 12, 1839; Chouteau Collection, MoHS.

68. See John E. Sunder, *Joshua Pilcher, Fur Trader and Indian Agent,* 159–65. See also Ramsay Crooks, New York, to Pierre Chouteau, Jr., St. Louis, March 12, June 27, and July 11, 1841, in Chouteau Collection, MoHS.

69. Sunder, *Joshua Pilcher,* 162–67; Ray H. Mattison, "David Dawson Mitchell"; and Charles E. Hanson, Jr., "Charles Keemle," in *Mountain Men and the Fur Trade,* ed. Hafen, 2:241–46; 8:203–209.

70. See Ray H. Mattison, "David Dawson Mitchell"; and Lecompte, "Pierre Chouteau Junior," in *Mountain Men and the Fur Trade,* ed. Hafen, 2:241–46; 9:110.

71. See William H. Goetzmann, "The Mountain Man as Jacksonian Man," *American Quarterly,* 15:3 (autumn 1963), 402–15.

72. "Invoice of merchandise imported by the American Fur Company, New York, . . . to be consigned to Pierre Chouteau, Jun. . . . for a/c and risk of said Company's Western Department," Chouteau Collection, MoHS.

73. "Persons Employed for the Upper Missouri Outfit for the Year 1830," and "Inventory of Stock belonging to Upper Missouri Outfit at Fort Union 10th June 1831," both in Chouteau Collection, MoHS.

74. W. B. Astor, New York, to Pierre Chouteau, Jr., Saint Louis, December 23, 1829, Chouteau Collection, MoHS.

75. "Post Accounts Current, Ledger D, 1831–1836," Fur Trade Ledgers, AFC West, MoHS (Roll 6, Vol. V).

76. Inventory sheet for several Western Department posts, dated Fort Pierre, July 9, 1832, Chouteau Collection, MoHS.

77. "Inventory of Stock at Fort Union, June 18, 1832," Chouteau Collection, MoHS.

78. "Account Sales of Sundry Furs & Skins Rec'd and Sold for account of Upper Missouri Outfit 1834 by the American Fur Company," in Sales & Accounts Current, Vol. 1, American Fur Company Papers, New York Historical Society, hereafter cited as NYHS (Roll 19); inventory figures appear in "Post Accounts Current," Fur Trade Ledgers, AFC West, MoHS, 167, 188.

79. Furs & Skins, vol. 1, 1835–1837, and Furs & Skins, vol. 2, 1836–1839, American Fur Company Papers, NYHS (Roll 18).

80. Invoices Out, 1834–1839, and Invoice Blotter No. 1, 1839–1841, Fur Trade Ledgers, MoHS (Roll 7, Vol. Y; Roll 9, Vol. DD).

81. Ledger, 1853–1857, Fur Trade Ledgers, MoHS (Roll 19, Vol. 7).

82. Pierre Chouteau & Co. No. 3, Journal No. 2, 1856–1858, Fur Trade Ledgers, MoHS (Roll 16, Vol. WW).

83. Pierre Chouteau & Co., New York, Sales Book, 1859–1864, Fur Trade Ledgers, MoHS (Roll 21, Vol. 17).

CHAPTER ONE

1. Hiram Martin Chittenden and Alfred Talbot Richardson, eds., *Life, Letters, and Travels of Father Pierre-Jean De Smet, S.J., 1801–1873,* 1:244; 2:604, 652; 3:857; "Stay at Fort Union, Description of the Fort and the Surrounding Area and the Assiniboin Indians," Prince Maximilian Journals, chapter 5, typescript courtesy of the Joslyn Art Museum, Omaha, Nebraska; Edwin T. Denig, "Description of Fort Union," July 30, 1843, in *John James Audubon and His Journals,* ed. Maria R. Audubon, 2:180–88; Coues, *Forty Years a Fur Trader,* 108–109; "Persons Employed for the Upper Missouri Outfit for the Year 1830," Chouteau Collection, MoHS.

2. Chittenden, *American Fur Trade,* 1:327–28. Chittenden cites a number of documents no longer extant in collections, including letters from McKenzie, at Vermillion River, to Pierre Chouteau, Jr., October 2, 1828; from McKenzie, at Fort Tecumseh, [to Chouteau?], December 26, 1828; and from McKenzie, at Fort Tecumseh, [to Chouteau?], March 15, 1829 (2:958–59). A letter from Pierre

Chouteau, Jr., Saint Louis, to William B. Astor, April 19, 1830, indicates that three
posts were in operation in the upper country, "at the Mandans, at the mouth of
the Yellowstone, and Fort Union two hundred miles further up" (2:959).

3. McKenzie, Fort Tecumseh, May 1829, to Laidlaw and Lamont, in Chouteau
Collection, MoHS.

4. Lynelle A. Peterson and William J. Hunt, Jr., *The 1987 Investigations at
Fort Union Trading Post: Archeology and Architecture*, 107. See also William J. Hunt,
Jr., "Fort Floyd: An Enigmatic Nineteenth-Century Trading Post," *North Dakota
History* 61:3 (Summer 1994), 7–20.

5. "A Tabular Statement Showing the number and names of the American
citizens who have been killed or robbed while engaged in the Fur Trade or the
Inland Trade to Mexico, Since the late war with Great Britain . . . ," OIA, LR,
Saint Louis Superintendency, 1824–51 (M234, Roll 749). Three more names
were added by 1831, and more men died in 1832.

6. "Inventory of Stock remaining on hand at Fort Floyd, April 29, 1829";
"Inventory of Stock belonging to Upper Missouri Outfit 1828 at Fort Tecumseh
7th May 1829"; and "Inventory of Merchandise remaining on hand at Vermillion
River 18th May 1829 the property of the Upper Missouri Outfit," Chouteau
Collection, MoHS.

7. "Journal of Fort Tecumseh, January 31, 1830 to June 10, 1830," May 19,
22, 23, 1830; and Kenneth McKenzie, Fort Union, May 5, 1830, to "Gentlemen
in charge of Fort Tecumseh," Chouteau Collection, MoHS. See also "Persons
Employed for the Upper Missouri Outfit for the Year 1830," Chouteau Collection, MoHS. About 120 men, nearly half of 258 engaged that year, went to Fort
Union in 1830, making it the most heavily staffed. Many engagés were listed as
voyageurs, or canoemen/laborers, but a number probably remained at the post
during their one-year engagements. About 40 signed contracts at Fort Union,
while some came from Saint Louis and 38 came from Montreal.

8. Entries for July 15–25 and August 25, "Journal of Fort Tecumseh, June
14, 1830, to April 8, 1831," Chouteau Collection, MoHS, 1830.

9. Entry for January 8, 1831, "Journal of Fort Tecumseh, June 14, 1830 to
April 8, 1831," Chouteau Collection, MoHS. ("Lemay, Vachard, and Hibert
returned from hunting the horses lost by Mr. McKenzie and party in Route from
St. Louis to this place. They saw no signs of them.")

10. Larpenteur says that by 1834, McKenzie was "considered the king of the
Missouri" (Coues, *Forty Years a Fur Trader*, 65).

11. Entries for December 18 and 28, 1830, "Journal of Fort Tecumseh, June
14, 1830 to April 8, 1831," Chouteau Collection, MoHS.

12. Excavations since 1986 have revealed architectural features and construction details absent from historical documentation for the site. See Hunt,
"Origins of Fort Union," 377–93.

13. George Catlin, *Letters and Notes on the Manners, Customs, and Conditions of the North American Indians*, 1:14, 15, 21.

14. See William H. Goetzmann, David C. Hunt, Marsha V. Gallagher, and William J. Orr, *Karl Bodmer's America*, 191, plate 193.

15. This discussion is based on Peterson and Hunt, *1987 Investigations at Fort Union*, 105–109, and Hunt, "Origins of Fort Union."

16. On French architecture in the Mississippi Valley, see Charles E. Peterson, "The Houses of French St. Louis," in *The French in the Mississippi Valley*, ed. John Francis McDermott, 17–40.

17. Hunt, "Origins of Fort Union," 382–83.

18. Coues, *Forty Years a Fur Trader*, 61–62.

19. Sills on the east and north palisades of Fort Union II "were integrated directly into the foundation walls of the Northeast Bastion," suggesting that "the palisade was constructed before the building of the Northeast Bastion" (Peterson and Hunt, *1987 Investigations at Fort Union*, 21, 111).

20. "Chevaux de-frise" may imply that the tops of the palisade poles were sharpened, since no elaborate structure is evident in Bodmer's sketch. Quote is from Maximilian's journal.

21. Peterson, "Houses of French St. Louis," 19; also Maximilian's journal.

22. Prince Maximilian's comments, from his journal.

23. George R. Brooks, ed., "The Private Journal of Robert Campbell," *Bulletin of the Missouri Historical Society*, October 1963 and January 1964, 6.

24. Kenneth McKenzie, Fort Union, February 14, 1832, to D. D. Mitchell, Fort Clark, Chouteau Collection, MoHS.

25. See Ewers, ed., *Five Indian Tribes of the Upper Missouri*, xiv; Hewitt, *Kurz Journal*, 101, 120, 123

26. Audubon, *Audubon and His Journals*, 181; Hewitt, *Kurz Journal*, 122, n. 42.

27. A competitor at the time, Robert Campbell, wrote on "Sabbath December 15—Last night two sides of McKenzies new fort was leveled with the ground." Maximilian, at Fort Clark, heard that "the wind had blown down all the pickets at Fort Union" (Brooks, "Private Journal of Robert Campbell," 111 n. 80; Peterson and Hunt, *1987 Investigations at Fort Union*, 111–13).

28. Hewitt, *Kurz Journal*, 122 n. 42.

29. Hunt, "Origins of Fort Union," 387; and "A List of Men to be employed . . . in the Upper Missouri and to be transported on Board the Steamer Yellow Stone," April 15, 1831, and Fort Union Letterbook, 1833–1835, both in Chouteau Collection, MoHS.

30. Audubon, *Audubon and His Journals*, 2:186.

31. McKenzie wrote on September 17 that "one bastion is roofed & shingled & pointed, the other built up as high as the pickets. Luteman has made his arrangements for the kitchen, and has erected & shingled five compartments

under the intended gallery" (Fort Union Letterbook, September 17 and October 9, 1834, Chouteau Collection, MoHS).

32. Audubon, *Audubon and His Journals*, 2:181–82. A painting of Fort Union attributed to J. B. Moncravie is in Hunt, "Origins of Fort Union," 378. Numerous flags were ordered over the years, some for Fort Union, others to be given to Indians. Fourteen flags in three sizes appear on a list of merchandise ordered for 1833. See "Post Accounts Current, Ledger D, 1831–1836," Fur Trade Ledgers, AFC West, MoHS.

33. Hunt, "Origins of Fort Union," 386–87.

34. Audubon, *Audubon and His Journals*, 2:181–82.

35. Ibid., 186–87.

36. Carl Wimer and Father Jakob Schmidt made illustrations of Fort Union in 1858 depicting the new flagpole structure, and an 1866 photograph shows the same structure.

37. Audubon, *Audubon and His Journals*, 2:184–85; and Peterson and Hunt, *1987 Investigations at Fort Union*, 114–20.

38. Audubon, *Audubon and His Journals*, 2:185–86. On August 15, 1843, the day he left Fort Union, Isaac Sprague noted that the pickets stood "20 feet high made of hewn cottonwood 1 ft. square. . . . the gate is 14 ft high by 12 wide Flag staff in center 60 feet . . . The ground is very muddy when wet, but soon dries hard enough for bricks" (Diary of Isaac Sprague, courtesy of the Boston Athenaeum).

39. Audubon, *Audubon and His Journals*, 2:185. For a bird's-eye perspective image of the fort, showing the painting and many other details (also possibly Moncravie's work), see Hunt, "Origins of Fort Union," 378.

40. Hewitt, *Kurz Journal*, 244. There was a room of this description already in service at the fort. In October 1851, Kurz drew Le Tout Piqué (Cree) and his retinue holding council with Baptiste (an interpreter), Denig, and Kurz in such a room. See Ernst J. Kläy and Hans Läng, *Das Romantische Leben der Indianer malerisch darzustellen . . . Leben und Werk von Rudolf Friedrich Kurz (1818–1871)* (AARE: Solothurn, 1984), 99.

41. Audubon, *Audubon and His Journals*, 2:183–84.

42. Ibid., 184.

43. Peterson and Hunt, *1987 Investigations at Fort Union*, 12, 47, 86, 120.

44. Audubon, *Audubon and His Journals*, 2:187.

CHAPTER TWO

1. Mary Lee Spence and Donald Jackson, eds., *The Expeditions of John Charles Frémont* 1 (Urbana: University of Illinois Press, 1973): 37, 45–46, 87–90, and elsewhere.

2. The six-hundred-odd-volume library of Auguste Chouteau, grandfather of Pierre Chouteau, Jr., included historical, scientific, ecclesiastical, and literary works. John Francis McDermott, *Private Libraries in Creole St. Louis*, Part one and 128ff.

3. John E. Sunder, *The Fur Trade on the Upper Missouri, 1840–1865*, 175–78.

4. Chouteau's company also assisted the cartographer Joseph N. Nicollet during 1838–39. See Edmund C. Bray and Martha Coleman Bray, eds., *Joseph N. Nicollet on the Plains and Prairies*, 5 n. 9, 10, 27, 34; and Sunder, *Fur Trade on the Upper Missouri*, 176.

5. E. T. Denig, Fort Union, December 1, 1849, to Alexander Culbertson, in Chouteau Collection, MoHS. Specimens included beavers, a white wolf, a "War Eagle," an antelope head, and "sundry other smaller matters." John C. Ewers considered Denig "better qualified than any other man of his generation to write on the history and ethnology of the Indian tribes of the Upper Missouri" (Denig, *Five Indian Tribes of the Upper Missouri*, xxxii, xxxv–xxxvi). See also William H. Goetzmann, *Exploration and Empire: The Explorer and Scientist in the Winning of the American West*, 309–310, 491.

6. Denig, "Indian Tribes of the Upper Missouri"; Denig, *Five Indian Tribes of the Upper Missouri*; Thaddeus A. Culbertson, *Journal of an Expedition to the Mauvaise Terres and the Upper Missouri in 1850*, ed. John Francis McDermott, "Introduction."

7. Michael Stephen Kennedy, ed., *The Assiniboines: From the Accounts of the Old Ones Told to First Boy (James Larpenteur Long)*, lxi–lxv, 162, 177. Some mixed-blood descendants of traders became anthropologists or informants. Shoots Them, a half-Assiniboine born at Fort Union, the son of Philip Alvarez, worked for Chouteau and later for Hubble & Hawley. James Larpenteur Long, or First Boy, was Charles Larpenteur's grandson.

8. Savoie Lottinville, ed., *Paul Wilhelm, Duke of Württemberg; Travels in North America, 1822–1824* (Norman: University of Oklahoma Press, 1973), "Editor's Introduction"; and William H. Goetzmann, *Exploration and Empire: The Explorer and Scientist in the Winning of the American West*, 191–93. A few AFCo and UMO accounts, memorandums, and receipts related to "Prince Paul" are in the Chouteau Collection, MoHS (March–September, 1830).

9. See Loyd Haberly, *Pursuit of the Horizon: A Life of George Catlin* (New York: Macmillan Company, 1948), 23–35.

10. Catlin, *Letters and Notes*, 1:3.

11. Ibid., 14.

12. Ibid., 14, 29, 42. The UMO ordered several small cannons in 1832 and 1833, some of which were used at Fort Union (see note 34, chapter 3).

13. Ibid., 21.

14. Ibid., 26 plate 9, 42.

15. Ibid., 60. Surviving records show that from June 25 to July 11, 1832, Catlin purchased $61.63 worth of goods at Fort Union (including $25.00 for

the skiff he used to go downriver). Two paintings, valued at $30.00, were taken
as partial payment of this bill. Between May 28 and August 15 he purchased
$22.88 worth of goods at Forts Clark and Pierre (Chouteau Collection, MoHS).

16. Brian W. Dippie, *Catlin and His Contemporaries: The Politics of Patronage*,
60 n. 29; Catlin, *Letters and Notes*, 2:194–200 (Letter 55). Kennedy, in his *Recollections of an Assiniboine Chief*, 21, recalls the name as Asan-Zan-na, or "In the Light"
(20).

17. George Catlin, Pittsburgh, January 29, 1833, to Pierre Chouteau, Jr.,
Chouteau Collection, MoHS. Catlin's last published letter condemned "monopolies," noting that "long and cruel experience has well proved that it is impossible for enlightened Governments or money-making individuals to deal with
these credulous and unsophisticated people, without the sin of injustice" (Catlin,
Letters and Notes, 2:225, 251).

18. Dippie, *Catlin and His Contemporaries*, 58, 186–88.

19. Catlin, *Letters and Notes*, 1:62; 2:223.

20. William H. Goetzmann, "The Man Who Stopped to Paint America," in
Willam H. Goetzmann *et al.*, *Karl Bodmer's America* (Lincoln: Joslyn Art Museum
and University of Nebraska, 1984), 1–23; and William H. Goetzmann, *New
Lands, New Men: America and the Second Great Age of Discovery* (New York: Viking,
1986), chapter 5.

21. Goetzmann, "The Man Who Stopped to Paint America," 5–6.

22. Ibid., 8.

23. Maximilian Journals, March 27, 1833.

24. Ibid., March 28, 1833.

25. Ibid., March 30 and April 1, 1833.

26. Goetzmann, "The Man Who Stopped to Paint America," 10; Maximilian
Journals, April 1–9, 1833.

27. Alexander Culbertson, from Chambersburg, Pennsylvania, joined the
UMO on March 16, 1833, for three years as "commis traiteur" (clerk-trader) for
two thousand dollars. Contract in Chouteau Collection, MoHS.

28. Goetzmann, "The Man Who Stopped to Paint America," 10–11, plates
140–52.

29. Maximilian's Journals, June 24, 1833.

30. Ibid., June 24–25, 30, 1833. The prince noted that the UMO had "twenty-
three trading posts in all," producing annually about 25,000 beavers, 2,000–
3,000 otters, 40,000–50,000 bison, 500–600 each of fishers and martens, 1,000–
2,000 each of wildcats and lynxes, 2,000 red foxes, 200–300 cross foxes, 20–30
silver foxes, "several thousand" minks, 100,000–1,000,000 muskrats, and 20,000–
30,000 deerskins.

31. Ibid., June 24–26, 1833.

32. Ibid., June 14 and 27 and July 4, 1833. Glass, Edward Rose, and Menard
were murdered by some Arikaras "a few miles below the mouth of the Big Horn"

in the winter of 1832–33 while taking furs down the Yellowstone. Glass worked several years as a hunter for Fort Union. Aubrey L. Haines, "Hugh Glass," in *Mountain Men and the Fur Trade*, ed. Hafen, 6:168–69.

33. Maximilian Journals, June 24–28 and July 4, 1833.

34. Ibid., July 5, 1833. An invoice dated January 11, 1833, New York, indicates that $140.37 worth of fireworks purchased from John Dick were packed in three boxes destined for the Rocky Mountains (Chouteau Collection, MoHS).

35. Sources for the 1843 trip include Audubon, *Audubon and his Journals;* John Francis McDermott, ed., *Audubon in the West;* John Francis McDermott, ed., *Up the Missouri with Audubon: The Journal of Edward Harris;* and Diary of Isaac Sprague.

36. Audubon considered combining his Missouri River trip with one to the Rockies with Stewart but decided against it. Audubon declared in a letter: "I am told that [Stewart] would give a great deal that we should join him. If so why does he not proffer some $10,000 . . . ?" (McDermott, *Up the Missouri with Audubon*, 6, 13–14. See also McDermott, *Audubon in the West*, 57; Audubon, *Audubon and His Journals*, 1:452–54).

37. Sprague Diary, March 12–April 25, 1843; Audubon, *Audubon and His Journals*, 1:456. LaBarge and Sire are treated in Hiram Martin Chittenden, *History of Early Steamboat Navigation on the Missouri River: Life and Adventures of Joseph LaBarge.*

38. Sprague Diary, May 10, 1843; Audubon, *Audubon and His Journals*, 1:478–80; Chittenden, *Early Steamboat Navigation*, 141–48. For a refutation of this story, see McDermott, *Audubon in the West*, 88–89 n. 10.

39. Audubon, *Audubon and His Journals*, 1:507; Chittenden, *Early Steamboat Navigation*, 148–49, McDermott, *Up the Missouri with Audubon*, 69.

40. Chittenden, *Early Steamboat Navigation*, 152–53. Though this story may be apocryphal, Audubon wrote of William Sublette, Thomas Fitzpatrick, and Robert Campbell that "not one knows one animal from another beyond a Beaver, a Bear, a Raccoon, or an Otter," suggesting that he had alienated them. McDermott, *Audubon in the West*, 69; McDermott, *Up the Missouri with Audubon*, 6–8.

41. Audubon, *Audubon and His Journals*, 2:29, 34. Harris also treated several patients at Fort Pierre for venereal disease ("the infernal disease which I dare not name," according to Audubon) and other problems (McDermott, *Audubon in the West*, 105, 119). Harris's diary is silent on this matter.

42. Audubon, *Audubon and His Journals*, 2:33–35, 71. Harris says it was Edwin Denig playing the "clarionet," and Francis Chardon the drum. The Chouteau mentioned is Auguste Liguest Chouteau, nephew of Pierre Chouteau, Jr. (McDermott, *Up The Missouri with Audubon*, 101 n. 32).

43. Audubon, *Audubon and His Journals*, 2:35.

44. Ibid., 36, 53, 73, 87, 89.

45. Ibid., 74–84, 107, 139; Sprague Diary, July 11, 1843. Sprague's and Harris's journals contain notes on the numbers of birds and mammals killed, many of which were too mutilated to be useful.

46. Audubon, *Audubon and His Journals*, 2:77, 89, 112.

47. Dippie, *Catlin and His Contemporaries*, 59–60. Audubon complained to his journal on July 23, 1843, that the British at HBC posts supplied Indians with alcohol, while Fort Union had "none for them, and very little for anyone," adding, "if our Congress will not allow our traders to sell whiskey or rum to the Indians, why should not the British follow the same rule? Surely the British, who are so anxious about the emancipation of the blacks, might as well take care of the souls and bodies of the redskins" (Audubon, *Audubon and His Journals*, 2:109). Two days before leaving Saint Louis, Audubon, in a letter to his wife, said he would "give Mr. Sarpy an acknowledgment for what we have purchased of the firm, and will settle with them on our return. . . . Our letters will procure us everything at Cost" (McDermott, *Audubon in the West*, 65, 67). According to Harris, the cost for the trip up and down the Missouri came to $1,640.18 (McDermott, *Up the Missouri with Audubon*, Appendix v, 214–17).

48. Hewitt, *Kurz Journal*, 3, 130–31, 291, 361, and elsewhere.

49. Ibid., 65. Previously unpublished Kurz images appear in Kläy and Läng, *Das Romantische Leben*.

50. Stevens's report is titled *Narrative and Final Report of Explorations for a Route for a Pacific Railroad near the Forty-Seventh and Forty-Ninth Parallels of North Latitude from St. Paul to Puget Sound*, hereafter cited as Stevens, *Final Report*.

51. Stevens, *Final Report*, 78, 86, 88.

52. Ibid., 86.

53. Ibid., 74; Robert Taft, *Artists and Illustrators of the Old West, 1860–1900*, 12–13.

54. Stevens, *Final Report*, 88; H. Exec. Doc. 129, 33rd Cong., 1st sess., 217–37.

55. Goetzmann, *Exploration and Empire*, 265–302.

56. William F. Raynolds, *Report on the Exploration of the Yellowstone River*, 77–78; John E. Wickman, "Robert Meldrum," in *Mountain Men and the Fur Trade*, ed. Hafen, 9:279–81.

57. Raynolds, *Report on the Exploration of the Yellowstone River*, 10–11, 20–21; William H. Goetzmann, *Army Exploration in the American West, 1803–1863* (New Haven: Yale University Press, 1959), 417–426.

58. Raynolds, *Report on the Exploration of the Yellowstone River*, 77–78.

59. Ibid., 11, 110–14.

60. Ibid., 114.

61. Ibid., 146.

62. Ibid., 114, 147.

63. Ibid., 148.

64. Rick Stewart, Joseph D. Ketner, II, and Angela L. Miller, *Carl Wimer: Chronicler of the Missouri River* (Norman: University of Oklahoma Press, 1984), 84–85.

65. Ibid., 112.

66. Hays to his mother, July 21, 1860, quoted in Taft, *Artists and Illustrators of the Old West*, 43–44; see 36–52 and plate 18 for data on Hays. See also Coues, *Forty Years a Fur Trader*, 306 n. 2.

67. Mildred D. Ladner, *William de la Montagne Cary: Artist on the Missouri River*, 17.

68. Cary's illustration of the event was published in *Recreation* magazine in 1895. See Ladner, *William de la Montagne Cary*, 39–41.

69. Ladner, *William de la Montagne Cary*, 46–85; W. H. Schieffelin, "Crossing the Plains in '61," *Recreation* 3, nos. 1–3 (July–September 1895): 15. Cary's illustration of this raid appeared in *Frank Leslie's Illustrated Newspaper*, May 30, 1868. See also Pierre Chouteau, Jr., St. Louis, to Charles Primeau, Fort Pierre, February 6, 1861, Chouteau Collection, MoHS.

70. Taft, *Artists and Illustrators of the Old West*, 52.

71. *Solitary Rambles and Adventures of a Hunter in the Prairies* (London: John Murray, 1853). I cite a later edition, *Solitary Rambles; or, Sporting Adventures in the Prairies* (London: G. Routledge & Co., 1857), 59.

72. For an undeservedly sympathetic account, see Jack Roberts, *The Amazing Adventures of Lord Gore, A True Saga from the Old West* (Silverton, Colo.: Sundance Publications, 1977).

73. Alfred Vaughn, Fort Pierre, November 9, 1856, to Alfred Cummings, Saint Louis; Cummings to George H. Manypenny, Washington, December 12, 1856, OIA, LR (M234, Roll 885).

74. [Unknown] to Department of the Interior, January 16, 1857 OIA, LR (M234, Roll 885).

75. Marshall Sprague, *A Gallery of Dudes* (Boston: Little, Brown, 1966), 95–117, 215–46.

76. Leslie A. White, ed., *Lewis Henry Morgan: The Indian Journals, 1859–62*, 166–200.

77. Ibid., 9–12.

78. Robert C. Carriker, *Father Peter John De Smet: Jesuit in the West*, 21–30.

79. Ibid., 36–37, 54–55.

80. Chittenden and Richardson, *Life, Letters, and Travels of Father De Smet*, 1:244; 2:604, 652; 3:857.

81. P. Chouteau, Jr., & Co., Saint Louis, April 22, 1841, to De Smet, De Smet Papers, Jesuit Missouri Provincial Archives, Saint Louis, Missouri. In Chittenden and Richardson, *Life, Letters, and Travels of Father De Smet* (3:1062–63), De Smet refers to "intelligent traders who have resided a number of years among the

various tribes" such as "my principal informers and kind friends, Messrs. [Edwin] Denig, [Robert] Meldrum, and [Alexander] Culbertson."

82. De Smet, May 1852, to Edwin T. Denig, and De Smet, September 27, 1852, to Rev. P. J. Verhaegen, S.J., in Chittenden and Richardson, *Life, Letters, and Travels of Father De Smet*, 4:1481, 1483, 1491–97. See also Carriker, *Peter John De Smet*, 64–65, 140.

83. Chittenden and Richardson, *Life, Letters, and Travels of Father De Smet*, 1:81–83. See also George E. Tinker, *Missionary Conquest: The Gospel and Native American Cultural Genocide* (81–86), which employs interpretive leaps and decontextualized evidence to argue that De Smet and the traders conspired to execute a deliberate program of labor exploitation and cultural destruction of Indians.

84. For Point, see Joseph P. Donnelly, S.J., ed., *Wilderness Kingdom: Indian Life in the Rocky Mountains: 1840–1847; The Journals and Paintings of Father Nicolas Point.*

85. I follow Point's recital. Chittenden says that Fort Lewis was dismantled in "spring of 1846" and moved "to where the village of Fort Benton now stands." The fort was christened Fort Benton in 1850. Donnelly, *Wilderness Kingdom*, 212; Chittenden, *Early Steamboat Navigation*, 234–35.

86. Donnelly, *Wilderness Kingdom*, 177, 214–15, 222, 243, 248.

87. Gerhard Schmutterer, *Tomahawk and Cross: Lutheran Missionaries among the Northern Plains Tribes, 1858–1866*, 8, 117.

88. Ibid., 19–20, 135.

89. Ibid., 135–45.

90. Ibid., 150.

91. Ibid., 66–69, 78–79, 101–106; Raynolds, *Report on the Exploration of the Yellowstone River*, 75–76.

CHAPTER THREE

1. Rudolph Friederich Kurz was probably the only man who worked at Fort Union for the sake of "experience." Hewitt, *Kurz Journal*, 65, 130–31, 217.

2. Ibid., 225.

3. Porter, *John Jacob Astor*, 2:691, 694–95, 703, 723 n. 52; Chittenden, *American Fur Trade*, 1:310.

4. See Gabriel Franchère, *A Voyage to the Northwest Coast of America*, ed. Milo Milton Quaife (Chicago: Lakeside Press, 1954); and Carl P. Russell, "Gabriel Franchère," in *Mountain Men and the Fur Trade*, ed. Hafen, 1:281–86.

5. Hewitt, *Kurz Journal*, 123; Ramsay Crooks, New York, March 15, 1832, to Pierre Chouteau, Jr., Saint Louis; Chouteau Collection, MoHS. Of forty-one Canadians contracted in 1832, only one, James Boyle, had an English surname. Included were thirty-five boatmen, two carpenters, two blacksmiths, and a

cooper ("List of Men engaged at Montreal for Western Department, 1832," Chouteau Collection, MoHS).

6. William Clark, Superintendent of Indian Affairs, Saint Louis, to Pierre Chouteau, Jr., March 26, 1832, in Chouteau Collection, MoHS.

7. Kenneth McKenzie, Fort Tecumseh, July 7, 1829, to Pierre Chouteau, Jr., Saint Louis. Sandoval appears as employee number 50 in "Persons Employed for the Upper Missouri Outfit for the Year 1830" and in an engagement contract dated Saint Louis, August 23, 1831. Both items are in Chouteau Collection, MoHS. Harvey worked for the UMO in the late 1830s, but violent behavior brought his dismissal. He returned to Fort Union in 1840, and a year or two later he killed Sandoval (Coues, *Forty Years a Fur Trader*, 167–70.

8. See Coues, *Forty Years a Fur Trader*, 163–66, 167–70; and Audubon, *Audubon and His Journals*, 2:65.

9. Coues, *Forty Years a Fur Trader*, 331; "Fort Union 15th July 1836," Larpenteur MS Journals, MnHS; and Gregory, Bruguier, and Geowey Papers, MnHS. See also Hewitt, *Kurz Journal*, 120–21. A man named "Alvarisse" is mentioned in "Journal of Fort Tecumseh, January 31, 1830 to June 10, 1830," May 16, 1830, Chouteau Collection, MoHS.

10. See Daybooks 1 through 7, May 29, 1866, to July 4, 1867, Gregory, Bruguier, and Geowey Papers, MnHS; Pierre Chouteau, Jr., & Co., "Journal, 1864–1868," Fur Trade Ledgers, MoHS (Roll 19, Vol. 12); and Larpenteur MS Journals, MnHS, vol. 3, June 27 and August 21, 1867.

11. See Elinor Wilson, *Jim Beckwourth: Black Mountain Man and War Chief of the Crows* (Norman: University of Oklahoma Press, 1972); T. D. Bonner, ed., *The Life and Adventures of James P. Beckwourth, Mountaineer, Scout, Pioneer, and Chief of the Crow Nation of Indians* (New York: Harper and Brothers, 1856; reprint, Williamstown, Mass.: Corner House Publishers, 1977).

12. Coues, *Forty Years a Fur Trader*, 70, 121–22; and "Post Accounts Current, Ledger D, 1831–1836," Fur Trade Ledgers, AFC West, MoHS, 18.

13. Hewitt, *Kurz Journal*, 101–102, 244.

14. Engagement contracts for 1833–38 (of which there are several hundred), Chouteau Collection, MoHS. For a study of UMO engagés, see William R. Swagerty, "A View from the Bottom Up: The Work Force of the American Fur Company on the Upper Missouri in the 1830s," *Montana: The Magazine of Western History* 43, no. 1 (Winter 1993).

15. Fort Union Letterbook, Chouteau Collection, MoHS, September 10, 1835.

16. Denig, "Indian Tribes of the Upper Missouri," 380; Hewitt, *Kurz Journal*, 123–24.

17. Miller's first name appears in a note dated Fort Union, September 16, 1833, from McKenzie to Pierre Chouteau, Jr., to pay twenty dollars, to be charged to the UMO, to a Mrs. Feulke at Saint Louis on behalf of a Peter Miller. See also

James A. Hamilton, Fort Union, October 30, 1833, to Kenneth McKenzie, and letters dated September 17 and October 9, 1834, all in Fort Union Letterbook, Chouteau Collection, MoHS.

18. Antoine Luteman was hired on March 14, 1832, for a term of eighteen months at $250 as "Boatman, hunter, carpenter" (Engagement of Antoine Luckman [sic], and "A List of Men to be employed . . . ," March 24, 1832; also Fort Union Letterbook, December 10, 1835; both in Chouteau Collection, MoHS).

19. Kenneth McKenzie, Fort Union, December 15, 1833, to H. Picotte; James Archdale Hamilton to Kenneth McKenzie, September 17, 1834; and James Archdale Hamilton to William Laidlaw, December 10, 1834, all in Fort Union Letterbook, Chouteau Collection, MoHS. Also see "An order for various articles of Merchandize to be forwarded to Fort Union U.M.O. in the Spring 1832," Chouteau Collection, MoHS.

20. Audubon, *Audubon and His Journals*, 2:181–82.

21. Hamilton to Pierre Chouteau, Jr., & Co., March 26, 1835, Fort Union Letterbook, Chouteau Collection, MoHS.

22. Larpenteur MS Journals, MnHS; Audubon, *Audubon and His Journals*, 2:183; Hewitt, *Kurz Journal*, 229, 234.

23. Hewitt, *Kurz Journal*, 86, 88, 93, 259. For examples of artifacts Kurz collected, see Kläy and Läng, *Das romantische Leben*, 103, 111, 116.

24. See Hewitt, *Kurz Journal*, 125, 134.

25. Describing a buffalo hunt in spring 1835, Larpenteur wrote: "On such occasions all their families also went into camp to make dried meat for their own use, and also as a kind of recreation" (Coues, *Forty Years a Fur Trader*, 79–80).

26. Coues, *Forty Years a Fur Trader*, 1; Denig, *Indian Tribes of the Upper Missouri*, 380–81.

27. Hewitt, *Kurz Journal*, 235.

28. See "Invoice of Sundry Merchandise . . . shipped on board the Ship Talma . . . February 9, 1833"; William B. Astor, New York, September 6, 1832, to Pierre Chouteau, Jr., & Company; William B. Astor, New York, March 30, 1833, to Pierre Chouteau, Jr., & Company; William B. Astor, New York, May 6, 1833, to Pierre Chouteau, Jr., & Company; William B. Astor, New York, October 11, 1833, to Pierre Chouteau, Jr. & Company; Joshua Pilcher, Fort Mitchell, October 28, 1838, to Jacob Halsey; Kenneth McKenzie, Fort Union, December 16, 1833, to Ramsay Crooks, Fort Union Letterbook, all in Chouteau Collection, MoHS; also J. Pilcher, Eau que River [sic], to W. Clark, Oct. 27, 1838, OIA, LR (M234, Roll 884).

29. Leslie A. Perry, "Frontier Subsistence: An Example of Nineteenth Century Fur Trade Food Procurement," M.A. thesis, University of Nebraska, Lincoln, 1981, 111.

30. Coues, *Forty Years a Fur Trader*, 331 n. 1.

31. Hewitt, *Kurz Journal*, 194–95.

32. Perry, "Frontier Subsistence," 103.

33. Audubon, *Audubon and His Journals*, 2:33, 36. James Kipp told Audubon that he had caught "upwards of one hundred" wolves by "fishing" for them.

34. Perry, "Frontier Subsistence," 28–31.

35. In 1833, Maximilian was told conditions were too dry to grow crops, but by 1835, Larpenteur had a successful garden and made reference to it in his journals (Perry, "Frontier Subsistence," 85; Denig, *Five Indian Tribes of the Upper Missouri*, 68 n. 3). A box of garden seeds arrived in 1839 ("Fur Trade Ledgers," MoHS [Roll 9, Vol. DD], p. 24).

36. See Perry, "Frontier Subsistence," 86. Denig's comment is in *Five Indian Tribes of the Upper Missouri*, 68. See also Larpenteur MS Journals, MnHS, August 24–25, 1835; Audubon, *Audubon and His Journals*, 2:187–88; and Hewitt, *Kurz Journal*, 159. Twenty-six types of garden produce were grown at Fort Union between 1829 and 1867.

37. "Inventory of Stock Belonging to Upper Missouri Outfit at Fort Union 10th June 1831"; "Sketch of order for sundry Merchandize required for the trade of Fort Union U.M.O. Season 1834–1835"; "An order for various articles of Merchandize to be forwarded to Fort Union, U.M.O. in the Spring 1832," all in Chouteau Collection, MoHS.

38. Jacob Halsey, Fort Pierre, August 25, 1834, to William Laidlaw, Saint Louis, UMO Letterbook B, Chouteau Collection, MoHS. Kenneth McKenzie made a special order in December 1835 for luxury items that included brandy, gin, capers, a half-dozen quarts of "best Catchup," pearl barley, herrings, and a box of "Segars" (McKenzie to Henry K. Ortley, Esq., December 10, 1835, Fort Union Letterbook, Chouteau Collection, MoHS). Five canisters of oysters were sent in April 1833, as indicated in a shipping list dated April 9, 1833, Chouteau Collection, MoHS.

39. Papers of Pierre-Jean de Smet, S.J., Book C-4, Jesuit Missouri Province Archives, Saint Louis; Chittenden and Richardson, *Life, Letters and Travels of Father De Smet*, 1:244, 2:604, 652; 3:857; Larpenteur MS Journals, MnHS, Vol. 2 (1864–66). Daguerreotype images are mentioned in an account of "sundries" dated June 15, 1852, in Fur Trade Ledgers (Microfilm roll 15, volume SS), MoHS.

40. Hewitt, *Kurz Journal*, 240.

41. Abel, *Chardon's Journal*, 109, 164, 173; Hewitt, *Kurz Journal*, 166.

42. E. T. Denig, Fort Union, to Jacob Halsey, Fort Pierre, March 25, 1837, Chouteau Collection, MoHS.

43. Hewitt, *Kurz Journal*, 101, 120, 123.

44. Denig, "Indian Tribes of the Upper Missouri," 380; Hewitt, *Kurz Journal*, 136 n. 50; Denig, *Five Indian Tribes of the Upper Missouri*, xxiii–xxiv.

45. Hewitt, *Kurz Journal*, 222, 224.

46. Ray H. Mattison, "Alexander Culbertson," in Hafen, *Mountain Men and the Fur Trade*, 1:253–58. De Smet stood as godfather to at least one Culbertson

daughter, Francisca, in 1851 (Pierre-Jean De Smet Papers, Book C-4, July 20, 1851, courtesy Jesuit Missouri Provincial Archives, Saint Louis).

47. Hewitt, *Kurz Journal,* 78, 83, 123, 364.

48. Chittenden, *American Fur Trade,* 1:387.

49. James A. Hamilton, Fort Union, to Kenneth McKenzie, Saint Louis, September 17, 1834, also July 4, 1835, Fort Union Letterbook, Chouteau Collection, MoHS; Coues, *Forty Years a Fur Trader,* 77, 87, 90, 95–97; Hewitt, *Kurz Journal,* 278, 293.

50. Larpenteur MS Journals, MnHS, Vol. 2, August 19, 1835.

51. Kenneth McKenzie believed that "it was not good policy to buy out opposition, rather work them out by extra industry and assiduity," and added: "I have encountered various opposition traders in my time & it has always been to their cost, if I can make nothing myself I will at least spoil the market for others" (McKenzie, Fort Union, December 14, 1833, to James Kipp; and McKenzie, Fort Union, November 24, 1835, to Bellehumeure, Fort Union Letterbook, Chouteau Collection, MoHS).

52. Hewitt, *Kurz Journal,* 124–25, 243.

53. Larpenteur's published and manuscript journals include many incidents of drunken violence, as does Kurz's journal. Hewitt, *Kurz Journal,* 238.

54. In December 1831 an order was placed for "1 # pounded zinc or amalgum for electrifying machine," to be sent to Fort Union ("Particulars of Mdze to be shipped at St. Louis on board Steam Boat Yellow Stone for Fort Union, U.M.O. in Spring 1832 . . ."; Chouteau Collection, MoHS). See Fort Union inventories in Chouteau Collection and Fur Trade Ledgers, MoHS microfilm (Roll 11, Book JJ; Roll 12, Book LL).

55. "Invoice of Sundry Merchandise . . . shipped on board the ship Talma," New York, February 9, 1833; "Invoice of one Box Merchandise . . . to be delivered . . . to Kenneth McKenzie," New York, March 12, 1833, both in Chouteau Collection, MoHS. In January 1833 the AFCo bought $140.37 worth of fireworks in New York (Invoice to John Dick and "Invoice of Sundry Merchandize . . . for account of . . . Western Department," January 30, 1833, Chouteau Collection, MoHS; Audubon, *Audubon and His Journals,* 2:74).

56. Tenpins appear in a list of goods sent to UMO posts aboard the *Assiniboine,* March 21, 1833 (Chouteau Collection, MoHS). Backgammon appears in Audubon, *Audubon and His Journals,* 2:76. Playing cards appear in an 1831 inventory and an 1833 order. Ten dozen decks were ordered for 1834–35 ("Inventory of Stock belonging to Upper Missouri Outfit at Fort Union, 10th June 1831"; "Order for Several Articles of Merchandize to be sent to fort Union in the Spring 1833"; "Sketch of order for Sundry Merchandize required for the trade of Fort Union U.M.O. Season 1834–1835," all in Chouteau Collection, MoHS). See also Hewitt, *Kurz Journal,* 148, 263, 282, 299–300.

57. Larpenteur MS Journals, MnHS, Vol. 2; Hewitt, *Kurz Journal*, 145, 153, 182–83, 199, 205, 222–23, 227, 239, 327; Sunder, *Fur Trade on the Upper Missouri*, 75, 175.

58. Audubon reported a musical performance in 1843 (see Audubon, *Audubon and his Journals*, 2:33, 35); Kurz said that Denig fiddled at a ball in 1851 (Hewitt, *Kurz Journal*, 124). An 1845 inventory shows "One Brass Key C. Clarinett," "2 violins, no longer strings," and "1 Military Drum." The drum first appears in an order in 1833. An 1847 inventory included a tambourine and a triangle. By 1850, only the drum remained on inventory lists ("Sketch of order for Sundry Merchandize required for the trade of Fort Union U.M.O. Season 1834–1835," Chouteau Collection, MoHS; "Inventory of Stock the Property of Pierre Chouteau Jr. & Co Upper Missouri Outfit 1844, on hand at Fort Union 20 May 1845," and similar inventories for 1846–51, all in Fur Trade Ledgers, MoHS [Roll 11, Vol. JJ; Roll 12, Vol. LL]). For the bugle, see Pierre Chouteau, Jr., & Co., "Invoice Blotter No. 1, 1839–1841," Fur Trade Ledgers, MoHS (Roll 9, Vol. DD). See also "Inventory of Stock belonging to Upper Missouri Outfit at Fort Union 10th June 1831," Chouteau Collection, MoHS.

59. Coues, *Forty Years a Fur Trader*, 215–16.

60. "Invoice of Sundry Merchandise . . . shipped on board the ship Talma," New York, February 9, 1833, Chouteau Collection, MoHS; Pierre Chouteau, Jr., & Co., "Post Accounts Current, Ledger D, 1831–36," Fur Trade Ledgers, MoHS (Roll 6, Vol. V); "An order for various articles of Merchandize to be forwarded to Fort Union, U.M.O. in the Spring 1832," Chouteau Collection, MoHS; and Pierre Chouteau, Jr., & Co., "Invoice Blotter No. 1, 1839–1841," Fur Trade Ledgers, MoHS (Roll 9, Vol. DD). Clyde D. Dollar, in "The High Plains Smallpox Epidemic of 1837," *Western Historical Quarterly* 8, no. 1 (January 1977): 22, identifies the medical tome as Robert Thomas, *The Modern Practice of Physic, Exhibiting the Character, Causes, Symptoms, Prognostics, Morbid Appearances, and Improved Methods of Treating the Diseases of All Climates* (8th American Edition, 1825). See also Larpenteur MS Journals, MnHS, Vol. 1; and Audubon, *Audubon and His Journals*, 2:81–82.

61. Chardon, Fort Clark, August 17, 1836, to Halsey, Chouteau Collection, MoHS.

62. Hewitt, *Kurz Journal*, 232, 247, 299.

63. "Post Accounts Current, Ledger D, 1831–1836," Fur Trade Ledgers, AFC West, MoHS; Larpenteur MS Journals, MnHS, June 8, 1835.

64. Abel, *Chardon's Journal*, 118 n. 481.

65. Larpenteur MS Journals, MnHS, Vol. 1. Edwin Denig, like others, believed that "there is also great risk in giving [Indians vaccine and] medicines, for should the patient die the whites would be blamed for poisoning him" (Denig, "Indian Tribes of the Upper Missouri," 428).

66. Crooks, New York, to Chouteau, Philadelphia, March 4, 1838, Chouteau Collection, MoHS.

67. Details in the two preceding paragraphs come from Larpenteur's unpublished journals and are corroborated by Jacob Halsey (Halsey, Fort Pierre, November 2, 1837, to Pratte, Chouteau, & Co., Chouteau Collection, MoHS). See also Arthur J. Ray, "Smallpox: The Epidemic of 1837–38," *The Beaver*, outfit 306:2 (Autumn 1975), 9.

68. W. Raymond Wood, "An Interpretation of Mandan Culture History," Bureau of American Ethnology, Bulletin 198 (Washington: GPO, 1967), 141; Halsey, Fort Pierre, November 2, 1827, to Pratte, Chouteau & Co., Saint Louis; Chardon, Fort Clark, November 28, 1837, to P. D. Papin; and Mitchell, Fort Union, December 1, 1837, to P. D. Papin, all in Chouteau Collection, MoHS; Abel, *Chardon's Journal*, 137.

69. Wood, citing David Thompson, notes an epidemic near the end of the eighteenth century (Wood, "An Interpretation of Mandan Culture History," 140). Others occurred in 1803–1804, 1837, and 1856. See notes below and Annie Heloise Abel, ed., *Tabeau's Narrative of Loisel's Expedition to the Upper Missouri* (Norman: University of Oklahoma Press, 1939), 99–100, 123–24.

70. Kipp, Fort Union, January 29, 1857, to Pierre Chouteau, Jr., & Co., Chouteau Collection, MoHS. Kipp blamed Joseph Picotte's opposition company for bringing the disease up the Missouri by failing to put ashore people who already had smallpox when the steamer passed Jefferson City, Missouri (Charles E. Galpin, Fort Pierre, March 20, 1857, to Pierre Chouteau, Jr., & Co., Chouteau Collection, MoHS). An unidentified writer at Fort Berthold informed Chouteau that he was in "great hopes" that the Hidatsa would "entirely escape" the small pox ([unknown], Fort Berthold, March 30, 1857, to Pierre Chouteau, Jr., & Co., Chouteau Collection, MoHS).

71. William Laidlaw, Fort Pierre, October 30 and November 3, 1833, to Colin Campbell, William Dickson, and Charles DeGray, UMO Letterbook B; Joshua Pilcher, "Near the Bluffs," August 21, 1833, to Pierre Chouteau, Jr., both in Chouteau Collection, MoHS. See also Chittenden, *Early Steamboat Navigation*, 32–33, 189–93; Coues, *Forty Years a Fur Trader*, 280, 289; and Denig, "Indian Tribes of the Upper Missouri," 425.

72. See Ann F. Ramenofsky, *Vectors of Death: The Archeology of European Contact*, 130–36.

73. Hewitt, *Kurz Journal*, 230.

74. "Upper Missouri Outfit 1830, to Retail Store Am. Fur Company," Chouteau Collection, MoHS.

75. W. D. Hodgkiss, Fort Pierre, February 14, 1850, to Pierre Chouteau, Jr., & Co., Saint Louis, Chouteau Collection, MoHS.

76. Coues, *Forty Years a Fur Trader*, 94–96; Alexander Ross, *The Red River Settlement*, 36–38. Coues, echoing Larpenteur, says that the Deschampses had

"twice robbed Fort Union, robbed Mr. Jeanisse and threatened to kill him; robbed and whipped Indians; murdered a young man in 1834; and habitually committed adultery with their sisters-in-law" (Coues, *Forty Years a Fur Trader*, 96 n. 4).

77. Coues, *Forty Years a Fur Trader*, 87–90.

78. Details for the preceding paragraphs come from "Destruction of the Des Champs Family at Fort Union the 28th of June 1836," in Larpenteur MS Journals, MnHS, Vol. 1. See also Coues, *Forty Years a Fur Trader*, 87–101. In his manuscript journal Larpenteur names the dead man "Jack Kipling," but in Coues's edition he becomes "Jack Rem," presumably the man called "Jack Ram."

79. William N. Fulkerson, Mandan Sub-Agency, to William Clark, Saint Louis, September 1836, OIA, LR (M234, Roll 751).

80. This incident is detailed in Larpenteur MS Journals, MnHS, Vol. 1, July 15, 1836. See also Coues, *Forty Years a Fur Trader*, 101–105.

81. Different versions of this tale appear in Larpenteur MS Journals, MnHS, Vol. 1, and in Coues, *Forty Years a Fur Trader*, 118–23. See also "Duplicate List of Men Shipped & Engaged for a/c U.M.O. 1832," Chouteau Collection, MoHS.

82. In Larpenteur's original journal, this event strongly reflects the issues of community safety and law. In Coues's edition, which was consciously directed toward popular appeal and publication, it takes the tone of a ribald tale.

83. Hewitt, *Kurz Journal*, 237.

84. Ibid., 77–78, 103.

85. "Journal of Fort Tecumseh, June 14, 1830, to April 8, 1831," Chouteau Collection, MoHS.

CHAPTER FOUR

1. See Prucha, *Documents of United States Indian Policy*, 8–10, 14–15; Thomas Elliot Norton, *The Fur Trade in Colonial New York* (Madison: University of Wisconsin Press, 1974), especially chapter 5.

2. "An Act for establishing Trading Houses with the Indian Tribes," in Prucha, *Documents of United States Indian Policy*, 16–17. Twenty-eight trade houses came and went in twenty-seven years (Prucha, *Documents of United States Indian Policy*, 87).

3. Prucha, *American Indian Policy in the Formative Years*, 88; Prucha, *Documents of United States Indian Policy*, 22.

4. "An Act to regulate trade and intercourse with the Indian tribes, and to preserve peace on the frontiers" (1802), in Prucha, *Documents of United States Indian Policy*, 17–21.

5. Ibid., 24.

6. "An Act to amend an act, entitled 'An act to regulate trade and inter-course with the Indian tribes and to preserve peace on the frontiers'" (1822), in ibid., 34.

7. Ibid., 43–44. Emphasis in original.

8. "An Act to provide for the appointment of a commissioner of Indian Affairs, and for other purposes," 1832, in ibid., 62.

9. Ibid., 68–71.

10. Ibid., 64–68.

11. "Regulating the Indian Department (To accompany bills H. R. Nos. 488, 489, 490)," May 20, 1834. The three bills, "A bill to provide for the organization of the Department of Indian Affairs," "A bill to regulate trade and intercourse with the Indian tribes, and to preserve peace on the frontiers," and "A bill to provide for the establishment of the Western Territory, and for the security and protection of the emigrant and other Indian tribes therein," are reprinted in ibid., 64–71.

12. U.S, Congress, House, "Regulating the Indian Department," 23rd Cong., 1st sess., H. Exec. Rep. 474, May 20, 1834.

13. Ibid., 11. See also Robert W. McCluggage, "The Senate and Indian Land Titles, 1800–1825," *Western Historical Quarterly* 1, no. 4 (October 1970): 415–25.

14. LeRoy R. Hafen, *Broken Hand: The Life of Thomas Fitzpatrick, Mountain Man, Guide and Indian Agent* (revised ed., Denver: The Old West Publishing Company, 1973), 136–37. The HBC faced destructive competition too, though not until World War I, when the British Board of Trade temporarily suspended London fur auctions. This led to immediate and intense competition in acquiring and marketing furs. By 1920 the speculative frenzy collapsed, with heavy losses for the HBC and its competitors. See Arthur J. Ray, *The Canadian Fur Trade in the Industrial Age*, 96–103.

15. U.S. Congress, House, "Regulating the Indian Department," 95, 97.

16. U.S. Congress, Senate, 18th Cong., 1st sess., S. Exec. Doc. 56, March 18, 1824.

17. Ibid.

18. Letter from Thomas S. Jessup, Quartermaster General, February 18, 1824, to Secretary of War John C. Calhoun, in ibid.

19. Joshua Pilcher, Upper Missouri, September 15, 1838, to William Clark, Saint Louis; Thomas H. Harvey, Superintendent of Indian Affairs, Saint Louis, August 23, 1848, to William Medill, Commissioner of Indian Affairs; Kenneth McKenzie, Saint Louis, July 27, 1848, to Harvey; D. D. Mitchell, Saint Louis, July 27, 1848, to Harvey, all in OIA, LR (M234, Roll 884). See also Chittenden, *American Fur Trade*, 2:696.

20. U.S. Congress, House, "Report of the Commissioner of Indian Affairs, November 26, 1853," 33rd Cong., 1st sess., H. Exec. Doc. 1, 357.

21. See W. J. Rorabaugh, *The Alcoholic Republic: An American Tradition* (New York: Oxford University Press, 1974).

22. Prucha, *Documents of United States Indian Policy*, 67.

23. Lt. J. Freeman, Fort Leavenworth, December 8, 1832, to William Clark, Saint Louis, OIA, LR (M234, Roll 750). Freeman says the *Yellow Stone* first arrived "early in the last season" with a license to carry "about 1,500 gallons" of liquor; she again arrived on August 2, 1832. See also Prucha, *American Indian Policy in the Formative Years*, 135.

24. Clark based his action on a letter from Thomas L. McKenney dated January 10, 1828, stating that the secretary of war and Governor Lewis Cass authorized traders to carry one gill per day, per man, for each "boatman" going into the Indian country. Clark permitted Valois & Leclerc to carry up 262 gallons for 32 men for a year, roughly 8.2 gallons for each man. Copies of permission, statement of quantities, and extract from McKenney letter in OIA, LR (M234, Roll 750).

25. William Davenport, Cantonment Leavenworth, September 25, 1831, to Lewis Cass, Secretary or War, OIA, LR (M234, Roll 883). Clark permitted John B. D. Valois & Co. to carry 102 gallons of liquor. John Dougherty, agent at Bellevue, said that Leclerc once worked for Cabanné (Lucien Fontenelle, Council Bluffs, February 26, 1829, to John Dougherty, Cantonment Leavenworth, OIA, LR [M234, Roll 883]; Deposition of John Dougherty, Saint Louis District Court, 1833, OIA, LR [M234, Roll 750]).

26. J. P. Cabanné, Saint Louis, March 18, 1833, to William Clark, OIA, LR (M234, Roll 750).

27. Leclerc, Belle Vue, September 25, 1832, to John Dougherty, U.S. Indian Agent, OIA, LR (M234, Roll 750).

28. Chittenden, *American Fur Trade*, 1:349.

29. Alexander G. Morgan was Fort Leavenworth's sutler from about 1830 until 1835 and served as postmaster from 1831 to 1838 (Louise Barry, ed., *The Beginning of the West*, 176, 205, 285, 306; A. G. Morgan, Fort Leavenworth, February 25, 1833, to J. P. Cabanné, OIA, LR [M234, Roll 750]).

30. Possibly Antoine Payne, as identified in Barry, *Beginning of the West*, 415, 418.

31. Bean's deposition to Saint Louis District Court, 1833, OIA, LR (M234, Roll 750).

32. Bean, Sioux Sub-Agency, October 10, 1832, to William Clark, Saint Louis, OIA, LR (M234, Roll 750). For Bean's bad relationship with the UMO, see Abel, *Chardon's Journal*, 203 n. 21.

33. Bean's deposition to Saint Louis District Court, 1833, OIA, LR (M234, Roll 750).

34. Gordon in 1831 complained to Secretary of War Lewis Cass that monopolistic British traders sold goods cheaper than Americans could manage, because of high import duties and uncompetitive American goods (Letter from Gordon to Cass, October 3, 1831, reprinted in Abel, *Chardon's Journal*, 343–49). Gordon, like Leclerc and Pilcher, served the Missouri Fur Company and was employed by the UMO in 1830–31 (See Charles E. Hanson, Jr., "William Gordon," in Hafen, *Mountain Men and the Fur Trade*, 9:157–64).

35. "Subsequent to obtaining the license for carrying on the trade . . . one of the undersigned [Gordon] became a partner by purchase." Valois, Leclerc, and Gordon, Saint Louis, January 11, 1833, to Lewis Cass, Secretary of War, OIA, LR (M234, Roll 750).

36. Cabanné said Gordon was "altogether a volunteer in this business. . . . He had no interest in the boat or Cargo. . . . He has purchased the privilege of complaining." Astor, the most prestigious man involved, wrote that Gordon had "lately purchased an interest therein on *speculation* hoping to make profit out of it by the heavy damages they expect to obtain through the Courts of Justice" (J. P. Cabanné, Saint Louis, March 18, 1833, to Lewis Cass, Secretary of War; William B. Astor, New York, March 12, 1833, to same; and Gordon, Saint Louis, August 12, 1833, to Clark, all in OIA, LR (M234, Roll 750). See also Barry, *Beginning of the West*, 235.

37. A. G. Morgan, Fort Leavenworth, February 25, 1833, to Cabanné, OIA, LR (M234, Roll 750). Morgan wrote two letters on the same day, February 25.

38. Chittenden assumed Cabanné's career was permanently ruined, but William Clark offered to reinstate Cabanné's trading privileges by August 1834. Cabanné, in or out of the country, retained his company partnership for several years (Chittenden, *American Fur Trade*, 1:349; Clark, Saint Louis, August 14, 1834, to Elbert Herring, Commissioner of Indian Affairs, OIA, LR (M234, Roll 750); Ray H. Mattison, "John Pierre Cabanné Sr." in Hafen, *Mountain Men and the Fur Trade*, 2:72–73).

39. W. B. Astor, New York, February 11, 1833, to Pierre Chouteau, Jr., and Crooks to Chouteau, February 17, 1833, both in Chouteau Collection, MoHS. See also Louis McLane, Department of State, July 1, 1833, to W. B. Astor; Lewis Cass, Washington, October 19, 1833, to W. B. Astor; Louis McLane, October 20, 1833, to Lewis Cass, all in Nute, *Calendar of the American Fur Company's Papers*, 2:1–2.

40. John S. Galbraith, *The Hudson's Bay Company as an Imperial Factor, 1821–1869*, 54–55.

41. W. B. Astor, New York, March 12, 1833, to Pierre Chouteau, Jr., Saint Louis; and Ramsay Crooks, New York, February 17, 1833, to Pierre Chouteau, Jr., both in Chouteau Collection, MoHS.

42. William B. Astor, New York, March 12, 1833, to Pierre Chouteau, Jr., Saint Louis, Chouteau Collection, MoHS.

43. Cabanné, Saint Louis, March 18, 1833, to Lewis Cass, Secretary of War, OIA, LR (M234, Roll 750).

44. F. G. Young, ed., *The Correspondence and Journals of Captain Nathaniel J. Wyeth, 1831–6*, 212–13. For Wyeth's travels, see Bernard DeVoto, *Across the Wide Missouri*. DeVoto assumes that Wyeth turned in McKenzie (p. 120). Wyeth's journal makes no mention of harsh treatment at Fort Union, nor does he mention a complaint tendered at Leavenworth (p. 219).

45. President Andrew Jackson appointed Ellsworth one of three special commissioners to deal with emigrating Indians under an act of July 14, 1832. Ellsworth arrived at Fort Leavenworth on August 3, 1833, remaining until early September (Barry, *Beginning of the West*, 217, 240, 242). Elbert Herring (1777–1876), a famous New York jurist with no previous Indian affairs experience, was the first commissioner of Indian affairs at Washington, D.C. (Charles Lanman, *Biographical Annals of the Civil Government of the United States During its First Century* (Washington, D.C.: James Anglim, 1876), 201; Ronald N. Satz, "Elbert Herring, 1831–36," in Robert M. Kvasnicka and Herman J. Viola, eds., *The Commissioners of Indian Affairs, 1824–1977*, 13–16).

46. Henry L. Ellsworth, Fort Leavenworth, November 8, 1833, to Elbert Herring, Washington, D.C., copy of letter in Indian Collection, MoHS (Box 2).

47. Chouteau, Saint Louis, November 22, 1833, to Clark, OIA, LR (M234, Roll 750). No additional evidence has surfaced concerning experiments the company authorized.

48. Crooks, Washington, February 17, 1833, to Chouteau, Chouteau Collection, MoHS.

49. McKenzie, Fort Union, December 16, 1833, to Chouteau, in Fort Union Letterbook, Chouteau Collection, MoHS.

50. McKenzie, Fort Union, December 16, 1833, to Crooks, in Fort Union Letterbook, Chouteau Collection, MoHS.

51. McKenzie, Fort Union, January 21, 1834, to D. D. Mitchell, in Fort Union Letterbook, Chouteau Collection, MoHS. In December 1833, McKenzie's distiller, name unknown, was "attacked with inflammatory rheumatism & pleurisy." Consequently, the distillery was shut down, and McKenzie feared the man might die, terminating the operation (McKenzie, Fort Union, January 8, 1834, to Samuel Tullock, in Fort Union Letterbook, Chouteau Collection, MoHS).

52. This must be John Palmer Bourke, a veteran Red River man acquainted with Robert Dickson, an original partner in McKenzie's Columbia Fur Company. Chittenden, generally unsympathetic to the AFCo, strongly suggested that Bourke was "fabricated" as part of McKenzie's "feeble invention" (Gilman, Gilman, and Stultz, *Red River Trails*, 4, 13; Chittenden, *American Fur Trade*, 1:361).

53. McKenzie, Fort Union, March 18, 1834, to Chouteau, in Fort Union Letterbook, Chouteau Collection, MoHS.

54. McKenzie, Fort Union, March 20, 1834, to Chouteau, in Fort Union Letterbook, Chouteau Collection, MoHS.

55. Crooks, New York, February 23, 1834, to Chouteau, Chouteau Collection, MoHS.

56. Crooks, New York, March 28, 1834, to Chouteau, Chouteau Collection, MoHS. Emphasis in original.

57. See Chittenden, *American Fur Trade*; DeVoto, *Across the Wide Missouri*; and Berry, *Majority of Scoundrels*. Berry, following Chittenden, thought that Bourke,

McKenzie's associate at Red River, was "imaginary" (p. 341), and he never mentions Commissioner Herring, though he suspected Sublette as a likely informer. DeVoto places guilt squarely on McKenzie's shoulders, following the trail of complicity backward no further than to company officials (pp. 121–22). Since so many writers have relied on Chittenden, it is his work that I deal with most closely in this regard.

58. Chittenden, *American Fur Trade*, 1:354–62. Chittenden must have read the original document while examining the Chouteau Collection at MoHS, but he failed to note Herring's tacit, if not explicit, approbation for continuing AFCo liquor imports into the Upper Missouri.

59. Ibid., 362, 385.

60. William Laidlaw, Fort Pierre, September 27, 1835, to Chouteau & Co.; McKenzie, Fort Union, September 19, 1836, to P. D. Papin, [Fort Pierre?]; Pierre Chouteau, Jr., Saint Louis, April 16, 1837, to P. D. Papin, Fort Pierre, all in Chouteau Collection, MoHS. The distillery was probably no longer at Fort Union in 1835, but according to Charles Larpenteur, its "house" remained. Larpenteur MS Journals, MnHS, Vol. 2, June 12, 1835.

61. Coues, *Forty Years a Fur Trader*, 217–19. This affair took place in the winter of 1843–44 and damaged Chardon's career in the Upper Missouri. Larpenteur, or his editor, Elliott Coues (p. 237), says that McKenzie remained at Fort Union until spring of 1846, but it seems more likely that the year was 1845 (McKenzie, Saint Louis, October 8, 1844, to "My dear Wife"; McKenzie, Fort Pierre, October 27, 1844, to "My dear Wife," both in Chouteau Collection, MoHS). See also Andrew Drips notebook, 1843–45, Drips Collection, MoHS.

62. *Kenneth McKenzie* vs. *Pierre Chouteau, John B. Sarpy, Joseph A. Sire, John F. A. Sandford* [*sic*], *Felix Vallé, and Luther C. Menard*, Saint Louis Circuit Court, November 20, 1849, Chouteau Collection, MoHS. See also affidavit dated June 13, 1859, signed by Pierre Chouteau, Jr., and James Harrison in Kenneth McKenzie Papers, June 13, 1859, MoHS.

63. In 1860 and 1861, McKenzie received confidential information about prices expected from furs sales at New York ("Memorandum of Prices likely to be realized, in New York, for Furs and Skins, in the year 1860," November 1, 1859; and "Memorandum of Prices likely to be obtained in New York, for Furs and Skins, in the year 1861," November 23, 1860, both in Chouteau Collection, MoHS). See also Ray H. Mattison, "Kenneth McKenzie," in Hafen, *Mountain Men and the Fur Trade*, 2:217–24.

64. Chouteau & Company records indicate that liquor was brought upriver in quantities ranging from a few hundred to several thousands of gallons each year. See, for example, "Invoices Out, 1834–1839," and "Invoice Blotter No. 1, 1839–1841," Fur Trade Ledgers, MoHS (Roll 7, vol. Y; Roll 9, vol. DD). Also see T. H. Harvey, Saint Louis, October 8, 1844, to T. Hartley Crawford, Washington, OIA, LR (M234, Roll 750).

65. Bent, St. Vrain & Co., Fort William,, Arkansas River, January 1, 1842, to D. D. Mitchell, Saint Louis, OIA, LR (M234, Roll 753). For Simeon Turley, see Janet Lecompte, "Simeon Turley," in *Mountain Men and the Fur Trade*, ed. Hafen, 7:301–14. For Bent, St. Vrain & Company's order for the stills, see Ledger Z, 426–33, and Ledger DD, 76–89, Chouteau Collection, MoHS. See also Janet LeCompte, *Pueblo, Hardscrabble, Greenhorn: The Upper Arkansas, 1832–1856*, 98, 104–105, 148–49. For a detailed study of the Platte River liquor trade and the government's prohibition program, see Barton H. Barbour, "Special History Study: The Fur Trade at Fort Laramie National Historic Site," National Park Service, Santa Fe, New Mexico, 2000.

66. Much correspondence from Drips and his assistant, Joseph V. Hamilton, to superintendents Mitchell and Harvey and other federal officials can be found in OIA, LR (M234, Roll 753).

67. Some details concerning this case are in OIA, LR (M234, Roll 755). Harvey's opposition is treated in chapter 5 herein.

68. A. H. Redfield, aboard steamer *Twilight*, June 21, 1858, to Mix, OIA, LR (M234, Roll 885). Emphasis in original.

69. Denig, "Indian Tribes of the Upper Missouri," 466.

70. Again, the HBC offers an excellent comparison. As late as 1945, despite intense competition after 1914, the HBC remained northern Canada's dominant institutional presence. With the government "extremely reluctant to shoulder the burden of native relief," the HBC developed nutrition and craft programs for natives facing changing conditions. "However," Arthur J. Ray points out, "the time had passed when the company could expect that these actions would buy loyalty to the extent they had in earlier days. . . . In retrospect, the northern natives were better off with the company than with government bureaucrats. Even though the old order had many flaws, the strong personal ties that developed between Indians and traders served to protect each other's basic needs. Government agents did not establish these bonds, and they operated in a very different institutional context" (Ray, *Canadian Fur Trade in the Industrial Age*, 226–27).

CHAPTER FIVE

1. Charles L. Kappler, ed., *Indian Treaties, 1778–1883*, 594–95.

2. For military conditions, see Francis Paul Prucha, *The Sword of the Republic: The United States Army on the Frontier, 1783–1846*, 319–95; David Michael Delo, *Peddlers and Post Traders: The Army Sutler on the Frontier*.

3. Prucha, *Sword of the Republic*, 240–48, 365–70; Roger L. Nichols, *General Henry Atkinson: A Western Military Career*, 184–85; Harold McCracken, *George Catlin and the Old Frontier* (New York: Bonanza Books, 1959), 134, 143–56; Barry, *Beginning of the West*, 269–70.

4. See Smits, "Frontier Army and the Destruction of the Buffalo."

5. Robert M. Utley, *Frontier Regulars: The United States Army and the Indian, 1866–1890*, 432 n. 20.

6. Clokey, *William H. Ashley*, 169.

7. See Brooks, "Private Journal of Robert Campbell."

8. Campbell's papers are housed at the Mercantile Library Association, University of Missouri, St. Louis. A full-length biography was published in 1999 by William R. Nester, *From Mountain Man to Millionaire: The 'Bold and Dashing Life' of Robert Campbell* (Columbia: University of Missouri, 1999). For William Sublette, see John E. Sunder, *Bill Sublette: Mountain Man*.

9. Chittenden, *American Fur Trade*, 2:960–61.

10. Sunder, *Fur Trade on the Upper Missouri*, 37–38, 40, 53–55.

11. Coues, *Forty Years a Fur Trader*, 179–80.

12. Ibid., 174–75.

13. Audubon, *Audubon and His Journals*, 2:70; McDermott, *Audubon in the West*, 119, 123.

14. McDermott, *Up the Missouri with Audubon*, 127; Audubon, *Audubon and His Journals*, 2:82, 86.

15. McDermott, *Up the Missouri with Audubon*, 127.

16. Chittenden, *American Fur Trade*, 1:369.

17. Audubon, *Audubon and His Journals*, 2:31.

18. Coues, *Forty Years a Fur Trader*, 183–84.

19. Ibid., 191–92.

20. Ibid., 216.

21. Sunder, *Fur Trade on the Upper Missouri*, 72, 75.

22. Coues, *Forty Years a Fur Trader*, 223–24; Sunder, *Fur Trade on the Upper Missouri*, 52–77.

23. Ledger entries from Pierre Chouteau, Jr., & Company from April to July 1846 show goods purchased from Fox and Livingston amounting to about twenty-eight hundred dollars, the bulk of which was credited to Fort Union on June 3 (AFCo Ledger JJ, 255, 262, 264, 270, 281; Fur Trade Ledgers [Roll 11, Vol. JJ], MoHS).

24. Coues, *Forty Years a Fur Trader*, 236.

25. Sunder, *Fur Trade on the Upper Missouri*, 78–80, 85.

26. Coues, *Forty Years a Fur Trader*, 167–70. Harvey, fired around Christmas 1839, set off with only a dog for Saint Louis to plead his case before Chouteau. Impressed with Harvey's grit, Chouteau reengaged him in March 1840.

27. Ibid., 217–19; Abel, *Chardon's Journal*, xxxv–xxxvi, nn. 186–88; Sunder, *Fur Trade on the Upper Missouri*, 61; Anne McDonnell, ed., "The Fort Benton Journal, 1854–56, and the Fort Sarpy Journal, 1855–56," *Contributions to the Historical Society of Montana*, vol. 10 (Helena: Naegele Printing Co., 1940), 302–305. Paul Kane heard more details about this incident in 1848 while with HBC

traders on the Saskatchewan. The Blackfeet held Big Snake responsible for causing the problem by murdering Reese. In anger, he killed two men and wounded two others. A few months later a Cree enemy, finding Big Snake alone, killed him on the prairie (J. Russell Harper, ed., *Paul Kane's Frontier*, 148–49, 152).

28. *Kenneth McKenzie* vs. *Pierre Chouteau, John B. Sarpy, Joseph A. Sire, John F. A. Sandford* [*sic*], *Felix Vallé, and Luther C. Menard*, Saint Louis District Court, November 20, 1849, Chouteau Collection, MoHS.

29. Sunder, *Fur Trade of the Upper Missouri*, 87–89.

30. Chouteau, Saint Louis, December 5, 1848, to William Medill, OIA, LR (M234, Roll 755). Kipp remained in the Upper Missouri until 1865; Culbertson left a few years earlier. See Mattison, "James Kipp" and "Alexander Culbertson," in *Mountain Men and the Fur Trade*, ed. Hafen, 1:253–56, 2:201–205.

31. Chouteau, Saint Louis, January 12, 1849, to T. H. Harvey and J. J. Gantt, OIA, LR (M234, Roll 755).

32. "Register of Traders' Licenses, 1847–1873," NA, RG75, OIA, Records of the Miscellaneous Division. Chouteau applied for a license on February 15, 1849 (approved on March 20) that listed Alexander Culbertson, James Kipp, and Andrew Drips as employees. Few records concerning Harvey and Gantt's case survived. Record Group 206, Records of the Solicitor of the Treasury, Letters Received, U.S. Attorneys, Clerks of Courts and Marshals, Kansas City Regional Center, National Archives, has letters dated February 12, March 16, and July 5, 1849, that mention damage amounts.

33. See Campbell Family Papers, Mercantile Library Association/University of Missouri at Saint Louis, also published as *Papers of the Saint Louis Fur Trade, Part 3: Robert Campbell Family Collection from the St. Louis Mercantile Library Association*, University Publications of America, 1994. I refer to a ledger book (listed as "Folder 2-7, Ledger Book" in the collection) containing 1849 and 1850 accounts with Harvey, Primeau, & Co., and an account dated August 17, 1855, listing assets of Harvey, Primeau, & Co. See also Berry, *Beginning of the West*, 751, 875.

34. Sunder, *Fur Trade of the Upper Missouri*, 164–65; and "Register of Traders' Licenses, 1847–1873," NA, OIA, Records of the Miscellaneous Division. When Joseph Picotte & Co. applied for a license on June 2, 1856, he named Kenneth McKenzie and Robert Campbell as sureties. Mckenzie was at this time involved in his lawsuit against Chouteau & Company, which was not settled until June 1859 ("6-13-1859," Kenneth McKenzie Papers, MoHS).

35. Sunder, *Fur Trade of the Upper Missouri*, 182–84, 208–209.

36. Chittenden, *Early Steamboat Navigation*, 210–15, 287–91.

37. Donald Jackson, ed., *The Journals of Zebulon Montgomery Pike* (Norman: University of Oklahoma Press, 1966) 1:89.

38. For Fort Snelling, see Theodore C. Blegen, *Minnesota: A History of the State*, 85–123; William Watts Folwell, *A History of Minnesota*, 1:135–40; and Robert

G. Ferris, ed., *Soldier and Brave: Historic Places Associated with Indian Affairs and the Indian Wars in the Trans-Mississippi West* (Washington: United States Department of the Interior, National Park Service, 1971), 170–71.

39. Folwell, *History of Minnesota,* 1:106–108.

40. Ibid., 1:351–52, 359–60.

41. Gilman, Gilman, and Stultz, *Red River Trails,* 87.

42. Ross, *Red River Settlement,* 339–40.

43. See Blegen, *Minnesota,* 183–96. Alexander Ross counted 5,391 people at the Red River settlement in 1849 and estimated a population of about 6,500 in 1855 (Ross, *Red River Settlement,* 409). See also Dale Miquelon, "A Brief History of Lower Fort Garry," *Canadian Historic Sites, Occasional Papers in Archeology and History* No. 4 (Ottawa: National Historic Sites Service, Department of Indian Affairs and Northern Department, 1970), 17–19.

44. Chambers, *Old Bullion Benton,* 85, 110–11, 263, 304, 306; Ralph Emerson Twitchell, *The Leading Facts of New Mexico History* 2 vols. (Cedar Rapids: The Torch Press, 1912) 2:101 n. 70.

45. Clokey, *William H. Ashley,* 190–96.

46. Ibid., 232, 272–75.

47. Kvasnicka and Viola, *Commissioners of Indian Affairs,* 13–15.

48. Ibid., 18–20, 23–25.

49. Ibid., 32–33.

50. Ibid., 71–73, 84–85.

51. For Minnesota politics from 1845 to 1865, see Blegen, *Minnesota,* 213–56; and Folwell, *History of Minnesota,* 1:231–65, 365–421; 2:1–36. For unscrupulous Minnesota fur traders, see Robert A. Trennert, Jr., *Indian Traders on the Middle Border: The House of Ewing, 1827–1854,* 176–201.

52. Chittenden, *Early Steamboat Navigation,* 216–20, 234–35.

53. Ibid., 273–76.

54. Helen McCann White, ed., *Ho! For the Gold Fields: Northern Overland Wagon Trains of the 1860s* (St. Paul: Minnesota Historical Society, 1966), 23.

CHAPTER SIX

1. Barry, *Beginning of the West,* 1147; J. W. Whitfield, Washington, July 1856, to [unknown], and R. M. Clelland, Secretary of Interior, January 6, 1857, to Jefferson Davis, Secretary of War, both in OIA, LR (M234, Roll 885). Chouteau claimed a loss of $13,145.53; additional claims totaled nearly $18,000.

2. Alfred J. Vaughn, Saint Joseph, Missouri, March 6, 1854, to Alfred Cumming, Saint Louis, OIA, LR (M234, Roll 885).

3. Alfred J. Vaughn, Saint Louis, April 1, 1854, to Alfred Cumming, Saint Louis, OIA, LR (M234, Roll 885).

4. Pierre Chouteau, Jr., & Co., Saint Louis, May 20, 1854, to Alfred Cumming, Saint Louis, OIA, LR (M234, Roll 885).

5. Coues, *Forty Years a Fur Trader*, 419–20; Alfred J. Vaughn, Fort Union, July 3, 1854, to Alfred Cumming, Saint Louis, OIA, LR (M234, Roll 885).

6. Alfred J. Vaughn, Fort Union, July 3, 1854, to Alfred Cumming, Saint Louis, OIA, LR (M234, Roll 885).

7. Alfred J. Vaughn, Fort Pierre, November 21, 1854, to Alfred Cumming, Saint Louis; Cumming, Saint Louis, to George W. Manypenny, Washington, January 2, 1855; May 21, 1855; July 29, 1856; Vaughn, Fort Pierre, February 17, 1855, to Cumming, Saint Louis, all in OIA, LR (M234, Roll 885).

8. Alfred Vaughn, Saint Louis, to Alfred Cumming, Saint Louis; and Alexander Culbertson, Saint Louis, to Alfred Cumming, Saint Louis, May 19, 1855, OIA, LR (M234, Roll 885).

9. Alfred Vaughn, Fort Clark, September 29, 1855, to Alfred Cumming, Saint Louis, OIA, LR (M234, Roll 885).

10. Alfred J. Vaughn, Fort Pierre, February 15, 1856, to Alfred Cumming, Saint Louis, OIA, LR (M234, Roll 885). In September 1853 Vaughn complained to Commissioner of Indian Affairs George W. Manypenny about "reckless, renegade white men . . . travelling from one Indian village to another, poisoning and corrupting [their] minds." In the same letter Vaughn wrote: "I must say, in justice to the American Fur Company [that is, the UMO] since my arrival in this agency, they have done all in their power to make me comfortable, and have shown every disposition to aid me in my official duties when required" (U.S. Congress, House, *Report of the Commissioner of Indian Affairs, November 26, 1853*, 33rd Cong., 1st sess., H. Exec. Doc. 1, 358–59.

11. Alfred J. Vaughn, Fort Union, September 10, 1856, to Alfred Cumming, Saint Louis, in *Report of the Commissioner of Indian Affairs . . . for the Year 1856* (Washington: A. O. P. Nicholson, 1857), 77–85.

12. C. E. Galpin, Fort Pierre, March 20, 1857, to Pierre Chouteau, Jr., & Co., Saint Louis, Chouteau Collection, MoHS.

13. Major Frederick T. Wilson, U.S.A., "Old Fort Pierre and Its Neighbors," *South Dakota Historical Collections*, 1:279–81, 348–50; anonymous, "Official Correspondence Relating to Fort Pierre," *South Dakota Historical Collections*, 1:400, 404; Robert G. Athearn, *Forts of the Upper Missouri*, 42; "Memorandum of Agreement made and entered into this 14th day of April 1855 between Major General Th. S. Jessup . . . and General Charles Gratiot on behalf of Pierre Chouteau & Co. . . . ," Chouteau Collection, MoHS.

14. Joseph LaBarge, [1855], to Pierre Chouteau, Jr., & Co., Chouteau Collection, MoHS.

15. Historians usually cite a figure of $45,000 dollars; most criticize the "Company" for ripping off the government. See Pierre Chouteau, Jr., New York, February 9, 1856, to John B. Sarpy, [Saint Louis?], Chouteau Collection, MoHS.

In translation, the relevant portion of the letter reads: "I received your letters of the 28 and 29 of the past month, to which I do not have time to respond today. This [letter] is to inform you that I just received a warrant from the treasury at New York for $36,500 which Sanford, after two weeks of debate has consented to take for Fort Pierre. It is still better than to have to run the delay and risk of a legal process."

16. Athearn, *Forts of the Upper Missouri*, 48–50; Dee Alexander Brown, *The Galvanized Yankees* (Urbana: University of Illinois Press, 1963), 116–17; C. E. Galpin, Fort Pierre, March 20, 1857, to Pierre Chouteau, Jr., & Co., Saint Louis, Chouteau Collection, MoHS.

17. Alfred J. Vaughn, Saint Louis, March 8, 1857, to Alfred Cumming, Saint Louis, OIA, LR. (M234, Roll 885). Vaughn estimated the agency would cost two thousand dollars to build, but no funds materialized.

18. Coues, *Forty Years a Fur Trader*, 417–18; John C. Ewers, *The Blackfeet: Raiders on the Northwestern Plains*, 226–35.

19. A. H. Redfield, Washington, February 3, 1858, to Charles E. Mix, acting commissioner of Indian affairs; Redfield, Steamer *Twilight,* June 21, 1858, to Mix; Redfield, Fort Randall, October 4, 1858, to Superintendent of Indian Affairs at Saint Louis, all in OIA, LR (M234, Roll 885); Sunder, *Fur Trade on the Upper Missouri*, 203.

20. Bernard S. Schoonover, Fort Union, August 20, 1860, to A. M. Robinson, Saint Louis; Schoonover, Fort Pierre, October 22, 1859, to Robinson, Saint Louis, both in OIA, LR (M234, Roll 885).

21. T. H. Harvey wrote that the Sioux had ridiculed white soldiers as "squaws" during the 1823 Leavenworth expedition against the Arikaras. Despite complaints in 1846–47, nothing was done because of the Mexican War; Harvey believed a volunteer force would be expensive and ineffective (T. H. Harvey, Saint Louis, February 4, 1847, to William Medill, Washington, OIA, LR [M234, Roll 754]). See also letter from UMO employees Pierre Beauchamp and Charles Patinaud to Agent Schoonover on September 28 and 30, 1859, OIA, LR (M234, Roll 885).

22. Pierre Chouteau, Jr., Saint Louis, January 2, 1861, to A. M. Robinson, Saint Louis, OIA, LR (M234, Roll 885).

23. Latta, Leavenworth City, January 8, 1863, to William P. Dole, OIA, LR (M234, Roll 885); Sunder, *Fur Trade on the Upper Missouri*, 230–33.

24. Athearn, *Forts of the Upper Missouri*, 47, 80; Wilson, "Old Fort Pierre and Its Neighbors," 294–96; George E. Hyde, *Red Cloud's Folk: A History of the Oglala Sioux*, 79–82.

25. Samuel N. Latta, August 27, 1862, to William P. Dole, in U.S. Department of the Interior, Office of Indian Affairs, *Report of the Commissioner of Indian Affairs for the Year 1862* (Washington: Government Printing Office, 1863), 196–97. No evidence in the Chouteau materials I have examined supports Latta's claim (see note 36 below).

26. *Report of the Commissioner of Indian Affairs for the Year 1862*, 196–97.

27. For the rise of commercial activities in Iowa, see William Silag, "Gateway to the Grasslands: Sioux City and the Missouri River Frontier," *Western Historical Quarterly* 14 (October 1983): 4, 397–414.

28. *Report of the Commissioner of Indian Affairs for the Year 1862*, 192–96.

29. See Kenneth Carley, *The Sioux Uprising of 1862* (St. Paul: Minnesota Historical Society, 1976).

30. Despite successes at White Stone Hill in September 1863 and Killdeer Mountain in July 1864, Sully's expeditions further irritated the Sioux. The federal government, "having started a small fire, was now obligated to put out a major one" that lasted for three decades (Athearn, *Forts of the Upper Missouri*, 115).

31. Athearn, *Forts of the Upper Missouri*, 143.

32. See "Morton S. Wilkinson," in Lanman, *Biographical Annals of the Civil Government*, 464.

33. Wilkinson, Crow Creek Agency, July 14, 1864, to Hon. Jas. Harlan, U.S.S., OIA, LR (M234, Roll 885). For James Harlan, see Lanman, *Biographical Annals of the Civil Government*, 186–87. Fellowes D. Pease appears later in this chapter in connection with the North Western Fur Company. Nepotism was common in the Indian service; Lewis Henry Morgan in 1862 observed that the system was "not only a failure but disgraceful for the immorality and dishonesty with which the business is managed" (White, *Lewis Henry Morgan*, 138–39, 156).

34. Athearn, *Forts of the Upper Missouri*, 155–74; Brown, *Galvanized Yankees*, chapter four.

35. Athearn, *Forts of the Upper Missouri*, 155–74.

36. Morgan's quote is from White, *Lewis Henry Morgan*, 152. See also Chittenden, *Early Steamboat Navigation*, 260–62. James B. Hubbell discussed Dimon's actions in "Trading with the Indians in the Stirring Days of the Early Sixties," Saint Paul Dispatch, August 3, 1901. Charles Larpenteur noted that Chouteau, "having been reported as a rebel . . . could not obtain a license, and was obliged to sell out all his trading posts" (Coues, *Forty Years a Fur Trader*, 366). Pierre Chouteau, Jr., owned five slaves in 1860 (undoubtedly house servants), but there is no evidence that he or his men actively supported the Confederate cause (Sunder, *Fur Trade on the Upper Missouri*, 221 n. 12). John Francis McDermott observed that many better-off Saint Louis families held slaves although the town was not an agricultural center, inferring that slave ownership signified high status rather than possible Confederate sympathies. See McDermott, *Private Libraries in Creole Saint Louis*, part one.

37. Athearn, *Forts of the Upper Missouri*, 155–74, 206. Dimon later "admitted that his suspicions about subversion among the traders had proved to be incorrect" (312 n. 18).

38. See William E. Lass, "The Moscow Expedition," *Minnesota History* 39, no. 6 (Summer 1965): 227–40; and William E. Lass, "The History and Significance

of the Northwest Fur Company, 1865–1869," *North Dakota History* 61, no. 3 (Summer 1994): 21–40. See also James A. Smith Papers and James Boyd Hubbell Papers, MnHS.

39. In 1868, Hubbell's uncle, James Boyd, wrote that he was still a "Radical," though he disliked the leadership of Benjamin Butler and Thaddeus Stevens. In 1867–68 Boyd helped Hubbell apply for a tax collector's job in Montana Territory by persuading a neighbor, E. S. Woodford, to write his senator, Orris S. Ferry, who served on the Committee on Territories. Woodford wrote that Hubbell's "radical record is untarnished, his business talent, adequate to any position" (James Boyd, West Winsted, Connecticut, September 8, 1868, to James B. Hubbell; and E. S. Woodford, West Winsted, March 28, 1868, to Hon. O. S. Ferry, Hubbell Papers, MnHS). Alpheus Fenn Hawley was from Jamestown, Chautauqua County, New York. At one time, probably 1853, the Know-Nothing party ran Hawley for Congress, but he lost to Reuben E. Fenton, later governor of New York. Hubbell and Hawley both arrived at Mankato in 1857 (Anonymous, *Mankato: Its First Fifty Years* (Mankato, Minn.: Free Press Printing Company, 1903), 228; Lanman, *Biographical Annals of the Civil Government*, 144).

40. *Mankato*, 166; J. B. Hubbell, "Red Men Smoke Pipe of Council," *Saint Paul Dispatch*, September 7, 1901.

41. "Register of Traders' Licenses, 1847–1873," NA, OIA, Records of the Miscellaneous Division, 50. Other Missourians were also denounced. Joseph LaBarge was allegedly told by Secretary of the Treasury Salmon P. Chase that "all Missourians were prima facie Rebels." Chittenden, *Early Steamboat Navigation*, 342–43.

42. Agreement to sell Chouteau's Missouri River forts, Washington, D.C., March 2, 1865; and bill of sale for forts Pierre, Berthold, Union, and buildings at Fort Sully, May 19, 1865, Smith Papers, MnHS. The North Western Fur Company paid Pierre Chouteau, Jr., & Co. $13,041.21 on January 13, 1866. See "Sales for a/c of N.W. Fur Co.," [January 13, 1866], Hubbell Papers, MnHS.

43. Articles of partnership, New York, March 23, 1865, with amendment dated March 5, 1866, Hubbell Papers, MnHS; C. Francis Bates, New York, February 27, 1866, to J. A. Smith, Chicago, Smith Papers, MnHS.

44. Chouteau, Saint Louis, July 26, 1865, to A. J. [*sic*] Smith & Co., Chicago, Smith Papers, MnHS

45. Pierre Chouteau, Jr., & Company, "Journal, 1864–1868," Fur Trade Ledgers, MoHS (Roll 19, Vol. 12, 1140–41); Chouteau, Saint Louis, July 26, 1865, to A. J. [*sic*] Smith & Co., Chicago, Smith Papers, MnHS; Lass, "The Northwest Fur Company in the Fort Union Region," *Fort Union Fur Trade Symposium Proceedings, September 13–15, 1990* (Williston: Friends of Fort Union Trading Post, 1994), 6; D. N. Cooley, Commissioner of Indian Affairs, April 16, 1866, to James Harlan, Secretary of Interior; Cooley, September 29, 1866, to O. H. Browning, OIA, Report Books, 1838–85 (M348, Roll 15); "Profit & Loss a/c [1869], Smith Papers, MnHS; [J. B. Hubbell], "Trading with the Indians in the

Stirring Days of the Early Sixties," *Saint Paul Dispatch*, August 3, 1901 (courtesy MnHS). Pierre Chouteau, Jr., died on September 6, 1865.

46. Pierre Chouteau, Jr., & Company, "Journal, 1864–1868," Fur Trade Ledgers, MoHS (Roll 19, Vol. 12).

47. The company calculated its own freight charges to be about three cents per pound; the government paid between five and eight cents per pound. See undated [1854] notes dealing with various bid proposals and rationales for calculating charges (Chouteau Collection, MoHS).

48. Articles of agreement between Charles E. Mix and Pierre Chouteau, Jr., & Co., March 15, 1859, and bills of lading dated May 26, 1859, OIA, LR (M234, Roll 885); Pierre Chouteau, Jr., & Company, "Journal, 1864–1868," Fur Trade Ledgers, MoHS (Roll 19, Vol. 12).

49. [Hubbell], "Trading with the Indians," *Saint Paul Dispatch*, August 3, 1901. The *Yellow Stone* arrived at Fort Union "with a company of soldiers from Fort Rice" on May 19, 1865 (Coues, *Forty Years a Fur Trader*, 432).

50. Trial Balance, July 1, 1866, Hubbell Papers, MnHS.

51. "Sales for a/c of N.W.Fur Co," [Aug. 3–Oct. 31, 1865], Hubbell Papers; "Mssrs. James A. Smith & Co fur a/c in a/c & Interest a/c to December 31, 1866 with Martin Bates Jr. & Co," Smith Papers; "List of furs delivered to D. W. Marsh Agent for Durfee & Peck at Fort Stevenson, D.T., May 16, 1868 . . . ," Smith Papers, MnHS.

52. The NWFCo's business consisted of "supplying miners at Fort Benton and Helena, adding new Indian trading posts, and engaging in the transportation, by steamboats and wagon trains, of government supplies, as well as the goods of the corporation. . . . The Company's collection of peltries alone amounted to 24,000 robes per annum and small furs in proportion" (*Mankato: Its First Fifty Years*, 240).

53. W. S. Harney, September 7, 1868, to James A. Smith and C. K. Peck; Profit & Loss a/c [1865–68], both in Smith Papers, MnHS.

54. A. Bassett, Fort Totten, to J. A. Smith & Co., Chicago, January 27 and March 2, 1868; James Blake, Fort Totten, February 13, 1869, to Frank M. Smith, all in Smith Papers, MnHS. Adams Bassett is identified in Coues, *Forty Years a Fur Trader*, 387.

55. Bassett, Fort Totten, to J. A. Smith, Chicago, May 29 and June 20, 1868, Smith Papers, MnHS.

56. See Lass, "'Moscow Expedition'"; Edmund J. Danziger, Jr., "The Indian Office during the Civil War: Impotence in Indian Affairs," *South Dakota History* 5, no. 1 (Winter 1974): 52–72; and George H. Phillips, "The Indian Ring in Dakota Territory, 1870–1890," *South Dakota History* 2, no. 4 (Fall 1972): 345–67.

57. Affidavits dated March 26 and April 7, 1866; and Wilkinson, Fort Berthold, September 26, 1866, to D. N. Cooley, Smith Papers, MnHS. In fact, three affidavits, each with differing amounts of provisions, were made out.

58. Undated declaration and transcript of treaty talks signed by A. B. Smith, Smith Papers, MnHS.

59. Ibid.

60. John Geowey had been in the area since at least October 1863; Gregory's first name may have been Shaw; and "Bruguier" may be Theophile Bruguiere, whom Charles Larpenteur described as "my old friend . . . an old Indian trader, and the first settler at the mouth of the Big Sioux River" (Coues, *Forty Years a Fur Trader*, 297). See Boskowitz, April 14, 1877, to Geowey; and Daybooks numbers 1 (May 29–June 25, 1866) and 3 (July 16–September 2, 1866), both in Gregory, Bruguier, and Geowey Papers, MnHS.

61. "Invoice of goods furnished C. E. Galpin & Co. by Mr. John Geowey at Chouteau Creek October 7, 1863"; "Shipments from Fort Union May 31 to Oct 14, 1866"; "Fort Expenses outside of mess," October 1866 to April 1867; J. A. Boskowitz, Chicago, April 20, 1865, to John Geowey; and Daybook number 6 (June 12–June 27, 1867), all in Gregory, Bruguier, and Geowey Papers, MnHS.

62. An August 1866 inventory showed $15,079.22 in goods on hand at Fort Union for Gregory, Bruguier, and Geowey ("Balance Sheet, August 16, 1866"; and Kerler, Fort Union, January 17, 1867, to John Geowey, both in Gregory, Bruguier, and Geowey Papers, MnHS).

63. "Balance Sheet Fort Union April 9, 1867," in Gregory, Bruguier, and Geowey Papers, MnHS.

64. D. N. Cooley, Washington, March 16, 1866, to James Harlan, Washington, OIA, Report Books, 1838–85 (M348, Roll 15).

65. Coues, *Forty Years a Fur Trader*, 363, 365, 369–75.

66. Coues, *Forty Years a Fur Trader*, 382–84.

67. Athearn, *Forts of the Upper Missouri*, 232–34.

68. Sworn statement of Charles W. Hoffman, Gallatin County, Montana, December 29, 1902, Hubbell Papers, MnHS.

69. Ibid.

70. Ibid.;"Indian Depredation Claims," September 26, 1904, Hubbell Papers, MnHS.

71. U.S. Congress, Senate, Committee on Indian Affairs, 41st Cong., 3rd sess., S. Rep. 337, 1871. Hubbell persisted with the claim until 1904, about one year before his death. See "Indian Depredation Claims," September 26, 1904, Hubbell Papers, MnHS, in which he advised H. P. Hall that he had Senators Nelson and Clapp on his side and that he wished Hall to "help me and yourself a little," too.

72. Undated manuscript [carries incorrect date of May 13, 1865]; A. H. Wilder, Saint Paul, October 8, 1868, to Hubbell; and "Notes by Judge Hubbell," 15–16, all in Hubbell Papers, MnHS. See also contract dated June 2, 1865, between NWFCo and A. B. Smith to make "Red Stone Indian Pipes"; and "Profit & Loss a/c" [1869], both in Smith Papers, MnHS.

73. Undated declaration and transcript of treaty talks signed by A. B. Smith, Smith Papers, MnHS.

74. Daybooks numbers 1 through 7 (May 29, 1866–July 4, 1867), Gregory, Bruguier, and Geowey Papers, MnHS.

75. Engagement contract for Pierre Hawk, May 27, 1866, Daybooks numbers 6 and 7 (June 12–July 4, 1867), Gregory, Bruguier, and Geowey Papers, MnHS. Dr. Washington Matthews described Ramsey as a "tall, good looking old man of Spanish type" who lived among the Assiniboines in 1871 (Coues, *Forty Years a Fur Trader*, 331–32). See also Charles Larpenteur MS Journals, MnHS, Vol. 3, July 5, 1867; and Pierre Chouteau, Jr., & Co., "Journal, 1864–1868," Fur Trade Ledgers, MoHS (Roll 19, Vol. 12).

76. Coues, *Forty Years a Fur Trader*, 355–61; Larpenteur MS Journals, MnHS, Vol. 2. The families were as follows:

1.	Joseph Ramsey [Ramusio?]	1 wife 1 girl 5 years old
2.	Joseph Lesperance	1 wife 1 girl 3 years old
3.	[same]	1 wife 2 boys, 5 and 7 years old
4.	Guiteau [?]	1 wife
5.	St. Arneau	1 wife 1 girl 4 years old
6.	Mr. Nelson	1 boy 1 year old, 1 girl 3 years old
7.	Mr. Theodor [?]	1 boy 4 months old
8.	Mr. Reilor [?]	1 boy 4 years old, 1 girl 3 years old
9.	Henry [?]	1 wife
10.	Boleau	1 wife, 1 girl 6 years old
11.	[same]	1 wife, 1 girl 7 months old
12.	Joseph Dagneau	1 wife, 1 boy 15 years old, 1 boy 6 years old, 1 girl 3 years old
13.	Philipe	1 wife, 1 boy 4 years old
14.	Thomas Campbell	1 wife
15.	Robert Lemon	wife and child, boy 2 1/2
16.	Louis Bompart	wife & 2 children, 7 & 4 years old

77. Coues, *Forty Years a Fur Trader*, 364–65, 369, 375–77. It is unaccountable that Larpenteur named A. B. Smith, who had sworn out a blistering affidavit against James A. Smith. Perhaps there was some confusion. Editor Elliott Coues said A. B. Smith was the "younger Mr. Smith, son of the head of the firm of Hubbell, Hawley & Co.," adding, "I know nothing to speak of about the firm or their affairs."

78. Articles of agreement between NWFCo and Durfee & Peck, New York, October 4, 1867, Smith Papers, MnHS.

79. Coues, *Forty Years a Fur Trader*, 379, 388–90.

80. Larpenteur MS Journals, MnHS, Vol. 3.

81. Ibid.

82. Ibid.

83. Ibid.; A. Bassett, Fort Totten, September 24, 1867, to J. A. Smith & Co., Chicago, Smith Papers, MnHS.

84. Larpenteur MS Journals, MnHS, Vol. 3.

85. Gregory L. Fox, "The Garden Coulee Site (32WI18): A Late Nineteenth Century Village of a Band of Dissident Hidatsa," United States Department of the Interior, National Park Service, Midwest Archeological Center, Lincoln, Nebr., 1982.

Bibliographical Essay

In the interest of economy, not all cited sources are herein listed; rather, this is meant to identify the most important documents, books, and articles used for this study. Among archival sources, no collection was more useful than the Chouteau Collection in the Missouri Historical Society at Saint Louis. Also useful were microfilm copies of the American Fur Company Papers. Likewise, the Missouri Historical Society's Fur Trade Collection, Kenneth McKenzie Collection, and Andrew Drips Papers all proved valuable. I also consulted the Robert Campbell Family Papers, Mercantile Library Association, University of Missouri at Saint Louis, recently published in microfilm as Martin P. Schipper, ed., *Papers of the St. Louis Fur Trade, Part 3: Robert Campbell Family Collection—From the St. Louis Mercantile Library Association* (Bethesda, Md.: University Publications of America, 1994).

The Montana Historical Society's Bradley Papers also provided useful information. The Boston Athenaeum holds Isaac Sprague's diary of his 1843 trip to Fort Union with John Audubon. The Minnesota Historical Society in Saint Paul provided several important collections: the Great Northern Railroad Collection; the Gregory, Bruguier, and Goewey Collection; the James A. Smith Collection; the James Boyd Hubbell Papers; and the Larpenteur Family Papers, including Charles Larpenteur's original manuscript diaries that differ considerably from the version edited by

Elliott Coues. The Jesuit Missouri Provincial Archives at Saint Louis, Missouri, hold the Pierre-Jean De Smet Papers, which detail De Smet's activities around Fort Union and his associations with the fur traders. The Joslyn Museum of Art in Omaha, Nebraska, holds the Maximilian-Bodmer Collection, which includes illustrations and notebooks from Maximilian's trip to Fort Union in 1833. I also consulted the American Fur Company Papers, New York Historical Society, and the Astor Papers, New York Public Library.

The National Archives house much useful material; almost all the citations appearing in this book are available on microfilm. Of special importance to this study were Office of Indian Affairs, Letters Received, Upper Missouri Agency, 1824–74 (M234, Rolls 883–87), and Office of Indian Affairs, Letters Received, Saint Louis Superintendency, 1824–51 (M234, Rolls 747–56). Additional material was culled from Office of Indian Affairs, RG 75, Report Books, 1838–85 (M348, Roll 15), and Office of Indian Affairs, NA, RG 75, OIA, Records of the Miscellaneous Division,"Register of Traders' Licenses, 1847–73."

Government publications of a variety of types offered the official view of Upper Missouri affairs. Reports of the commissioner of Indian affairs from 1853 through 1865 shed light on agents' duties, the difficulties they encountered, and their views on policy and the fur trade. All of these reports are found in the Congressional Serial Set.

A number of congressional documents also cast light on the attitudes of policy makers regarding the fur trade and the government's desire to regulate it. Of special interest were "Regulating the Indian Department (To Accompany Bills H.R. Nos. 488, 489, 490)," May 20, 1834 (Washington: Gales & Seaton, Printers) [Serial Set 263]; U.S. Congress, House, 23rd Cong., 1st sess., H. Exec. Rep. 474, "Regulating the Indian Department"; U.S. Congress, House, 33rd Cong., 1st sess., H. Exec. Doc. 1, "Report of the Commissioner of Indian Affairs, November 26, 1853"; U.S. Congress, Senate, 18th Cong., 1st sess., S. Exec. Doc. 56; U.S. Congress, Senate, 20th Cong., 2d sess., S. Exec. Doc. 67; U.S. Congress, Senate, 20th Cong., 1st Sess., S. Exec. Doc. 90; and U.S. Congress, Senate, 41st Cong., 3rd sess., S. Exec. Rep. 337. Also useful were William F. Raynolds, *Report on the Exploration of the Yellowstone River* (1868), U.S. Congress, Senate, 40th Cong., 1st sess., S. Exec. Doc. 77; and *Reports of Explorations and*

Surveys to Ascertain the Most Practicable and Economical Route for a Railroad from the Mississippi River to the Pacific Ocean, 12 vols. (Washington: Government Printing Office, 1855–61), vol. 12, part 1; Isaac Ingalls Stevens, *Narrative and Final Report of Explorations for a Route for a Pacific Railroad near the Forty-Seventh and Forty-Ninth Parallels of North Latitude from St. Paul to Puget Sound*, U.S. Congress, House, 36th Cong., 1st sess., H. Exec. Doc. 56.

A number of publications from the Smithsonian Institution likewise aided my research. Most important were Edwin Thompson Denig's "Indian Tribes of the Upper Missouri," ed. J. N. B. Hewitt, *Forty-Sixth Annual Report of the Bureau of American Ethnology, 1928–29* (1930); J. N. B. Hewitt, ed., *Journal of Rudolph Friederich Kurz*, Bureau of American Ethnology Bulletin 115 (1937); and Thaddeus A. Culbertson's *Journal of an Expedition to the Mauvaises Terres and the Upper Missouri in 1850*, ed. John Francis McDermott, Bureau of American Ethnology Bulletin 147 (1952). Background on Upper Missouri Indians appears in John C. Ewers, *The Horse in Blackfoot Indian Culture*, Bureau of American Ethnology Bulletin 159 (1955); Frederick W. Hodge, ed., *Handbook of American Indians North of Mexico*, 2 vols., Bureau of American Ethnology Bulletin 30 (1907, 1910); John R. Swanton, *The Indian Tribes of North America*, Bureau of American Ethnology Bulletin 145 (1952); and John A. Walthall and Thomas E. Emerson, eds., *Calumet and Fleur-de-lys: Archeology of Indian and French Contact in the Midcontinent* (Washington, D.C.: Smithsonian Institution Press, 1992).

Other useful sources include John C. Ewers, *The Blackfeet: Raiders on the Northwestern Plains* (Norman: University of Oklahoma Press, 1958); Edwin Thompson Denig, *Five Indian Tribes of the Upper Missouri*, ed. John C. Ewers (Norman: University of Oklahoma Press, 1961); Dan Kennedy (Ochankugahe), *Recollections of an Assiniboine Chief* (Toronto and Montreal: McClelland and Stewart, 1972); Michael Stephen Kennedy, ed., *The Assiniboines: From the Accounts of the Old Ones Told to First Boy (James Larpenteur Long)* (Norman: University of Oklahoma Press, 1961); George E. Hyde, *Red Cloud's Folk: A History of the Oglala Sioux* (Norman: University of Oklahoma Press, 1937); David G. Mandelbaum, *The Plains Cree: An Ethnographic, Historical and Comparative Study*, Canadian Plains Studies 9 (Regina: Canadian Plains Research Center, University of Regina, 1979); Robert H. Lowie, *The Crow Indians* (New York: Holt, Rinehart and

Winston, 1935, reissued 1956); and Virginia Irving Armstrong, *I Have Spoken: American History through the Voices of the Indians* (Chicago: Sage Books, 1971).

For the development of Indian policy, I consulted Charles L. Kappler, ed., *Indian Treaties, 1778–1883* (New York: Interland Publishing Inc., 1972); Robert M. Kvasnicka and Herman J. Viola, eds., *The Commissioners of Indian Affairs, 1824–1977* (Lincoln: University of Nebraska Press, 1979); Ora Brooks Peake, *A History of the United States Indian Factory System, 1795–1822* (Denver: Sage Books, 1954); Francis Paul Prucha, *American Indian Policy in the Formative Years: The Indian Trade and Intercourse Acts, 1790–1834* (Cambridge: Harvard University Press, 1962; reprint, Lincoln: University of Nebraska Press, 1970); Francis Paul Prucha, ed., *Documents of United States Indian Policy* (Lincoln: University of Nebraska Press, 1975); Francis Paul Prucha, *The Sword of the Republic: The United States Army on the Frontier, 1783–1846* (Toronto, Ontario: Macmillan Company, 1969); and S. Lyman Tyler, *A History of Indian Policy* (Washington: Bureau of Indian Affairs, 1973). Useful articles on this topic include Edmund J. Danziger, Jr., "The Indian Office during the Civil War: Impotence in Indian Affairs," *South Dakota History* 5, no. 1 (Winter 1974); Reginald Horsman, "Scientific Racism and the American Indian in the Mid-Nineteenth Century," *American Quarterly* 27 (May 1975); Ray H. Mattison, "The Indian Reservation System on the Upper Missouri, 1865–1900," *Nebraska History* 36, no. 3 (September 1955); Robert W. McCluggage, "The Senate and Indian Land Titles, 1800–1825," *Western Historical Quarterly* 1, no. 4 (October 1970); George H. Phillips, "The Indian Ring in Dakota Territory, 1870–1890," *South Dakota History* 2, no. 4 (Fall 1972); Robert A. Trennert, "The Fur Trader as Indian Administrator: Conflict of Interest or Wise Policy?" *South Dakota History* 5, no. 1 (Winter 1974); John C. Ewers, "When Red and White Men Met," *Western Historical Quarterly* 2, no. 2 (April 1971); and Thomas F. Schilz, "Robes, Rum, and Rifles: Indian Middlemen in the Northern Plains Fur Trade," *Montana: The Magazine of Western History*, 40, no. 1 (Winter 1990).

Archeological and architectural information on Fort Union is found in Lynelle A. Peterson and William J. Hunt, Jr., *The 1987 Investigations at Fort Union Trading Post: Archeology and Architecture*, U.S. Department of the

Interior, National Park Service (Lincoln, Nebr.: Midwest Archeological Center, 1990). Articles on this topic include Mary Shivers Culpin and Richard Borjes, "The Architecture of Fort Union: A Symbol of Dominance," in *Rendezvous: Selected Papers of the Fourth North American Fur Trade Conference, 1981*, ed. Thomas Buckley (Saint Paul, Minn.: North American Fur Trade Conference, 1984); Gregory L. Fox, "The Garden Coulee Site (32WI18): A Late Nineteenth Century Village of a Band of Dissident Hidatsa," unpublished report, U.S. Department of the Interior, National Park Service, Midwest Archeological Center, Lincoln, Nebr., 1982; William J. Hunt, Jr., "Origins of Fort Union: Archeology and History," in Jennifer S. H. Brown, W. J. Eccles, and Donald P. Heldman, eds., *The Fur Trade Revisited: Selected Papers of the Sixth North American Fur Trade Conference, Mackinac Island, Michigan, 1991* (East Lansing and Mackinac Island: Michigan State University Press and Mackinac Island State Parks, 1994); William J. Hunt, Jr., "Fort Floyd: An Enigmatic Nineteenth-Century Trading Post," *North Dakota History* 61, no. 3 (summer 1994), 7–20; and Charles E. Peterson, "The Houses of French St. Louis," in John Francis McDermott, ed., *The French in the Mississippi Valley* (Urbana: University of Illinois Press, 1965). Another good source for Upper Missouri fur forts is Frank H. H. Roberts, ed., *River Basin Surveys Papers*, numbers 15–20, Smithsonian Institution, Bureau of American Ethnology Bulletin 176 (1960), especially Alan R. Woolworth and W. Raymond Wood, "The Archeology of a Small Trading Post (Kipp's Post, 32MN1) in the Garrison Reservoir, North Dakota."

Grace Lee Nute, ed., *Calendar of the American Fur Company's Papers*, Annual Report of the American Historical Association for the year 1944 (Washington: GPO, 1945) 2 vols., offers a cursory guide to this massive collection, although some of the cited material, such as Astor's correspondence with Daniel Webster, is not available on microfilm.

Useful primary accounts dealing with affairs at and around Fort Union include Maria R. Audubon, ed., *John James Audubon and His Journals*, 2 vols. (New York: Charles Scribner's Sons, 1897); Annie Heloise Abel, ed., *Chardon's Journal at Fort Clark, 1834–1839* (Pierre, S.Dak.: Lawrence K. Fox, 1932); Elliott Coues, ed., *Forty Years a Fur Trader on the Upper Missouri: The Personal Narrative of Charles Larpenteur, 1833–1872*, 2 vols. (New York:

Francis P. Harper, 1898; reprint, Minneapolis: Ross & Haines, 1962); and John Palliser, *Solitary Rambles; or, Sporting Adventures in the Prairies* (London: G. Routledge & Co., 1857).

Additional information can be found in Ray H. Mattison, "Fort Union: Its Role in the Upper Missouri Fur Trade," *North Dakota History* 29, nos. 1–2 (January–April, 1962); and Erwin N. Thompson, *Fort Union Trading Post: Fur Trade Empire on the Upper Missouri* (Medora, SD: Theodore Roosevelt Nature and History Assoc., 1986). See also Sister Dolorita Marie Dougherty, "A History of Fort Union (North Dakota), 1829–1867," Ph.D. diss., Saint Louis Univ., 1957; and Myron L. Koenig, "Fort Union as a Missouri River Post," M.A. thesis, Univ. of Iowa, 1933.

Published primary documentation dealing with fur traders and their business includes Hiram Martin Chittenden, *History of Early Steamboat Navigation on the Missouri River: Life and Adventures of Joseph LaBarge*, 2 vols. (New York: Francis P. Harper, 1903; reprint, Minneapolis: Ross & Haines, 1962); John C. Luttig, *Journal of a Fur-Trading Expedition on the Upper Missouri, 1812–1813*, ed. Stella M. Drumm (Saint Louis: Missouri Historical Society, 1920, reprint with preface and notes by Abraham P. Nasatir, New York: Argosy-Antiquarian Ltd., 1964); Donald McKay Frost, *Notes on General Ashley, the Overland Trail, and South Pass* (Barre, Mass.: Barre Gazette, 1960); Abraham P. Nasatir, *Before Lewis and Clark: Documents Illustrating the History of the Missouri, 1785–1804*, 2 vols. (Saint Louis: Saint Louis Historical Documents Foundation, 1952); and W. Raymond Wood and Thomas D. Thiessen, eds., *Early Fur Trade on the Northern Plains: Canadian Traders among the Mandan and Hidatsa Indians, 1738–1818* (Norman: University of Oklahoma Press, 1985).

Among many works that treat the fur trade, I found the following items pertinent to this study: Don Berry, *A Majority of Scoundrels: An Informal History of the Rocky Mountain Fur Company* (New York: Harper & Brothers, 1961); Hiram Martin Chittenden, *The American Fur Trade of the Far West*, 2 vols. (New York: Francis P. Harper, 1902; reprint, Stanford: Academic Reprints, 1954); Bernard DeVoto, *Across the Wide Missouri* (Boston: Houghton Mifflin, 1947); William H. Goetzmann, *Exploration and Empire: The Explorer and Scientist in the Winning of the American West* (New York: Alfred A. Knopf, 1966); David Lavender, *The Fist in the Wilderness* (Garden City, N.Y.: Doubleday and Company, 1964); Janet LeCompte, *Pueblo, Hardscrabble, Greenhorn: The Upper Arkansas, 1832–1856* (Norman: University of Oklahoma Press, 1978); Paul Chrisler Phillips, *The Fur Trade*, 2 vols. (Norman: University of Oklahoma Press, 1961); Kenneth Wiggans Porter, *John Jacob Astor, Business Man*, 2 vols. (Cambridge: Harvard University Press, 1931); John E. Sunder, *The Fur Trade on the Upper Missouri, 1840–1865* (Norman: University of Oklahoma Press, 1965); David J. Wishart, *The Fur Trade of the American West, 1807–1840: A Geographical Synthesis* (Lincoln: University of Nebraska Press, 1979); and an article, Phil E. Chappell, "A History of the Missouri River," *Transactions of the Kansas State Historical Society, 1905–1906*, vol. IX (Topeka: State Printing Office, 1906).

Background on individual fur traders came from Richard M. Clokey, *William H. Ashley: Enterprise and Politics in the Trans-Mississippi West* (Norman: University of Oklahoma Press, 1980); William E. Foley and C. David Rice, *The First Chouteaus: River Barons of St. Louis* (Urbana and Chicago: University of Illinois Press, 1983); John C. Haeger, *John Jacob Astor: Business and Finance in the Early Republic* (Detroit: Wayne State University Press, 1991); LeRoy R. Hafen, ed., *The Mountain Men and the Fur Trade of the Far West*, 10 vols. (Glendale: Arthur H. Clark Company, 1965–72); Ray H. Mattison, ed., *Henry A. Boller, Missouri River Fur Trader* (Bismarck: State Historical Society of North Dakota, 1966); Dale L. Morgan, ed., *The West of William H. Ashley, 1822–1838* (Denver: Old West Publishing Company, 1964); Richard E. Oglesby, *Manuel Lisa and the Opening of the Missouri Fur Trade* (Norman: University of Oklahoma Press, 1963); Donald Dean Parker, ed., *The Recollections of Philander Prescott, Frontiersman of the Old Northwest, 1819–1862* (Lincoln: University of Nebraska Press, 1966); James P. Ronda, *Astoria and Empire* (Lincoln: University of Nebraska Press, 1990); John E. Sunder, *Bill Sublette, Mountain Man* (Norman: University of Oklahoma Press, 1959); John E. Sunder, *Joshua Pilcher, Fur Trader and Indian Agent* (Norman: University of Oklahoma Press, 1968); Robert A. Trennert, Jr., *Indian Traders on the Middle Border: The House of Ewing, 1827–54* (Lincoln: University of Nebraska Press, 1981); and F. G. Young, ed., *The Correspondence and Journals of Captain Nathaniel J. Wyeth, 1831–6* (Eugene, Ore.: University Press, 1899). Articles on this topic include George R. Brooks, ed., "The Private Journal of Robert Campbell," *Bulletin of the Missouri Historical Society* (20: 1, 2) October 1963 and January 1964, and J. Ward Ruckman, "Ramsay Crooks and the Fur Trade of the Northwest," *Minnesota History* 7, no. 1 (March 1926).

Books on artists and scientists include George Catlin, *Letters and Notes on the Manners, Customs, and Conditions of the North American Indians*, 2 vols (London, 1844; reprint, New York: Dover Publications, 1973); Brian W. Dippie, *Catlin and His Contemporaries: The Politics of Patronage* (Lincoln: University of Nebraska Press, 1990); Joseph P. Donnelly, S.J., ed., *Wilderness Kingdom: Indian Life in the Rocky Mountains: 1840–1847; The Journals and Paintings of Father Nicolas Point* (Chicago: Holt, Rinehart and Winston, 1967); William H. Goetzmann, David C. Hunt, Marsha V. Gallagher, and William J. Orr, *Karl Bodmer's America* (Lincoln: Joslyn Art Museum and University of Nebraska Press, 1984); Mildred D. Ladner, *William de la Montagne Cary: Artist on the Missouri River* (Norman: University of Oklahoma Press, 1984); Rick Stewart, Joseph D. Ketner II, and Angela L. Miller, *Carl Wimar: Chronicler of the Missouri River* (Fort Worth: Amon Carter Museum, 1991); Robert Taft, *Artists and Illustrators of the Old West, 1860–1900* (New York: Charles Scribners Sons, 1953); Leslie A. White, ed., *Lewis Henry Morgan: The Indian Journals, 1859–62* (Ann Arbor: University of Michigan Press, 1959); John Francis McDermott, ed., *Audubon in the West* (Norman: University of Oklahoma Press, 1965); John Francis McDermott, ed., *Private Libraries in Creole St. Louis* (Baltimore: Johns Hopkins Press, 1938); John Francis McDermott, ed., *Up the Missouri with Audubon: The Journal of Edward Harris* (Norman: University of Oklahoma Press, 1951); and Edmund C. Bray and Martha Coleman Bray, eds., *Joseph N. Nicollet on the Plains and Prairies* (Saint Paul: Minnesota Historical Society, 1976). Articles include Friedrich Bauser, "The Journeys of Duke Paul, the Records Concerning Them and Their Literary Value," in *South Dakota Historical Collections*, vol. 19 (Pierre, S.Dak.: Hipple Printing Company, 1939); and W. H. Schieffelin, "Crossing the Plains in '61," *Recreation* 3, nos. 1–3 (July–September 1895).

General background information can be found in Louise Barry, ed., *The Beginning of the West* (Topeka: Kansas State Historical Society, 1972); Theodore C. Blegen, *Minnesota: A History of the State* (Saint Paul: University of Minnesota Press, 1975); William Watts Folwell, *A History of Minnesota*, rev. ed., 4 vols. (Saint Paul: Minnesota Historical Society, 1956); and William E. Lass, *A History of Steamboating on the Upper Missouri River* (Lincoln: University of Nebraska Press, 1962).

As one of the UMO's most persistent competitors, and for comparative purposes, I refer frequently to the Hudsons's Bay Company and, to a lesser extent, the North West Company. Among the sources I cite for these outfits are Marjorie Wilkins Campbell, *The North West Company* (Toronto: Macmillan Company of Canada, 1957); John S. Galbraith, *The Hudson's Bay Company as an Imperial Factor, 1821–1869* (New York: Octagon Books, 1977); John Morgan Gray, *Lord Selkirk of Red River* (Toronto: Macmillan Company, 1963); J. Russell Harper, ed., *Paul Kane's Frontier* (Austin: University of Texas Press, 1971); Harold A. Innis, *The Fur Trade in Canada: An Introduction to Canadian Economic History*, rev. ed. (New Haven: Yale University Press, 1962); Douglas MacKay, *The Honorable Company: A History of the Hudson's Bay Company* (reprint, Freeport, N.Y.: Books for Libraries Press, 1970); Peter C. Newman, *Company of Adventurers*, vol. 1 (Markham, Ontario: Penguin Books, 1985), and vol. 2, *Caesars of the Wilderness* (Markham, Ontario: Penguin Books, 1987); Arthur J. Ray, *The Canadian Fur Trade in the Industrial Age* (Toronto: University of Toronto Press, 1990); Alexander Ross, *The Red River Settlement* (reprint, Minneapolis: Ross & Haines, 1957); Bruce G. Trigger, *Natives and Newcomers: Canada's "Heroic Age" Reconsidered* (Kingston and Montreal: McGill-Queen's University Press, 1985); and Rhoda R. Gilman, Carolyn Gilman, and Deborah M. Stultz, *The Red River Trails: Oxcart Routes between St. Paul and the Selkirk Settlement, 1820–1870* (Saint Paul: Minnesota Historical Society, 1979).

Two excellent recent articles on business connections in the North West Company are Heather Devine, "Roots in the Mohawk Valley: Sir William Johnson's Legacy in the North West Company," and Harry W. Duckworth, "British Capital in the Fur Trade: John Strettell and John Fraser," both in Jennifer S. H. Brown, W. J. Eccles, and Donald P. Heldman, eds., *The Fur Trade Revisited: Selected Papers of the Sixth North American Fur Trade Conference, Mackinac Island, Michigan, 1991* (East Lansing and Mackinac Island: Michigan State University Press and Mackinac Island State Parks, 1994).

For military history of the Upper Missouri region, I found the following books useful: Robert G. Athearn, *Forts of the Upper Missouri* (Englewood Cliffs, N.J.: Prentice-Hall, 1967); anonymous, "Official Correspondence

Relating to Fort Pierre," in *South Dakota Historical Collections,* vol. 1 (Aberdeen, S.Dak.: News Printing Company, 1902); David Michael Delo, *Peddlers and Post Traders: The Army Sutler on the Frontier* (Salt Lake City: University of Utah Press, 1992); Roger L. Nichols, *General Henry Atkinson: A Western Military Career* (Norman: University of Oklahoma Press, 1965); Roger L. Nichols, *The Missouri Expedition, 1818–1820: The Journal of Surgeon John Gale, with Related Documents* (Norman: University of Oklahoma Press, 1969); Robert M. Utley, *The Indian Frontier of the American West, 1846–1890* (Albuquerque: University of New Mexico Press, 1984); Robert M. Utley, *Frontier Regulars: The United States Army and the Indian, 1866–1890* (New York: Macmillan, 1973); Major Frederick T. Wilson, "Old Fort Pierre and Its Neighbors," in *South Dakota Historical Collections,* vol. 1 (Aberdeen, S.Dak.: News Printing Company, 1902); and Doane Robinson, ed., "Official Correspondence of the Leavenworth Expedition into South Dakota in 1823," in *South Dakota Historical Collections,* vol. 1 (Aberdeen, S.Dak.: News Printing Co., 1902). Articles include Ray H. Mattison, "The Indian Frontier on the Upper Missouri to 1865," *Nebraska History* 39, no. 3 (September 1958); Roger L. Nichols, "Backdrop for Disaster: Causes of the Arikara War of 1823," *South Dakota History* 14, no. 2 (Summer 1984); Francis Paul Prucha, "Army Sutlers and the American Fur Company," *Minnesota History* 40, no. 1 (Spring 1966); and Russell Reid and Clell G. Gannon, eds., "Journal of the Atkinson-O'Fallon Expedition," in *North Dakota Historical Quarterly* 4, no. 3 (October 1929).

Books dealing with missionaries and their work in the Upper Missouri include: Robert C. Carriker, *Father Peter John De Smet: Jesuit in the West* (Norman: University of Oklahoma Press, 1995); Hiram Martin Chittenden and Alfred Talbot Richardson, eds., *Life, Letters, and Travels of Father Pierre-Jean De Smet, S.J., 1801–1873,* 4 vols. (New York: Francis P. Harper, 1905); Gerhard Schmutterer, *Tomahawk and Cross: Lutheran Missionaries among the Northern Plains Tribes, 1858–1866* (Sioux Falls, S.Dak.: The Center for Western Studies, Augustana College, 1989); and George E. Tinker, *Missionary Conquest: The Gospel and Native American Cultural Genocide* (Minneapolis: Fortress Press, 1993).

Articles useful for my discussion of the decline in bison numbers and its probable causes include Merrill G. Burlingame, "The Buffalo in Trade and Commerce," *North Dakota Historical Quarterly* 3, no. 4 (July 1929);

James L. Clayton, "The Growth and Economic Significance of the American Fur Trade, 1790–1890," in *Aspects of the Fur Trade: Selected Papers of the 1965 North American Fur Trade Conference* (Saint Paul: Minnesota Historical Society, 1967); Dan Flores, "Bison Ecology and Bison Diplomacy: The Southern Plains from 1800 to 1850," *Journal of American History* 78, no. 2 (September 1991); Rudolph W. Koucky, M.D., "The Buffalo Disaster of 1882," *North Dakota History* 50, no. 1 (Winter 1983); Kenneth N. Owens and Sally L. Owens, "Buffalo and Bacteria," *Montana: The Magazine of Western History* 37, no. 2 (Spring 1987); and David D. Smits, "The Frontier Army and the Destruction of the Buffalo: 1865–1883," *Western Historical Quarterly* 25, no. 3 (Autumn 1994).

Useful analyses of the smallpox epidemic of 1837 include Clyde D. Dollar, "The High Plains Smallpox Epidemic of 1837," *Western Historical Quarterly* 8, no. 1 (January 1977); Ann F. Ramenofsky, *Vectors of Death: The Archeology of European Contact* (Albuquerque: University of New Mexico Press, 1987); Arthur J. Ray, "Smallpox: The Epidemic of 1837–38," *The Beaver*, Autumn 1975; Michael K. Trimble, "Chronology of Epidemics Among Plains Village Horticulturalists, 1738–1838," *Southwestern Lore* 54, no. 4 (December 1988); and Michael K. Trimble, "An Ethnohistorical Interpretation of the Spread of Smallpox in the Northern Plains Utilizing Concepts of Disease Ecology," *Reprints in Anthropology* 33 (Lincoln, Nebr.: J & L Reprint Company, 1988).

The best source for the origins of the Northwestern Fur Company (also known as Hubbell & Hawley) is a series of studies by William E. Lass: "The 'Moscow Expedition,'" *Minnesota History* 39, no. 6 (Summer 1965); "The Northwest Fur Company in the Fort Union Region," *Fort Union Fur Trade Symposium Proceedings, September 13-15, 1990* (Williston: Friends of Fort Union Trading Post, 1994); and "The History and Significance of the Northwest Fur Company, 1865–1869," *North Dakota History* 61, no. 3 (Summer 1994).

Several books and articles deal with fur trade social and legal history. Useful to this study were Walter O'Meara, *Daughters of the Country: The Women of the Fur Traders* (New York: Harcourt, Brace and World, 1968); Sylvia Van Kirk, *Many Tender Ties: Women in Fur Trade Society, 1670–1870* (Norman: University of Oklahoma Press, 1980); Carol M. Judd, "'Mixt Bands of Many Nations': 1821–70," in *Old Trails and New Directions: Papers of the Third North American Fur Trade Conference* (Toronto: University of Toronto Press, 1980); Jacqueline Peterson, "Women Dreaming: The Religiopsychology of Indian White Marriages and the Rise of a Métis Culture," in *Western Women: Their Land, Their Lives*, ed. Lillian Schlissel, Vicki Ruiz, and Janice Monk (Albuquerque: University of New Mexico Press, 1988); Kenneth W. Porter, "Negroes and the Fur Trade," *Minnesota History* 15, no. 4 (December 1934); Arthur J. Ray, "Indians as Consumers in the Eighteenth Century," in *Old Trails and New Directions: Papers of the Third North American Fur Trade Conference* (Toronto: University of Toronto Press, 1980); E. E. Rich, "The Fur Traders: Their Diet and Drugs," *The Beaver*, Summer 1976; William R. Swagerty, "A View from the Bottom Up: The Work Force of the American Fur Company on the Upper Missouri in the 1830s," *Montana: The Magazine of Western History* 43, no. 1 (Winter 1993); Sylvia Van Kirk, "Fur Trade Social History: Some Recent Trends," in *Old Trails and New Directions: Papers of the Third North American Fur Trade Conference* (Toronto: University of Toronto Press, 1980); and Bruce M. White, "Give Us a Little Milk: The Social and Cultural Meanings of Gift Giving in the Lake Superior Fur Trade," *Minnesota History* 48, no. 2 (Summer 1982).

Aspects of legal history can be found in John Phillip Reid, "Certainty of Vengeance: The Hudson's Bay Company and Retaliation in Kind against Indian Offenders in New Caledonia," *Montana: The Magazine of Western History* 43, no. 1 (Winter 1993), and "Principles of Vengeance: Fur Trappers, Indians, and Retaliation for Homicide in the Transboundary North American West," *Western Historical Quarterly* 24, no. 1 (February 1993). For foods used at Fort Union, see Leslie A. Perry, "Frontier Subsistence: An Example of Nineteenth Century Fur Trade Food Procurement," M.A. thesis, University of Nebraska, Lincoln, 1981.

Index

References to illustrations are printed in *italic* type.

Abbott, Samuel, 15
Adobe construction techniques, 116
AFCo. *See* American Fur Company
African-American workers, 116–17
Alcohol. *See* Liquor
Alexis, Grand Duke, 100
Alvarez, Philip, 234, 235
American Beaver and His Works, The (Morgan), 101
American Fur Company (AFCo), 11, 14–18, 21, *31*, 72–73, 83, 154, 195; and Fort Union, 41–42, 45; Leclerc-Cabanné affair, 160–64; and liquor regulations, 164–65, 172; McKenzie's distillery operation, 167, 170; Vaughn's praise of, 207; Wimar and, 95
American Fur Trade of the Far West (Chittenden), 170
American Indians. *See* Indians
Annuity contracts, 22, 29–34, 154, 192, 202, 223–24
Annuity goods, 205, 206, 207, 212
Arapahos, 180
Archdale, H. S., 227, 235
Arikaras, 16, 44, 79, 82, 206, 211, 215, 220, 252n.27; and North Western Fur Company, 227–28; North Western Treaty negotiations with, 222; smallpox epidemics, 138; treaty with U.S., 180
Army, U.S., 146, 178–81, 204, 225; bison slaughtered by, 28, 182; cavalrymen, 181–82; and demolition of Fort Union, 237; desertion rates, 181; and Hubbell's

bill for occupancy of Fort Berthold, 233; and Indian agents, 92, 219; and Indian cultural transformation, 11; liquor confiscations by, 159; liquor consumption in, 158, 181; military forts, 156, 179, 180, 194–95; purchase of Fort Pierre, 208–209; Sioux Wars, 204, 205, 207–209, 216, 230, 231; soldier-Indian relationships, 174, 182, 218; soldiers at Fort Union, 216, 233, 235; surveys by, 91–93; whiskey distribution by, 9
Artisans, 118–20
Ash Hollow, Battle of (1855), 208
Ashley, William H., 15, 23, 24, 116, 154, 170, 183, 184, 197–98
Asiatic cholera, 138–39
Assiniboine (steamboat), 37, 76, 78, 79, 244n.40
Assiniboines, 7, 9, 16, 23, 26, 28, 79, *80*, 81, 86, 108, 187; buffalo hide lodges, 49; and Crows at Fort Union, 230; daguerreotypes of, 90; Denig's report on, 68; and drunkenness, 106; gang rapes by, 129; Girl Band, 131; Hubbell's trade with, 220; Larpenteur and, 236; North Western Treaty negotiations with, 222; raids on garden at Fort Union, 125; railroad opposed by, 89; relations with Americans, 156, 157; and Sioux hostility, 207, 215, 230, 231, 237; skulls plundered from burial sites of, 79, 86; and smallpox epidemic, 137, 138; treaties with U.S., 180; Wi-jun-jon, 71
Astor, John, 3, 11, 14–18, 113, 177, 198